DEMOCRACY, WAR, AND PEACE IN THE MIDDLE EAST

INDIANA SERIES IN
ARAB AND ISLAMIC STUDIES

SALIH J. ALTOMA, ILIYA HARIK, AND MARK TESSLER
GENERAL EDITORS

DEMOCRACY, WAR, AND PEACE IN THE MIDDLE EAST

EDITED BY

DAVID GARNHAM
AND
MARK TESSLER

INDIANA UNIVERSITY PRESS
BLOOMINGTON AND INDIANAPOLIS

The paper used in this publication meets the minimum
requirements of American National Standard for Information
Sciences—Permanence of Paper for Printed Library Materials,
ANSI Z39.48-1984.

Manufactured in the United States of America

Library of Congress Cataloging-in-Publication Data

Democracy, war, and peace in the Middle East / edited by David Garnham
and Mark Tessler.
p.   cm. — (Indiana series in Arab and Islamic studies)
Includes bibliographical references and index.
ISBN 0-253-32549-8 (alk. paper). — ISBN 0-253-20939-0 (pbk. :
alk. paper)
1. Middle East—Politics and government—1979–   2. Democracy—
Middle East.   I. Garnham, David, date.   II. Tessler, Mark A.
III. Series.
DS63.1.D46   1995
320.956—dc20   94-27764
1 2 3 4 5   00 99 98 97 96 95

CONTENTS

Part Three: Domestic Politics and International Behavior

Part Four: Critical Cases

❖

NOTE ON TRANSLITERATION

SCHOLARLY PRACTICE HAS been followed in the transliteration of Arabic words, although several exceptions have been made for the benefit of general readers. Diacritical markings are not employed, unless they are present in quoted passages or bibliographic citations. Full diacritics would render the text cumbersome for non-specialists; and partial or modified diacriticals might be awkward as well, without necessarily being of major assistance in pronunciation. The absence of diacritical markings, by contrast, will not prevent specialists from recognizing the original Arabic word. Common English spellings, if they exist, are employed for Arabic names and terms. Thus, for example, the text uses King Hussein rather than King Husayn, Gamal Abdul Nasser rather than Jamal Abd al-Nasir, and sheikh rather than shaykh.

❖

INTRODUCTION

MARK TESSLER AND DAVID GARNHAM

THIS BOOK JOINS several of the most prominent research concerns from the fields of international relations and Middle East studies. Its general preoccupation is with patterns of governance and their relationship to interstate conflict. More particularly, it gives attention to the prospects for democracy in the Arab world and to the ways that Arab democratization might affect the Arab-Israeli conflict. In addressing questions about democracy, war, and peace in the Middle East, the volume seeks to make a contribution that is theoretical and analytical, as well as practical and substantive.

Democracy in the Arab World

The decade of the 1980s brought increased concern for issues of governance and democracy in the Middle East, particularly in the Arab world. Moreover, this concern emerged primarily in response to internal challenges and pressures, and only secondarily, if at all, as a result of developments taking place in other world regions. Popular dissatisfaction with authoritarian leaders and regimes grew steadily during the 1980s, with Morocco, Algeria, Tunisia, Libya, Sudan, Egypt, Jordan, and Syria all experiencing major public riots or other disturbances expressing opposition to the established political order (Tessler 1991). These outbursts of violence, which took place on more than one occasion in some countries, helped to place the issue of governance in a prominent position on the Middle East's political agenda.

Partially in response to these domestic pressures, a number of Arab countries began to experiment with political liberalization and democratization in the mid- and late 1980s. Among the countries where important progress was made are Morocco, Algeria, Tunisia, Egypt, Jordan, and Yemen. In each of these countries, the government eased restrictions on political activity and permitted elections in which there was at least some measure of competition. The political map of the Middle East consequently looked quite different in 1990 than it had in 1980. As expressed by Hudson (1990), writing about the Arab world in general, "however inadequate [its] polyarchal tendencies may be, political life is more complex and participant, and less authoritarian, than it used to be."

Movement toward meaningful political change has been slow and uneven. Most Arab countries that sought to liberalize during the 1980s continue to impose limits on political competition, usually with a view toward ensuring that expressions of dissent do not develop into challenges which might lead to the replacement of existing regimes. There has also been backsliding in some instances. Algeria, for example, a country where progress toward democracy was particularly impressive in the late 1980s, has suspended its experiment in political liberalization and returned to the authoritarian rule of a military government. The country has also seen a return of the anger and unrest of the 1980s. Tunisia is another country where the political opening initiated in the 1980s has not fulfilled its promise. Although not all earlier gains have been lost, the government has not hesitated to stifle dissent and suppress opposition, by force if necessary, when a threat to its continued dominance was perceived. Additional doubts about the prospects for democracy are also raised by the survival of authoritarian regimes in Libya, Saudi Arabia, Syria, Iraq, and several other countries.

The preceding demonstrates that there is at least as much continuity as change in Arab political life. It also suggests that an important battery of questions to be asked by those concerned with governance and democracy in the Middle East deals with the attitudes and behavior of present-day political leaders. To what extent are these leaders and the social classes they represent willing to permit genuine political liberalization? And to the extent they oppose change beyond that which they can orchestrate and control, will they be able to contain pressures for democratization, or will these pressures eventually push them aside?

On the other hand, despite continuing obstacles, the prospects are good for continued movement from authoritarianism toward democracy. The popular frustrations and anger that pushed many Arab regimes to liberalize in the 1980s remain central features of political life, and in the years ahead they will undoubtedly exert additional pressure for political change. So, too, will the gradual diffusion of democratic currents from other parts of the Third World, including Latin America and some parts of Asia and sub-Saharan Africa. As Zacek (1993) writes, "there is a 'contagion' of democratic development: events in some countries clearly impact on neighboring ones." Thus, while the experiments in political liberalization begun in the 1980s do not constitute a full break with the past, it seems certain that issues of governance will remain a major preoccupation in the Arab world, and it is probable in this context that movement toward democratization, however halting, will continue to take place.

Recognition of the need for continued democratization, and perhaps of its inevitability, is reflected in the political discourse of both the government and the opposition in much of the Arab world. As expressed by a Jordanian journalist writing in 1991, "there are everywhere signs of a profound desire for change—for democracy and human rights, for social equity, for regional economic integration, for accountability of public officials, for morality in public life" (Khouri 1991). Similar sentiments were expressed at an international conference held in Amman, Jordan, in 1991 and attended by sixty prominent Arab intellectuals. Participants declared in their final communique that "democracy should take priority in the pan-Arab national project. It should not be sacrificed for any other value or cause" (Halasa 1991). And yet again, as a well-known Kuwaiti lawyer wrote in 1991, more important than any other political objective is "bringing democracy and human rights to the Arab world" (Juwan 1991).

Official statements and actions lend additional support to the proposition that movement toward democracy will continue. For example, King Hussein told the people of Jordan in a November 1992 address, "We perceive Jordanian democracy as a model and an example . . . from which there will be no turning back," and a newsletter published by the Jordan Information Bureau accordingly announced in a January 1993 headline that "political parties signal the birth of a new, more pluralist political era in Jordan." Further, competitive parliamentary elections took place in Jordan in November 1993. Other indications of a continuing emphasis on political liberalization include the revival of parliamentary life in Kuwait late in 1992, and the conduct in Morocco in June 1993 of competitive parliamentary elections that for the most part appear to have been fair.

Finally, many of the obstacles to democratization that confront the Arab world are similar to those that have caused problems elsewhere, but which in many instances have nevertheless proved to be surmountable. There is no a priori reason to assume that it will be impossible to overcome these obstacles in the Arab case. As noted by many scholars, including O'Donnell and Schmitter

(1986, p. 72), transitions to democracy are almost invariably uneven; they are rarely linear and are often irrational. This proposition is supported by the experience of a number of countries in Asia, including the Philippines and South Korea, by many states in Latin America, although in some cases democracy is not new but is rather being reestablished after a long period of military rule, and in a few countries in sub-Saharan Africa, most notably Senegal and Zambia.

For all of these reasons, while there will be unavoidable disappointments and setbacks, it is reasonable to expect that Arab governments will gradually become more responsive to the men and women over whom they rule. And to the extent that this conclusion is valid, or at least plausible, it is important for scholars to inquire about the likely consequences of such a change in the patterns of governance prevailing in the region.

One important set of questions, in addition to those mentioned above pertaining to the intentions of present-day leaders, concerns the kind of government that would result from genuine political accountability in the Arab world. What sorts of preferences about patterns of governance and the broad goals of public policy are likely to be expressed by ordinary men and women, and what kinds of political norms and structures can be expected to come to prominence in response to these citizen demands? Will these resemble the norms and structures associated with democratic regimes in the West, or is there some different, perhaps Arab, or Islamic or Third World variety of democracy that is likely to emerge?

This issue is partly one of definition. If the essence of democracy is the ability of the governed to hold accountable those who rule over them, then the content of preferences which the former require the latter to respect need not be considered when determining whether a political system is democratic. The only exception would be a demand for the denial of civil and political rights to selected categories of the population. Otherwise, if the will of the majority has been freely expressed and the populace has the ability to remove leaders it considers unresponsive or incapable, then the essential elements of democracy would appear to be present.

Nevertheless, additional questions about the attitudes and beliefs of ordinary citizens cannot be avoided when assessing the prospects for democracy in a region where people have historically been denied the opportunity to select and hold accountable their political leaders. Specifically, can democracy take root and flourish in societies which lack, or may lack, a prior commitment at popular levels to freedom of expression and dissent, to organized partisan competition, to political tolerance and respect for diversity, and to other liberal political principles? Further, if these elements of popular political culture are indeed essential for democratic experiments to succeed, to what extent are they present in the Arab world, despite the absence of past experience with democracy? And finally, to the extent they are absent, will the civic norms and values necessary for democracy emerge once political socialization takes place within a democratic framework?

These questions are as important as those pertaining to elite intentions in evaluating the prospects for successful democratization. Indeed, they may be more important in the long term. And even in the more immediate future, as experiments in democratization go forward in an incremental fashion, they must be investigated by those seeking to assess the kinds of political systems and public policies that are likely to result from increased political accountability. None of this is unique to the Arab world, of course. Similar questions are being raised in other societies that have a long history of authoritarian rule but which at present are being buffeted by pressures for democratization.

The role of Islam in shaping those citizen attitudes to which democratic regimes will be required to pay attention is a particularly important issue that emerges in this context in the Arab world. Will men and women with strong religious attachments demand public policies that conform to Islam, as they understand it, and how will this shape the form and substance of political life? Additionally, will the Muslim majorities in Arab countries seek to be governed by the leaders of Islamist political movements, almost all of which oppose any separation of religion and politics, and how will the political process in general and the prospects for democracy in particular be affected should these Islamists indeed come to power through free and fair elections?

These questions call attention to the need to examine the relationship not only between democracy and citizen attitudes in general, but between democracy and the norms of Islam in particular. One immediate concern is the possibility that political liberalization will bring to power Islamist leaders with antidemocratic inclinations. The danger, as expressed by *The Economist* in a January 1992 article, is that the first people delivered to power by democracy will in fact be intent on dismantling it. Yet, can these individuals be prevented from governing, if freely elected, without progress toward democracy being compromised just as surely? And is it in fact a reasonable fear that Islamist leaders capable of attracting popular support would enact antidemocratic policies were they to come to power?

More broadly, it is necessary to ask about the relationship between Islamic attachments and political values among the public at large. Which Islamic practices and interpretations are likely to be most pronounced, both in general or under particular conditions, and in what ways, if any, will these orientations influence preferences about public policy and governmental activity? For example, is there any relationship between the degree of religious piety and the kinds of civic norms mentioned earlier, including political tolerance, respect for diversity, and a commitment to free expression and dissent? Similarly, is support for these and other democratic values either promoted or diminished by particular interpretations of Islamic law?

Democracy and Peace

In addition to these questions about the prospects for continued movement toward democracy in the Arab world, and about the character of the political systems that can be expected to emerge if significant progress does indeed take place, it is both useful and necessary to ask about the implications of democratization in the arena of foreign policy and international relations. Are democratic polities likely to have foreign policy objectives different from those of the more authoritarian regimes in the Arab world? Will democratic and authoritarian Arab regimes exhibit different patterns of behavior in their relations with other states?

Within the regional context of the Middle East, these concerns assume special significance in connection with the Arab-Israeli conflict. The conflict, which has persisted for almost half a century, has embroiled the Middle East in six major wars and cost thousands of lives, both Arab and Israeli. It has also caused the diversion of billions of dollars from productive investments to the purchase of armaments, and it has diverted energies as well as resources and blocked regional cooperation which would almost certainly increase economic development and permit a more rational and effective use of natural resources. Finally, the conflict has left the Palestinian people stateless and dispersed, creating frustration and anger that are an important source of regional tension.

The value of investigating a possible link between democratization in the Arab world and the future of the Arab-Israeli conflict is suggested by a growing body of international relations research which indicates that democracies almost never go to war against one another. Indeed, the reported absence of warfare between democratic states and the possible pacifying effects of democracy have been a particularly conspicuous focus of peace research since the late 1980s. As a result of this research, many scholars now contend that almost all interstate warfare occurs either among nondemocratic states or between democratic and nondemocratic political systems. Some analysts go so far as to state that the absence of war between democracies "comes as close as anything we have to an empirical law in international relations" (Levy 1988, p. 662).

Although there is debate about whether democracy will contribute to a resolution of the Arab-Israeli conflict, or even to a reduction in the likelihood of Arab-Israeli war, there are both practical and analytical reasons to investigate these possibilities. First, and most obviously, the extremely high direct and opportunity costs associated with the protracted struggle provide an obvious justification for seeking to identify conditions under which the intensity of the conflict might diminish. The domestic needs of the Arab states provide ample reason to encourage democratization. But the case of democracy would be even stronger were there an expectation that it would contribute to solving problems in the regional as well as the domestic political arena.

Further, questions about the relationship between democracy and peace are no longer of purely theoretical interest in the Middle East. Until recently, democracy's possible pacifying effects were largely irrelevant to Middle Eastern international relations. Research does not suggest that democracies never go to war, only that they do not go to war against other democracies. Thus, since Israel was the only democratic state in the region, inquiries about relations between Israel and one or more democratic Arab states were essentially hypothetical and speculative. At present, however, given the gains that have already been made, the Israeli-Egyptian dyad and the Israeli-Jordanian dyad, as well as some others, constitute pairs in which both states are democratic to at least some meaningful degree. It is therefore important to ask whether relations between these pairs of democratic or quasi-democratic states will be different than they were when one of the states was governed by a more authoritarian regime.

These questions are given additional salience by the change of government in Israel in 1992, and also by the signing of an accord between Israel and the PLO in September 1993. The present Labor-led coalition, headed by Yitzhak Rabin, has demonstrated genuine interest in achieving a peace based on territorial compromise and accommodation with the Palestinians. This contrasts with the position of the previous Likud-led government of Yitzhak Shamir, which rejected any withdrawal from occupied Arab lands and denied that Palestinians had legitimate political rights. While international relations research suggests that even the hard-line government of a democratic Israel would be unlikely to go to war against a democratic Arab state, the country's intransigent position under Likud and Shamir was nonetheless a major obstacle to peace. Now, however, with a more moderate government in Jerusalem, democratization in the Arab world raises the possibility not only that the likelihood of Arab-Israeli war will diminish, but also that meaningful progress toward resolving the conflict can be made.

Moreover, the Declaration of Principles signed by Israel and the PLO in September 1993 holds out the prospect of a genuine breakthrough in the lingering Middle East dispute. The document deliberately deferred decisions on difficult substantive issues, and it soon became clear that there would be disappointments and setbacks as the parties struggled to translate principle into practice. Nevertheless, the agreement is revolutionary in that it records the parties' recognition of their "mutual and legitimate political rights" and commits them to "put an end to decades of confrontation and conflict." Further, the signing of the accord was followed by movement toward the establishment of new cooperative relationships between Israel and a number of Arab states, including Qatar, Tunisia, Morocco, and Jordan. Thus, despite the serious problems that remain, the prospects for Arab-Israeli peace have never been brighter.

If there is to be continued progress toward a resolution of the conflict, and if advances are to build the confidence and mutual respect necessary for lasting peace, it is essential that quarrels and controversies be addressed without resorting to violence, especially at the interstate level. Otherwise, it is unlikely that Arabs and Israelis will be able to preserve whatever gains they have recently made, to say nothing of developing normal and harmonious relations over the longer term. It is in this context, again, that the practical importance of the relationship between democracy and peace may be seen. To the extent the Arab world is indeed becoming more democratic, and should this in turn reduce the likelihood that conflicts in the Middle East will lead to war, the gains to be realized from the September 1993 accord and other developments that bring Palestinians and Israelis closer to a settlement will be that much more significant.

Interestingly, a number of Israeli leaders have themselves called attention to the relationship between democracy and peace. For example, Shimon Peres, former prime minister and currently foreign minister in the Labor-led government, is reported to favor elections in the West Bank in part because greater democratization among the Palestinians would increase the chances for Arab-Israeli peace. According to a recent summary of Peres' views in *Yediot Aharonot* (May 7, 1993), "he relies, it seems, on the assumption currently held by researchers in political science that democratic societies do not fight each other.

They seek to settle their differences by non-violent means." Leaders of the more hawkish Likud opposition also appear to put stock in this thesis, although they are less inclined to welcome and encourage Arab democratization and tend rather to argue that Israel should not be asked to make concessions so long as antidemocratic tendencies remain in the Arab world. Benjamin Netanyahu, the current head of Likud, wrote in a recent article, for example, that "Israel should not give up territories in return for a peace treaty with non-democratic regimes . . . because dictatorships lack the same element of self-restraint [as democratic systems and consequently] there is no guarantee that a peace treaty with [a non-democratic regime] will be preserved" (*Ha'aretz,* June 21, 1993).

In addition to focusing on the Arab-Israeli conflict, it is important to inquire about the broader range of ways in which democratization might affect the regional international system of the Middle East. To the extent that the Arab world is indeed becoming more democratic, will the region as a whole become more pacific, with diminished likelihood that other disputes, in addition to the Arab-Israeli conflict, will lead to war? Also, might there perhaps be other changes in the character of bilateral and multilateral inter-Arab relations? Will the interaction between two or more democratic Arab states be different from the interaction between two or more authoritarian Arab states, and will the nature and political dynamics of the region's international subsystem be different as a result?

Finally, the Middle Eastern case offers an important opportunity to evaluate further, and if necessary to refine, the general analytical insights that have thus far emerged from international relations research on democracy and peace. To begin with, additional studies are needed in order to assess the general validity of the proposition that democracies do not go to war against one another. To date, despite a number of wide-ranging empirical investigations, relatively few exceptions to this proposition have been identified. On the other hand, the number of apparent exceptions is not insignificant, and this has led some to question statements that attribute "law-like" properties to findings about the absence of war between democracies.

Several scholars identify interstate conflicts that appear to involve war between democracies, citing examples that range as far back in time as the war between Athens and Syracuse in the fifth century B.C. Kenneth N. Waltz, for example, identifies three possible exceptions to the proposition that democracies do not fight one another: the War of 1812, the American Civil War, and Wilhelminian Germany before World War I (1991). Examining the period be-

tween 1816 and 1988, David A. Lake considers two additional apparent exceptions: the Spanish-American War and Finland's alliance with the Axis powers
during World War II (Lake 1992). A more recent example is the current war
between Serbia and other republics of the former Yugoslavia, all of which are
led by democratically elected governments. These are only some of the possible
exceptions that might be mentioned and which have been cited by various
authors.

Additional research is needed in order to assess both the relative importance
and analytical implications of these instances of war between democracies,
and the study of an increasingly democratic Middle East offers an important
opportunity to investigate the relationship between democracy and peace with
these objectives in mind. Should democratization in the Arab world be associated with an easing of the Arab-Israeli conflict, or of other regional disputes
that have been productive of interstate violence, then confidence will grow in
the hypothesized relationship between democracy and peace and there will be
less concern about exceptions to this pattern. Equally important, the locus of
applicability of the observation that democracies do not fight one another will
have been extended, since it will have been demonstrated that this proposition
holds for different world regions and for peoples and countries with dissimilar
political and cultural traditions. The latter consideration is particularly important because conclusions advanced to date are based primarily on data from
European and North American countries.

Alternatively, if democratization in the Middle East is followed by continued or intensified interstate violence, confidence in the democracy-produces-
peace hypothesis will be weakened and the exceptions that have been cited will
appear more important. It will be necessary in this case to reconsider the accuracy of the hypothesized relationship between democracy and peace, at least
as an insight about international behavior that purports to be universally applicable. It will also be necessary to consider the possibility that the hypothesized relationship between democracy and peace holds under some conditions
but not under others, with evidence from the Middle East serving as a stimulus
and making a contribution to the larger and more comparative research effort
that will be necessary to learn about such conditionalities.

If democracy does not have a pacifying effect in the Middle East, particularly with respect to the Arab-Israeli conflict, one possible reason may be the
increased influence of Islamist political leaders. It is by no means certain that
democracy will bring Islamist regimes to power in the Arab world. Nor is it
certain that democratic Arab countries governed by Islamist regimes would

take military action against Israel. But such a scenario is at least possible, and should this occur it will be necessary to refine analytical conclusions that purport to be general by incorporating insights about regime type and ideology. More specifically, it will be necessary to specify that democracy leads to pacific international behavior only if citizens do not choose to be governed by regimes with "fundamentalist" or "totalitarian" ideologies. Such a finding would be of considerable analytical importance, despite the disheartening conclusion that democracy in the Arab world would not be likely after all to foster movement toward Arab-Israeli peace.

An investigation of the impact of democratization on peace in the Middle East may also make other analytical contributions. One potentially relevant consideration is the possibility raised by some scholars that the relationship between democracy and peace is spurious. Most of the data supporting this hypothesis come from the study of European and North American democracies. Most of these countries are also relatively prosperous, so it must be asked whether their reluctance to fight other democracies is the result of shared cultural, historic or economic factors, rather than the character of their political systems (Maoz and Russett 1992). John E. Mueller advances an interesting variation on this theme. He suggests that many Western democracies have become averse to war, viewing war as "intolerably costly, unwise, futile and debased" (Mueller 1989; 1990, p. 321). Consequently, in this view, war becomes as unthinkable as slavery and duelling—other previously accepted but now obsolete practices. According to Mueller, an aversion to war is spreading with a time lag of about a century in regions and countries where processes of democratization occurred previously, and this more recent normative development, rather than democracy, is the principal determinant of any reluctance to go to war. Evidence from the Middle East can shed light on these and other speculations about the spurious nature of the relationship between democracy and peace. Specifically, the likelihood that pacific international behavior is wholly or partly the result of cultural, historic or economic factors, and that democracy is thus a less important causal agent, can be assessed by determining whether findings based on the study of European and North American countries are replicable with data from democracies characterized by different cultural, historic or economic circumstances.

Yet another analytical consideration is the need to investigate more fully the reasons that democracies rarely go to war against one another, and thereby to explicate the pathways connecting democracy to international behavior. For example, is this behavior determined primarily by the more procedural aspects of democracy, including processes and structures that govern the production of information and the making of decisions? Or is political culture of equal or even greater significance, with the commitments and principles embraced by ordinary citizens playing a particularly critical role? An inquiry about democracy and peace in the Middle East may shed valuable light on these questions, which have not yet been satisfactorily answered by international relations research. By moving from aggregate studies to the investigation of specific cases, and by examining a region with political and cultural traditions different from those of the United States and Europe, which have been the focus of most previous research, it may be possible to learn more about the factors that discourage democracies from fighting one another.

The Present Volume

The following chapters by students of comparative politics and international relations, most of whom are also specialists on the Middle East, attempt to answer many of the questions set forth above. The authors first presented the results of their investigations and inquiries at an international conference in Milwaukee, convened in April 1992 and sponsored by the University of Wisconsin-Milwaukee/Marquette University Center for International Studies. Subsequently, after three days of intense discussion, authors were asked to revise their papers for inclusion in the present volume.

Although most chapters deal with issues of both democracy and peace, and with the relationship between them, contributions have been divided into four categories in accordance with their general approach and principal focus. The first section of the volume contains three chapters devoted to pertinent theoretical issues and their relevance to the Middle East. In the opening chapter, James Lee Ray presents and analyzes the major arguments about the relationship between democracy and war. Ray traces the origins of a global trend toward democratization, assesses the peace-producing potential of this trend, and makes the case that democracy is likely to have a pacifying impact in the Middle East, as well as elsewhere.

Jo-Anne Hart's contribution covers similar ground but offers a somewhat different conclusion. Focusing on a particular subset of security issues, that of deterrence, she argues that differences between the foreign policy behavior of democratic and authoritarian regimes in the Middle East may turn out to be less pronounced than would be expected from the scholarly literature on democracy and peace. Noting that there is considerable variation in the behavior of both democratic and authoritarian regimes, she suggests that regime type itself may have only limited explanatory power. She also suggests that external circumstances, as well as domestic and individual-level attributes, will have to be taken into consideration if decisions related to deterrence and other security issues are to be fully understood.

Finally, concluding the first section, I. William Zartman situates these issues within the context of Middle Eastern political aspirations. He discusses the importance that people in the area attach both to more accountable government in the domestic sphere and to increased security in the region's international subsystem. Zartman examines the prospects and problems associated with each set of objectives, and he also reviews the challenges and opportunities associated with the simultaneous pursuit of more democratic patterns of governance and enhanced regional stability.

The second section deals in greater depth with issues of democracy, including issues of definition and the impact of the Arab world's major cultural and religious traditions. In the first of the three chapters in this section, Robert L. Rothstein reviews the defining elements of democracy that have emerged from the Western experience, giving particular attention to some of the difficulties and disagreements that characterize the pertinent scholarly literature. He then discusses the extent to which, and the conditions under which, available definitions of democracy are likely to be useful in the Middle East and other Third World areas where pressures for political change are currently in evidence. One of Rothstein's conclusions is that for the foreseeable future, political liberalization in the Arab world is likely to produce only weak democracies, hybrid regimes mixing together democratic and authoritarian characteristics. As a result, Rothstein also concludes that it may be some time before it is possible to determine whether democracies in the Middle East, except for Israel, behave in a manner similar to other democracies.

Jamal Al-Suwaidi continues this line of inquiry, using both historical material and public opinion data to assess the degree to which the political conceptions of people of the Arab world, particularly in the Arab Gulf, are likely to be conducive to successful democratization. Suwaidi also analyzes the impact of Islamic attachments on political attitudes and values, and he presents additional public opinion data in order to examine the interrelationships among attitudes toward democracy, Islamic political movements, and foreign policy issues, including those pertaining to Israel and the United States. One of Suwaidi's findings is that the relationship between support for democracy and foreign policy attitudes is not the same among men and women with differing attitudes toward political Islam. For example, anti-Israel attitudes diminish as a function of support for democracy among people who do not support Islamic political movements, but they are positively correlated with prodemocracy attitudes among those who do support such movements.

The last chapter in this section, by Shukri B. Abed, explores Islamic attitudes toward democracy in greater depth. Drawing on the writings of both liberal Muslim intellectuals and fundamentalist theoreticians and politicians, Abed makes it clear that Islam's attitude toward democracy and other political concepts of non-Muslim origin is not monolithic. He also shows that different points of view have been advanced in the name of Islam not only by Muslim political thinkers in general, but even by those who identify with fundamentalist Islam. Thus, Abed demonstrates, there is no "true" Islamic position, and this in turn makes it necessary to ask which of the available interpretations will gain legitimacy and become politically influential in a particular country at a particular time.

The third section of the volume returns to the theme of democracy and peace in the Middle East, looking with greater specificity at the connections between domestic politics and international behavior and presenting additional evidence with which to assess key hypotheses. The first chapter in this section, by Mark Tessler and Marilyn Grobschmidt, argues that democracy in the Arab world will indeed increase the chances for a peaceful resolution of the Arab-Israeli conflict. The chapter supports this assertion with a discussion of the pathways that link domestic politics to foreign policy in the Arab states and Israel, and also with a comparative analysis of public opinion data from three Arab societies. Tessler and Grobschmidt also argue that while democratization in the Arab world may increase the political importance of Islamic norms and institutions, this will not necessarily prevent progress toward Arab-Israeli peace.

Focusing not only on the Arab-Israeli conflict but on enduring rivalries in the Middle East more broadly, the chapter by Zeev Maoz presents additional empirical evidence with which to test hypotheses about the linkages between domestic politics and international behavior. Following a review of relevant scholarly literature, Maoz advances and then tests with time-series data from the Middle East a number of hypotheses about the relationship between domestic structures and processes and international conflict. Despite a few inconsistencies in the data, Maoz finds general support for the proposition that levels of international hostility are affected by changes in domestic political systems, and more particularly that movement toward democracy reduces the intensity of conflict interaction.

The final chapter in this section, by Michael C. Hudson, undertakes a comparative historical study, with particular attention to the cases of Egypt, Syria, Iraq, Jordan, and Lebanon. Hudson first asks whether it is possible to discern any relationship between democracy and foreign policy in the Arab world on those occasions when governments were at least somewhat more democratic. He then poses a speculative counterfactual proposition, asking whether it is plausible to think that Arab regimes, had they been more democratic, would have pursued different, less belligerent policies toward Israel. Hudson concludes that this would "probably not" have been the case. He also speculates about the relationship between democracy and several other foreign policy issues, including Arab unity and relations with the United States.

The fourth and final section of the book looks in depth at three critical cases, those of Egypt, the Palestinians, and Israel. In the first chapter in this section, Ann M. Lesch presents a careful assessment both of the degree to which Egypt has in recent years become more democratic and of the foreign policy orientations of the two most recent Egyptian regimes. Lesch concludes with respect to domestic politics that accomplishments to date have been limited, the result being a political system with both more liberal and more authoritarian characteristics. Moreover, she argues that this process of selective and partial democratization contains inherent contradictions. So far as foreign policy is concerned, Lesch does not see any clear relationship between the progress toward democracy that has been made and Egypt's more pacific posture toward Israel. She deems the arguments both for and against the democracy and peace hypothesis to be plausible, but concludes that democratization in Egypt has thus far been too incomplete to use the experience of that country to test competing positions.

The case of the Palestinians is taken up in the next chapter by Emile F. Sahliyeh, who examines both the political structures and processes of the PLO and the political life of Palestinians in the occupied West Bank and Gaza. Sahliyeh concludes that Palestinian politics contains both democratic and antidemocratic elements, with the former being particularly important in the West Bank and Gaza. He also reports that there is an association among Palestinians between support for democratic patterns of governance and a willingness to reach an accommodation with Israel. Looking toward the future, Sahliyeh argues that a Palestinian state in the West Bank and Gaza, were one to be established, would most likely be democratic and seek peaceful relations with its neighbors, including Israel.

In the last case study, dealing with Israel, Gabriel Sheffer discusses the structure of the country's democracy, including the relationship between public opinion and government policy, and then inquires about the ways that Israeli citizens and political elites perceive the attempts at liberalization taking place in some Arab countries. Sheffer reports that the Israeli public tends to attach little significance to Arab efforts at democratization, but adds that this may not be of much importance since public opinion in Israel has historically had little influence on crucial decisions concerning war and peace. Although the attitudes of elites are more important, Sheffer argues that most Israeli leaders are also skeptical about the possibility of significant progress toward democracy in the Arab world and that most believe such progress, were it to occur, would bring Muslim extremists to power and hence reduce the prospects for peace. Thus, he concludes, political liberalization in the Arab world is unlikely, for the time being at least, to bring a significant reduction in Israel's willingness to use force against its neighbors.

REFERENCES

Halasa, Serene. 1991. "Arab Scholars Call for New Order Based on Democracy, Urge End to Iraq Sanctions." *Jordan Times*, May 30–31.

Hudson, Michael C. 1990. "The Democratization Process in the Arab World: An Assessment." Paper presented at the annual meeting of the American Political Science Association, San Francisco, August 30–September 2.

Juwan, Hamed. 1991. "Democracy, Not Dictatorship." *Washington Post*, April 10.

Khouri, Rami G. 1991. "A Lesson in Middle East History and Humanity." *Jordan Times*, May 28.

Lake, David A. 1992. "Powerful Pacifists: Democratic States and War." *American Political Science Review* 86, no. 1 (March), pp. 24–37.

Levy, Jack S. 1988. "Domestic Politics and War." *Journal of Interdisciplinary History* 18, no. 4 (Spring), pp. 653–73.

Maoz, Zeev, and Bruce M. Russett. 1992. "Alliance, Contiguity, Wealth, and Political Stability: Is the Lack of Conflict among Democracies a Statistical Artifact?" *International Interactions* 17 (February), pp. 245–68.

Mueller, John E. 1989. *Retreat from Doomsday: The Obsolescence of Major War.* New York: Basic Books.

————. 1990. "The Obsolescence of Major War." *Bulletin of Peace Proposals* 21, no. 3 (September), pp. 321–28.

O'Donnell, Guillermo, and Philippe C. Schmitter. 1986. "Tentative Conclusions about Uncertain Democracies. In Guillermo O'Donnell, Philippe C. Schmitter, and Laurence Whitehead, eds., *Transitions for Authoritarian Rule: Prospects for Democracy*, Part Four. Baltimore: Johns Hopkins University Press.

Tessler, Mark. 1991. "Anger and Governance in the Arab World: Lessons from the Maghrib and Implications for the West." *Jerusalem Journal of International Relations* 13, no. 2 (September), pp. 7–33.

Waltz, Kenneth N. 1991. Remarks at a meeting of the American Political Science Association.

Zacek, Jane S. 1993. "Prospects for Democratic Rule." *In Depth: A Journal for Values and Public Policy* 3, no. 1 (Winter), pp. 257–77.

PART ONE

THEORETICAL ISSUES

THE FUTURE OF INTERNATIONAL WAR
Global Trends and Middle Eastern Implications

JAMES LEE RAY

K. J. HOLSTI (1986, p. 356) has observed about international politics specialists in particular that "many of [their] theoretical arguments about the fundamental contours of our discipline are really debates about optimism and pessimism, our very general outlook toward the world in which we live." One enduring issue in the field of international politics that brings out optimistic and pessimistic streaks in most of its practitioners concerns the future role of international war in the global political system. In this century, one of the earliest, most important documents in the optimistic literature, first published in 1910, is *The Great Illusion* by Norman Angell. Angell's argument was an extension of the classical liberal argument that free trade would make war obsolete.[1] Both world wars produced a number of proposals for making the world more peaceful and hopes that such proposals might achieve the ultimate success, i.e., the elimination of international war altogether. The ending of another "war," perhaps, that is, the Cold War, has played a role in provoking a spate of optimism about the future of international politics in general, and international war in particular. The apogee of optimism about international politics in general was reached by Fukuyama (1989; 1992) in "The End of History." Mueller (1989) argues about international war in particular in *Retreat from Doomsday* that "major war," that is, among developed countries, is "obsolescent."[2]

This paper will analyze major arguments to the effect that international war may become obsolete, and will ultimately focus on a global trend toward democracy as the factor with perhaps the greatest peace-producing potential. It will also analyze the origins of the global democratizing trend, as well as the possible relevance of that trend to political developments and regime transitions in the Middle East. While acknowledging that the Middle East may be that region of the world most resistant to democratization, the conclusion will point out an impressive variety of theoretical approaches which suggest that democracy might have a pacifying impact even in that region of the world.

Toward the End of International War?

According to Cohen (1990, p. 8), "there are three core arguments for the dwindling importance of force in international politics . . . the horrific quality of modern military technology, the spread of democracy, and the rise of transnational issues and actors. . . . " Another important argument stresses the impact of ethics, legal principles, or norms on the use of force. Let us look first at the argument that economic factors, especially more intense interdependence, as well as higher levels of wealth, will make war obsolete.

Economics and Peace

It is a tribute, perhaps, to the influence of vulgar Marxism that theories tracing the real causes of war to economic forces are so influential, and that probably the notion regarding the obsolescence of war of longest standing also points in that direction. We have already mentioned the "free trade will lead to peace" idea of the Manchester liberals, as well as Norman Angell's argument in *The Great Illusion* that war had become illogical in an economic sense and therefore might become obsolete. Despite the fact that the First World War and the Second World War and virtually all the wars in between and after have provided a rather outrageously large number of anomalies for this idea, it has demonstrated a rather remarkable staying power.[3] Levi (1981), for example, propounds a thesis very similar to Angell's. Even though Russett and Starr (1989) point out that current levels of economic interdependence among the richer states of the world are not, by many measures, any higher than they were before the First World War (and that level did not, obviously, prevent that war), they still conclude that "for a war among [industrialized] countries, the prospective gains would not be high. . . . The costs of such a war . . . would likely be very high. . . . With such great prospective costs, war with another developed market economy just does not look cost-effective at all" (Russett and Starr 1989, p. 420).

Carl Kaysen (1990) makes a similar argument in his review of Mueller's *Retreat from Doomsday*. Until the Industrial Revolution, war was quite economically rational. War was relatively inexpensive, and "successful war yielded a clear gain: control over territory—additional land, and the associated labor force." But now, "in the economic sphere, land [has] greatly diminished in importance as a resource." In short, Kaysen (1990, pp. 49, 53) concludes that international war no longer pays economically, and that is one reason that it is significantly less likely to occur.

William Domke compares states that trade more with states that trade less, across space, within each of 31 years during which war occurred between 1871 and 1975. He discovers a significant negative relationship between the extent of trading activity (as a percent of GNP) and the likelihood that a state will become involved in a war. He explains that "growing foreign trade sectors will create stronger domestic interest groups that wish to avoid war. . . . The presence of a domestic foreign trade sector will constrain governmental choice" (Domke 1988, p. 138).

But there are good reasons to doubt, it seems to this writer, that international war will be made obsolete, at least directly, either by increasing levels of economic development, or more intense interdependence. Domke shows that across space in a given year in which a war is fought, states that trade more have been less likely to get involved in an international war. But the relationship is negative in only 23 of the 31 years he analyzes, and the negative relationship is "significant" in only 9 of those years (Domke 1988, p. 132). In any case, those cross-sectional relationships at the national level shed little light on the impact of increasingly intense international activity over time at the level of the international system. It would be perfectly possible for strong negative relationships between trade and war to show up in annual across space national level analyses, even though there is a strong positive relationship between the level of trade and the incidence of war at the system level over time.

The idea that economic interdependence will lead to the disappearance of war is also undermined by Waltz (1979, p. 138). He argues that "the fiercest civil wars and the bloodiest international ones are fought within arenas populated by highly similar people whose affairs are closely knit"; Gaddis (1986, pp. 111–12) observes that the ten bloodiest interstate wars in the last century and a half "grew out of conflicts between countries that either directly adjoined one another or were actively involved in trade with one another." And the assertion that relatively high levels of wealth will make war obsolete seems implausible in light of the fact that the richest states in the world, until the most recent decades, were in Europe, at the same time that Europe was the site of the longest and bloodiest interstate wars in the world.

Robert Jervis (1991/92, p. 51) has noted in a recent article about the future of international politics in general and international war in particular that "when states fear each other, interdependence can increase conflict." One can certainly speculate convincingly that under current conditions, increased economic interdependence between Arab states and Israel, for example, would not be likely to ameliorate conflict. It is possible that increased levels of economic well-being in the Middle East would strengthen any latent tendencies toward democracy, and thus indirectly, for reasons to be analyzed later in a discussion about the relationship between regime type and international conflict, contribute to a pacific trend in the region. In favor of this idea is the fact that in the wake of the collapse of communism in the Soviet Union and Eastern Europe, as well as the end of the Cold War, the "modernization" idea that economic development leads more or less naturally to political development in the form of more democratic forms of governance is making a comeback. Lucian Pye (1990, p. 7), for example, in his analysis of the crisis of authoritarianism, speaks of the "vindication of modernization theory" inherent in recent democratizing trends around the world, and Fukuyama (1992, p. 112) argues similarly that "looking around the world, there remains a very strong overall correlation between advancing socioeconomic modernization and the emergence of new democracies." But Fukuyama also notes that the Middle East contains virtually all the exceptions to this rule, because "income from petroleum has permitted states like Saudi Arabia, Iraq, Iran, and the UAE to acquire the trappings of modernity—without having had their societies go through the social transformations that come when such wealth is generated by the labor of their populations." Both Mueller (1989) and Ray (1989) make arguments to the effect that international wars seem increasingly unlikely in the developed world because of attitudinal changes regarding war in developed countries. But Fukuyama's pessimistic conclusion regarding the impact of modernization fueled by oil wealth on democratizing trends seems equally applicable to a roughly analogous argument that economic modernization seems to have had a catalytic or indirect effect on cultural attitudes about international war. In any case, the presence of substantial levels of oil-generated wealth does not appear to have had a very powerful pacifying effect on recent relationships between Iraq, Iran, and Kuwait, for example.

The Technological Road to Peace

On the surface, at least, the case for nuclear weapons as a cause of peace is compelling. Since the first ones were exploded in anger in 1945, major powers and developed industrialized states, have stopped fighting wars against each other. No two states possessing nuclear weapons have ever fought a war against each other, and formal allies of the superpowers between 1960 and 1980 did not fight wars, or even engage in low-level military conflict with one another (Weede 1983). In addition, no two formal allies of states with nuclear weapons and not allied to each other fought wars against each other from 1945 to 1986 (Ray 1986). Accordingly, such "realistic" theorists as Waltz (1979, 1982), and Bueno de Mesquita and Riker (1982) conclude that nuclear weapons have powerful peace-producing effects. And, of course, such writers as Feldman (1981) and Rosen (1977) some time ago developed arguments to the effect that nuclear proliferation in the Middle East could be an important key to peace in the region.

As Walt (1991, p. 225) points out, both Mueller and Ray argue that war is becoming obsolete (at least for certain kinds of states), but "their arguments are not based on dangers posed by nuclear weapons." Similarly, Melko (1992, p. 111) argues that "there is a good case to be made for the view that nuclear weapons have not been a major factor in the present peace." Mueller's main arguments against the relevance of nuclear weapons to an explanation of peace emphasize that the horrors of the First and Second World Wars would have sufficed to produce peace, had nuclear weapons not even been invented. Ray's argument against the idea that nuclear weapons have been responsible for peace, at least among the more industrialized countries of the world since the Second World War, focuses first on the long line of analogous arguments about the peace-producing impact of horrible weapons, all of which have proven to be wrong. It also emphasizes the apparent lack of impact on nuclear weapons on the resolution of international crises (Organski and Kugler 1980; Kugler 1984; Huth and Russett 1984; Gochman and Maoz 1984), as well as the irrelevance of nuclear weapons to an explanation of peace among the significant number of industrialized democracies. Melko's skepticism about the pacifying power of nuclear weapons is based on his idea that peace has been produced instead by a "world view" characteristic of the contemporary age.

Saddam Hussein may have come close to developing nuclear weapons before the Persian Gulf War. China seems willing to sell missile and possibly nuclear technology to several Middle Eastern states. The breakup of the Soviet Union may make nuclear technology and expertise available on the world market. The government of Pakistan has recently admitted that it has the knowledge (but not, it still insists, the desire) necessary to create nuclear weapons. In short, nuclear proliferation may have a "promising" future in the Middle East. But if there are at least some problems in the argument that nuclear weapons have produced peace among major, or developed states, surely it is even more difficult to argue persuasively that nuclear weapons are a key to peace in a region like the Middle East. Though they are aware of the difficulties and make valiant attempts to deal with them, writers like Waltz, Bueno de Mesquita and Riker, Feldman, and Rosen (the advocates of nuclear proliferation mentioned above), do not deal convincingly with at least a couple of the problems in their arguments supporting proliferation. These problems involve imbalances and monopolies that would be likely to result in the process of proliferation in the Middle East, and the vulnerability to pre-emptive strikes or technological breakthroughs of the necessarily small arsenals that would result from that process (Ray 1985, 1991; Betts 1985; Nye 1981).

Peace through "Moral Progress"

Neither economic factors nor military technology, perhaps, can be counted on to create conditions in which war will not pay with such overwhelming consistency that it will virtually never be fought. Perhaps international war might be more dependably eliminated by widespread, nearly universal acceptance of the norm that initiating war is unacceptable on arational, or ethical grounds. That, at least, is the kind of argument made by both Mueller (1989) and Ray (1989). But, according to Mueller (1991, p. 27), "If one arranges the areas of the world by . . . economic development, it seems that when ideas have filtered throughout the world in recent centuries, they have tended to do so in one direction, with what Europeans would a century ago have called the 'civilized world' at the lead." He goes on to point out that "sometimes ideas which have had a vogue and become 'passe' in the West can still be seen to be playing themselves out in the less developed world. . . . " This is the case, Mueller (1991, p. 28) concludes, with regard to "notions concerning the desirability and efficacy of war."

Ray's argument regarding the impact of cultural ideas on the incidence of war rests even more heavily than Mueller's on an analogy with the impact of "moral progress" on the abolition of slavery. "There are logical connections," according to this argument, "between the practice of slavery and the philosophical rationalizations developed in its defense on the one hand and the practice of war and its associated philosophical defense on the other . . . these connections suggest that if one comes to seem outmoded because of the developments in ethical thought, the other might soon suffer the same fate" (Ray 1989, p. 423). The developments in ethical thought referred to here have their roots most prominently in the Enlightenment and Western, liberal notions regarding equality and sanctity of human life. Similarly, Fukuyama (1992, p. 382) argues that "the root cause for the secular decline of slavery . . . and war is the same," i.e., developments in the area of political philosophy associated with the impact of the French Revolution on cultural and political attitudes.

It may be relevant, then, to point out that "the institution [of slavery] was finally outlawed by Saudi Arabia in 1962 and by the Sultanate of Muscat and Oman in 1970" (Davis 1984, p. 379), and that even more recently there has been a controversy about slavery in the Sudan (Mahmud and Baldo 1987). The relatively late disappearance of slavery in the Middle East might suggest that evolutionary trends in ethical attitudes about international war (as well as slavery) are even more unlikely to have an important impact on the incidence of war in that region than in other parts of the Third World.

Peace through Democracy

On the basis, in part, of findings reported by Rummel (1975–1981, 1983) and Doyle (1986), Jack Levy (1988, p. 662) declares that "the absence of war between democracies comes as close as anything we have to an empirical law in international relations." Maoz and Abdolali (1989, p. 3) provide important systematic empirical evidence supporting first, the idea that "democracies rarely clash with one another, and never fight each other in war," and, second, Russett's (1989, p. 245) assertion that "democratic states have not fought each other. This is one of the strongest nontrivial or nontautological statements that can be made about international relations."

Maoz and Russett (1991, 1992) generate quite persuasive evidence that the correlation between democracy and peace on the dyadic level of analysis is not spurious, at least for the period from 1946 to 1986, a finding reinforced by Bremer's (1992) analysis of over 200,000 dyad years from 1816 to 1965. Bueno de Mesquita and Lalman (1992) have developed a theory of international conflict interactions that supports a *liberal* (as opposed to a *realpolitik*) argument stressing the importance of regime type to an understanding of the outcomes of disputes between states. It provides a theoretical basis of impressive breadth and depth for anticipating the view that conflicts between democratic states are unlikely to end up in international war.

It can be inferred from the hypothesized peaceful nature of relationships between democracies that a world full of democracies would be peaceful, an inference especially profound in its implications if in fact there is a global trend toward democracy.[4] Harvey Starr (1991, p. 379), relying on data from Freedom House (Gastil 1983, 1989), shows that there was "a global movement towards democracy even prior to 1989/90." R. Bruce McColm (1991, p. 6) reports that according to Freedom House data on 1991, "of the 165 countries monitored . . .

formal liberal democracies account for 76 countries and another 36 (112 of the 165 monitored) could be said to be in varying stages of transition to a democratic system." And with respect to 1991, Freedom House has announced that the number of countries that qualify as "free" reached a record high (*Los Angeles Times Report* 1991, p. 25).[5]

Categorizing countries by regime type is typically a controversial business, of course, but by now there is a fairly widespread agreement that the number of democratic countries in the world has increased substantially in the last couple of decades. Samuel P. Huntington (1991a, p. 12), for example, asserts that "between 1974 and 1990, at least 30 countries made transitions to democracy, just about doubling the number of democratic governments in the world." Taking a more long-range look at the question, Gurr (1974, p. 1501) reported in his review of political systems from 1800 to 1971 that "marked increases were found between the 19th- and the mid-20th century polities in the extent of 'democratic' authority characteristics such as institutional constraints on chief executives and the openness of the process by which they attained office." It may be even more significant for the future of global politics and international war that, as Modelski (1990, p. 22) points out, over the last 500 years "there has been a progressive growth—via a massive learning diffusion process—of an increasingly weighty community of democracies." Modelski and Perry (1991) analyze this process in some detail; according to their data, 1 to 2 percent of the world's population lived in democratic states in the seventeenth century, a figure which reached 10 percent by 1900 and currently stands at about 40 percent.

The Global Origins of the Democratizing Trend

Whether or not the global trend toward democracy will ultimately extend to the Middle East depends in part on the origins of this trend. Do the sources and dynamics of that trend, to the extent that they can be accurately perceived, suggest that the currently undemocratic regimes in the Middle East will ultimately succumb to the forces at work in other parts of the globe?

To some extent, each of the regime transitions in the last ten to twenty years has had its idiosyncratic origins. However, it is this writer's impression that many and perhaps most attempts to account for regime transitions tend to rely too heavily on factors internal to the states being analyzed. For example, Gillespie (1987), O'Donnell, Schmitter, and Whitehead (1986), Baloyra (1987a, 1987b), Vanhanen (1990), virtually all chapters in Diamond, Linz, and Lipset

(1989), and all the works reviewed by Nef (1988) focus almost exclusively on internal structures and processes in their account of recent regime transitions.[6]

Daniel Levine (1988), in another review of several works on recent regime transitions, points out that most analysts have shifted their level of analysis away from global or regional elements in favor of the play of forces within national societies, reflecting their disenchantment with the failure of models emphasizing exogenous factors, such as world-system analysis and dependency theory, to predict or explain the recent crisis of authoritarianism. But this understandable disenchantment may have resulted in an overreaction, or an unwillingness to grant system level factors their due even when they have left quite visible traces. A fairly straightforward logic suggests that so many transitions away from authoritarian rule toward more democratic governance in so many different places at more or less the same time (in the last decade or so) are unlikely to have totally different, independent causal origins. The idea that they are essentially random, coincidences, all brought about by independently operating different causal processes within each of the different states in Latin America, Eastern Europe, Africa, Asia, or the Middle East, which just *happened* to produce similar results at essentially the same time, is inherently implausible (Ray 1982). There must be some common sources that account for all these virtually simultaneous changes in such far-flung corners of the globe.

Samuel Huntington agrees with the logic of that argument[7] and points out five factors which he feels have been most fundamental to the global democratizing trend in the last fifteen or twenty years: (1) legitimacy problems in authoritarian systems; (2) rapid economic growth in the 1960s; (3) changes in the doctrine and activities of the Catholic Church; (4) changes in the policies of the Soviet Union, the United States, and the European Community; (5) "snowballing," or diffusion of transitions from early democratizers to later ones (Huntington 1991b, pp. 45–46).

Huntington's discussion of the impact of each of these factors on the contemporary global democratizing trend is, for the most part, persuasive. But the thesis here suggests that in compiling that list of five factors, and even in a much longer list of possibly important causes of the global democratizing trend (Huntington 1991b, p. 37), Huntington overlooks a fundamental, and arguably the most important reason for the proliferation of transitions to democracy in the last twenty years. Surely one of the most important common sources of those transitions involves the impact of economic and political competition among the largest, most important states in the international system. The basic argument here is that this competition and the implications of its outcome are crucially important because of the tendency for states to emulate those who are perceived to be most successful in this competition. This imitative tendency has its most important basis, perhaps, in the anarchic nature of the international system. "Competitive systems," Waltz (1986, p. 66) points out, "are regulated, so to speak, by the 'rationality' of the more successful competitors. . . . Either their competitors emulate them or they fall by the wayside. . . . Competition spurs the actors to accommodate their ways to the . . . most acceptable and successful practices."[8] Francis Fukuyama (1992) is quite contemptuous of realism in general and of Waltz's neorealistic approach in particular (see, for example, p. 381), but he argues that "the possibility of war is a great force for the rationalization of societies, and for the creation of uniform social structures across cultures. Any state that hopes to maintain its political autonomy is forced to adopt the technology of its enemies and rivals. More than that, however, the threat of war forces states to restructure their social systems along lines most conducive to producing and deploying technology" (Fukuyama 1992, p. 73).[9] This argument may put more stress on the possibility of outright military conflict and less on the impact of more economically oriented competition than current global conditions warrant. And to develop this thesis more fully, one ought to emphasize that competitors also learn from the failures of others and attempt to avoid similar mistakes. If James Rosenau's (1990, pp. 387, 422) thesis about the emergence of "turbulence" in the current international system is valid, the analytic skills of leaders and citizens are much improved in the contemporary era. One of the effects of this improvement is a "trend toward performance [as opposed to traditional] criteria of legitimacy,"[10] a trend that would increase the pressure on governments to emulate successful methods and avoid failures based on contrasting methods and policies.

Competition among the major powers of the world helps to explain regime transitions among the other states. The Soviet Union's rise and fall over the last sixty years or so is a factor of particular importance to an understanding of trends in transitions during that time period. The Soviet Union began to build an image as a prototype or model for other countries to emulate in the 1930s. The Western industrialized countries were in the throes of the Great Depression, while the Soviet Union, according to the image it managed to project at any rate, was undergoing a period of dynamic economic change and progress under the beneficent guiding hand of Joseph Stalin. Although it was dealt a stunning blow by Hitler's surprise attack in 1941, the Soviet Union recovered and managed to establish a reputation as a first-rate military power by the end of the Second World War. This reputation was solidified when the Soviets developed an atomic bomb by 1949, more rapidly than most in the West had assumed was possible. The emergence of the Soviet economy in the 1950s as the world's second largest gave it natural prominence as a possible model to be emulated by all those countries hoping to duplicate its rapid rate of industrialization. Then, the launching of two sputnik satellites in the fall of 1957 made the Soviet Union, and socialism, appear to be the irresistible wave of the future.

The launching of the sputniks made an obvious impression on the outside world. "A leading Western ambassador" cabled a report to his government that "on October 4 [the day sputnik's launching was announced], the balance of political and diplomatic power shifted from Washington to Moscow" (*Newsweek* 1957, p. 29).[11] Ambassadors (and journalists) were by no means the only observers who were impressed by the stellar accomplishments of the Soviets. Hans Morgenthau (1958, pp. 133-34), for example, a few months after the launching of the sputniks, acknowledged that "the demonstration of American technological inferiority has greatly diminished the prestige of the United States among the uncommitted nations," and that "the prestige of the Soviet Union, by virtue of its accomplishments in one spectacular field of technology, has risen."[12]

In the decade or so after the sputniks, Western scholars developed theories of political development that built upon this insight in a way that could be viewed as providing rationalizations for dictatorship that were, in small part at least, self-fulfilling prophecies. Alexander Gerschenkron (1962) and Barrington Moore (1966), for example, both developed arguments to the effect that latecomers to the industrialization process needed to deal with different problems, problems which required governmental structures that were "different" from the bourgeois democratic forms of the early industrializers.[13]

Perhaps the most influential version of the thesis regarding the irrelevance of democracy to the problems of Third World countries was developed by Samuel Huntington in *Political Order in Changing Societies* (1968). One (anti-democratic) theme pervades the book. "The Lockean American is so fundamentally anti-government," according to Huntington, "that he identifies government with restrictions on government. . . . In many modernizing societies this formula is irrelevant. . . . The problem is not to hold elections but to create organizations" (Huntington 1968, p. 7).

So, in the 1960s and into the 1970s, the Soviet Union proclaimed itself as the regime most worthy of emulation by developing countries, and its claim seemed validated by its general economic performance, as well as the launching of the sputniks. At the same time, many (or most?) Western scholars of political development acknowledged that democracy was probably not appropriate for the problems facing most Third World countries.[14] Some of the dictatorships in the Third World that emerged during this time were tolerated and/or supported by the United States government because it feared that leftist authoritarian regimes were the likely alternatives. Others emulated the Soviet Union and/or the Chinese systems to a greater or lesser degree. Almost all of the modernizing dictatorships of the left or the right were influenced by the notion that the Soviet Union had demonstrated that dictatorship is both necessary and desirable in the face of the type and the number of problems confronting such regimes in the twentieth century. As Huntington (1968, pp. 137–38) explained:

> Today, in much of Asia, Africa, and Latin America, political systems face simultaneously the needs to centralize authority, to differentiate structure, and to broaden participation. It is not surprising that the system which seems most relevant to the simultaneous achievement of these goals is a one-party system. If Versailles set the standard for one century and Westminster for another, the Kremlin may well be the most relevant model for many modernizing countries in this century. . . . The primary need these countries face is the accumulation and concentration of power, not its dispersion, and it is in Moscow and Peking and not in Washington that the lesson is to be learned.

The Turning of the Worm

The world looks rather different in the 1990s. By the 1980s, the Soviet economy had not come close to surpassing the U.S. economy, either in total or per capita production. Furthermore, throughout most of the latter part of the 1980s, Mikhail Gorbachev argued repeatedly and persuasively that Stalin had imposed on the Soviet Union a political and economic system that needed to be drastically reformed if that country were not to be relegated to a position of permanent inferiority and irrelevance. This point has been dramatically reinforced by the fact that during the period when the Soviets had projected that they would surpass the United States economically, they were instead surpassed by democratic and non-Western Japan, which as recently as 1965 had an economy only about 25 percent as large as that of the Soviet Union. The importance of that profound transition among the major powers of the world has been reinforced by the fact that the economic success of democracies has not been limited to the United States or Japan. In 1989, for example, every country in the world with a GNP per capita of over $10,000 a year, and a life expectancy of

75 years or over (a pair of indicators that arguably reflect a desirable combination of economic dynamism and a high physical quality of life), was democratic (World Bank 1991, pp. 204–05).

The Soviet Union also ceased to seem worthy of emulation in the eyes of many because it achieved neither economic equity nor the development of legitimate political institutions. In addition to economic growth, equity and political institutionalization are basic goals for virtually all developing countries. Thomas Dye and Harmon Ziegler (1988) suggested that wealth was more inequitably distributed in the Soviet Union than in the United States. Their assertion was based on a source published some time ago (Ward 1978), and more recent data (Durning 1990, p. 138) suggest that incomes were more equally distributed in the Soviet Union (before its dissolution) than in the United States. But possession of money was not sufficient for the purpose of achieving access to goods and services in the Soviet Union. Communist Party membership, or some other basis of political power, was also necessary if one was to avoid long lines and empty store shelves. Even if money incomes were distributed more evenly in the former Soviet Union, access to goods and services, and therefore wealth (the focus on the data in Ward 1978) may have been more evenly distributed in the United States. Better, even if inadequate access to health services, for example, even for relatively disadvantaged groups in the United States, might account for the fact that "in 1985, a male infant born in the Soviet Union had an expected life span of 63 years . . . two less than a black baby boy [in the United States]" (Heise 1989, p. 36).

Huntington explained that Leninism, as a theory of political development, provided guidelines for political mobilization, political institutionalization, and the foundations of political order.[15] But now the Soviet Union has fallen apart, and Leninism seems to have failed, in the long run, at the crucial political tasks of political integration and concentration of power in the central government.

The deterioration of the Soviet Union as an authoritarian model to emulate is not a recent phenomenon. The reforms of Mikhail Gorbachev, and the dissolution of the Soviet Union, serve only to highlight, albeit quite dramatically, a process which became quite visible some time ago. Well-known Sovietologist Bialer (1981, p. 1001) observed more than ten years ago that "the Soviet Union['s] . . . model of rule and development . . . is increasingly considered irrelevant by both Marxists and non-Marxists, and the Soviet socioeconomic and political system is held in greater contempt than ever."[16] Rather oddly, in light of the extent to which Huntington (1968) stressed the influence of the Soviet example, his more recent work (Huntington 1991b) puts no stress on the impact of the Soviet Union's fate. This weakening of the Soviet model, in process now for ten or fifteen years, and the corresponding increase in the attractiveness of democratic models, accounts in large measure, I would argue, for the "deepening legitimacy problems of authoritarian systems" as well as the "snowballing, or demonstration effects . . . of the first transitions to democracy in the third wave," which Huntington (1991b, pp. 45–46) does emphasize. The impact of this competitive process among the major powers of the world also subsumes, or is arguably more fundamental to an understanding of the process of global democratization in the last two decades than the other three factors to which Huntington calls our attention (i.e., growth in the 1960s, changes in the policies of the Catholic Church, and changes in the policies of the Soviet Union, the United States, and the EC).

Democratization in the Middle East

Will the democratizing trend visible in virtually every part of the globe extend to the Middle East? There is a lot of skepticism on this point.[17] It would be futile to deny that there are good reasons for this skepticism. In 1989, for example, there were only twelve nations in the world that did not make the (admittedly minimal) symbolic commitment to "democracy" involved in an official policy of universal suffrage, and eight of those twelve were concentrated in the Middle East (Bahrain, Kuwait, Lebanon, Qatar, Saudi Arabia, Oman, the United Arab Emirates, and the Yemen Arab Republic) (*The World Factbook 1989*, 1989). By 1991 there were thirteen states without universal suffrage, and the Yemen Arab Republic had merged with the People's Democratic Republic of Yemen and adopted a policy of universal suffrage. So only seven of the thirteen states without universal suffrage were in the Middle East (unless Afghanistan is considered "Middle Eastern"); however, eleven of those thirteen were members of the Organization of the Islamic Conference (i.e., Afghanistan, Bahrain, Brunei, Burkina Faso, Kuwait, Lebanon, Qatar, Guinea, Oman, Saudi Arabia, and the United Arab Emirates).[18]

In 1990, a story in the *New York Times* declared that "Algeria is the Arab world's Eastern Europe. . . . It was a genuine revolution and had a moral authority within the Arab world" (Ibrahim 1990, p. 6). Even as recently as the beginning of 1992, Norton (1992, p. 38) asserted that "one of the most important and promising political experiments underway in the Arab world is in Algeria. . . . Algeria has become a bellwether for the possibility of a genuine political opening in the Arab world, and the results of the proposed elections are likely to inspire imitation elsewhere." But the elections in Algeria were canceled, out of fear of what Islamic fundamentalists would do if they won them. "Quite suddenly, from Riyadh to Rabat, fear of fundamentalism is back" (*Economist* 1992a, p. 45).

The dynamics of competition within the global political system might reinforce this trend in the Middle East toward fundamentalism and against democracy, as well as against the United States. After the Napoleonic Wars in the early nineteenth century, and after the First and Second World Wars, the victors in those wars constituted a "grand coalition" of almost everybody against almost nobody. According to the logic of the "size principle," rational actors will create coalitions that are just large enough to win, but no larger (Riker 1962, pp. 32–33). The necessity of sharing the "spoils" of victory so widely exerts a powerful pressure against the stability of grand coalitions, each of which, after the Napoleonic Wars of the nineteenth century and the World Wars of the twentieth century, fell apart.[19]

"In the last few years, we seem to have experienced something like the functional equivalent of World War III" (Mueller 1991, p. 6). So far, the "grand coalition" resulting from the end of the Cold War has held together pretty well; for example, when Iraq invaded Kuwait, "the five permanent members . . . acted in concert to enforce the international law governing the use of force against an aggressor state . . . [for] the first time since the adoption of the U.N. Charter in 1945" (Damrosch and Scheffer 1991, p. ix). But as Jervis (1991/92, p. 62) acknowledges, "If the standard rules of international relations were still to apply, the Soviet Union would be replaced as an American adversary by one of the most powerful states in the system."

China is the most obvious candidate for leader of an anti-American, and probably antidemocratic coalition, and China is showing signs of assuming that position already. Vietnam and China, usually antagonistic, have improved relations. More importantly, China and North Korea, another member of this nascent antidemocratic coalition, seem intent on supplying various sorts of advanced military technology to several states in the Middle East, such as Libya, Syria, and Iran. If the coalescence of the antidemocratic forces in the world continues apace, and Middle Eastern states are swept up into this process, that will likely reinforce fundamentalist, anti-American, and antiliberal regimes and political ideologies in that region.

Probably the most serious threat to any trend toward democracy in the Middle East, however, has the same origins as the threat to the global trend. Global democratization is most vulnerable to reversal for the same reasons that the recent surge came into being in the first place. It involves competition in the anarchic international system, and the resulting tendency for successes to be emulated. Even though the democratizing trend has not been entirely dependent on economic factors so far, "democracy" might be discredited to a crucial extent if few or none of the newer democratic regimes prove able to deal successfully with the economic challenges facing them in the future. Perhaps most crucial will be the fate of economic and political reforms in the Soviet successor states of the Commonwealth of Independent States. If those republics turn in large numbers to severe authoritarian tactics, say, in order to complete their moves in the direction of a market economy, or to reimpose Stalinist controls, that will constitute a serious blow to the trend toward democracy, in the entire world as well as the Middle East.

The fate of political reforms in China might also help to bring the global democratizing trend to a halt. Liu Binyan (1989, p. 22) a former member of the Chinese Communist Party, reports that Chinese leadership took the action it did in Tiananmen Square in June of 1989 on the grounds that Hong Kong, Singapore, South Korea, and Taiwan adhered to authoritarian tactics until after they had achieved considerable economic gains.[20] China may come to be seen as an important trendsetter in that direction in the coming years. The "Four Tigers" have great potential to play an important role in a process which might inspire an antidemocratic trend just because those East Asian countries have been so successful economically and because their success has not obviously been duplicated by rival prototypes or models relying on democratic political processes. In short, there is a clear danger that future circumstances will lead to the widespread conclusion (again) that democracy is a luxury that can only be afforded *after* a high level of economic development is achieved, and that the major shortcoming of previous authoritarian regimes that failed to duplicate the success of those in East Asia was that they simply adopted faulty strategies.[21]

Samuel Huntington (1991b, pp. 15–16) notes that there have been two previous waves of democratization, from 1828 to 1926, and from 1943 to 1962: "Each of the first two waves of democratization was followed by a reverse wave in which some but not all of the countries that had previously made the transition to democracy reverted to nondemocratic rule." The third wave may also be reversed to some substantial extent unless some of the newer democracies (especially the ones in the CIS and Eastern Europe), are soon able to demonstrate some real successes in dealing with their serious economic problems.

On the Bright Side

Although the "grand coalition" that has emerged in the wake of the end of the Cold War may fall apart, as previous grand coalitions have (after the Napoleonic Wars of the previous century and the World Wars of this one), Jervis (1991/92, p. 62) declares, "I do not believe that this will occur," at least partly because democratic states do not fight wars against each other, nor even engage in serious conflicts at the rates other states do, and the major powers of the world are within shouting distance at this time of being uniformly democratic. China is the most glaring exception (although democracy is far from secure in Russia) but some recent reports indicate that "reform is winning in China. . . . China is still far from free, but the omens for it are good" (*Economist* 1992b, p. 14). If China were to move in a market-oriented, and then a democratic direction in, say, the next five years or so, that would prevent the unification of antidemocratic forces in the world, perhaps, and also deprive those forces of yet another example in support of the argument that only authoritarian governments can deal successfully with the rigors of the early stages of economic development in the twentieth century.

Even if the "the third wave" of democratization is sustained, or at least not rolled back substantially, there are those who would argue, as we have seen, that the Middle East might be the only region in the world that would remain impervious to that trend. Most arguments to this effect point to the profound incompatibility between democracy and Islam, or at least Islamic fundamentalism. However, as Huntington (1991b, pp. 75–76, 310) points out, the first wave of democratization was concentrated in Protestant countries, and this evoked decades of theorizing that Catholicism was inherently antidemocratic. In recent decades, though, "the third wave [of democratization] of the 1970s and 1980s was overwhelmingly a Catholic wave" (Huntington 1991b, p. 76), leading Huntington and others (such as Karl 1990) to speculate that Catholicism, because of changes in the Church originating in the Second Vatican Council of 1963–1965, has now become an important force in favor of democratizing trends.

This turnabout is reminiscent, as Huntington acknowledges, of similar transformations in ideas about the relationship between culture and politics, as well as economics. For example, Asia's relative "backwardness" in comparison with Europe, led for centuries to speculation—at its most visible in the

writings of Max Weber—that there is a profound incompatibility between
Confucianism and modernization or dynamic economic growth. But the success of the East Asian "tigers" in recent decades now inspires theorists like Kahn
(1984, p. 78) to argue that "societies based upon the Confucian ethic may in
many ways be superior to the West in the pursuit of industrialization, affluence, and modernization."

Thanks also to the influence of Max Weber, Protestantism is often given
credit for the blooming of economic and political liberalism in both North-
western Europe as well as the United States. But read about John Calvin's Geneva in the middle of the sixteenth century:

> To regulate lay conduct a system of domiciliary visits was established: one or
> another of the elders visited, yearly, each house in the quarter assigned to him,
> and questioned the occupants on all phases of their lives. Consistory and
> Council joined in the prohibition of gambling, card-playing, profanity, drunk-
> enness, the frequenting of taverns, dancing . . . indecent or irreligious songs,
> excess in entertainment, extravagance in living, immodesty in dress. The al-
> lowable color and quantity of clothing, and the number of dishes permissible
> at a meal, were specified by law. Jewelry and lace were frowned upon. A woman
> was jailed for arranging her hair to an immoral height. Theatrical perform-
> ances were limited to religious plays, and then these too were forbidden. . . .
> Censorship was taken over from Catholic and secular precedents, and en-
> larged: books of erroneous religious doctrine, or of immoral tendency, were
> banned. . . . To speak disrespectfully of Calvin or the clergy was a crime. A
> first violation of these ordinances was punished with a reprimand, further vio-
> lation with fines, persistent violation with imprisonment or banishment. For-
> nication was to be punished with exile or drowning; adultery, blasphemy, or
> idolatry, with death. In one extraordinary instance a child was beheaded for
> striking its parents. . . . Torture was often used to obtain confessions or evi-
> dence. (Durant 1957, p. 474)

This was the cultural soil, so to speak, that was to be so nurturing, ultimately, to liberal political and economic values? Yes, according to Huntington
(1991b, pp. 310–11), for example, because "even if [a] culture . . . is at one point
an obstacle to democracy, cultures historically are dynamic rather than pas-
sive." That is one possible interpretation of the evidence regarding the linkage
between religious cultural background conditions and economic and/or political liberalization. Another interpretation would suggest that religious, cultural
traditions like Confucianism or Islam are such broad, ubiquitous, yet elusive

phenomena that they evoke numerous flexible, ad hoc, and even contradictory hypotheses which serve mainly to obscure more important relationships.

For example, Huntington (1991b), as we have seen, can argue plausibly that Catholicism has changed and is now an important force in support of the global democratizing trend. But it is also possible to argue, with at least equal logic and plausibility, that conservatives in the Catholic Church in Latin America have actually mounted an effective rearguard resistance to the decrees of the Second Vatican Council of the 1960s, and that the liberalizing trend in Latin America in the 1980s was not fostered by the Catholic Church but occurred in spite of the Catholic Church, because the Church is now so much less influential than it is generally presumed to be (Oxford Analytica 1991, pp. 129–34).[22]

Similarly, Fukuyama (1992, p. 217) can point out, plausibly, that because fundamentalist Islam is a totalistic religion which seeks to regulate every aspect of human life, both public and private, "it is not . . . surprising that the only liberal democracy in the contemporary Muslim world is Turkey, which was the only country to have stuck with an explicit rejection of its Islamic heritage. . . . " But Bill (1991, p. 4) can also observe that in the home of *the* Islamic fundamentalist Revolution, Iran, "there is a constitutional political system in place that includes an elected president, an elected 270-person parliament, [and] a cabinet appointed by the president but approved by the Majlis. . . . The Islamic Majlis is the site of spirited and wide-ranging debate. . . . No ideology, interest, or individual is immune from sharp criticism. The newspapers are often highly critical of the government and at times even of Rafsanjani. . . . " Bill explains, plausibly, that all this democratic activity is a result of the decrease in foreign threats to Iran (especially from Iraq), which has allowed "political participation and pluralism . . . to blossom as originally envisioned in the Islamic constitution," and he thus perceives, apparently, democratic impulses in that Islamic fundamentalist state which are bound to flourish if only Iran is freed from external menaces.

In other words, broad, religious cultural traditions are so multifaceted that whenever a political change takes place, such as democratization, one can always find some element within them which seems to have brought it about, *or* argue that the democratization has taken place because of the waning influence of that tradition. Possibly, the level of economic development is a more fundamental cause of democratization, and what has occurred is that Protestant, Catholic, and even, to some extent, Confucian countries have all proven capable of democratization when they, in turn, reached the requisite level of development. If so, then it may be significant that most of the undemocratic countries of the world entering into that range of development (as measured by GNP per capita) where most of the democratic transitions have taken place in recent decades are in the Middle East and North Africa. This leads Huntington (1991b, pp. 313–15) to declare that "the wave of democratization that . . . swept about the world from region to region in the 1970s and the 1980s could become a dominant feature of Middle Eastern and North African politics in the 1990s." In any case, whether one feels that Islam might change (like Protestantism and Catholicism have), or that perhaps religious cultural values are largely irrelevant to democratization, the conclusion with respect to the issue at hand is the same: Islam, even Islamic fundamentalism, is unlikely to be an insuperable barrier to democratization in the Middle East, especially if (the thesis here would suggest), the global environment continues to be receptive to the broad democratizing trend in place over the last twenty years.

And if the democratizing trend does ultimately extend into the Middle East, it would not be "unrealistic," either in the common or in the international relations theoretical meaning of that term, to anticipate that the trend would bring with it a significant pacifying effect. (We have already seen that the democratizing trend itself can be interpreted as congruent with neo-realistic principles.) Robert O. Keohane (1983) points out that the three assumptions that constitute the "hard core" of the realist research paradigm are: (1) States are the most important actors, (2) Global politics can be analyzed as if states were unitary rational actors, and (3) States calculate their interests in terms of power. The work of Bueno de Mesquita (1981, 1985), and most recently his work with Lalman (1992) is based on a state-centric assumption and the rationality assumption. And although Bueno de Mesquita rightly argues that his approach focuses on other considerations, power calculations certainly play an essential part in it.

Bueno de Mesquita and Lalman (1992) develop a *liberal* alternative to a *realpolitik* approach to the analysis of international conflict; the fundamental difference between the two is that the liberal alternative, which they ultimately find superior, focuses on domestic political processes as a major factor. This emphasis on the role of domestic factors in international conflict does represent a departure from "realistic" thinking, especially in its "neorealistic" version, a "key distinguishing characteristic" of which is that "the internal attributes of actors are given by assumption rather than treated as variables"

(Keohane 1983, pp. 508–09). However, since Bueno de Mesquita and Lalman (1992) do also focus on states, on the rationality of actors, and on power calculations in a "realistic" fashion, and deduce even so that democratic states are very unlikely to fight wars against each other, then even the most hard-bitten "realists" would have to take seriously the proposition that a more democratic Middle East might be significantly more peaceful.[23]

In fact, the proposition that a global trend toward democracy might contribute significantly to the end of international war in general receives support from an impressive variety of theoretical approaches, from the modified (albeit significantly) realpolitik approach of Bueno de Mesquita and Lalman, to the "intentional humanism" of Rummel (1975–1981), learning theory and Modelski's long cycle theory (Modelski 1990), classical liberalism (Doyle 1986), diffusion theory (Starr 1991), and decision-making theories (Mintz and Geva 1992). The proposition that a trend toward democracy might contribute significantly to peace in the Middle East would also receive support from all of these sources. The idea that these notions are valid everywhere in the world *except* the Middle East is pessimistic to an unwarranted degree.

Conclusion

International war might become obsolete because of the impact of economic growth or interdependence, nuclear weapons, "moral progress," or a global trend toward democracy. Of all these factors, the one with greatest pacifying potential, according to the thesis here, is the global trend toward democracy. Of all the regions in the world, the Middle East is arguably the most impervious to the global democratizing trend. Most arguments to that effect focus on the alleged profound incompatibility between Islamic culture and democratic political values. However, Protestantism, Catholicism, and Confucianism have in turn all been categorized as antidemocratic (or, in the case of Confucianism, antimodernizing); currently, however, it is argued that they are especially amenable or hospitable to democracy and modernization. As in virtually all broad religious, cultural traditions, Islam too has elements that might be considered "democratic," and these elements might come to seem more obvious and important as Middle Eastern countries reach higher levels of economic development. If so, a wide variety of theoretical approaches to international politics, including those with important characteristics of "realism," suggest that democracy might ultimately have a pacifying impact on the Middle East in particular, as well as the world in general.

NOTES

1. Morgenthau (1967, p. 49) asserts that "from Sir Andrew Freeport in the *Spectator* at the beginning of the eighteenth century to Norman Angell's *The Great Illusion* in our time, it has been the conviction of the capitalists as a class and most capitalists as individuals that 'war does not pay,' that war is incompatible with an industrial society, and that the interests of capitalism require peace and not war."

2. Mueller (1991, p. 1) specifies that this means "becoming [not being] obsolete."

3. Waltz (1954, p. 99) points out that "the expenses of conquering and holding cannot be balanced by advantages in trade, for the same advantages can be had, without expense, under a policy of free trade.... This reasoning is the root of the traditional war-does-not-pay argument, an argument dating back at least to Emeric Cruce early in the seventeenth century...."

4. According to Rothstein (1991, p. 47), Maoz and Abdolali (1989) report that "the proportion of democracies in the international system *positively* affects the number of disputes begun and underway," and concludes that there is not much support for the argument that "a system with more free or democratic states will also be peaceful...." However, especially if such people as Doyle (1986) and Bueno de Mesquita and Lalman (1992) are correct in their arguments that democratic states are especially likely to have conflictful relationships with nondemocratic states, one might expect to find such a positive relationship between the proportion of democracies in the system and the amount of conflict in the system (or at least expect that an increase in the number of democratic states would exert a pressure in that direction) as long as the addition of democracies increases the number of unbalanced dyads, i.e., pairs of states only one of which is democratic, in the system. But once the proportion of democratic states in the system reaches 50 percent (which would not have happened during the time period analyzed by Maoz and Abdolali), the addition of democratic states will increase the number of balanced, entirely democratic dyads, and thus exert a negative impact on the amount of conflict in the system.

5. However, Freedom House also announced at the same time that the proportion of the world's population living in "free" countries dropped in 1991, a result of their categorizing India as only "partly free" due to the violent election in the wake of the assassination of Prime Minister Rajiv Gandhi, and to "harsh repression" in Kashmir (*Los Angeles Times Report* 1991, p. 25).

6. Karl (1990, p. 5) neatly summarizes this point of view when she says "the search for causes rooted in ... international factors has not yielded a general law of democratization, nor is it likely to do so in the near future.... The search ... should probably

be abandoned and replaced by more modest efforts to derive a contextually bounded approach to the study of democratization."

7. "It does seem unlikely that the clustering of transitions within a decade and a half could be purely coincidental. It appears reasonable to assume that these transitions were produced in part by common causes affecting many countries" (Huntington 1991b, p. 44).

8. Waltz (1990, p. 7) updates this general theoretical point in his discussion of particular recent events when he asserts: "The changes taking place in the Soviet Union follow in good part from external causes. Gorbachev's expressed wish to see the Soviet Union enter the twenty-first century with dignity suggests this. One expects great powers to resist falling to lower international rankings. Brezhnev's successors, notably Andropov and Gorbachev, realized that the Soviet Union could no longer support a first-rate military establishment on the basis of a third rate economy. National economic reorganization, and the reduction of imperial burdens, became an international necessity, which in turn required internal political reform." (Deudney and Ikenberry 1991/92, p. 97, make a similar argument.) This explanation might seem suspect now that Gorbachev's policies have resulted in the dissolution of the Soviet Union rather than its revival, but it is certainly possible that the hope for revival was an important motive for perestroika and glasnost, and the dissolution of the country was an unintended result. And admittedly Waltz focuses on "great powers," while the argument here extends to all states in the system. Even smaller states have regional competitors to be concerned about, and the leaders of all states are anxious to secure their tenure as well as the prestige of their states with strong political institutions and high levels of economic performance. So, they also take their cues from successful competitors in the system.

9. And, again much like Waltz, Fukuyama (1992, p. 75) argues that "perhaps the most recent example of defensive modernization was the initial phase of Mikhail Gorbachev's own *perestroika*. It is quite clear from his speeches and those of other senior Soviet officials that one of the chief reasons that they initially considered undertaking a fundamental reform of the Soviet economy was their realization that an unreformed Soviet Union was going to have serious problems remaining competitive, economically and militarily, into the twenty-first century."

10. At another point, Rosenau (1990, p. 429) elaborates: "Just as people are increasingly inclined to demand that the claims of collectivities be grounded in persuasive evidence and proof, so they are more and more likely to insist that the legitimacy of leaders and their policies be grounded in appropriate and successful performances." Furthermore, Rosenau, unlike Waltz, applies this argument to all states, not just great powers.

11. For similar journalistic speculation along these lines, see Wallace 1957, and *Newsweek* 1958.

12. As Mueller (1989, p. 146) points out, "The impact of the space race can hardly be overstated. For the better part of a decade the Soviets scored triumph after triumph as the United States struggled desperately to get into the game. . . . These developments

made some Americans feel like losers. The Communists seemed to be on the march everywhere: winning hearts and minds left and right in the third world, and outclassing the West in important areas of technology."

13. Robert Heilbroner in *The Future as History*, published in 1959, nicely exemplifies the mood in much of American academia in that year. He points out that "until the present decade of world history, the generally accepted paragon of economic progress was the United States. This is no longer true" (Heilbroner 1959, p. 87). He points out that "the Russian over-all economy has been growing approximately twice as fast as our own; during the last recession it grew three times as fast" (p. 147). He refers repeatedly to the "worldwide retreat from capitalism" (p. 157) and concludes grimly that "the future holds out the grave threat of an ideological isolation of the American system" (p. 169). Heilbroner also points out in *The Future as History* that "in their situations of genuine frustration, one lesson will not be lost upon the underdeveloped nations. This is the fact that two peasant countries in the twentieth century have succeeded in making the convulsive total social effort which alone seems capable of breaking through the thousand barriers of scarcity, ineptitude, indifference, inertia. These are the Soviet Union and . . . China" (p. 86). See also Apter 1965. This idea was eventually reinforced by dependency theorists who typically concluded that highly centralized governments of the socialist type were necessary to deal with those problems (Frank 1968; Cardoso and Faletto 1978; Fagen 1978), and by theorists such as O'Donnell (1973), who argued that the economic difficulties faced by Latin American states in particular made "bureaucratic-authoritarian" regimes a more or less natural outcome.

14. Interesting evidence that scholarly ruminations of this kind can have practical consequences has surfaced in an article by Lucian Pye (1990, p. 17), who acknowledges that "theorists in both the Chinese Academy of Social Sciences and some of China's leading universities . . . came to the support of the official orthodoxy in 1988 by trying to develop what they call the theory of 'neo' or 'new' authoritarianism and which they thought might legitimize China's economic 'reforms' under conditions of political restriction. . . . They even sought to support their analysis by citing U.S. scholars who in the 1950s and 1960s suggested that dictatorial systems had some advantages in modernizing." Pye goes on to specify that the scholars the Chinese referred to were Samuel Huntington and members of the Social Science Research Council on Comparative Politics.

15. "The modernizers of the seventeenth century canonized the king, those of the twentieth century the party. But the party is a far more flexible and broad-gauged institution for modernization than the absolute monarchy. It is capable not only of centralizing power but also of expanding it. This is what makes the Leninist theory of political development relevant to the modernizing countries of Asia, Africa, and Latin America" (Huntington 1968, p. 342).

16. Three years later, reflecting what I would argue was already becoming an increasingly solid consensus on this point, which had not escaped the attention even of the leadership in the Soviet Union, Ford (1984, p. 1138) pointed out that "most knowledgeable Soviet officials . . . are aware . . . that the Soviet economic performance ap-

peals less and less to the outside world, and are in fact ashamed by the vast gap between their standard of living and that of the West." Less perspicaciously, Ford concluded this article with the following declarations: "We cannot change the Soviet system . . . alter their attitude toward human rights, weaken their hold on Eastern Europe, Mongolia or Afghanistan, or indeed change the rough military balance between the United States and the U.S.S.R. There is no hope of convergence of the two systems" (p. 1144).

17. For example, as Hudson (1990, p. 1) has pointed out, the editors of a recent multi-volume effort analyzing the spread of democracy in the Third World declare that "democracy is the only model of government with . . . broad ideological legitimacy and appeal in the world today," *except* in the "large portion of the world . . . where Islam is a major or dominant religion" (Diamond, Linz, and Lipset 1989, p. x). Fukuyama (1992) is extraordinarily optimistic about the global democratizing trend in general, but repeatedly comes up with assertions such as "the liberal revolution has left certain areas like the Middle East relatively untouched" (p. 45), and, even more pointedly, "Now, outside the Islamic world, there appears to be a general consensus that accepts liberal democracy's claim to be the most rational form of government" (p. 211). It is quite clear that "there is a tendency to presume that Arab societies are insulated from the global trend toward democratization" (Norton 1992, p. 37).

18. The only two countries in the world that did not have an official policy of universal suffrage and were not members of the Organization of the Islamic Conference were Fiji and Ghana, both of whom had such a policy in 1989, and, one can surmise, are likely to adopt it again in the not-too-distant future. Another statistic along these lines is provided by Huntington (1991, p. 308): "Between 1981 and 1990 only two of the thirty-seven countries in the world with Muslim majorities were ever rated 'free' by Freedom House in its annual surveys: The Gambia for two years and the Turkish Republic of Northern Cyprus for four."

19. As Riker (1962, p. 7) explains about the break-up of the coalition that was victorious in the Second World War, "Having defeated the Axis, the winners had nothing to win from unless they split up and tried to win from each other."

20. See also Pye (1990, p. 17) on this point.

21. Development economist Ronald Findlay, for example, argues that "the primary explanation for the difference between Latin American and East Asian trade regimes [is that] the East Asian countries are just more authoritarian. The East Asian governments are so much more authoritarian that they can simply impose the policies most conducive to growth with minimal accommodation to rent-seeking demands. The less authoritarian Latin American countries have to resort to import-substituting policies and money creation to buy political support" (cited in Woo 1990, p. 419).

22. "An estimated 90 percent of Latin Americans are baptized Catholic, yet only 10 to 15 percent attend mass regularly" (Oxford Analytica 1991, p. 129).

23. It might be relevant also to point out that Bueno de Mesquita (1981, pp. 138–39) finds that his expected utility approach to international conflict is applicable to the Middle East in particular, as well as to conflicts in general. (In fact, the proportion of

cases *not* conforming to predictions based on the model in that book is smaller in the Middle Eastern context than in Europe, the Americas, and Asia.)

REFERENCES

Angell, Norman. 1913. *The Great Illusion.* 4th ed. New York: Knickerbocker Press.

Apter, David. 1965. *The Politics of Modernization.* Chicago: University of Chicago Press.

Baloyra, Enrique, ed. 1987a. *Comparing New Democracies.* Boulder, CO: Westview.

———. 1987b. "Democracy Despite Development." *World Affairs* 150, pp. 73–92.

Betts, Richard K. 1985. "Surprise, Attack, and Preemption." In *Hawks, Doves, and Owls,* ed. Graham T. Allison Jr., Albert Carnesdale, and Joseph S. Nye, Jr. New York: Norton. Pp. 54–79.

Bialer, Seweryn. 1981. "The Harsh Decade: Soviet Policies in the 1980s." *Foreign Affairs* 59 (Summer), pp. 999–1020.

Bill, James A. 1991. "The New Iran: Relations with Its Neighbors and the United States." *Asian Update,* pp. 1–11.

Binyan, Liu. 1989. "Deng's Pyrrhic Victory." *New Republic* (October), pp. 21–24.

Bremer, Stuart. 1992. "Dangerous Dyads: Conditions Affecting the Likelihood of Interstate War, 1816–1965." *Journal of Conflict Resolution* 36 (June).

Brzezinski, Zbigniew. 1989. *The Grand Failure.* New York: Scribner's.

Bueno de Mesquita, Bruce. 1981. *The War Trap.* New Haven, CT: Yale University Press.

———. 1985. "The War Trap Revisited: A Revised Expected Utility Model." *American Political Science Review* 79 (March), pp. 156–77.

Bueno de Mesquita, Bruce, and David Lalman. 1992. *War and Reason.* New Haven, CT: Yale University Press.

Bueno de Mesquita, Bruce, and William Riker. 1982. "An Assessment of the Merits of Selective Nuclear Proliferation." *Journal of Conflict Resolution* 26 (June), pp. 283–306.

Cardoso, Fernando Henrique, and Enzo Faletto. 1978. *Dependency and Development in Latin America.* Berkeley: University of California Press.

Cohen, Eliot. 1990. "The Future of Force." *The National Interest* 21 (Fall), pp. 3–15.

Damrosch, Lori Fisher, and David J. Scheffer. 1991. Preface. In *Law and Force in the New International Order,* ed. Lori Fisher and David J. Scheffer. Boulder, CO: Westview.

Davis, David Brion. 1984. *Slavery and Human Progress.* New York: Oxford University Press.

Deudney, Daniel, and G. John Ikenberry. 1991/92. "The International Sources of Soviet Change." *International Security* 16 (Winter), pp. 74–118.

Diamond, Larry, Juan J. Linz, and Seymour Martin Lipset, eds. 1989. *Democracy in Developing Countries: Latin America*. Boulder, CO: Lynne Rienner.

Domke, William. 1988. *War and the Changing Global System*. New Haven, CT: Yale University Press.

Doyle, Michael W. 1986. "Liberalism in World Politics." *American Political Science Review* 80 (December), pp. 1151–70.

Durant, Will. 1957. *The Reformation*. New York: Simon and Schuster.

Durning, Alan B. 1990. "Ending Poverty." In *State of the World 1990*, ed. Lester Brown et al. New York: Norton. Pp. 135–53.

Dye, Thomas R., and Harmon Ziegler. 1988. "Socialism and Equality in Cross-National Perspective." *PS: Political Science and Politics* 21 (Winter), pp. 45–56.

Economist. 1992a. "Fear of Fundies." February 15. Pp. 45–46.

Economist. 1992b. "Upbeat China." March 21. Pp. 14–15.

Fagen, Richard. 1978. "A Funny Thing Happened on the Way to the Market." *International Organization* 32 (Winter), pp. 287–300.

Feldman, Shai. 1981. "A Nuclear Middle East." *Survival* 23 (May/June), pp. 107–16.

Ford, Robert A.D. 1984. "The Soviet Union: The Next Decade." *Foreign Affairs* 62 (Summer), pp. 1132–44.

Frank, Andre Gunder. 1968. *Development and Underdevelopment in Latin America*. New York: Monthly Review Press.

Fukuyama, Francis. 1989. "The End of History?" *National Interest* 16 (Summer), pp. 3–18.

———. 1992. *The End of History and the Last Man*. New York: Free Press.

Gaddis, John Lewis. 1986. "The Long Peace: Elements of Stability in the Postwar International System." *International Security* 10, no. 4 (Spring), pp. 99–142.

Gastil, Raymond. 1983. *Freedom in the World*. New York: Freedom House.

———. 1989. *Freedom in the World*. New York: Freedom House.

Gerschenkron, Alexander. 1962. *Economic Backwardness in Historical Perspective*. Cambridge: Harvard University Press, Belknap Press.

Gillespie, Charles C. 1987. "From Authoritarian Crisis to Democratic Transition." *Latin American Research Review* 22, pp. 165–85.

Gochman, Charles S., and Zeev Maoz. 1984. "Militarized Interstate Disputes, 1816–1976: Procedures, Patterns, and Insights." *Journal of Conflict Resolution* 28 (December), pp. 585–615.

Gurr, Ted Robert. 1974. "Persistence and Change in Political Systems, 1800–1971." *American Political Science Review* 68 (December), pp. 1482–1504.

Heilbroner, Robert. 1959. *The Future as History*. New York: Harper.

Heise, Lori. 1989. "Life and Death in the U.S.S.R." *Worldwatch* 2, pp. 26–37.

Holsti, K. J. 1986. "The Horsemen of the Apocalypse: At the Gate, Detoured, or Retreating?" *International Studies Quarterly* 30 (December), pp. 355–77.

Hudson, Michael C. 1990. "The Democratization Process in the Arab World: An Assessment." Presented at the annual meeting of the American Political Science Association, San Francisco, August 30–September 2.

Huntington, Samuel P. 1968. *Political Order in Changing Societies*. New Haven, CT: Yale University Press.

———. 1991a. "Democracy's Third Wave." *Journal of Democracy* 2 (Spring), pp. 12–34.

———. 1991b. *The Third Wave: Democratization in the Late 20th Century*. Norman, OK: University of Oklahoma Press.

Huth, Paul, and Bruce M. Russett. 1984. "What Makes Deterrence Work? Cases from 1900 to 1980." *World Politics* 36 (July), pp. 496–526.

Ibrahim, Youssef. 1990. "An Affluent Kuwait Joins the Arab Trend Toward Democracy." *New York Times*, March 11, sec. A, p. 6.

Jervis, Robert. 1991/92. "The Future of World Politics: Will It Resemble the Past?" *International Security* 16 (Winter), pp. 39–73.

Kahn, Herman. 1984. "The Confucian Ethic and Economic Growth." In *The Gap Between Rich and Poor*, ed. Mitchell A. Seligson. Boulder, CO: Westview. Pp. 78–80.

Karl, Terry Lynn. 1990. "Dilemmas of Democratization in Latin America." *Comparative Politics* 23 (October), pp. 1–21.

Kaysen, Carl. 1990. "Is War Obsolete? A Review Essay." *International Security* 14 (Spring), pp. 42–64.

Keohane, Robert O. 1983. "Theory of World Politics: Structural Realism and Beyond." In *Political Science: The State of the Discipline*, ed. Ada Finifter. Washington, DC: American Political Science Association. Pp. 503–40.

Kugler, Jacek. 1984. "Terror without Deterrence." *Journal of Conflict Resolution* 28 (September), pp. 470–506.

Levi, Werner. 1981. *The Coming End of War*. Beverly Hills, CA: Sage.

Levine, Daniel. 1988. "Paradigm Lost: Dependence to Democracy." *World Politics* 40 (April), pp. 377–94.

Levy, Jack S. 1988. "Domestic Politics and War." *Journal of Interdisciplinary History* 18, no. 4 (Spring), pp. 653–73.

Los Angeles Times Report. 1991. "Freedom Watchers Find 13 More Nations Qualify in '91." *Tampa Tribune*, December 19, sec. 1, p. 25.

Mahmud, Ushore Ahmad, and Suleyman Ali Baldo. 1987. *Al Dien Massacre: Slavery in the Sudan*. Khartoum: University of Khartoum.

Maoz, Zeev, and Nasrin Abdolali. 1989. "Regime Types and International Conflict, 1816–1976." *Journal of Conflict Resolution* 33 (March), pp. 3–35.

Maoz, Zeev, and Bruce M. Russett. 1991. "Normative and Structural Causes of Peace." Presented at the annual meeting of the Peace Studies Society, Ann Arbor, MI, November 15–17.

———. 1992. "Alliance, Contiguity, Wealth, and Political Stability: Is the Lack of Conflict among Democracies a Statistical Artifact?" *International Interactions* 17 (February), pp. 245–68.

McColm, R. Bruce. 1991. "The Comparative Survey of Freedom: 1991." *Freedom Review* 22, pp. 5–6 and 12.

Melko, Matthew. 1992. "Long-Term Factors Underlying Peace in Contemporary Western Civilization." *Journal of Peace Research* 29 (February), pp. 99–114.

Mintz, Alex, and Nehemia Geva. 1992. "Why Don't Democracies Fight Each Other? An Experimental Study." Presented at the Fourth World Peace Science Congress. Rotterdam, the Netherlands, May 18–20.

Modelski, George. 1990. "Is World Politics Evolutionary Learning?" *International Organization* 44 (Winter), pp. 1–24.

Modelski, George, and Gordon Perry III. 1991. "Democratization in Long Perspective." *Technological Forecasting and Social Change* 39, pp. 23–34.

Moore, Barrington Jr. 1966. *Social Origins of Dictatorship and Democracy.* Boston: Beacon Press.

Morgenthau, Hans. 1958. "Russian Technology and American Policy." *Current History* 34, pp. 133–34.

———. 1967. *Politics Among Nations,* 4th ed. New York: Knopf.

Mueller, John E. 1989. *Retreat from Doomsday: The Obsolescence of Major War.* New York: Basic Books.

———. 1991. "Is War Still Becoming Obsolete?" Presented at the annual meeting of the American Political Science Association, Washington, DC, August 29–September 1.

Nef, Jorge. 1988. "The Trend toward Democratization and Redemocratization in Latin America." *Latin American Research Review* 23, pp. 131–53.

Newsweek. 1957. "Satellites and Our Safety: Stepping up the Pace." October 21, p. 29.

Newsweek. 1958. "A World at Stake." January 20, p. 69.

Norton, Augustus Richard. 1992. "Breaking through the Wall of Fear in the Arab World." *Current History* (January), pp. 37–41.

Nye, Joseph S. 1981. "Sustaining Non-Proliferation in the 1980s." *Survival* 23 (May/June), pp. 98–106.

O'Donnell, Guillermo. 1973. *Modernization and Bureaucratic-Authoritarianism.* Berkeley: University of California, Institute of International Studies.

O'Donnell, Guillermo, Philippe C. Schmitter, and Laurence C. Whitehead, eds. 1986. *Transitions from Authoritarian Rule: Comparative Perspectives*. Baltimore: Johns Hopkins University Press.

Organski, A. F. K., and Jacek Kugler. 1980. *The War Ledger*. Chicago: University of Chicago Press.

Oxford Analytica. 1991. *Latin America in Perspective*. Boston: Houghton Mifflin.

Pye, Lucian. 1990. "Political Science and the Crisis of Authoritarianism." *American Political Science Review* 84 (March), pp. 3-20.

Ray, James Lee. 1982. "Designing Research on the World-System." *Comparative Political Studies* 15 (October), pp. 364-70.

———. 1985. *The Future of American-Israeli Relations*. Lexington: University Press of Kentucky.

———. 1986. "The Impact of Nuclear Weapons on the Escalation of International Conflicts." Presented at the annual meeting of the International Studies Association, Anaheim, CA, March 25-29.

———. 1989. "The Abolition of Slavery and the End of International War." *International Organization* 43 (Summer), pp. 405-39.

———. 1991. "The Future of International War." Presented at the annual meeting of the American Political Science Association, Washington, DC, August 29-September 1.

Riker, William. 1962. *The Theory of Political Coalitions*. New Haven, CT: Yale University Press.

Rosen, Stephen J. 1977. "A Stable System of Mutual Deterrence in the Arab-Israeli Conflict." *American Political Science Review* 71 (December), pp. 1367-83.

Rosenau, James N. 1990. *Turbulence in World Politics: A Theory of Changes and Continuity*. Princeton: Princeton University Press.

Rothstein, Robert L. 1991. "Democracy, Conflict, and Development in the Third World." *Washington Quarterly* 14 (Spring), pp. 43-66.

Rummel, Rudolph J. 1975-1981. *Understanding Conflict and War*. 5 vols. Beverly Hills, CA: Sage.

———. 1983. "Libertarianism and International Violence." *Journal of Conflict Resolution* 27 (March), pp. 27-71.

Russett, Bruce M. 1989. "Democracy and Peace." In *Choices in World Politics: Sovereignty and Interdependence*, ed. Bruce M. Russett, Harvey Starr, and Richard Stoll. New York: W. H. Freeman. Pp. 245-60.

Russett, Bruce M., and Harvey Starr. 1989. *World Politics: Menu for Choice*. New York: W. H. Freeman.

Starr, Harvey. 1991. "Democratic Dominoes: Diffusion Approaches to the Spread of Democracy in the International System." *Journal of Conflict Resolution* 35 (June), pp. 356–81.

Vanhanen, Tatu. 1990. *The Process of Democratization.* New York: Crane Russak.

Wallace, Robert. 1957. "First Hard Facts on All Russian Science." *Life,* November 16, pp. 109–22.

Walt, Stephen M. 1991. "The Renaissance of Security Studies." *International Studies Quarterly* 35 (June), pp. 211–40.

Waltz, Kenneth N. 1979. *Theory of International Politics.* New York: Random House.

———. 1982. "The Spread of Nuclear Weapons: More May Be Better." *Adelphi Papers* 171. London: International Institute of Strategic Studies.

———. 1986. "Reductionist and Systemic Theories." In *Neorealism and Its Critics,* ed. Robert O. Keohane. New York: Columbia University Press. Pp. 47–69.

———. 1990. "On the Nature of States and Their Recourse to Violence." *United States Institute of Peace Journal* 3 (June), pp. 6–7.

Ward, Michael. 1978. *The Political Economy of Distribution.* New York: Elsevier.

Weede, Erich. 1983. "Extended Deterrence by Superpower Alliance." *Journal of Conflict Resolution* 27 (June), pp. 213–54.

Woo, Wing Thye. 1990. "The Art of Economic Development: Markets, Politics, and Externalities." *International Organization* 44 (Summer), pp. 403–29.

World Bank. 1991. *World Development Report 1991.* New York: Oxford University Press.

World Factbook 1989, The. 1989. Washington, DC: Central Intelligence Agency.

World Factbook 1991, The. 1991. Washington, DC: Central Intelligence Agency.

2

DEMOCRACY AND DETERRENCE

JO-ANNE HART

Introduction

NUMEROUS STUDIES ADDRESS the question of whether domestic political freedom promotes international peace (Doyle 1983a; Lake 1992; Rummel 1983;
Maoz and Abdolali 1989; Chan 1984; Weede 1984). The importance of this research extends beyond its immediate findings and methods, however. First, for
theorists, it provokes debate over international relations paradigms: specifically,
whether structural realist models or state-level behaviorist models have more
explanatory power. Additionally, for regional specialists, it invites speculation
about whether the democratization trends currently sweeping the globe will
make states less prone to war and thereby alter the interstate dynamics of con-
flict-laden areas. The latter question is important for the Middle East; although
no full democracies have emerged in the region,[1] recent developments reflect
the growing popular appeal of participatory government.

The present chapter considers the question of regime type and war and
peace with particular reference to one subset of security issues—that of deterrence. The discussion highlights some of the presuppositions that undergird
the assertion of democratic pacifism and examines their applicability and consequences with reference to the Middle East. In addition, more specifically, it
asks whether democratic states have structural advantages which make them
better able than autocratic regimes to deter attacks and avoid war. Finally, the
chapter examines other factors that affect deterrence and shape deterrence
strategies. Prior to addressing these issues, however, it is necessary to define
deterrence and to explicate briefly the calculation of deterrence strategies.

Deterrence may be defined as a strategy undertaken by a state or set of states
to prevent another state or set of states "from taking actions it is considering
but has not already initiated" (Huth and Russett 1990). Understood as a re-

gime's strategy for preventing attack, deterrence thus differs from a regime's calculus for initiating war. Because a decision to use force is normally based on a cost-benefit assessment, a deterrer must be able to persuade a challenger that the actual use of force will be more costly than advantageous. For example, if a state can be persuaded that it will lose too many troops (cost) in the pursuit of desired territory (benefit), then the challenger will be unlikely to initiate an attack and hence will be deterred. In general, although it acknowledges that democratic and authoritarian regimes have different advantages and disadvantages with respect to deterrence, this chapter will argue that regime type alone is not sufficient to determine the incentives to use force and the calculation of tolerable costs. Under some conditions, both democracies and authoritarian regimes find it useful to go to war; and under other conditions, both pursue strategies of deterrence. Policies relating to war and deterrence thus are shaped not only by patterns of domestic governance but by other factors as well, including both mass and elite perceptions regarding costs and benefits, decision-making structures, and military capabilities.

Civilian Burden and Public Opinion

It is often asserted that the direct accountability of democratic leaders to their citizens limits the use of force in international relations. This proposition rests on several interrelated assumptions. First, because civilian populations bear the costs of war, they are normally expected to resist armed conflict among states. Second, since public support is imperative to a democratic regime, its leaders will similarly be disinclined to initiate war. For these reasons, democratic leaders may be more reluctant to assume the risks of war than the leaders of states whose citizens have no institutional mechanisms for registering dissent and holding the government accountable.

Electoral politics is particularly important in this connection, forcing democratic leaders to concern themselves with relatively short-term public opinion. As expressed by one scholar, incumbents are typically "driven by the necessity of securing enough votes to remain in office," and accordingly "insist upon evidence of a clear and present danger and usually require several provocations" before resorting to war (Schweller 1992). A related consideration is the role played by opposition parties in competitive political systems. Knowing that wars can create an opening for critics may stay the hand of leaders who would themselves have preferred the war option (Bueno de Mesquita and Lalman 1990).

While these arguments have some validity, they are not the whole story. They tend to underestimate both the power of political elites to mold public opinion and the sacrifices that civilian populations will often accept for the sake of some higher principle or cause. Nor do electoral considerations always bring opposition to international adventures. On the contrary, war situations can be used by incumbents to rally the electorate, especially if presented as requiring only quick and low-risk operations. Indeed, political science research provides a near consensus on the substantial connection between domestic needs and involvement in international conflict, and between election cycles and involvement in such conflict (Russett 1987; Nincic and Cusack 1985; Nordhaus 1975; Page and Shapiro 1983; Russett and Graham 1989).

Public opinion may also prevent governments from implementing rational deterrence strategies, prompting rather than constraining conflict. In the recent Gulf war, for example, the Arab regimes that were more sensitive to popular attitudes tended not to support U.S. interventionism and this may have encouraged Saddam Hussein to believe that the coalition ranged against him would collapse. Here, then, greater government accountability weakened rather than strengthened efforts at deterrence. One can also speculate that had Saudi Arabia been more democratic it would have been unable to accept 500,000 American troops on its soil, again reducing the ability to deter Iraqi aggression. And yet another potential problem was the strong desire of the Israeli public for retaliation in the face of Iraqi Scud missile attacks, even though this, too, might have undermined the coalition needed to deter the Baghdad regime. While these problems and potential problems in the end were not decisive, they indicate that war avoidance is not always made easier by greater accountability to public opinion.

Because authoritarian leaders are relatively unconstrained by public opinion, their decision-making is highly centralized and usually covert. This permits decisive and flexible decisions based more baldly on rational self-interest, or realpolitik, that often reinforces deterrence. Decisiveness and flexibility can allow authoritarian regimes to make difficult decisions on either side of the deterrence equation: They are free either to assume risk or to submit to a deterrent threat. In both instances, authoritarian leaders need offer fewer explanations for their actions than the leaders of democratic regimes.

There are times, however, when not even authoritarian regimes can ignore the desires of their subjects. Nondemocratic leaders do not systematically offer their citizens policy options regarding war and peace, but neither do they always disregard the potential civilian burden of initiating war. Although publics without representation or interest articulation are more vulnerable to assuming the costs of war, authoritarian regimes may nonetheless conclude that they must shield their civilian populations from significant war sacrifices. This may lower deterrent costs by preserving internal stability and consequently the authoritarian leader's position of power. Iraq's domestic strategy during its war with Iran is illustrative. By sustaining at least $80 billion in external debt, the regime provided a substantial consumer safety net which mitigated public sacrifice, at least in the short run. Presumably, this made an eight-year war more possible for Saddam Hussein. It would thus be a mistake to discount entirely the elements of accountability that may constrain authoritarian leaders.

There is also a deeper question concerning a society's willingness to bear costs related to war. To understand the conditions under which leaders will risk potentially great civilian burdens by attacking or deterring, it is necessary to bear in mind the principles and causes that frame the justification for such actions. Throughout history, civilians have often willingly endured enormous costs in order to achieve their goals. This is especially true when these goals are associated with matters of principle, such as legitimacy, justice, national self-esteem, or religious integrity.[2] Nor is there any inherent reason to suspect that democracy inhibits the willingness to sacrifice for popular ends. Historian Michael Eliot Howard (1976, pp. 110–11) reports that conflicts arising from nineteenth-century European nationalism were not tempered by democratization, since greater political participation led more citizens to see the state as embodying "higher values." Similarly, there is no shortage of causes and principles for which the Arab masses might be willing to fight, if the choice was theirs. As much or perhaps even more than Arab dictatorships, Arab democracies would likely be sensitive to the justice of the Palestinian cause, the redemption of Arab-Islamic pride, and freedom from Western dominance.

Some deterrence analysis suggests that when international conflict is discussed in the emotional language of self-esteem, there is an increased likelihood of "rationality" failures in foreign policy decision-making and, therefore, deterrence failures (Stern 1989; Russett 1989). This analysis would seem to have considerable relevance to the Middle East, and particularly to the Israeli-Palestinian conflict. Therefore, even if Arab regimes democratize, it seems unlikely that rational political considerations would preclude Arab regimes from initiating wars on the grounds of some important principle.

This discussion suggests that public opinion, both in its content and influence, has similar effects on deterrence in democratic and authoritarian regimes. It can compel both democratic and autocratic leaders to act either belligerently or judiciously, depending upon the principles behind the action and the importance of maintaining domestic stability. Admittedly, the collective pressure of the masses normally is not strong enough to make a difference in policies of national security and international relations. But here again there are similarities between democratic and authoritarian regimes; in both systems it is primarily the political and military elites who hold the power to formulate policies of national security and international relations. Consequently, it is necessary to go beyond an analysis that contrasts public opinion in democratic and authoritarian polities. To detect differences in deterrence between the two types of political systems, attention must be turned to the decision-making structures of each.

Decision-Making

National security decision-making is highly centralized and restricted in virtually all regimes. Decisions of war and peace, whether or not they are shared with state bureaucracies and representative assemblies, are made by the highest ranking political and military leaders. There are, however, some obvious differences in the way that democratic and authoritarian regimes make these decisions.

Decision-making is typically more open in democracies. Accountability and information exchange entail a degree of transparency. Contending opinions are openly expressed, and democratic political and military leaders frequently engage in at least limited public debate over security options. Authoritarian leaders, by contrast, are better able to limit decision-making input as well as public disclosure. This is especially true since they typically control the media and the flow of available information. These contrasting decision-making structures may have differing influences on the effectiveness of deterrence strategies in democratic and authoritarian regimes.

The inherent openness of democratic decision-making creates several disadvantages for democracies with respect to deterrence. International adversaries can regard the relatively exposed decision-making processes of democracies as a "window" on expected cost-benefit calculations, and this provides adversaries with the upper hand in formulating deterrence strategies. They can determine at what point war initiation becomes too costly for a democracy and then attempt to keep the stakes high enough to prevent war initiation by that democracy. Dealing with nondemocratic states, on the other hand, involves much more guesswork because their perceptions of costs and benefits are concealed.

By signalling a lack of resolve or credibility, the displays of discord and uncertainty that take place in democracies can similarly undermine a deterrence threat. Some speculate, for example, that Saddam Hussein's perception of American resolve during the 1990 Gulf crisis was negatively affected by the ongoing American debate about whether to go to war against Iraq. The Congressional hearings prior to the Gulf War are a good illustration. While political leaders publicly debated the advantages and disadvantages of sanctions and force to obtain the liberation of Kuwait, they confronted charges that the debate itself aided Iraq. Conversely, the ability of authoritarian regimes to deter a challenger is enhanced by the signs of resolve and genuine public commitment that stem from the secrecy of their decision-making process.

It should be added that countervailing influences may undo some of the advantages of concealed decision-making structures. Closed circles of authoritarian decision-making may increase the likelihood of incompetence and misjudgment and thus result in less effective policies. There is speculation, for example, that the isolated and sycophantic character of Saddam Hussein's closest advisors contributed to his mistakes and miscalculations in the 1990–91 Gulf crisis. Yet any firm conclusions about this possibility must await further investigation. Indeed, a variety of mistakes can defeat deterrence, and empirical work has demonstrated that both democratic and authoritarian regimes are subject to miscalculation, misjudgment, and misperception (Lebow 1989; Parker 1993). The relationship between authoritarianism and poorly conceived and implemented deterrence strategies is a promising arena for further inquiry, with the potential to contribute to a fuller understanding of the importance of regime type for international behavior.

Military Capabilities

Military capability is a key component of deterrence, both in the ability to deter and to initiate war.[3] Therefore, a key question is whether authoritarian or democratic states tend to have greater military capabilities.

Authoritarian regimes may be thought to have an advantage over democracies with respect to military capabilities. Authoritarian leaders often maintain excessively large standing armies and other military capabilities. Unlike elected leaders, the tenure of autocratic leaders depends largely upon repressing domestic opposition, and the role of checking internal subversion and maintaining domestic stability is usually assigned to the military. In addition, Lake (1992) attributes an inherent expansionist bias to autocracies, which may also predispose them to add military capabilities.[4] Finally, autocratic leaders can acquire and maintain such significant military capabilities because they are not accountable. In authoritarian systems, the public is less able to resist societal militarization, despite its burdens, meaning that authoritarian regimes may more easily implement such practices as conscription and heavy taxation.

Nevertheless, despite these advantages, authoritarian regimes do not necessarily have the upper hand in military capability. Democracies are typically wealthier than authoritarian systems and thus have more resources to devote to military expenditures. In addition, since World War II, public tolerance of defense spending has consistently been sufficient to sustain high standards of defense preparedness and highly advanced arsenals, despite the domestic opportunity costs that this entails. Thus, democracies seem to possess equal or even superior military strength compared to authoritarian regimes.

Many democracies have also found a successful counterpart to coercive conscription. Although conscription is generally unpopular and can act as an obstacle to protracted conflict, some democracies, such as France and Germany, have nonetheless implemented it successfully. Other democracies are able to maintain standing armies large enough to initiate and sustain the use of force by offering generous salaries and benefits for military service. By and large, however, because they are often reluctant to hold large numbers of troops under arms, and also because of the financial resources available to them, democracies tend to rely more on weaponry than on standing armies for deterrence. Weapons deployment can make threats to inflict retaliatory civilian pain highly credible and thus, in turn, dissuade challengers from initiating hostilities. For example, President Eisenhower deliberately chose to deploy U.S. nuclear weapons in Europe rather than sustain the burden of larger American troop deployments there.

Weapons that credibly threaten an adversary's civilian population are especially effective deterrents, regardless of regime type. This is particularly true for nuclear weapons. The Cold War illustrated that neither superpower could attain a deterrence monopoly in the nuclear age. The current Middle Eastern proliferation of other unconventional arsenals, such as ballistic missilry and chemical weapons, enhances this type of capability, regardless of the character of the regime. Yet even the ability to harm civilian populations is not a strictly reliable form of deterrence. Empirical evidence from modern wars is mixed as to the correlation between population losses and decisions to surrender or refrain from attack (Pape 1991 and Rosen 1972). American ability, and willingness, to devastate Vietnam was not determinative, for example. Similarly, the missile "war of the cities" that Iran and Iraq conducted during the latter stages of their war eroded public morale but was not decisive for either side. To be determinative, casualty rates probably must exceed some threshold, but estimating this threshold in particular instances has often proven elusive.

This also raises a larger and more challenging question about the foundation of deterrence. To what extent does behavior conform to the rational expected utility assumptions of classic deterrence theory? There is a substantial empirical basis for the argument that when states use force they are typically driven by indigenous needs, rather than by a precise reading of their adversaries' actions and intentions (Gross-Stein et al. 1985). Strategies that attempt to deter primarily through threats and displays of force may underestimate this key aspect of deterrence dynamics. Deterrence, in sum, is very difficult in the face of a decision to initiate conflict that is internally driven, such as the Japanese attack at Pearl Harbor (Russett 1989). This goes to the very basis of deterrence theory and, again, is a consideration that is not likely to be affected by regime type differences.

The Transition to Democracy

In the short run, transitions to democracy are often unstable, with protracted struggles between declining elites and aspiring democratic forces, and the ambiguity and uncertainty of this situation may complicate deterrence. A divisive milieu may undermine both credibility and resolve. Domestic upheaval may also increase external perceptions of vulnerability, appearing to offer a fortuitous opportunity to attack. Such was the case during Iran's systemic shift from the Shah's authoritarianism to the Islamic Republic.[5] During this transition, Iran could not credibly deter Iraq because the government lacked tight control over the military. Consequently, Iraq invaded to capitalize on Iran's perceived weakness.

While the uncertainty associated with regime transitions can complicate deterrence, a variety of outcomes are in fact possible. Transitions can invite opportunistic attack, as noted, but ambiguity can also reduce a potential challenger's incentive to attack by threatening the possibility of unwanted or unintentional escalation. Still another possibility is that weak, unstable, and vulnerable regimes in transition may calculate a need for external aggression. Viewed in isolation, then, instability is an indeterminate factor. It may encourage war initiation by either a regime or its adversary, and it may also sometimes discourage the initiation of hostilities.

Liberalism

Liberalism is predicated on the notion of morally autonomous individuals and the "cosmopolitan law of access" which extends equal rights to the international domain (Doyle 1983b). The key theoretical foundation for the peacefulness of democracies lies in their liberal state institutions and their liberal conception of citizen-state relations.[6] Democracies are presumably less likely to initiate war against each other because of shared commercial interests, constitutional restraints, and international respect for individual rights (including rights of sovereignty and noninterference).[7] The international behavior of autocracies is unconstrained by such considerations. They are seen to have an imperialist bias.

One might expect the emergence of additional democracies to decrease the occurrence of warfare. This is not necessarily the case, however, for democracy and liberalism are not synonymous. A representative government does not ensure that individual rights will be protected either domestically or internationally. In the Arab world, democratic empowerment is likely to significantly diverge from traditional liberal conceptions of democracy. Islamic influences on participatory government may be incompatible with liberal notions of sovereignty and rights. Islamic political principles may delegitimize national borders between Muslims, and erect other distinctions between Muslims and non-Muslims regardless of international boundaries. Other transnational ideologies, such as Arab nationalism, may also challenge liberal norms. It is impossible to know whether and how this might affect a non-liberal democratic regime's willingness to initiate war or its ability to deter.

Also deserving attention is the theory that while autocracies have an imperialist bias, liberal regimes feel compelled to check expansionist and aggressive tendencies. Consonant with Doyle's argument that democracies need each other for security, Lake (1992) expects democracies to form "overwhelming countercoalitions" to meet imperialist threats. Lake's argument follows a structural interpretation of system behavior. Since autocracies have prevailing expansive incentives, and since their behavior would injure democratic citizens, democracies have an overwhelming incentive to resist autocrats.

But this system-level explanation assumes the conventional calculation of cost-benefit utility. For Lake, for example, the "overlarge" democratic coalition should deter autocratic expansion by raising the costs of conquest, and it should be more likely to win in the event that deterrence fails. Indeed, given the greater wealth and extractive capability of the individual democratic states, as well as the alliance among them, the democratic coalition should be "virtually invincible" (Lake 1992, p. 31). This structural view omits part of the story, however.

Empirical evidence supports the argument that democracies will defeat authoritarian regimes, but the bearing of regime type on deterrence, which precedes war, remains indeterminate. It is also necessary to consider the political, cultural, and economic forces that comprise the costs and benefits embedded in particular deterrence calculations, and then to ask whether these might not be of such a nature that potential aggressors will remain undeterred despite the threat of high costs? Moreover, it is clear that aggression will not always be deterred. For example, the U.S.-led coalition that defeated Iraq in the 1991 war was overlarge in Lake's terms yet it failed completely to deter Iraq. The coalition was required to fight a war which devastated Iraq's military capabilities and its civilian population because *threats* of high costs did not compel Iraq.

War against Non-Democrats

The pacifism attributed to democracies does not apply to their relations with nondemocracies. This is an important distinction; democratic dyads may be less war-prone, but individual democracies are not inhibited from warfare with non-democratic states. The frequency of war involvement is unrelated to regime difference: "only in their relations with each other does the relative pacifism of democracy appear" (Lake 1992, p. 32).

Doyle (1983b, p. 325) argues that liberal democracies restrict their ideas of sovereignty and rights to other liberal regimes and in this way explains how democracies can tend toward interventionism: "There is a perception by liberal states that non-liberal regimes are in a permanent state of aggression against them," he notes, and for this reason the legitimacy of non-liberal regimes is largely discounted. They are not entitled to freedom from intervention because it is assumed that they do not respect the political independence and territorial integrity of other states. If this is indeed a major reason that democracies sometimes initiate wars against nondemocracies, then it is also possible that Western liberal democracies will not extend peacefulness to inchoate Arab democracies that do not take liberal forms.

Another analysis of the tendency toward interventionism among democracies is offered by Lake (1992, p. 30), who argues that democratic regimes often turn international conflicts into "ideological crusades." Lake also reports that democracies are "significantly more likely to win the wars they fight against autocracies," which is partly attributable to the societal support associated with such a crusade, as well as to greater wealth and the ability to form effective coalitions.

Although democracies are not inhibited from warfare with nondemocratic states, available evidence is as yet inconclusive on the question of whether they initiate wars less frequently than nondemocracies (Levy 1989). Some scholars, however, argue that democracies are comparatively unlikely to engage in anticipatory self-defense. This argument is advanced by Schweller (1992), for example, who also offers an interesting discussion of the reasons why attacks initiated by Israel constitute "allowable exceptions" due to the "unique systemic pressure" on the Jewish state. Because of this pressure, Schweller reasons, Israeli citizens avoid a critical pitfall of other democracies: they do not mistakenly transfer the dynamics of civil society to the international system. Of course, other representative governments and publics may also perceive their international or regional system as hostile, and war initiation may accordingly be considered legitimate in democracies far more often than Schweller and some others believe to be the case.

If Schweller's formulation of "unique systemic pressure" were to be applied more broadly in the Middle East and extended to democratic or democratizing Arab states, the prospect of a reduction in armed conflict in the region would become even more uncertain. Collective and specific traumas could plausibly lead democratic Arab publics to support an assertive foreign policy, and subsidies from oil-rich states might even make defense expenditures less burdensome. Situational variables are obviously critical, but this abstract scenario could hold for Arab states, as well as for Israel, meaning that democracy in the Arab world might have only a limited impact on the potential for violent interstate conflict in the Middle East.

Conclusion

No characteristic of regime type is determinative. States have a range of motivations for initiating external conflict, and under given circumstances, both democratic and authoritarian regimes can bear the costs associated with such behavior. Critically important interests can induce conflict or summon the ability to deter. Some characteristics of democracies are conducive to persuasion and, therefore, deterrence, but authoritarian regimes have an edge in decision-making flexibility. Further, there is also the possibility of countervailing pressures in each of these cases so that, in the final analysis, the influence of regime type on deterrence is dependent on context and situation.

In the absence of other variables, it is impossible to conclude that democratic decision-making structures and the calculations of expected utility related to them are superior to those of authoritarian regimes so far as war avoidance is concerned. A pervasive concern in international relations theory is the conditions under which foreign policy is guided by external circumstances rather than by domestic imperatives. The difficulty of assessing the relationship between democracy and deterrence may be seen against this background. Do system-level variables explain more than domestic and individual-level attributes? The debate is just beginning.

Researchers should consciously pursue this line of inquiry, employing a broad range of approaches and devoting particular attention to areas where existing work is thin. Cases of deterrence failure do not imply that research on regime pacifism is of no value. Rather, they highlight the importance of deterrence analyses, both empirical and theoretical, which go beyond structural calculations of military costs and instead shed light on the dynamics of perception and on internal incentives for war or peace. Similarly, reliance on liberalism's assumptions to assess the implications of democratization in the Middle East, without corresponding attention to contextual considerations, will limit both theoretical insight and our understanding of the real-world possibilities emerging in the region.

NOTES

1. Israel is fully democratic only for its Jewish inhabitants.

2. As Stern (1989) notes, it is especially risky to deter governments, or to challenge their interests, when there is strong domestic support for foreign policy positions perceived in terms of justice or national self-esteem. Russett's work (1989) has contributed most to this line of inquiry. His discussion of the effectiveness of foreign action for increasing domestic support points out that widely held notions of justice and injustice, even if originally promoted by leaders for their own political purposes, can constrain a government's action.

3. Military capabilities alone are of indeterminate influence on deterrence. Local military superiority increases the immediate likelihood that deterrent threats will succeed. However, overall strategic superiority has been found to make little contribution

to deterrence success once a challenge has arisen. Levy (1989) argues that a challenger's estimate of the military balance may influence but does not determine whether it initiates a challenge.

4. Lake (1992) also proposes, however, that democratic states should be expected to form overwhelming countercoalitions against authoritarian strength.

5. It is worth noting that in 1980 there was still the possibility of a liberal and democratic Islamic regime, led by Mehdi Bazargan. Furthermore, it is arguable that even the Islamic Republic moved Iran closer to legitimate participatory government than had been the case under the Shah.

6. There are at least two interrelated types of arguments for the impact of democracy. One is a structural and institutional (state-system) explanation. The other concerns the role of citizen attitudes and behavior in democratic political systems (Warren 1992).

7. Peaceful relations among democracies are also valued because of a need to balance other threats, particularly since democracies usually prefer other democracies as defense alliance partners.

REFERENCES

Bueno de Mesquita, Bruce, and David Lalman. 1990. "Domestic Opposition and Foreign War." *American Political Science Review* 84 (September); pp. 747–65.

Chan, Steve. 1984. "Mirror, Mirror on the Wall: Are Freer Countries More Pacific?" *Journal of Conflict Resolution* 28 (December), pp. 617–48.

Doyle, Michael W. 1983a. "Kant, Liberal Legacies, and Foreign Affairs [Part 1]." *Philosophy and Public Affairs* 12, no. 3 (Summer), pp. 205–35.

———. 1983b. "Kant, Liberal Legacies, and Foreign Affairs [Part 2]." *Philosophy and Public Affairs* 12, no. 4 (Fall), pp. 323–53.

Gross-Stein, Janice, Robert Jervis, and Richard Ned Lebow. 1985. *Psychology and Deterrence*. Baltimore: Johns Hopkins University Press.

Howard, Michael Eliot. 1976. *War in European History*. London: Oxford University Press.

Hudson, Michael C. Chapter 9 this volume.

Huth, Paul, and Bruce M. Russett. 1990. "Testing Deterrence Theory: Rigor Makes a Difference." *World Politics* 42, no. 4 (July), pp. 466–501.

Lake, David A. 1992. "Powerful Pacifists: Democratic States and War." *American Political Science Review* 86, no. 1 (March), pp. 24–37.

Lebow, Richard Ned. 1989. "Deterrence: A Political and Psychological Critique." In *Per-

spectives on Deterrence, Paul C. Stern et al., eds. New York: Oxford University Press. Pp. 25–51.

Levy, Jack S. 1989. " 'The Causes of War' A Review of Theories and Evidence." In *Behavior, Society, and Nuclear War,* vol. 1, Philip E. Tetlock et al., eds. New York: Oxford University Press, 1989. Pp. 209–333.

Maoz, Zeev. Chapter 8, this volume.

Maoz, Zeev, and Nasrin Abdolali. 1989. "Regime Types and International Conflict, 1816–1976." *Journal of Conflict Resolution* 33 (March), pp. 3–35.

Nincic, Miroslav, and Thomas Cusack. 1985. "The Political Economy of U.S. Military Spending." *Journal of Peace Research* 22, no. 4, pp. 101–15.

Nordhaus, William. 1975. "The Political Business Cycle." *Review of Economic Studies* 42, no. 1, pp. 169–89.

Page, B. I., and R. Shapiro. 1983. "Effects of Public Opinion on Policy." *American Political Science Review* 77, no. 1, pp. 175–90.

Pape, Robert. 1991. "A Theory of Military Coercion." Manuscript draft, p. 22.

Parker, Richard B. 1993. *The Politics of Miscalculation in the Middle East.* Bloomington: Indiana University Press.

Rosen, Steven. 1972. "War Power and the Willingness to Suffer." In *Peace, War, and Numbers,* ed. Bruce M. Russett. Beverly Hills, CA: Sage. Pp. 167–83.

Rummel, Rudolph J. 1983. "Libertarianism and International Violence." *Journal of Conflict Resolution* 27, no. 1 (March), pp. 27–71.

Russett, Bruce M. 1987. "Economic Change as a Cause of International Conflict." In *Peace, Defence, and Economic Analysis,* ed. Frank T. Blackaby and Christian Schmidt. London: Macmillan.

———. 1989. "Democracy, Public Opinion, and Nuclear Weapons." In *Behavior, Society, and Nuclear War,* vol. 1, Philip E. Tetlock et al., eds. New York: Oxford University Press. Pp. 174–208.

Russett, Bruce M., and T. W. Graham. 1989. "Public Opinion and National Security Policy: Relationships and Impacts." In *Handbook of War Studies,* ed. Manus I. Midlarsky. London: Allen & Unwin. Pp. 239–57.

Schweller, Randall L. 1992. "Domestic Structures and Preventative War: Are Democracies More Pacific?" *World Politics* 44 (January), pp. 235–69.

Stern, Paul C., et al., eds. 1989. *Perspectives on Deterrence.* New York: Oxford University Press.

Warren, Mark. 1992. "Democratic Theory and Self-Transformation." *American Political Science Review* 86, no. 1 (March), pp. 8–23.

Weede, Erich. 1984. "Democracy and War Involvement." *Journal of Conflict Resolution* 28, no. 4 (December), pp. 649–64.

3

A SEARCH FOR SECURITY
AND GOVERNANCE REGIMES

I. WILLIAM ZARTMAN

THE MIDDLE EAST states are caught up in another round of their long search for systems of governance and security. There are internal and regional causes for this which are augmented by the extraordinary changes introduced by the end of the Cold War. The principal pressures come from within: popular disillusionment with current regimes and forms of government, rising cries for participation by the ruled in the determination of their own affairs, resentment against the growing gap between state and society, and a breakdown of effective and legitimate regional interstate relations.[1] These pressures are also reinforced from without: global movement toward democratization, potential opportunities to resolve regional conflicts, and the transitory appearance of a pragmatic spirit replacing ideology in dealing with problems. Consequently, the Middle East again turns to reexamine its domestic and regional regimes.

Regimes are rules and routines governing behavior around specific issues that reflect and regulate power structures.[2] They are the expectations by which relations are conducted. Even when not formalized in a treaty or constitution, they are broadly implicit in an underlying structure of norms and behaviors. Regimes can range from systems of world order, regional security communities, and patterns of international economic relations, to the rules of a domestic political game. Once established, regimes tend to persist, for their purpose is stable and predictable relations.

Yet regimes are always at risk. A regime is reaffirmed when the parties to it successfully overcome challenges and reassert its structures and habits. But at times, conditions change, challenges accumulate, and new parties gain influence in response to structural shifts, new issues, or an exhaustion of established political formulas. Parties favored by the existing regime expand their efforts to resist these challenges. When they begin to be less successful, however, there appears an interregnum during which alternative arrangements are proposed, debated, tried, defended and discarded. Power relations usually continue to shift during this period, until gradually the basis of a new regime is formed. In the domestic arena, this may be accomplished by revolution, by seizure of authority, or by a constitutional convention in political relationships. In interstate relations, negotiation is often necessary to create the replacement regime and to have it accepted. This is true since no international authority or decision rule exists to formalize a new order outside of a negotiated agreement among the parties involved.

The Middle East has been engaged in a long process of testing and discarding both domestic and regional security regimes. Since the end of colonial rule, the states of the region have sought to establish viable and effective arrangements for the management of domestic political activity. Most of these regimes have been judged by the governed to have performed poorly, however, creating a postcolonial record marked by challenge, response and challenge again. Since World War II and the creation of Israel, there has been an equally unstable pursuit of regional security. The nature and interconnections between these two pursuits at the present historical moment are the subjects of the discussion to follow. What are the pressures and prospects associated with the search for governance and the search for regional security, and how do developments in one sphere influence developments in the other?

Domestic Regimes of Governance: Democracy and Political Islam

The Middle East today is at the juncture of two historical political currents.[3] Both address the highest question of political life: How should individuals and societies decide their own future? One answer is, "By repeated and updated acts of choice in a rapidly evolving world," whereas the other states, "By a single affirmation of faith in millennial verities." On one side, then, is democracy, flowing from the West since classical Athens, which has suddenly resurged as a popular demand and central political criterion in response to failed authoritarian rule. On the other side, by contrast, there is an Islamic revival and its extension as a political formula which has arisen in reaction to the failures of modernization and secular socialism.

The currents of democracy and Islam both constitute systems of thought and action with their own integrity. Neither incorporates the precepts of the other; each has a particular history and meaning in the Middle East that give special acuteness to the current struggle to shape a domestic regime. Yet it is difficult to examine either alone, without considering the other's effect in the current world. The two sets of ideas and practices challenge and contaminate each other wherever they meet.[4]

Many stirring and insightful treatises on democracy exist, and from them one can draw two defining but apparently contradictory elements. On the one hand, democracy is procedural. It is choosing rulers, at regular intervals, from among contending candidates. It does not, in this context, guarantee immediate results; it is not synonymous with good government in the short run. It produces both good results and mistakes, and the procedure may not be annulled merely because of a momentary mistake. In the longer run, however, democratic procedures offer the only guarantee of accountability and responsibility by the governors, the only way of correcting mistakes, the only way both to get the rascals out and to reduce rascaldom while they are in. From this perspective, democracy is the ability both to choose and to repent.

On the other hand, democracy is not just procedure. It is government conducted by democrats, by people who live within a set of rules that provide for repeated choice, and who believe that losing does not threaten their security nor winning guarantee their privilege. While not guaranteeing good results at any one point in time, it is based on the deeper belief that only open debate will bring the best alternatives to light, even if there may sometimes be a little lag time. Perhaps the most problematic aspect of democracy in this connection concerns the conditions necessary for its emergence. Social preconditions may include such attributes as literacy and urbanization,[5] but they also include adherence to the previously mentioned ideals and values, the origins of which are unclear. Indeed, there appears to be a chicken-and-egg dilemma, since adherence to democratic values is hard to come by without experience in democracy.

In the Middle East, as elsewhere in the Third World, this dilemma appeared to be resolved by nationalist movements which embodied mass democracy, or Rousseau's General Will, targeted against the colonial order. These were exercises in national self-determination, taking over government and restoring it to the people, often appropriating institutions that the colonizer had imported and left behind. But mass nationalist movements did not evolve throughout the region. They existed only in Egypt after World War I, and in Morocco, Algeria, Tunisia, Israel and, eventually, Palestine, after World War II. And even where present, nationalist movements found self-government an elusive and frustrated goal. In Egypt, for example, an alliance between the monarchy and remnants of the colonial power destroyed the nationalist movement, and in

Morocco the monarchy alone presided over its fragmentation. Elsewhere in North Africa, nationalist movements came to power so encumbered with legitimacy and unity that democracy was virtually impossible. Unable to condone division, debate, parties, and repeated elections among competing candidates, they failed to provide for succession to the "Fathers" of the emancipated countries. The democracy of the colonial succession thus remained a dead letter in the Middle East, a truncated exercise.[6] Only in Israel did nationalism pave the way for democracy, and then only for an exclusive, ascriptively defined portion of the population that some considered colonial.

Now, at the end of the millennium, half a century or so after independence, a new wave of democracy is sweeping the world. The renewed pressure for popular sovereignty has a special meaning for the Middle East. The current wave of democracy began in the late 1980s. It coincided with the collapse of the communist system of social or totalitarian democracy in the Soviet Union and Eastern Europe,[7] and with the culmination of the colonial liberation movement, in the collapse of South Africa's apartheid system. In the Middle East, the renaissance of democracy fulfills the logic and promise of nationalist movements and represents the culmination of self-determination under which government is determined by the people at regular intervals, rather than by a sole, initial vote in favor of independence.

Beyond its importance as the culmination of the nationalist movement, the current wave of democratization gains significance from two other aspects of postcolonial states. One is the enormous expansion of state functions into areas of socioeconomic services and regulations that far exceed the scope of state activities in precolonial or even colonial times.[8] Typically, in the Third and especially the Muslim Worlds, the state is the largest employer and the largest investor; nearly all university faculties are civil servants and all students live on state subsidies, expecting (and sometimes guaranteed) state jobs upon graduation. Basic food staples are subsidized to preserve low consumer prices, and medical treatment (like education) is free or provided at low cost. The state is also a source of intrusive regulations, as a legislator of labor laws, currency controls, exit visas, curriculum reforms, and social norms. As a result, the state is an important prize for political control, whether democratic or not.

Yet the state is also seen, in the Arab World and elsewhere in the Third World, as the hunting preserve of the few. The rulers are isolated from the people, ruling less by coercion than by manipulation. They are unlike the charismatic leaders who dominated Arab politics in the 1950s and 1960s. The decade of the 1980s saw significant outbursts of popular disapproval in most Middle

Eastern countries, which addressed not only shortfalls in goods and services provided by the government but a profound lack of trust and faith in the leaders themselves. Prominent examples include the Iranian revolution in 1979, riots in 1981 and 1984 in Casablanca and 1990–91 in northern Morocco, unrest in 1986 in Constantine and then in 1988 throughout Algeria, in 1984 in Tunis, in 1986 in Cairo and other cities of Egypt, in 1989 in Amman, and the 1986 riots in the Great Mosque in Mecca. Strident and bloody expressions of popular protest against the governors of the Muslim Middle East occurred on these occasions.

Remote rulers controlling powerful states have thus coincided explosively with a sudden rise in pressures for democracy as the consummation of nationalist self-determination. Unfortunately for a lasting commitment to democratic values, however, democracy is not viewed merely as a healthy procedure, it is considered a guarantee of the results that the previous system failed to produce. That is a tough challenge to throw in the face of a new system of government, especially when its practitioners have had little experience and when foreign aid is falling, terms of trade are unfavorable, and investment funds are shrinking. Middle Eastern democracy threatens to become yet another system of government which "didn't produce," because so much is expected of it. Moreover, while democratic resurgence threatens incumbent authoritarians in the Muslim world, charismatic demagogues threaten to deform democracy into xenophobic populism.

Political Islam is the most powerful challenge to democracy. It promises morality, authenticity, earthly success, and the exclusion of corruption and error, backed by God's word as a guide and as a guarantee. Arab writers and Western analysts have long debated two poles of attraction for Muslim society in its search for a model for the kingdom of believers on earth. One is an Arab-Islamic model of revealed values, calling for a return to religious inspiration to bring the kingdom of God to His followers. The other is a worldly model of materialistic values, designed to bring modern success to the community of believers. Some see the first as authentic but traditional and outmoded. Others consider the second modern but secular, foreign, and thus alien. This dichotomy represents more than a clash of conceptions and criteria for desirable conduct. It is the basis of a dialectic, that is, a dynamic process of conflict and reaction.[9]

From this clash between thesis and antithesis comes, in time, a synthesis of the two cultures into a political system that combines the material values of the state with religious values of the individual. Eventually, the synthesis itself is attacked, usually by a new antithesis in the form of a religious revival that castigates the incumbent political culture for its materialism and worldliness. The confrontation reopens, and it is resolved in turn, not by a clear defeat of one side or the other but rather by a new synthesis combining elements of both models. The dynamic continues.

This dialectic was the basis of the famous analysis by Abdurrahman ibn Khaldun,[10] the fourteenth-century Arab philosopher, who saw the dynamic of history as a conflict between desert zealots and urban materialists. The rulers of Arab society became corrupted by the material culture of their capitals, which then stimulated the corrective zealotry of the hardy desert communities. The latter emerged from the wild to conquer the city and install an austere government based on religious principles. But in time, urban life corrupted them, and their rule became a synthesis of the two cultures. In a cyclical fashion, new zealot groups, bound together in their coarse life by a strong spirit of solidarity, again came over the mountains to clean out the urban fleshpots and, in turn, to fall into them.

In the coming of Western colonialism, the dialectic took on a new meaning. The materialistic thesis became the colonial society which drew in imitators fascinated by Western material success, but which offended the colonized society because of its foreign and secular worldliness. The antithesis during this era also reflected influences from abroad, through contact with Europe, and produced reform governments in the Ottoman core (Tanzimat) and in Tunisia at the end of the nineteenth century. In the Arab world, the clash of values produced a notable synthesis of faith and reason in the works of Jamal al-Din al-Afghani at the same time. However, the corruption of this synthesis through association with reinforced colonial rule during World War I produced a new antithesis in the ideas of Hassan al-Banna and the organization he founded in 1928, the Muslim Brotherhood.

Throughout the Depression and World War II, Arab nationalism and Islam combined to form a powerful message to be used against colonial rule. However, the most successful nationalist leaders could both wield that message and also talk the language of the colonizer and negotiate an agreement for independence to create a modern society based on both national and modern values. North African nationalist leaders such as Allal al-Fassi, the *alim* (doctor of theology) from Qarawiyin University in Fes who led the Moroccan Independence Party, or Habib Bourguiba, the French-trained lawyer from Monastir who founded the New Constitution Party and for 30 years was Tunisia's president, embodied the new synthesis of modern Western and Arab-Muslim national values.

In time, however, this synthesis was attacked by a new wave of corrective zealotry from the margins of modern society. Bourguiba, President Anwar Sadat of Egypt, King Hassan II of Morocco (and outside the Arab world, Iran's Shah Reza Pahlevi) were attacked as too modern, materialistic and secular, and also for subordinating the interests of their citizens to the demands of the West.[11] Their governments were charged with corruption, impiety, and neglect of the national culture and heritage, as well as with disrupting traditional national society in the name of modernization without fulfilling their promises to provide compensating material benefits: Basic values were destroyed, the city corrupted the soul, poverty became more pervasive than in traditional times, the wealth of the few was more ostentatiously flaunted, and the developed world surged ahead, mocking the house of Islam.

These moments of confrontation and challenge to a former synthesis do not arrive by chance. It is no accident that Islamism is rising at the end of the twentieth century. Such events occur when the current order is no longer a source of stability and satisfaction. When order, identity and resources collapse, believers flock back to their religion. They seek more than salvation in the afterlife; they also want an answer and solution to the unsatisfactory conditions of their earthly life. Previously, regional orders collapsed with the coming of colonialism at the turn of the century and then with its destruction after the world wars. The colonization and decolonization of the Muslim world disrupted the sense of identity in the region; people literally no longer knew who they were in the clash between authenticity and modernity.[12]

But these moments of confrontation are not merely philosophic matters; they also involve material conditions. When the economy no longer fulfills its inhabitants' needs, when modernization dismantles the peasant and traditional urban commercial economies, and when the state falls short in assuming the colonial promise of providing specific social services and ensuring the general welfare, believers see the cause in divine retribution for adopting alien models of social organization and for the corrupt and indulgent deviance of their rulers. The remedy is a return to the straight path revealed in God's word.

The antithesis comes in the form of a religious utopia,[13] which promises jobs and good government here and now, because its economic and political program "is in the Quran," in the words of Islamist campaigners from Algeria and Tunisia to Sudan and Iran. This response bears the stamp of religious legitimacy which guarantees successful governance. If success is delayed, moreover it is not because the formula is incorrect but because its application has been thwarted by the incompletely eradicated forces of impiety. In the best dialectic terms, the antithesis does not seek a compromising synthesis; it seeks to prevail.

What is required for a new synthesis, therefore, is a vigorous confrontation between modernist and Islamist forces and, eventually, a new charismatic figure who can combine their best features into a nationalist-modernist program for society. If the synthesis comes too early, it will weaken the force of the debate that is needed to reveal and purge both the depths of corruption and irresponsibility in the modernist thesis and the shallowness of the utopian and atavism of the religious antithesis. Time is needed to combine the scientific understanding of modernism and the mobilizing inspiration of nationalism in order to produce a program of commitment and productivity that will meet society's need for order, identity, and resources.

Democracy seems ready made for this sort of confrontation, yet it operates with a deep flaw. If the rules of the game are adhered to by believers in pluralistic competition and open debate, and if most of the participants see their interests served by a continuation of that process, the battles to compete democratically and to preserve (or attain) democracy can be waged simultaneously. But this is usually not the case. Morocco, Egypt, Sudan in the mid-1960s and mid-1980s, possibly Jordan in the 1990s, Tunisia in the late 1980s, and Lebanon in an earlier time, for all their differences and imperfections, may be considered examples of such conditions, at least up to a point. Elsewhere, however, the modernists have no experience in democracy.

This problem has other important dimensions as well, and they may be even more fundamental than lack of experience. Modernist governments have a tarred record in the past and only a dim vision of the future, creating tensions between whatever interest in democracy they may possess and their natural desire to remain in power. Additionally, Islamist challengers, for their part, deploy powerful social symbols to brand their opponents as illegitimate, thereby raising fears that they will end pluralist competition should they prevail in the electoral arena.

The contest under democracy thus becomes a contest *over* democracy, in which neither of the two competing historical currents is likely to "win" totally in the struggle for the definition of domestic political regimes. More likely, the result will be a turbulent mixture in varying proportions of democracy, with its commitment to incrementalism and replicated and updated acts of choice on the one hand, and, on the other, the Islamists' view that for the faithful there is in reality no choice at all, only continuing affirmation of the religion's eternal truth. The outcome of this competition and the way in which the mix between pluralism and religious conformity is constructed will have momentous consequences for the people of the Middle East, and also for the rest of the world. Moreover, in addition to giving shape to domestic regimes of governance, it will also affect the prospects for regional security in the Middle East.

International Regimes of Security: Conflict and Management

Since the creation of Israel, the Middle Eastern conflict system has sharply divided Israel from the Arab states with a clear structure of mobile relations among Egypt, Syria, Iraq and Saudi Arabia.[14] National security is assured by unilateral military measures augmented by shifting alliances of political and military cooperation among Arab states and external allies. Both unilateral policies and multilateral cooperation are governed by implicit norms and expectations for both sides.

Palestine's partition in 1947 created a new situation. Regional security was sharply defined by Israel's superiority in the first three Arab-Israeli wars, in 1947–48, 1956 and 1967, and by the Three Nos—no recognition, no concessions, no negotiation—of the Arab Summit in Khartoum after the war of June 1967. While the regional power relations established in the first three military confrontations were shaken by Egypt in the Arab-Israeli war of October 1973, leading to partial conflict management in the 1970s, they were not contested effectively by Israel's other neighbors. Limited security cooperation between Egypt and Israel, which had been established in 1956, was thus restored in greater complexity in 1974 and 1975. There was also a significant additional expansion in 1979,[15] although that process petered out under the Reagan administration after the death of Sadat in 1981 and war in Lebanon in 1982.

Additional developments followed the second Gulf War of 1990–91, with a number of factors converging to produce a cautious reassessment of regional norms and expectations. Of particular importance were a weakening of the Palestine Liberation Organization (PLO) as a regional actor and the fact that the major Arab states were on the same side as Israel against Iraq, which was supported by the PLO. Also important were Israeli restraint in the face of Iraqi attacks, which reflected a respect for Arab sensitivities and helped avoid a wider conflagration of uncertain proportions, and the U.S.'s role in pursuing the peace process with persistence and even-handedness.

Rather than a sharp line of noncommunication and conflict, relations between Israel and the Arab states range from the peace between Israel and Egypt to Israel's more conflictive relationship with the PLO and Syria. Aspects of these relationships are recorded in formal documents, in the 1979 peace treaty, the Camp David agreements, and UN Security Council Resolution 242. In addition, there are equally important aspects of the evolving regime that lie below the written level in the domain of norms and expectations. These include the "cold peace" of limited and "correct" relations between Egypt and Israel, the spheres of influence and contact avoidance between Syria and Israel in Lebanon, and the regularly held but until recently denied contacts between Jordan and Israel.

As this variety suggests, the Middle East is searching for a regional security regime that will establish new norms and expectations about relations, communications, and behavior among regional actors. This regime should provide for security based on conflict management rather than conflict itself. Power relations are still contested, and the search for a corresponding regime continues inconclusively, both along the Israeli borders and among the states in the region. Yet it is clear that an evolution is taking place, that the security regime in the region is evolving from one of conflict to one of management.

On the other hand, the results of this evolution are not fully clear and could be problematic. As long as conflicting parties consider their security unthreatened by the current situation and retain a hope of winning or of escalating their way out of the stalemate, a negotiated or even a mediated transformation of regimes is unlikely. The "decade of decision" in the 1970s showed that either a mutually hurtful stalemate or a mutually enticing opportunity is needed to push or pull the parties into negotiations. A mutually hurtful stalemate, optimally associated with a recent or impending catastrophe, blocks the possibility of a unilateral solution to the security dilemma. It forces the parties to search for an alternative through joint efforts.[16] A mutually enticing opportunity uses the chance for improved relations with a powerful mediator to draw parties away from the conflict among them and into a more constructive outcome.[17]

The timing of security regime change may relate more to the notion of enticing opportunity than hurtful stalemate. Regime change is stimulated as much by the exhaustion of alternatives and the stabilization of shifting power relations as by the actual relations in the current Middle East conflict. For the transformation to be consummated, and for the peace process to produce a new regime that assures security and the management of conflict, certain pre-negotiatory functions must be fulfilled:

(1) Parties must come to an understanding about the *costs and risks* involved in an agreement, and preferably to a realization that gains by one party need not inevitably be at the expense of the other. They must also agree that the purpose of negotiations is to generate the movement necessary to produce compromise and concessions from all participants, not to justify opposition to an adversary with whom one is unwilling to conclude an accord.

(2) Parties also need an agreement on *requitement*, the understanding that concessions will be reciprocated rather than banked. Negotiation is based on conventions of reciprocation in which free gifts—such as handshakes, bows, tipped hats, and wavers—are answered with similar gestures. No party makes such a gesture without the knowledge that it will be reciprocated in some measure.

(3) For a meeting to occur, the *parties* and the *agenda* must be agreed upon. Conflicts often include disagreement over the parties and issues that are amenable to negotiation, and uncertainty about both considerations must be reduced before invitations can be issued and the agenda presented. The major question with regard to parties is that of appropriate Palestinian representation. A particularly important agenda item is the status of Jerusalem, the most visible issue on which efforts in the late 1980s foundered.

A final set of items relates to the circumstances of the parties themselves. On the one hand, each party must build political support for the negotiation process. Each must mobilize domestic support for its own engagement. Somewhat ironically, each party may also be required to expend considerable effort convincing the other party's supporters that negotiation is the appropriate path. On the other hand, bridges between the parties must be constructed as well. To communicate effectively when they finally meet, the two parties must start communicating beforehand and must begin to know and understand one another.

Until September 1993, all parties to the Madrid peace process neglected these requirements, which illustrated the tentativeness of their commitment to establishing a regime shift. Official spokesmen for Israelis, Palestinians, and the Arab states failed to send signals to reassure the publics of the other parties. Nor did they build meaningful relationships with the others' spokesmen.

Sadat's trip to Jerusalem in 1977 and his message while there reached directly into the opponent's camp and delivered a clear signal of his willingness to negotiate. The same thing is now occurring between Israel and its other neighbors, including the Palestinians.

Domestic and International Regimes

The Middle East has suddenly been thrown into a search for both domestic and international regimes. And while it may not be possible to analyze the two searches simultaneously in order to predict a single outcome, they can be juxtaposed in order to illuminate and more fully comprehend the dynamics of each.

The domestic search involves confrontation and conflict in which negotiation currently plays little role. Negotiation analysis indicates that such confrontations between competing formulas of governance are resolved either by reframing the conflict in different terms so that the contending parties can be satisfied, even if none achieves its preferred outcome, or by one side's victory over the other. The former result may be possible only when Islamist movements agree to play within the rules of democratizing political systems, which they have done when relatively weak compared to other parties or to the holders of central power. In recent years, this has occurred in Egypt, Jordan, and Morocco, which accordingly are instances of participatory cooperation contributing to a change in the domestic regime. By contrast, when Islamists have been within reach of taking power and imposing their own governing formula, as in Algeria and Sudan, they have used all means to openly challenge the system—including its democratizing aspects. The result, in these cases, has been open confrontation and a fight to win.

The regional search has moved far beyond a direct conflict of two clear formulas into a phase of reframing and synthesizing. Attempts to reduce propositions to "the Jordanian (federal) option" and the "Israeli (autonomy) option" hide important nuances. During its first nine months, Secretary of State Baker's initiative was clearly hindered by the nature of the Israeli regime under Yitzhak Shamir and the Likud party. Labor's victory in June 1992 opened up new prospects, which Norway's government successfully exploited. However, the direction the peace process will take given the range of possible alternatives—from partial implementation (of West Bank autonomy, for example) to the installation of an ongoing process marked by the implementation of successive agreements—remains open.

Meanwhile, both searches are stuck at the stage of revision—or hoped-for revision—of power relations. It is premature to focus on a formula for Middle East peace and security so long as rank and relations between Israel and Syria are unresolved, an ironic judgment since the dyad has been relatively stable since 1973. The uncertainty introduced by Iraq, less as a direct participant than as an ingredient in the Israeli-Syrian and Israeli-Jordanian dyads, also prevents the emergence of a stable regional power structure. Similarly, governments vying with Islamist movements are still trying either to break their opponents or to outlast them as they peak and decline. This is exemplified by the crisis in Algeria, which has been provoked by the government's struggle with the Islamic Salvation Front (FIS). The FIS' refusal to peak in 1992 has also reopened debate about whether En-Nahda in Tunisia actually peaked in 1989, as claimed. Since democracy is based on the continuous testing of shifting political fortunes, such uncertainty is endemic—indeed, crucial—to the system, although it remains a problem for the regime.

The relationship between the search for domestic and international regimes is ambiguous. While greater Islamist influence in domestic politics might reduce the chances for Arab-Israeli peace, political Islam is actually pluralistic, with no clear position on the peace process. The tactical agility with which Islamist parties greeted the evolving Gulf War—Tunisians say that En-Nahda first missed the train, then turned around and tried to take over the locomotive—shows that regional relations are not matters of fixed positions and immutable principle. Islamists tend to be poor negotiators; however, like Menachem Begin, they may be in a better position to make the right agreement than other, more power-sensitive governments.

Democracy is similarly complex and may favor many different types of outcomes. At best, limited democracy in Egypt and Israel permitted—and possibly enabled—a bilateral peace treaty but blocked any deeper reconciliation between the parties, and indeed fed a deep disillusionment on both sides. Certain functions of pre-negotiations appear to benefit from democratic conditions; others may not. In the current peace process, democracy's demagogic possibilities may be as much a potential impediment as conflict fatigue and enticing opportunities are potential facilitators. The key to progress in the peace process would thus appear to lie less in domestic regime type than in the ability of negotiators to devise innovative formulas that will reduce uncertainty and stabilize structural relations. And this will demand much help from the mediator.

NOTES

1. See Adeed Dawisha and I. William Zartman, eds., *Beyond Coercion: The Durability of the Arab State* (London: Croom Helm, 1988).

2. Stephen Krasner, ed., *International Regimes* (Ithaca, NY: Cornell University Press, 1985).

3. The argument of this section has been explored in greater detail in Charles Butterworth and I. William Zartman, eds., "Political Islam," special issue of *The Annals of the American Academy of Political and Social Science* 522 (November 1992).

4. Jacob Leib Talmon, *The Origins of Totalitarian Democracy* (London: Secker & Warburg, 1952).

5. Seymour Martin Lipset, *Political Man* (New York: Doubleday, 1960).

6. See I. William Zartman, "Revolution and Development," *Civilizations* 20, no. 2 (1970): 181–99.

7. This is not to say that Islam is the successor to Communism as a threat to the West, as some U.S. government spokesmen have suggested. Islam as a personal religious belief has no necessary consequences for either domestic governance or foreign relations, despite the inherent unity of social and religious life in Islamic teaching. It is only when the religious beliefs about piety and correct behavior are promoted as the basis of the political system that they shape the practices of domestic governance and international relations. Even then, regimes which call themselves Islamic may pursue their interests in cooperation with Western states, as governments in Saudi Arabia, Pakistan, and Mauritania have done. Others, also calling themselves Islamic, may see themselves necessarily and primarily in conflict with the West, as governments in Iran and Sudan have done. And in all of these states, opposition parties calling themselves Islamic have contested their own governments.

8. See Hassan Beblawi and Giacomo Luciani, eds., *The Rentier State* (London: Croom Helm, 1988).

9. There are many such works. See, for example, Nadav Safran, *Egypt in Search of Political Community* (Cambridge: Harvard University Press, 1961); David Gordon, *The Passing of French Algeria* (New York: Oxford, 1966); and Clement Henry Moore, *The Politics of North Africa* (Boston: Little Brown, 1970). See also I. William Zartman, "Political Dynamics in the Maghrib: The Cultural Dialectic," in Halim Barakat, ed., *Contemporary North Africa* (Washington: Center for Contemporary Arab Studies, Georgetown University, and London: Croom Helm, 1985).

10. Abdurrahman ibn Khaldun, *An Arab Philosophy of History*, ed. Charles Issawi (New York: Grove Press, 1950); Abdurrahman ibn Khaldun, *The Muqaddimah: An Introduction to History*, Franz Rosenthal and N.J. Dawood, eds. (Princeton: Princeton University Press, 1967).

11. Mohammed Tozy, "Islam and the State in North Africa," in I. William Zartman and W. Mark Habeeb, *Polity and Society in Contemporary North Africa* (Boulder, CO: Westview, 1992); Douglas Magnuson, "Islamic Reform in Contemporary Tunisia," in I. William Zartman, ed., *Tunisia: The Political Economy of Reform* (Boulder, CO: Lynne Rienner, 1991).

12. See Albert Memmi, *The Colonizer and the Colonized* (Boston: Beacon, 1967); and Frantz Fanon, *Black Skin, White Mask* (New York: Grove Press, 1967).

13. Lahouari Addi, "Islamicist Utopia and Democracy," in Charles Butterworth and I. William Zartman, eds., "Political Islam," special issue of *The Annals of the American Academy of Political and Social Science* 522 (November 1992).

14. Classic analyses include Malcolm H. Kerr, *The Arab Cold War, 1958–1967: A Study of Ideology in Politics* (London: Oxford University Press, 1967); and Patrick Seale, *The Struggle for Syria: A Study of Post-War Arab Politics, 1945–1958* (London: Oxford University Press, 1965).

15. Janice Stein, ed., *Peacemaking in the Middle East* (New York: Barnes & Noble, 1985). See also William B. Quandt, *The Middle East: Ten Years After Camp David* (Washington, DC: Brookings Institution, 1988).

16. I. William Zartman, *Ripe for Resolution* (New York: Oxford University Press, 1989); and Saadia Touval and I. William Zartman, eds., *International Mediation in Theory and Practice* (Boulder, CO: Westview, 1985).

17. I. William Zartman, "Beyond the Hurting Stalemate," paper presented at the 1992 annual meeting of the International Studies Association, Atlanta, GA, March 31–April 4, 1992.

PART TWO

DEMOCRACY IN CONTEXT

4

DEMOCRACY IN THE THIRD WORLD
Definitional Dilemmas

ROBERT L. ROTHSTEIN

Introduction

DEMOCRACY IS A classic example of an "essentially contested concept" (see Connolly 1974, pp. 22–32). There are profound disagreements about the appropriate theoretical framework, about whether democracy is simply an institutional arrangement for choosing rulers or an end in itself, about how to measure and evaluate democracy and democratic behavior, and about the importance of various empirical prerequisites for democracy. Seeking a universally acceptable meaning of democracy under these circumstances is probably futile since the disagreements cannot be resolved either by intellectual debate or by prolonged investigation of the "real" world.[1] Indeed, the conflicts seem so intractable that one theorist has recently noted that "the perennial dispute about the *definition* of democracy seems to me largely fruitless, and I hope to avoid it altogether" (Beitz 1989, p. 17).

Democracy seems especially difficult to define because it is not a given or a thing in itself but rather a form of government and a process of governance that changes and adapts in response to circumstances. Any 'universal' definition is likely to ignore differences in detail or to need constant redefinition and adjustment. Moreover, since all democracies are more or less imperfect, finding a single definition that indicates precisely where "more or less" becomes "either/or" (a democracy or not a democracy) seems impossible (see Bollen 1990, pp. 7–24).

The temptation to avoid the definitional wars, to adopt any generally acceptable definition, and to get on with the analytical task at hand is surely strong. There is, after all, one widely recognized definition of democracy that has been accepted not only in much of the Western world but also in much of the Third

World—at least rhetorically. In addition, my purpose here is not to provide a new definition of democracy but to point out the problems raised for understanding the emergence and consolidation of Third World democracies by accepting the conventional Western definition of democracy. And to understand these problems we must explore at least some aspects of the connotative meaning of democracy.[2] The purpose of this discussion is to indicate some practical consequences that ensue from adopting (or not adopting) one or another definition and to raise questions about whether an alternative definition is more appropriate in a Third World context.

Failure to clarify disagreement about meaning implies that we lack a generally accepted standard by which to evaluate democratic performance. For example, Third World intellectuals may see democracy as a means to achieve equality; the masses may see it as a means to end repression and facilitate prosperity; the ruling elites and the upper classes may see it as a threat to economic growth and their own perquisites; many Western scholars may see it as the most effective way to resolve internal disputes peacefully, and the policy-making community may see it as a means to end international wars or to increase the number of "like-minded" states in the international system.

Each interpretation could be true in different circumstances. Moreover, different policy choices result from the different meanings ascribed to democracy. Without agreement on which meaning of democracy is appropriate in a particular context, almost any outcome—good or bad—can be attributed to "democracy." One sees the danger in current circumstances. Democracy has become almost a euphemism for the decline of authoritarianism—two very different phenomena—without any particular meaning apart from some kind of promise to hold elections. The unexamined premise is that new democracies will behave as established democracies behaved in the past, but this is a potentially dangerous assumption that needs very careful analysis, not mere expressions of faith.

Definitions of Democracy

There are profound disagreements about the meaning of democracy, especially between theorists who emphasize its procedural and institutional elements and theorists who emphasize its egalitarian component. Nonetheless, one definition with essentially similar elements has become dominant in the Western world and internationally. There is little disagreement with what is contained in the mainstream definition of democracy; the disagreements largely relate to what else can or should be included in the definition.

Huntington has argued that a political system is democratic to the extent that its most powerful collective decision makers are selected through periodic elections in which candidates freely compete for votes and in which virtually all adults are eligible to vote (Huntington 1984, p. 195). This definition "stands to reason" to most citizens of Western countries. A primary purpose of this version of democracy is to dampen and resolve group conflict by diverting it into peaceful channels. Achievement of this goal is facilitated by the dominance of the rule of law and the protection of civil and political rights. The permanent tension between the government's need to govern and its need to be responsive to its citizens is moderated through various procedures and institutions (elections, parties, strong legislatures, etc.). This definition excludes any connection to socioeconomic conditions or to any particular outcome of the democratic process.

Pluralist democracy in the Western world is of course imperfect. There are differences in economic and social power, large and influential bureaucracies, disparities in access to information, and extreme apathy among large groups of citizens. This gives great power to economic and political elites, and some analysts assert that Western democracy is best described as a kind of "legitimate oligarchy." Still, the political system remains more than nominally democratic because the elites are committed to maintaining a pluralist system and sharing power.

Criticisms of the pluralist model of democratic politics must be even more strongly stated in reference to the Third World. Vast inequalities in power, wealth, and information constitute one set of problems. The power and influence of the state and the central bureaucracies are massive, which gives them a virtual monopoly in allocating resources and determining policies. Moreover, these disparities seem to be growing. An even more fundamental obstacle to full-fledged democratization in many Third World countries is the attitude of political elites toward opening the political system to meaningful participation and competition.

Third World elites often oppose increased participation as a threat to their control and stability. Huntington and Nelson (1976, p. 29) have argued that most elites view participation not as an end in itself but as a means to achieve other elite goals, such as maintaining power or facilitating development policy. High levels of participation may increase legitimacy and efficacy over the long term but generate demands that cannot be met in the short term. Moreover, voting gives primary political weight to numbers, and the numbers are largely in rural areas or in urban slums. Elites fear that populism will inevitably result, that savings and investment will be sacrificed to consumption, and that elite patterns of allocation to friends or necessary allies (especially the military) will be threatened. These real or imagined threats to development and to control have provided the rationale for a great deal of autocracy—and restraints on participation.[3]

Fears about the dangers of mass participation in a Third World context are not entirely irrational. Nor are they merely a reflection of self-interested desires to retain power by ruling elites. Demands for immediate economic betterment from an unsophisticated electorate, battered by decades of failed hopes and promises, are an obvious threat to any incumbent government that must balance a wide range of competing domestic and external interests. The long-run survival of democratic systems involves so many difficulties that some analysts advocate a strategy of short-run accommodation with the rich and powerful, clear restraints on redistribution, and policies that seek to make haste slowly (Di Palma 1990, pp. 86–108). This strategy is inherently plausible and may appeal to the leaders of many new democracies.

Although displacement of many authoritarian regimes is sharply increasing the prospects for participation, elite support for giving meaningful political influence to ordinary citizens often remains forced and reluctant. The resulting contained and limited participation is unlikely to stabilize Third World democracies. A formal democracy controlled by the rich and powerful differs little from past oligarchies. Under such circumstances, the differences in degree between developed democracies and new democracies are likely to become differences in kind.

Elites hope to avoid sharing power and to inhibit the development of an active opposition. One reason for this is the desire to avert the escalation of expectations. In addition, political conflict in many developing countries is simply too bitter, intense, and violent. The struggle to control the state is especially virulent when resources are scarce, allocations are made in a biased way, and divergent groups must compete for a shrinking pie. The political game is zero-sum, and the absence of a culture of accommodation and tolerance reinforces the dangers associated with unrestrained competition.[4] The Middle East is illustrative of the problem: massive and powerful national security states, often dominated by minority groups (Alawites, Tikritis) or by royal families, are intent on retaining power and are willing to use any means to do so; political culture is tribalized, hierarchical, and prone to divide the world into "we versus they" categories; and there is almost no willingness to accept the risks and uncertainties implicit in playing by the rules of the democratic political process.

Moreover, the power of the ruling elites is frequently insufficient to achieve certain national aims or to generate sufficient confidence to permit the risk of rejecting demands from influential groups. There is a persistent record of policy failure or of lofty rhetoric followed by inept or only partial implementation of policies. The insecurity produced by this poor performance record creates doubts about survival in office, or about regime survival itself. Therefore, competition can only exacerbate the fears and tensions of ruling elites. While much power has been abused or dissipated by elites for their own purposes, the very situation in which they find themselves generates paranoia about competition. Because they have insufficient power, elites genuinely committed to economic and political development face the prospect that they will be unable to contain centrifugal tendencies and implement national policies. In this universe of risk, competition—like participation—can thus seem either a luxury or a danger to elites that do not feel that they have enough power to contemplate sharing it or dispersing it or, above all, losing it. Since competition and participation are crucial dimensions of pluralist democracy, the prognosis for Third World democracy is problematic.

Enabling Conditions and the Civic Culture Debate

To predict the direction in which a system is headed, attention must be paid to those contextual factors that affect the prospects for the establishment and continuation of democracy. Strictly speaking, these factors are not part of the definition, but they can help to explain why democracies succeed in certain countries but not in others.

Discussions of background conditions or prerequisites for democracy are often inconclusive (see Dahl 1971; Huntington 1989; Di Palma 1990). We are told that, other things being equal, the chances for democracy are probably greatest in countries that have high levels of economic development and low levels of inequality, where ethnic and other cleavages are not severe, where the middle class is large and relatively prosperous, where there are autonomous groups and associations, where the political culture values compromise and tolerance of others, and where external supporters are democratic and generous. It is not clear, however, whether any of these conditions is necessary, and certainly none is likely to be sufficient. Moreover, democracy sometimes survives when few of these conditions are fulfilled, and it sometimes fails in countries where many of the preconditions are met.

A major concern is whether a civic culture, i.e., one that values the qualities of compromise and tolerance, is necessary to establish democracy or whether it results from the continued practice of democratic processes. Schmitter and Karl (1991, p. 83) reject the notion that democracy must initially be based upon a supportive civic culture. They argue that

> waiting for such habits to sink deep and develop lasting roots implies a very slow process of regime consolidation—one that takes generations—and it would probably condemn most contemporary experiences *ex hypothesi* to failure.

On the other hand, Schmitter and Karl (ibid.) assert that rules of prudence make it possible for democratic values to "emerge from the interaction between antagonistic and mutually suspicious actors." Two major principles are "contingent consent" and "bounded uncertainty." Contingent consent refers to how winners and losers in the political game will behave and the conditions necessary to justify citizen acceptance of governmental decisions. Bounded uncertainty refers to a certain degree of policy consistency and predictability between administrations. The success of new democracies, and the gradual development of democratic values, depends on establishing these norms which are products, rather than producers, of democracy.

This subtle and sophisticated argument does away with the need to analyze prerequisites or enabling conditions for democracy. It provides powerful support for classifying regimes that emerge from authoritarianism as democracies—provided they meet the narrow terms of the definition. Schmitter and Karl's analysis also has prescriptive implications. It may indirectly call for a strategy of accommodation with the rich and powerful that many see as prudent or necessary during the immediate posttransition period, assuming that the rich and powerful pay some heed to the rules of prudence.

This approach also offers strong support for the efforts of organizations such as the National Endowment for Democracy that seek to "export" democratic institutions to the Third World and Eastern Europe. Some theorists sharply criticize this "top-down" approach to democracy.[5] Nevertheless, in a situation where the background conditions cannot be exported, where discredited and displaced authoritarian regimes have prevented the development of a civic culture and an autonomous civil society, and where there is a strong desire to help new democracies survive, efforts to create or strengthen appropriate institutions and to familiarize citizens with them can be useful and important building blocks for democracy. This approach seems to offer an "easy" solution to an apparently insoluble problem: how to establish and consolidate genuinely democratic regimes quickly.

India, Costa Rica, and Israel illustrate Schmitter and Karl's argument. None began with a democratic culture, despite the residual effect of India's British colonial experience. The civic cultures that evolved in these countries during decades of democratic governance are surely imperfect, yet they survived as democracies despite daunting challenges and threats. Whether the characteristics that we associate with a democratic culture result from democracy or are a preface to it is uncertain and perhaps varies greatly in individual cases. It is most plausible that cause and effect are interactive: democracy is facilitated by the presence of certain character traits but also facilitates the development of compatible traits.

Unfortunately, waiting for a democratic culture to establish roots is a slow process, as is the effective establishment of their rules of prudence. In a Third World context, it may require almost as long to establish prudential rules as to establish the beginnings of a democratic culture. How then can contingent consent and bounded uncertainty emerge and become internalized behavioral rules in a context where experience with democracy is very limited, where internal conflicts are intense, and where trust and loyalty toward the government are rarely present?

During the transition period and the early years of consolidation, support for democracy is likely to be highly instrumental and focused primarily on winning immediate benefits for one's own group. Moreover, after decades of frustrated hopes and the association of democracy with prosperity, it will be difficult for both elites and masses to understand the necessity of moderation, of making haste slowly, and of accepting compromises. For these reasons, circumstances in the Third World "would probably condemn most contemporary [democratization] experiences *ex hypothesi* to failure" (Schmitter and Karl 1991, p. 83).

The relationship between political culture and democracy is difficult to discern because many other factors can impinge, including level of development and other quality of life considerations. There are also divergent opinions, different values, and different degrees of influence even within a common culture (Laitin 1988, pp. 589–90). For example, the political cultures of the Weimar Republic and Nazi Germany were strikingly different, even though both emerged from the same history and culture. Similarly, the same Confucian traits that once seemed to explain why the East Asian states would never effectively compete in the international economy are now used to explain their competitive success. Culture alone is rarely a determinative variable. Some Third World democracies have survived for decades with cultural traits that seem incompatible with democracy, while Third World democracies with compatible cultural traits may be overthrown. Although few new democracies will begin with a democratic culture, and will consequently need to develop that culture over time, it is difficult to draw firm conclusions about the implications for a successful transition to democracy.

Because of socioeconomic discontinuities, initial changes in political culture are usually weak and formless. The 'old' culture which opposed democracy loses some of its power to influence, but the new culture which supports democracy is not yet fully formed or strongly supported. (On changes in political culture, see Eckstein 1988.)

The crucial questions are tactical and not metaphysical: How do individuals divest themselves of the old culture and become more receptive to the new? Do different groups or generations confront these issues differently? Democracy may be possible without a democratic culture, as Schmitter and Karl assert, but democracy is more likely to succeed if some elements of that culture can be developed quickly.

The crux of the civic culture controversy concerns whether minimum enabling conditions affect the survival chances of new democracies. However, enabling conditions affect more than prospects for democracy. They also shape perceptions of democracy's definition and purpose. This raises significant questions about the likely behavior of new democracies and about appropriate policies in dealing with them.

Democracy, even where only recently established, may have some principled and internalized support because of its reputation and its association with prosperity and peace. But the citizenry's initial expectations (or perhaps hopes) are usually high—because of their own country's past failures and the economic success of developed democracies. Consequently, citizens may be quickly disillusioned with democracy. To moderate expectations, and to convert instrumental support into the required degree of trust and legitimacy, citizens must be convinced that democracy is preferable to the alternatives. This is not likely if governments take citizen support for granted and fail to actively cultivate an image of themselves as effective problem-solvers. This is not easily accomplished. Insufficient resources often block the most enlightened policies, and Third World governments often lack sufficient autonomy to implement policies that would generate public support. These factors inevitably affect prospects for democracy in the Third World.

All nation-states have lost some decision-making autonomy as a result of greater interdependence within an increasingly integrated world economy. Nevertheless, the difference between developed and developing countries is so great that it verges on becoming a difference in kind. Third World states, whether democratic or authoritarian, are increasingly governed by global economic trends and developments and by international agencies and major powers. This is true in a multitude of ways: the need for foreign aid and loans, problems in gaining access to foreign markets and technology, dependence on World Bank and IMF support, and vulnerability to patterns of recession in major markets. Moreover, the Third World is strongly affected by, but only marginally able to affect, decisions made by the developed market economies. The authority structure of most international economic agencies is also weighted against the Third World. This situation undermines the essential principle of democratic governance: rule by the people. If decisions made democratically can be thwarted by the actions of external actors, democratic governance in many poor countries may appear increasingly hollow.

Definitional Compromises: Living with Ambiguity

A loose and permissive definition of democracy suggests that movements away from authoritarianism constitute a "triumph" for Western liberal democracy. A tight and restrictive definition suggests that many of the new "democracies" are bogus, what the Nigerian novelist Wole Soyinka calls "voodoo" democracy. Different definitions will also generate different expectations for and about new democracies. If the wrong factors are emphasized, disenchantment and disappointment among the citizenry will quickly arise. This danger is especially severe in the Third World because of the gap between what most citizens expect from democracy and what most theorists suggest democracy is likely to produce.

The minimalist political definitions of democracy that we have been discussing focus on accountability, competition, some degree of participation, and the guarantee of important civil and political rights. They are certainly useful in understanding Western democracy, perhaps relatively useful or at least not harmful in attempting to understand democracy in some advanced Latin American and Eastern European cases, but much more problematic in attempting to understand democracy in other parts of the Third World. The minimalist definition assumes background conditions that are favorable, or will become so, as a result of democracy itself. These background conditions include: meaningful rules, procedures, and rights; sufficient development so that there are reasonable opportunities to prosper; an open and diversified social structure; peaceful resolution of internal conflicts; and awareness of the costs and dangers of the alternatives to and benefits from even imperfect democracy. In the Third World, none of this can be taken for granted.

It is potentially dangerous or costly to describe as democratic a large number of countries that have established few of the pertinent background conditions. These regimes may be relatively more democratic and less repressive than they were previously, but they are not genuinely democratic in the Western sense. We risk misunderstanding their probable behavior if we simply assume that they are "like us," or nearly so. A new definition of democracy is not the solution. The definition is not the problem but the absence of conditions that support it. Deemphasizing the significance of some of these conditions, as Schmitter and Karl have done, is important and useful, but it is not a solution.

Two conclusions follow. First, in the Third World context we should seek not a new definition of democracy but a specification of how to generate the background conditions that make the existing definition viable. In particular, we need to focus on conditions that are of concern to citizens of poor countries desperate for material betterment, freedom from repression, and an end of endemic governmental failure. New democracies do have some insulation from socioeconomic failure because of the other benefits of democracy, but only up to a point. Prolonged failure will undermine even strong democracies. After decades of failure, the citizens of these countries are profoundly skeptical, if not cynical, about what government will do for them. We risk a profound backlash against democracy if it, too, fails to perform and if new governments focus too exclusively on benefiting the rich and powerful.

The second conclusion is more controversial. Polyarchy is a useful term to describe advanced democracies that are relatively, but incompletely, democratized. We need a different term to describe states that are even less completely democratized. Absent a new concept, there is no alternative but to add a qualifying term to democracy for regimes that are still far from being genuine democracies. Schmitter and Karl (1991, p. 75) tried unsuccessfully to avoid this step by devising a universally relevant definition of democracy. I shall use the term "weak democracy," in contrast to the "strong democracy" of the developed countries. Weak democracies are Third World countries that are not yet polyarchies but are significantly less authoritarian in dimensions important for democracy. These are hybrid regimes with increasing degrees of political liberalization, persisting elements of authoritarianism (especially strong elite dominance, restrictions on participation), and perhaps some movement toward a market economy.[6]

Whether weak democracies become more democratic, retreat into authoritarianism, or oscillate between the extremes depends on several factors, including global economic trends, the generosity of the world community, and the effects of post-Cold War international relations. They are unlikely to become strong any time soon.[7]

Illustrating the Ambiguities: The Middle East

In attempting to assess the process of liberalization and ultimately of democratization in the Middle East, one needs to set the standard of reference carefully. The standard should not be the performance of developed country democracies. The appropriate standard is the performance of other Third World countries experiencing the arduous process of a simultaneous "double liberalization," toward democracy and the market. Even more significantly, the assessment must consider the preceding regime and its legacy, a legacy that usually impedes the transition.

Virtually all Islamic Middle Eastern regimes will begin as very weak democracies, hybrid regimes mixing democratic and authoritarian characteristics. As such, their behavior may not conform to the behavior of other democracies. Given this situation, we should not assume that the absence of warfare between Western democracies will be matched by new democracies—whether in the Middle East or elsewhere, although we can surely hope that this will be true. But without a clear explanation of *why* democracies have not fought other democracies, and evidence of whether these factors operate in the new democracies, the argument will be inconclusive. Not every country that has elections or permits opposition parties is a "democracy." The forms and procedures of democracy can be exported, but the enabling conditions cannot be. Some of the world's most brutal regimes have had elections with nominal opposition; this has hardly made them paragons of democratic virtue. The adoption of democratic forms and procedures is important, for democracy must begin somewhere. But these forms and procedures may be arrested or used by reactionary forces of the old order (especially the military) to disguise continued oligarchic control. They may also be subverted by forces intent on using democratic procedures to undermine democracy: this is potentially true for some Islamic fundamentalists.

Perhaps a simple classification scheme can clarify this discussion. Individual states vary greatly in how closely they resemble genuine polyarchies, including the enabling conditions that provide support for democratic forms and procedures. Current polyarchies, which are mostly advanced Western countries, come closest to meeting both the formal terms of most definitions and the deepest achievement of the background conditions. The gaps between the definition and the conditions that give the definition its fullest meaning widen as one descends the scale. A small group of established Third World democracies closely approximates the formal terms of the mainstream definition but has a very mixed and inconsistent record on the background conditions. Some see these countries—including India, Costa Rica, Jamaica, Israel, and perhaps Sri Lanka—as models for other Third World countries or as way stations on the road toward deeper democratization.[8] Regrettably, the classification scheme is as imperfect as the entities it seeks to encompass.

The countries in the next group are generally described as "new democracies." They include many countries in Latin America, most of Eastern Europe and the former Soviet Union, some countries in Asia, and perhaps a few elsewhere. In these cases, the "democracy" label is problematic. As discussed above, I prefer the designation "weak democracy." These countries have little or no experience with democracy; there is usually a persisting need to accommodate powerful and (at best) reluctantly democratic groups; and mass participation is sharply constrained by fears of populism and "uncontrolled" democracy. Levels of development are low; culture and social structure may be hostile to democracy; society may be ethnically or communally polarized; and elite unanimity on "rules of prudence" may be contingent or nonexistent. The classic problem of rising demands and insufficient resources is present in full force, perhaps exacerbated by slower growth in the world economy and growing indifference to Third World concerns. If this is recognized as a dilemma, it could be helpful to continue calling these regimes (weak) democracies—as a form of encouragement and perhaps also in order to generate greater external support.

The obstacles to Middle Eastern democracy are illustrated by the fact that no Arab government falls within the category of even the weak democracy. There are signs of political liberalization throughout the region, including elections, the emergence of opposition parties, and the appearance of relatively autonomous groups and associations. However, these movements away from authoritarianism remain rudimentary. When they threaten existing regimes, the response is swift and brutal. The suspension of elections in Algeria because of fears of a victory by Islamic fundamentalists is perhaps the best example.

There are many reasons to be pessimistic about the short-run prospects for Middle Eastern democracy. States based primarily on concerns of ruler security exist throughout the region. They very effectively repress dissent and terrorize their citizens. They will not relinquish power easily, especially where a minority group rules (as in Iraq and Syria) and fears destruction if it loses total control of the country. This situation unifies the ruling elites and helps to prevent the kind of destabilizing coups that might open up opportunities for opposition forces. Moreover, most Arab states have not seen the evolution of a civil society based on autonomous groups and associations which serve as intermediaries between the government and the people and provide some training in grass-roots democracy.

Middle Eastern regimes also dominate their economies to a considerable extent. This creates political advantages because they are well positioned to distribute economic benefits in return for political loyalty. Dissent is rare because of the fear of antagonizing the state or undermining its ability to provide benefits. This is especially true for the Gulf states, where resources are more plentiful. In these instances, rulers have substituted material benefits for political liberalization.

All of this suggests that the "brittleness" of some authoritarian states that collapsed rather quickly despite apparent stability may be less significant in the Middle East. Most Arab regimes remain resistant authoritarians. There are, however, significant variations within this group. The ruling families of the Gulf states are much more secure than other Middle Eastern regimes; they are able to buy off dissent and to contain it through an effective security apparatus. Both democracy and Islamic fundamentalism seem threatening to these regimes, and to many of their citizens. They fear losing access to riches which have frequently not been earned through effort and talent. Ironically, some of the background conditions for democracy are met in these cases, especially levels of development and the emergence of a middle class. There is, however, very little movement toward meeting any of the terms of the formal definition. Elsewhere, too much poverty retards democracy. In the Gulf, too much wealth has a similar effect. Economic downturns are perilous for these regimes, which may explain why, after the Gulf War, they borrowed so heavily to maintain high standards of living.

Other authoritarian regimes vary greatly across a number of dimensions: Jordan is not Egypt, and neither matches the barbarism of Iraq or Syria. However, none of these regimes meets either the definitional or the background conditions. Some apparent movement toward liberalization is either cynical (elections in Iraq and Syria) or a reluctant response to external pressure. The road to democracy is likely to be long, bumpy, and possibly bloody.

This rather crude classification scheme indicates why a simple contrast between democracies and nondemocracies is inadequate. The landscape is actually complex and shifting, with some states moving toward democracy (but still far from it), while others resist. There are very different relationships between the formal definition and the background conditions and great uncertainty about future prospects, with much depending on factors outside the control of the states involved. What is most likely to determine the fate of these regimes is not whether they hold elections but whether their citizens' needs are effectively met. The Middle Eastern regimes stand out primarily because liberalization has been so minimal. This bears sad testimony to brutally effective repression, and perhaps also to the pervasive influence of Islam, especially that of radical Islam.

Why has Islamic fundamentalism become an important *political* problem? There have always been fundamentalists around in many Western and non-Western societies. These "true believers" are impervious to compromise, indifferent to the values of others, and intent on creating a society governed only by their own beliefs. In the past, however, most citizens were more concerned with material progress and not greatly attracted to fundamentalism. Unfortunately, in much of the Middle East, deteriorating economic conditions and a loss of faith in the idea that existing regimes would improve conditions and act fairly have generated massive frustration and discontent. In some places the discontent has manifested itself as a demand for fundamentalism (which implies a shift from material to largely nonmaterial goals), in other places as a demand for democracy, and in yet others as some mixture of the two. The discontent has been galvanized by the Gulf War, Saddam's spurious promises to share the wealth of the regime more equitably, and by the specter of yet another Arab military humiliation.

There is also, of course, the additional complication of the conflict with Israel. As a functioning democracy, a supposedly alien intrusion in the Arab heartland, and a successful military power, it has become a symbol of Arab defeats and an explanation of too many failures in the Arab world. Thus fundamentalism, especially in its willingness to pursue dangerously destabilizing policies (terrorism, jihads, the acquisition of deadly weapons), has seemed a threat to Israel, to the developed world, to existing rulers in the region, and to democracy itself—insofar as Islamic movements use democratic rules and procedures to overthrow democracy itself.[9] These fears are exacerbated by the belief that fundamentalists will not "respond to reason."

Mass support for fundamentalism reflects the experience of repeated failures and disappointments which translates into demands for an entirely different kind of society with a new set of goals. The fundamentalist surge is not likely to be stemmed as a mass movement until material conditions improve for the majority of the population, and perhaps not until the Arab-Israeli conflict is assuaged.

As noted above, Schmitter and Karl have argued that a democratic culture is not a prerequisite for stable democracy. The culture can—or will—emerge from the experience of democratic governance, and prudential rules of political behavior can substitute effectively for a compatible civic culture. This implies that Islam, as a religion and culture, is not an insuperable obstacle to democracy if political elites learn to protect and pursue their interests by the rules of the democratic game. Moreover, cultural and religious effects are usually indirect. They may frame the discussion and delimit the range of alternatives considered, but they rarely impose a single choice of action. For true believers, the connection between religion and politics may be direct and unmediated by more worldly conditions. For followers, however, the effect is less direct and mediated by the circumstances of their daily lives. And without mass support, religious or cultural movements are likely to remain relatively unimportant politically. The support of mass followers is contingent and ultimately depends on how well the movement meets their daily needs. Doctrinal interpretations alone provide inadequate evidence of whether Islam is an obstacle to democratization. Socioeconomic performance inevitably affects patterns of belief, perhaps encouraging secularism and materialism, and thus compelling religion and culture themselves to adapt to new circumstances.

The Middle East cannot isolate itself from trends that are powerful and important everywhere else. Nonetheless, fundamentalist Islam does make it more difficult for a democratic culture to form, for "rules of prudence" to take hold, and makes stable democracy problematic until the people are persuaded that democracy can provide for their needs more effectively than any alternative. These caveats are reinforced by other considerations: the Middle East's tribalized, patriarchal, and xenophobic social structure is also inhospitable to democratization, and most states remain powerful, in control of access to wealth, and hostile to liberalization. None of these factors preclude Middle Eastern democracy, but they do explain why the Middle East lags behind other areas in movement toward democracy. Nevertheless, significant liberalization is likely in the Middle East, perhaps in the next decade, and the transition process may be less bloody if external powers increase their pressures for meaningful—and relatively rapid—political change. External powers cannot impose democracy on the region, but internal forces alone may be too weak to establish democracy. Only by working together will the prospects for success improve.

NOTES

1. As one theorist notes, "no definition of democracy can be found by gazing at the real world, no matter how meticulous the inspection" (Lively 1975, p. 146).

2. If "denotative" refers to the formal, explicit meaning of a term and "connotative" to the broader meaning or implications of a term apart from the thing it explicitly describes, the distinction is significant here because democracy often seems to imply something different to Third World intellectuals, practitioners, and citizens than to their Western counterparts. Even a universally accepted definition of democracy may imply different things in different settings.

3. For an earlier discussion of "departicipation," see Kasfir (1976).

4. One sees this even among established Third World democracies in the Caribbean. Thus, politics there exhibits "a tendency toward very intense, almost life-and-death patterns of party competition—the absence of a relatively peaceful mode of party competition is one of the most striking features of Caribbean political systems . . . " (Henry and Stone 1983, p. xxi).

5. Barber (1992, p. 63) thus notes, "Democracy grows from the bottom up. . . . Civil society has to be built from the inside out. The institutional structure comes last." This argument is probably true in an ideal sense, but it offers little guidance about dealing with new democracies forced to devise their own sequence of democratization.

6. I will not address the complex issue of short-run incompatibilities between movement toward democracy, with its egalitarian bias, and movement toward the market, with its inegalitarian bias. The group of weak democracies is quite heterogeneous, with different mixes of characteristics and with countries at different stages of departure from authoritarianism or toward polyarchy.

7. There is a need to resist the euphoria, even arrogance, about this wave of democratization. The forces of reaction have been discredited, but not completely destroyed. The military, the traditional elites, the fundamentalists, and others wait in the wings for democracy to fail and for "disaster myopia" to set in—that is, for memories of past disasters to recede as the problems of the present mount. Dealing with these problems will be difficult enough without attaching to countries labels that are at least partially misleading.

8. Several small Caribbean countries might also qualify, as well as Colombia, Venezuela, and Malaysia.

9. Democracy and fundamentalism are, in a sense, all that is left as alternatives to

authoritarianism. Whether they can become compatible remains unclear, but remember the obvious: just as there are many kinds of democracy, there is great variety in the Islamic world. The pattern of relationships between democracy and Islam is also likely to be varied: incompatible and hostile in some places, compatible and friendly in others, and mixed and shifting in yet others.

REFERENCES

Barber, Benjamin R. 1992. "Jihad v. McWorld." *Atlantic Monthly* (March).

Beitz, Charles. 1989. *Political Equality: An Essay in Democratic Theory.* Princeton: Princeton University Press.

Bollen, Kenneth A. 1990. "Political Democracy: Conceptual and Measurement Traps." *Studies in Comparative International Development* 25, no. 1 (Spring), pp. 7–24.

Connolly, William E. 1974. *The Terms of Political Discourse.* Lexington, MA: D. C. Heath.

Dahl, Robert A. 1971. *Polyarchy: Participation and Opposition.* New Haven, CT: Yale University Press.

Di Palma, Giuseppe. 1990. *To Craft Democracies: An Essay on Democratic Transitions.* Berkeley: University of California Press.

Eckstein, Harry. 1988. "A Culturalist Theory of Political Change." *American Political Science Review* 82, (September), pp. 789–804.

Henry, Paget, and Carl Stone, eds. 1983. *The Newer Caribbean: Decolonization, Democracy, and Development,* Introduction. Philadelphia: Institute for the Study of Human Institutions.

Huntington, Samuel P. 1984. "Will More Countries Become Democratic?" *Political Science Quarterly* 99, no. 2 (Summer).

———. 1989. "The Modest Meaning of Democracy." In *Democracy in the Americas: Stopping the Pendulum,* Robert A. Pastor, ed. New York: Holmes & Meier.

Huntington, Samuel P., and Joan M. Nelson. 1976. *No Easy Choices: Political Participation in Developing Countries.* Cambridge: Harvard University Press.

Kasfir, Nelson. 1976. *The Shrinking Political Arena: Participation and Ethnicity in African Politics.* Berkeley: University of California Press.

Laitin, David. 1988. "Political Culture and Political Preferences." *American Political Science Review* 82, no. 2 (June).

Lively, Jack. 1975. *Democracy.* New York: St. Martin's Press.

Przeworski, Adam. 1991. *Democracy and the Market: Political and Economic Reforms in Eastern Europe and Latin America.* New York: Cambridge University Press.

Schmitter, Philippe C., and Terry Lynn Karl. 1991. "What Democracy Is . . . and Is Not." *Journal of Democracy* 2, no. 3, pp. 75–88.

5

ARAB AND WESTERN
CONCEPTIONS OF DEMOCRACY
Evidence from a UAE Opinion Survey

JAMAL AL-SUWAIDI

Democratization in the Gulf

DESPITE THE GROWTH of intellectual interest in democracy in the Arab world, there remain serious gaps in our understanding of the dynamics that foster democratization in this region. The present chapter examines the prospects for democracy in the Arab world, with particular attention to the states of the Gulf, and also considers whether or not any movement toward democracy is likely to increase the prospects for a peaceful resolution of regional interstate conflicts. It offers both a theoretical and an empirical examination of the factors that can determine the success or failure of democracy in the Arab world. Specifically, it contrasts Arab and Western conceptions of democracy, giving particular attention to cultural factors; examines the prospects for greater democratization in a political environment characterized by competition between authoritarian governments and quasi-totalitarian Islamic opposition movements; and considers the possibility that the chances for peace in the Middle East would be improved should some measure of democratization in fact occur. The discussion of these theoretical issues is followed by the presentation and analysis of public opinion data from the United Arab Emirates, the purpose being to examine the interrelationships among attitudes toward democracy, Islamic political movements, and foreign policy issues, including those pertaining to Israel and the United States.

In the aftermath of the Gulf War and the disintegration of the Soviet Union and Eastern Europe, democracy and political participation have become major topics in world politics. Authoritarian regimes all over the world, including those in the Middle East, find themselves under pressure today to establish or at least to promise democratic governance. The increasing sentiments shown in Gulf Arab media by political activists, scholars, and businessmen raise important questions about the prospects for democracy in the Arab world and the need to address the question of political reforms in the Gulf Arab region.[1] Major questions about the legitimacy of the Gulf states and the maintaining of political power have been raised. In particular, how did the Gulf regimes maintain their political power without viable political institutions? Gulf states have managed the issue of governance through unofficial mechanisms relating to the tribe, the sect, and religion (Al-Naqeeb 1990). Yet, the changing international and regional scene, including the Iraqi invasion of Kuwait, the collapse of the Soviet Union, the global role of the United States, and the worldwide movement toward democratization, are exerting pressure on the traditional monarchies of the Gulf to move toward democratic reform.[2]

Demands for political participation in the Gulf states began as early as the 1930s, but the ruling families have been successful in suppressing these demands. The implementation of these demands did not begin until 1963, when Kuwait established its first National Assembly. However, Kuwait's democratic path was precarious and the Kuwaiti National Assembly has been dissolved several times. Elections for a new National Assembly took place in October 1992.

In 1973, Bahrain followed the Kuwaiti example by establishing its first National Assembly. By 1975, however, the National Assembly had been dissolved and it is yet to be resurrected. On the other hand, a Consultative Council, or *Majlis al-Shura*, was established in Qatar in 1972, and the United Arab Emirates National Federation Council was established in 1971. More recently, two Gulf states have taken steps in the direction of participatory government—King Fahd of Saudi Arabia announced on March 1, 1992, that a Consultative Council would soon be established, and in 1991 Oman replaced its appointed State Consultative Council with a new elected Council.

Despite renewed calls for participatory governments in the Gulf Arab states, political reforms have in fact been minimal since the Gulf crisis of 1990–91. As Halliday (1991, p. 228) explains, the Gulf royal families "have in the past made promises of reform when under pressure, but have not implemented them later on." With the exception of Kuwait, parliaments and councils have no legislative power and are limited to an advisory role. Moreover, the Kuwaiti democratic experience is very restricted because a large number of Kuwaitis, including women and naturalized citizens, are not permitted to vote.[3]

While the Gulf states' response to demands for political participation has

been limited, making it evident that there will not be a quick and radical political transformation, a process of evolutionary change toward democratization could nonetheless take place.[4] As Dahl (1971, p. 45) concludes, "stable
polyarchies and near-polyarchies are more likely to result from rather slow evolutionary processes than from revolutionary overthrow of existing hegemo-
nies." Internal and external pressures may thus eventually lead to the democratization in the Gulf. Internally, educated elites have been demanding more
political reform, as newspaper articles, lectures and meetings indicate. Externally, global political and economic transformations may exert additional pressure for liberalization and political reform. This analysis has been advanced by
a number of scholars, who suggest that the external pressure on Gulf regimes
could have a profound effect (see e.g., Hudson 1991, p. 407).

Other analyses suggest, however, that the Gulf states are more secure than
ever due to the defeat of Saddam Hussein, who posed a major regional threat
to the status quo. The Gulf states have also signed cooperation and security
agreements with the United States and other Western powers in order to protect themselves from some of the additional regional pressures that buffet the
area. In addition, there has been no serious confrontation between the general
public and the ruling families on the issue of political participation. Thus, governments in the Gulf may not feel compelled to make major concessions toward establishing participatory forms of government, at least for the time being.

Democratization in the Gulf states, as in the rest of the Arab world, has
traditionally been hindered by authoritarian regimes and quasi-totalitarian opposition.[5] In the postcolonial era, the Arab world has tended to develop and
foster authoritarian ideas and ideologies, such as Arab nationalism, Ba'athism,
and religious extremism. Arab nationalism and political Islam have the effect
of halting movement toward democracy. For example, the call for Arab unity
led by the Egyptian president Gamal Abdul Nasser was accompanied by statements and rhetoric directed against imperialism, Zionism, and the West. Democracy, freedom of expression, and representative government were set aside
for higher causes, such as Arab unity, domestic development, and the defeat of
Israel.

Since the demise of Arab nationalism as a viable ideology, Arab political life
has been dominated by political Islam, which is articulated by radical, sometimes fanatical, groups that stand against change, tolerance, and democracy. In
a system where rulers are accountable only to God, democracy ceases to exist.
As one scholar explains:

Opposition has little place in a system where the ruler is accountable only to God and where it is the ruler's responsibility to guarantee the continued harmonious integration of each individual and group into the community. (Anderson 1987a, p. 221)

Constitutional rule and tolerance of opposing ideas thus are likely to be absent in a state dominated by the ideologies of contemporary religious movements. Some of these groups might join the democratic process as a tactic to gain control of the state, but this does not mean that they are committed to democratic values. On the contrary, their goal remains the establishment of a theological, quasi-totalitarian political system. By itself, therefore, movement from Arab nationalism to political Islam does not bring the Arab world closer to democratic patterns of governance.

The present study is designed to assess the relationship between Islam and democracy on the one hand, and between both factors and foreign policy considerations on the other hand. To provide an empirical foundation for assessing these relationships, survey data from the United Arab Emirates will be employed. In addition, however, since it is important to recall that "data must be viewed within the framework of a certain logic" (Rosenberg 1968, p. xi), the next sections of this chapter will seek to provide both a conceptual framework and a substantive foundation for the data analysis to follow. The discussion includes an examination of Arab and Western conceptions of democracy, an account of political conflict in the Arab world today, and consideration of religious groups' attitudes toward democracy.

Democracy and Culture: Arab and Western Conceptions of Democracy

The choice of democracy is not a political decision that can be taken by political leaders or political elites; it is, rather, a form of political culture. The crisis of democracy in the Arab world stems primarily from the lack of democratic traditions in Arab culture and history. Samuel Huntington (1984, p. 214) argues that an important precondition for the development of democracy is "a culture that is less monistic and more tolerant of diversity and compromise." One might argue that when Europe was moving toward democracy, it had no democratic cultural base. Yet European movement toward democracy developed along secular lines. In the Arab world, on the other hand, movement toward democracy points toward religious values. Unequivocally stated, secularism as a cultural base for democracy is extremely difficult to develop in the Arab world, due to the organic nature of Islam and the radical interpretations of Islamic doctrine that have gained prominence (Smith 1974, p. 7).

Democracy is the best known method for protecting individuals' civil and political rights (Pateman 1970; Nagel 1987; Huntington 1984; Arat 1991). It provides for freedom of speech, press, faith, opinion, ownership, and assembly, as well as the right to vote, nominate and seek public office. Freedom from arbitrary arrest, imprisonment, torture, and inhuman punishment are also guaranteed in democratic political systems. The presence or absence of these rights serves as a criterion by which to evaluate the degree of democratization in any state and, needless to say, all but a few Arab countries have constitutions that affirm respect for a broad range of civil and political rights.

Given the centrality of civil and political rights, there is a fundamental difference between Western and Arab conceptions of democracy. The sharp distinction between religion and politics in Western culture has a historical context and ideological rationale that are different from those that have arisen from the experience of non-Western Arab culture. The analysis of Max Weber, for example, examines the evolution of Christianity from its early forms to its modern Protestant forms and stresses its movement toward a worldly religion with emphasis on economic rationality and secular political values.[6] Extending this Weberian thesis, Talcott Parsons also calls attention to the connection between Christian religious values and the secular social structure of Western societies.[7] Furthermore, there are differences not only in the religious traditions but also in the developmental experience of Western and non-Western societies. As Huntington (1968, p. 46) writes:

> In the modernization of the non-Western parts of the world, however, the problems of the centralization of authority, national integration, social mobilization, economic development, political participation, and social welfare have arisen not sequentially but simultaneously. The "demonstration effect" which the early modernizers have on the later modernizers first intensifies aspirations and then exacerbates frustration.

In the Western experience, secularism thus became a fundamental and necessary component of democracy and political development. Although the Christian church had been a distinct institution years before its association with the political authority of the Roman Empire in the fourth century, and while it continued to dominate sociopolitical life for many years after the demise of the Roman Empire, secular rulers eventually challenged and reduced the church's influence. As Strayer (1958/59, p. 39) asserts, "What we call struggles between state and church were often purely political conflicts between two states, an old clerical state and a new secular state." The result is a disassociation of religion and politics in Western democratic societies; religion deals with individual and spiritual matters and is concerned primarily with private affairs, whereas politics is a secular phenomenon concerned with physical and material life and with public affairs.

The Muslim world, by contrast, never experienced this kind of differentiation. Secularism and the privatization of religion are alien to the Muslim conception. Muslims have continued to assume that only a "religious leader" can provide good government for the Muslim community and that the main function of an Islamic government is to ensure obedience to God's law as explained in the *Quran* (Islam's Holy Book) and the *sunnah* (the sayings and doings of the Prophet Muhammad). As expressed by Hudson (1980, p. 3), in the Muslim view, "politically developed Islamic society is a lawful society. Rulers and the ruled alike are governed by the *Shariah* [Islamic law], as interpreted and applied by the learned scholars of Islam, the *ulama*, and the *fuqaha* [the jurists]." Consequently, in Islam, the religious sphere is clearly political and the political sphere is deeply religious.

Is Islam an obstacle to the development of democracy? Does the absence of a secular tradition in Muslim history constitute an important obstacle to the emergence of democratic systems of governance in the present-day Arab world? In order to address such questions adequately, it is necessary to avoid viewing the relationship between Islam and democracy in terms of the Western paradigm. At the very least, it is essential for scholars and others concerned with democracy in the Arab states to develop and employ approaches which reflect a recognition that Muslims do not consider religion to be a private or personal activity.

Yet an effort to place the relationship between Islam and democracy within the historic experience and normative framework of the Muslim world does not mean that problems and tensions should be ignored. For example, can democracy occur if the ulama or jurists have sole charge of legal interpretation? Might not the ulama's ability to declare laws compatible or incompatible with the teachings of the shariah lead to abuse? There are numerous examples of ulama manipulating Islamic teachings to the advantage of political leaders.[8] Indeed, the religion has been dominated by the state since its inception and the ulama have often played a role similar to that of the Christian clergy: motivated by political rather than religious considerations, they have offered doctrinal interpretations that are deliberately designed to justify the behavior of political leaders.

The potential for this kind of abuse, although present in secular democratic societies, is limited by certain traditions and values that are an institutionalized and essential part of Western political life. The most important of these is the principle that the individual citizen, not God's commands as interpreted by religious scholars and jurists, is the source of law, sovereignty, legitimacy, and political action (Anderson 1987a; Esposito and Piscatori 1991). In other words, at the heart of democracy is a belief that rulers must be accountable to the ruled.[9] This notion of accountability is far from being realized in Middle Eastern Islamic societies, however. Throughout Islamic history, Muslim rulers have insisted that they carry out God's command and need not be concerned with the wishes of those they rule. This is perhaps the main distinction between Western and Arab conceptions of democracy, a distinction reflecting the application of different normative criteria to questions about "the proper relationship between popular sovereignty and divine sovereignty" (Esposito and Piscatori 1991, p. 438).

Although Islamic theology emphasizes the organic unity of state and society, thus leaving no room for secular policies that separate the sphere of religion from that of politics, a number of Muslim and other scholars have sought to reinterpret Islamic teachings in an effort to accommodate the secular principles necessary for democracy.[10] Those sympathetic to this effort cite the writings and the philosophy of such Muslim modernists as Khayr al-Din al-Tunisi (1810–1890), Jamal al-Din al-Afghani (1839–1896), Muhammad Abdu (1849–1905), and Abdu Rahman al-Kawakibi (1849–1903), as well as many others (Kedourie 1966; Imara 1974; Voll 1982). These and many liberal Muslim thinkers argue that the true nature of Islam is reformist and progressive and that the religion is thus capable of incorporating modernist policies. Among the prescriptions of the modernists is a call for ulama to be trained in the modern sciences and philosophy, as well as in Islamic theology. Many modernists also favor a degree of secularism, meaning some separation of religion and politics, not only to reduce the influence of conservative Islamic teachings but to minimize the exploitation of religion by the ruling elites and the ulama.

According to Muslim modernists, secularism may take different paths in the Arab and Islamic world and need not necessarily involve the total elimination of religion from national political life. For instance, as in nineteenth-century experiments in modernization carried out by Egypt, Turkey, and several other Muslim countries, Islam could be granted official status as a source of national culture and could be championed by secular authorities as a force for social integration. Indeed, this may be particularly important at present, given the need to cope with major societal dislocations and rapid socioeconomic change. Thus, rather than restricting religion to matters of personal status, the construction of political systems that are secular in important respects may nonetheless look to Islam to perform social functions that are appropriate and even necessary in democratic societies.

Current proponents of Islamic modernism offer such formulations, but there are a number of reasons why their prescriptions may have only limited impact in the Arab and Islamic world. For one thing, Islamic history lacks democratic traditions, which means that modernist proposals will not strike a familiar chord. Along the same lines and possibly even more important, Islamic modernism itself has never been a major ideological force in Arab political processes. Unlike the Muslim Brotherhood, for example, Islamic modernism has not been a mass-oriented movement and has not had mass appeal. On the contrary, its emergence in the nineteenth century was based on individual scholarly effort and centered around a small number of thinkers and theoreticians, such as Abdu and al-Afghani, which may explain why there is a lack of mass support for the modernist message today.

Muslim modernists have also been placed on the defensive by conservative ulama and the *assulia* (fundamentalist) movements, which accuse them of articulating a distorted view of Islam and of manipulating the religion to fit Western values and conceptions. Unlike Islamic modernists, fundamentalist groups in the Middle East today are unwilling to tolerate dissent and political pluralism. Examples include the regimes in Iran and Sudan, where Islamic movements have assumed power, and the Muslim Brotherhood.[11] These religious movements reflect the gap between theory and practice in Islam caused by a failure to understand the Quran as a unified whole. They insist upon giving literal interpretation to Quranic verses and text and this obscures the real meaning of Islam's message; they interpret the Quran in a vacuum, ignoring the contextual factors and sociocultural conditions that give meaning to Quranic verses. While this tendency creates misinformation and a misunderstanding of Islam,[12] it is nonetheless widespread in the Arab world today and further limits receptivity to the proposals advanced by Muslim modernists.

A final difficulty confronting Muslim modernists lies in the historic and theological limitations of the formulation advanced by some scholars to demonstrate the compatibility of Islam and democracy. Specifically, some equate *shura* (consultation) with democracy, arguing that shura constitutes an authentic Islamic institution that ties rulers to those they govern. Shura, these modernists contend, provides for popular political participation and citizen influence in policy-making, resource allocation and succession. Yet such arguments confuse the meaning of both shura and democracy. Early Muslim scholars and jurists considered shura to be a voluntary political procedure rather than a requirement derived from the political rights of the governed. In addition, shura has been largely ignored throughout Muslim history, primarily because state domination over religion prevented its development. For these reasons, the procedure has not been standardized and institutionalized within Islam and no clear, established and widely practiced system of political participation has emerged within an Islamic framework. There is at present no coherent vision of how to implement the principles of shura in order to construct political systems that are both democratic and Islamic.

In addition to the cultural obstacles associated with history and religion, there are two other important impediments to the development of democracy in the Arab world today: the ineffective role of the middle class and the lack of adequate associational life.[13]

The existence of a middle class is crucial for transforming political systems into democracies. A major historical factor in the movement toward democracy in the West was the role played by the middle class. Yet the middle class in non-Western societies, including the Arab world, is often weak because the state dominates the economy; the governed are therefore capable of exerting no more than limited pressure for government accountability. As Huntington (1984, p. 204) states:

> The failure of democracy to develop in Third World countries despite their economic growth can, perhaps, be related to the nature of that growth. The leading roles have been played by the state and by multinational enterprises. As a result, economic development runs ahead of the development of a bourgeoisie. In those circumstances where a bourgeoisie has developed, however, the prospects for democracy have been greater [e.g., Turkey].

Nor has the middle class in the Arab world displayed the same political attitudes and made the same contribution to the development of democratic values as its counterpart in the West. As one scholar explains, "The Western bourgeoisie was involved in a class struggle against privileged aristocracy and absolute monarchy to protect its economic power and promote its social and political status" (Arat 1991, p. 38). In contrast, the middle class in most Arab societies has not had to struggle against a privileged aristocracy that controlled state authority. Rather, this class has itself been "supported by the state and given a privileged position in the economy" (Arat 1991, p. 39). This observation applies broadly but is illustrated particularly clearly by the situation in the oil-producing Gulf Arab states.

The weakness of associational life poses similar problems for democratization.[14] While the existence of active unions, professional societies and other economic and political associations tends to undermine authoritarian rule and produce pressures for governmental accountability, political regimes in the Arab world are very suspicious of any associational activity they cannot control. Again, this is particularly clear in the Gulf Arab states, where, according to one scholar, "leaders have tried to constrain associational life. Many forms of [voluntary associations] are simply banned. For groups to be effective, they must have institutions, for associations to flourish, people must be allowed to associate" (Crystal 1992, p. 25). These factors, along with the normative considerations discussed above, highlight the differences between Arab and Western experiences that bear on the issue of democratization.

Authoritarian Regimes and Quasi-Totalitarian Opposition

Two types of political regimes predominate in the Arab world today: authoritarian regimes that came to power through a national war of independence or a military coup, and absolute monarchies.[15] Institutionalized patterns of political participation and political freedom are lacking in both. Most Arab states ban political organizations, do not tolerate political dissent, and limit civil and political rights. Political repression is institutionalized and the secret police is the most sophisticated and effective institution in many Arab countries. Opposition may mean imprisonment, in some cases a sentence of death. Thus, as Anderson (1987a, p. 230) writes, "Much of the opposition faced by the regimes of the Middle East and North Africa stems from their failure to institute and respect regular procedures for recruiting political leaders and debating and determining policy."

This situation has created strong movement for political change in the present-day Arab world. The previous generation of Arabs who rallied behind charismatic leaders and accepted traditional authoritarian regimes is now being replaced by a young and better-educated generation that is more aware of the challenges and opportunities facing modern societies. Moreover, the young generation will not accept authoritarian rule and secret police tactics. These pressures for change do not portend an orderly transition to democracy, however. Rather, they appear to signal an upcoming wave of violence and instability in the region.

The emerging political conflict is between an old authoritarian state and a new Islamic opposition that is quasi-totalitarian in character. As long as Arab governments resist political participation and refuse to tolerate different political opinions, the strength of Islam as an alternative political ideology will continue to grow. Indeed, militant Islamic groups have been able to gain popular support in the Arab world in large measure precisely because of the violent and reactionary policies of many Arab regimes. In the case of Tunisia, for example:

> A few years ago a Tunisian group was unusual in publishing a manifesto, declaring itself in favor of political and religious pluralism and ready to work within the constitution. Repression, including the imprisonment or expulsion of the faction's leaders, strengthened the hardliners. Now they have the upper hand. (*Economist* 1992, p. 13)

The ideological vacuum in the Arab world also contributes to the emergence of Islamic opposition movements. Socialism is increasingly discredited and nationalism has lost much of its appeal among both ruling elites and political opposition groups. Thus, ideological developments as well as political reaction have contributed to the increasing strength of popular Islamic opposition movements and to the challenge these movements will pose for existing regimes in the 1990s.

With few exceptions, the programs and activities of religious opposition groups are similar in important respects to those of the authoritarian regimes that are currently in power. Although the content of their ideology is different, the end result is largely the same. If they gain power, religious groups will restrict public discourse and the free flow of information and will tolerate little if any dissent. They will also impose on society their narrow interpretation of Islam in sociopolitical life, for example, in such areas as women's role in society; they will enforce regulations of *halal* (religiously permissible action) and *haram* (religiously forbidden action), alternatively requiring or banning various sociopolitical activities in the name of Islam. Finally, religious groups will insist upon the establishment of Islamic economic institutions, such as Islamic banks.

There is thus little likelihood that religious opposition groups will promote liberal democratic values. While democracy requires pluralism, tolerance and the acceptance of political dissent, it is unlikely that religious groups will actively embrace these values or even reluctantly tolerate opposing political parties, beliefs, or values, especially those of secular groups or socialist organizations. The ideology of these groups precludes compromise since they believe that their own prescriptions are divine commandments. The word *kafir* (infidel) will be used to discredit competing ideologies and movements, with religious groups insisting that these ideas must be suppressed because they are anti-Islamic and hence immoral.

An important reason for the quasi-totalitarian character of current Islamic opposition movements is the fact that their leaders are not scholars of Islamic jurisprudence or even of Islamic history. Whereas early Muslim modernists, such as Abdu, al-Afghani and others, were intellectual political activists with a clear understanding of the conditions of modern societies, the leaders of today's Islamic groups lack the knowledge and the qualifications to provide viable alternatives to the political systems they seek to replace (David 1984, pp. 134–57). They offer only a vague and emotional reaction to unsatisfactory social, economic, and political conditions. For all these reasons, the authoritarianism of the current Arab regimes will become the quasi-totalitarianism of a theological state if religious opposition groups seize power.

Despite the current importance of Islamic opposition movements, the narrow platform and antidemocratic character of most groups is likely to limit their long-term appeal. If they would broaden their platform to include women and liberal segments of the population, religious groups could more seriously challenge the current governments of the Arab world. It is more likely, however, that they will continue to resist socioeconomic change and fail to modernize their political programs and tactics, eventually causing much of their appeal to wither away.

The ideology and sociopolitical programs of religious groups are too political to appeal to traditional mainstream Muslims. Their ideology is not only confusing but also insensitive to the need for socioeconomic change. Although religious groups demand total transformation of the present sociopolitical, legal, and economic circumstances of the Arab world, they do not provide a realistic or workable alternative. Most religious groups do not go beyond a call for "pure Islam" based on the Quran and the sunnah; they tend to ignore the need for continuous socioeconomic transformation and to use tactics and ideas that are far removed from present-day life. In contrast to current religious movements, which have no model for socioeconomic change, Muslim modernists presented such a model over a century ago. Modernist Islamic thinking encourages movement in a direction that does not hinder democracy and sociopolitical development. In addition, Islamic modernism would broaden the appeal of Muslim movements by attracting alienated segments of the population to which current religious groups do not appeal, including the educated, the middle class, and women. But the flexible, dynamic, and progressive vision of Islam presented by Muslim modernists has been totally ignored by most of the current Islamic movements.

If current religious groups came to dominate the government, the first question that would have to be asked concerns the nature of the Islamic political system they would establish. The platforms these groups espouse rarely extend beyond the realm of ideals; they express abstract and utopian values attached to political Islam and the khalifa system. Moreover, not only do they offer no specific model of government compatible with the challenges of modern society, the writings of their leaders suggest that their rule would be as authoritarian in character as that of existing regimes. Although some leaders promise to respect democratic principles, and discuss in this context such concepts as *ijmaa* (consensus), *baya* (consent), and *shura* (consultation), there is little agreement about the practical and real-world meaning of these concepts. In fact, there has never been a universally accepted model of government in Islam.

Several factors contribute to the lack of consensus on the nature of government in Islam. First, and most important, there is no direct or detailed model of government in the Quran, the sunnah, or the practice of the early caliphs. Although the Quran and the sunnah provide general guidelines for the political conduct of the Islamic *umma* (community of believers), they do not call for any particular form of government. Second, there has been no attempt to implement or institutionalize such Islamic political concepts as ijmaa, baya, and shura. After the death of the Prophet and the brief period of the Rightly Guided Caliphs, political authority was justified on the basis of tribal solidarity, or *asabiyah*. The approval or disapproval of the Islamic umma was ignored and eventually rulers started to name their own successors.

The lack of precision in their platform, as well as its narrow and antidemocratic character, will also tend to reduce the long-term appeal of current religious opposition groups. Without a clear and broadly accepted alternative model of government, Islamic groups are unlikely to be politically successful in the Arab world.[16] In the short term, however, these groups may make gains not because the substance of their message is persuasive but because dissatisfaction with the political and economic policies of existing regimes is creating pressure for change. In other words, although Islam will remain a salient factor for years to come, the religion alone will not determine the political future in the Arab world. Whether or not Islamic groups come to power will depend on economic and political factors. Economic and political crises have increased frustration among the Arabs and played a major role in producing support for current Islamic opposition movements. And unless these crises can be resolved, political Islam will gain popularity among the poorer classes and the result will be greater turmoil in the Arab world.

A UAE Opinion Survey

The literature on the role of Islam in sociopolitical change has for the most part been descriptive and vague, failing to specify the patterns of interaction among religious and sociopolitical orientations at the individual level of analysis. The lack of data-based research has resulted in speculative and subjective studies on Islam and democracy. In addition, there are virtually no major empirical studies of the relationship between Islam and democracy on the one hand and international and foreign policy considerations on the other. The present study attempts to address these needs. It seeks to make a contribution to theoretical knowledge by presenting and analyzing empirical evidence about some of the relationships among Islam, democracy and foreign policy in the Arab world today.

The data examined in this chapter were collected through survey research in the United Arab Emirates. The survey consisted of a sixty-item Arabic-language questionnaire; 500 questionnaires were distributed to a random sample of students at the UAE University in Al-Ain in May and June 1991. Of the returned questionnaires, 399 were usable, representing about 4 percent of the total UAE university student population. The timing of the survey is notable in that it permits assessment of the immediate impact of the Gulf War on the attitudes of the UAE's educated elite.

Respondents are distributed evenly among the four undergraduate classes and in appropriate proportions among the seven colleges of the university. Slightly more than half (55.4 percent) are female and all are between 19 and 26 years of age, with 22 years the median age. Not surprisingly, almost 90 percent of the respondents are unmarried. The overwhelming majority, 88 percent, are UAE nationals and they represent every Emirate in the federation. The balance of 12 percent are nationals of other Arab countries, presumably children of expatriate faculty members and government workers. Finally, respondents report monthly family incomes ranging from under 3,000 to more than 25,000 dirhams (approximately $800–$10,000), although almost 80 percent report a monthly income of less than 9,000 dirhams ($2,500).

On the basis of these characteristics, it can be assumed with a high degree of confidence that the UAE university students whose opinions have been sampled are broadly representative of the educated and middle class sectors of the society at large. In other words, it is unlikely that the results of the survey would have been significantly different had the respondents been a random sample of the UAE educated elite. In addition, given the political, economic, and cultural similarities between the UAE and other Gulf Arab states, it is probable that the survey's conclusions will also shed light on other Gulf states.

There are three broad objectives to the analysis of these data. First, the research examines the relationship between attitudes toward political Islam and toward democracy. Second, the nature of the relationship between attitudes toward political Islam and attitudes toward foreign policy will be discussed. Finally, the interrelationship among all three sets of attitudes—toward democracy, political Islam and foreign policy—will be presented. Based on the preceding discussion, it is hypothesized that respondents who strongly support current religious groups will have more negative attitudes toward democracy. It is also expected that they oppose Western culture, cooperation with the West, and a peaceful settlement of the conflict with Israel. In contrast, respondents who oppose religious groups are more likely to support democratic values, to be less antagonistic toward the West, and to be more favorably disposed to Arab-Israeli peace. The analysis will also examine the assumption that positive attitudes toward democracy are related to support for peace with Israel.

The univariate distributions presented in table 1 show how respondents answered a series of items dealing with attitudes toward political Islam, democracy, and foreign policy, the key variables to be investigated. The question about political Islam asks about support for current religious movements, the platforms of which call for the establishment of an Islamic state and a rejection of governance based on secular values. Questions about patterns of governance ask about the importance of popular political participation as well as about support for democracy. A series of foreign policy questions examines attitudes and orientations toward Western countries and toward Israel.

Survey Findings

This section analyzes the UAE student survey data in order to investigate relationships among attitudes toward political Islam, democratic and participatory patterns of governance, and issues of foreign policy.

Table 1. Attitudes toward Political Islam, Democracy, and Foreign Policy

Item	Number	Percent
1. Political Islam: Do you support current organized religious groups? Do you support the position of religious groups on the Gulf crisis?		
a. Strongly support religious groups	133	33.3
b. Support religious groups	128	32.1
c. Oppose religious groups	130	32.6
No response	8	2.0
Total	399	100.0
2. Political Participation: Do you consider political participation a national priority in the UAE today?		
a. Priority	215	53.9
b. Not a priority	176	44.1
No response	8	2.0
Total	399	100.0
3. Democratic Reforms: Do you support democratic reforms in society today?		
a. Strongly support democracy	198	49.6
b. Less supportive of democracy	190	47.6
No response	11	2.8
Total	399	100.0
4. Foreign Policy: "What is the main threat (danger) to my country?"		
a. The United States	73	18.3
b. Israel	203	50.9
c. Iran	33	8.3
d. Others	82	20.5
No response	8	2.0
Total	399	100.0
5. Foreign Policy: Do you approve of U.S. policy during the Gulf crisis?		
a. Approve	241	60.4
b. Somewhat approve	110	27.5
c. Disapprove	39	9.8
No response	9	2.3
Total	399	100.0

Table 1. *Continued*

6. Foreign Policy: Attitudes toward foreign (Western) assistance during the Gulf crisis		
a. Approve	311	77.9
b. Disapprove	80	20.1
No response	8	2.0
Total	399	100.0
7. Foreign Policy: Attitudes toward foreign (Western) assistance after the Gulf crisis		
a. Approve	136	34.1
b. Disapprove	255	63.9
No response	8	2.0
Total	399	100.0
8. Foreign Policy: Gulf security depends on		
a. Gulf states alone	122	30.6
b. Gulf states and Iran	59	14.8
c. Arab states	64	16.0
d. Western countries	48	12.0
e. Muslim states	106	26.6
Total	399	100.0

Political Islam and Democracy

To assess the prospects for democracy in the Gulf Arab states, it is essential to understand the attitudes about patterns of governance held by supporters of religious groups. Do those who sympathize with these Islamic political movements differ from other respondents in their views about the importance of democracy and political participation? Some analysts assume that those who support religious groups are also likely to support the quest for democratization in the Arab world.[17] Some of the reasons why this may not be the case were reviewed in the previous conceptual discussion. These competing propositions may be assessed using survey data from the UAE, and table 2 accordingly compares the attitudes toward democracy and political participation of respondents with different levels of support for religious groups. It may be noted that the views expressed by university students are quite significant. Radical Islamic teachings appeal primarily to younger individuals, those under the age of thirty, and religious groups are very active on university campuses in the Middle East, including the UAE.

Table 2 shows how attitudes toward political Islam interact with attitudes

Table 2. Political Islam, Political Participation, and Democracy

Political Islam	Political Participation			Democracy		
	High Priority	Not High Priority	Total	Strongly support democracy	Less supportive of democracy	Total
Strongly support religious groups	45.1% (N = 60)	54.9% (N = 73)	100.0 (N = 133)	36.2% (N = 47)	63.8% (N = 83)	100.0 (N = 130)
Support religious groups	56.3% (N = 72)	43.7% (N = 56)	100.0 (N = 128)	49.2% (N = 63)	50.8% (N = 65)	100.0 (N = 128)
Oppose religious groups	63.8% (N = 83)	36.2% (N = 47)	100.0 (N = 130)	67.7% (N = 88)	32.3% (N = 42)	100.0 (N = 130)

toward political participation and democracy. There is considerable support for political participation in the UAE. However, respondents who strongly support religious groups are less likely than others to consider political participation a high priority. Most religious groups and opposition religious scholars call for the establishment of an Islamic political order, regardless of the means employed to achieve this goal, and respondents who support Islamic groups are consequently more likely to consider the implementation of shariah (Islamic law) to be the first priority. Conversely, 63.8 percent of those who oppose political Islam are strongly in favor of political participation.

Table 2 also examines respondent attitudes toward democracy, and here there is an even more clear-cut distinction between supporters and opponents of religious groups. Sixty-four percent of those who strongly support religious groups are less likely to support democracy. In contrast, 67.7 percent of those who oppose religious groups support democracy. Religious groups argue against democracy in favor of shura; they consider democratic values an essential part of Western secular culture which must be resisted. More specifically, democracy is problematic for religious groups because it allows for different ideas and opinions to be heard, because it permits various groups to join the political process, and above all because it questions the validity of what these groups consider to be absolute truth and divine commands. Thus, a number of respondents who sympathize with organized religious groups perceive democracy as a Western phenomenon and a vehicle for the unwanted transmission of "Western cultural influence," or what they consider to be *al-quazw al-thaqafi*.

In sum, there is a clear relationship between attitudes toward political Islam and attitudes toward patterns of governance. Those who strongly support religious movements are less likely to attach importance to political participation and democratic reforms, whereas participation and democracy are judged to be much more important by those opposed to political Islam.

Political Islam and Foreign Policy

Religious groups have a specific stance on foreign policy issues, especially relations with the United States and peace talks with Israel. For example, religious groups in the Arab world strongly opposed U.S. involvement in the Gulf crisis, especially the military role of the U.S. Thus, many supporters of religious groups in Algeria, Tunisia, Sudan, Egypt, and Jordan supported Saddam Hussein during the Gulf War. In the UAE, however, respondents strongly supported the U.S. policy during the Gulf crisis, regardless of their attitudes toward religious groups. As shown in table 3, 67.4 percent of those who strongly support religious groups approve of U.S. involvement in the Gulf crisis, which is actually slightly greater than the level of support among those who oppose religious groups.

There is no important relationship between support for religious groups and attitudes toward U.S. involvement in the Gulf crisis because the experience of religious groups in the Gulf states differs fundamentally from that of such groups in other Arab states. In the Gulf states, including the UAE, Islamic revivalist groups are not in formal opposition to existing regimes but are rather legal organizations that emphasize socioreligious reform. Moreover, the Gulf states have developed special policies to deal with political Islam. According to Bill (1984, p. 123), the Gulf states

> reinforce institutions of establishment Islam while attempting to divide and co-opt the forces of [political] Islam. Sunni fundamentalist groups have been courted and encouraged. Saudi Arabia has poured large sums of money into the al-Islah organizations active in Kuwait, Bahrain, and the United Arab Emirates. Gulf officials have also helped finance and promote Islamic education.

Therefore, religious groups tend to compromise with the ruling elites in the Gulf. Unlike many Arab countries, the Gulf states have never had a violent confrontation with religious groups.

There are a number of reasons for the peaceful relationship between Gulf governments and religious groups. First, as noted, Gulf governments have a policy of supporting and funding religious groups; for instance, the UAE government actively supports Islamic causes and teachings. Second, in response, religious groups have rarely criticized Gulf governments. Third, the high standard of living in the Gulf has minimized conflict between the interests of governments and those of Islamic groups. In short, the unique political experience of Islamic groups in the Gulf has contributed to similarities between their position and those of Gulf governments toward the Iraqi invasion of Kuwait and the Gulf crisis.

When respondents were asked about the source of major threats to UAE national security, a majority selected Israel, despite the geographic distance between the two countries, the consequences of the Gulf crisis, and the start of peace talks between the Arabs and the Jewish state. Moreover, this observation holds regardless of respondents' support for religious groups. These findings are shown in table 4. The country that is next most likely to be seen as a threat to UAE national security is the United States, and in this instance there is a difference associated with levels of support for religious groups. Specifically, as also shown in table 4, the view that the U.S. is a threat is more common among those who support political Islam.

Table 3. Political Islam and Foreign Policy: Attitudes toward U.S. Policy during the Gulf Crisis

U.S. Involvement in the Gulf Crisis	Approve	Somewhat approve	Disapprove	Total
Political Islam:				
Strongly support religious groups	67.4% (N = 89)	18.2% (N = 24)	14.4% (N = 19)	100.0 (N = 132)
Support religious groups	54.7% (N = 70)	39.1% (N = 50)	6.2% (N = 8)	100.0 (N = 128)
Oppose religious groups	63.1% (N = 82)	27.7% (N = 36)	9.2% (N = 12)	100.0 (N = 130)

Table 4. Political Islam and Foreign Policy: Respondents' Opinions on the Countries that Constitute a Major Threat to UAE National Security

Country	U.S.	Israel	Iran	Others	Total
Political Islam:					
Strongly support religious groups	23.3% (N = 31)	50.4% (N = 67)	6.8% (N = 9)	19.5% (N = 26)	100.0 (N = 133)
Support religious groups	19.5% (N = 25)	54.7% (N = 70)	5.5% (N = 7)	20.3% (N = 26)	100.0 (N = 128)
Oppose religious groups	13.1% (N = 17)	50.8% (N = 66)	13.1% (N = 17)	23.0% (N = 30)	100.0 (N = 130)

The absence of a relationship between attitudes toward Israel and support for religious groups is somewhat surprising, since the groups themselves tend to have strong anti-Israel positions. Islamic opposition to Israel stems, in part, from a strong religious belief that Palestine is part of the Islamic umma and, in particular, that Jerusalem must be liberated. Jerusalem is the third holiest place in Islam—especially al-Masjid al-Aqsa (al-Aqsa Mosque); Jerusalem is the first of two kiblahs, i.e., the first place toward which a Muslim turns in prayer. Islamic groups also use Israel as a legitimizing factor in their opposition to Arab states. Israel provides a living example of the failure of Arab regimes to establish strong states. In fact, religious groups cite a willingness to begin peace talks with Israel as an indication of the failure and weakness of Arab governments. Thus, as one scholar writes, "Israel, as it stands today, strongly backed by the United States, is a legitimizing model for Islamic states or minimally for governments with fundamentalist (even fanatic) religious representation" (El-Guindi 1986, p. 32). Seen from this perspective, it may be noted that harsh Israeli policies toward the Palestinians may bring additional popular support to religious groups seeking to challenge current governments in the Arab world.[18] Nevertheless, despite these considerations, anti-Israel sentiments among UAE respondents are equally pronounced among those who support and oppose religious groups.

Turning to attitudes toward the United States, Washington's position on the question of democracy in the Arab world may be one factor influencing the views of respondents. The U.S. position on this issue remains unclear, however, the ambiguity arising from a number of contradictory messages. The U.S. has supported the transition to democracy in Eastern Europe and Latin America, but it fought a war to restore the traditional monarchy in Kuwait and has not subsequently exerted pressure on the Gulf states for democratization and political change. The fact that Washington does not recognize the internal pressures on these regimes for political reform may be partially responsible for America's lax attitude. The U.S. has ignored political reforms because the Gulf states appear to be politically stable, at least for now; Washington is apparently unwilling to risk its relationships with current political regimes that, in its view, are not faced with internal pressures for increased political participation.

As the preceding suggests, the U.S. is perceived as a major force in the preservation of the status quo, which makes it unpopular among many respondents despite its role in the liberation of Kuwait. Opposition to the U.S. may also reflect anger at American support for Israel and, in addition, a general antipathy toward Western values. All of these considerations are articulated with special force by religious groups, which may explain why anti-U.S. sentiments are more common among UAE respondents who support political Islam. As one study reports, religious groups equate "Western values with the corruption, materialism and immorality that they find in their own society; many see their own rulers as Western stooges; they long to purge their societies, even if the purging involves repression" (*Economist* 1992, p. 13).

Table 5 shows that most respondents think cooperation with the U.S. is not a priority, despite the U.S. role in the liberation of Kuwait. A majority of respondents is opposed to any military or security cooperation between the U.S. and the Gulf states after the Gulf crisis. In this instance, however, opposition to the U.S. role after the Gulf crisis is not connected to attitudes toward political Islam. Sixty-three percent of those who oppose religious groups also oppose cooperation with the U.S. after the Gulf crisis. When asked about the source of military assistance needed in the Gulf, respondents expressed a preference for troops from the Gulf Cooperation Council, followed by troops from Muslim countries and then Arab troops. Military assistance from Western countries was least often preferred.

Democracy, Political Islam, and Foreign Policy

Research in international politics suggests that democratic states are less likely than authoritarian states to resort to war in international conflict, at least to the extent that conflicts among two or more democracies are unlikely to be resolved through the application of force. Many of the chapters in this volume summarize the literature which supports this proposition.

Table 5. Attitudes toward U.S. Assistance during and after the Gulf War

Political Islam	During the Gulf Crisis			After the Gulf Crisis		
	Approve	Disapprove	Total	Approve	Disapprove	Total
Strongly support religious groups	72.2% (N = 96)	27.8% (N = 37)	100.0 (N = 133)	32.3% (N = 43)	67.7% (N = 90)	100.0 (N = 133)
Support religious groups	83.6% (N = 107)	16.4% (N = 21)	100.0 (N = 128)	35.2% (N = 45)	64.8% (N = 83)	100.0 (N = 128)
Oppose religious groups	83.0% (N = 108)	17.0% (N = 22)	100.0 (N = 130)	37.0% (N = 48)	63.0% (N = 82)	100.0 (N = 130)

Nevertheless, a number of factors need to be considered when dealing with the relationship between democracy and war. First, due to the complexity of the causes of war, it is inappropriate to focus on a single variable. As Dougherty and Pfaltzgraff (1981, p. 130) suggest:

social collectivities have gone to war throughout history for a variety of reasons—territory, dominion, security, wealth, prestige, the triumph of an idea, reunifying an ethnic-cultural system, and preserving a set of values.

Second, while democracy in the liberal tradition may be associated with peace, this may not be the case in religious cultures, where it is even possible that democracy will increase the probability of conflict. When applying the proposition that democracies are less war-prone than other forms of government to Middle East politics, it is essential to include the role of political Islam as an intervening variable. Muslim scholars divide international affairs into two distinct spheres: *Dar al-harb* (House of War) and *Dar al-Islam* (House of Islam). In a democracy, religious groups may gain political influence and, consequently, the intolerance and hostility of these groups toward other religions and ideologies may increase the likelihood of conflict. It is thus possible that religious democracies will be more war-prone than liberal democracies.

The preceding follows to the extent that the relationship between democracy and war is determined by the nature of political culture rather than by domestic political structure. And as Morgan and Campbell (1991, p. 208) write:

> liberal democracies are more peace loving than other states, not because their political structure constrains decision makers directly, but because the citizenry of such states develop norms and expectations regarding proper methods of conflict resolution.

So far as religious-democratic systems are concerned—systems in which democratization permits religious groups to gain political power or influence, decisions, policies, and state goals are likely to be established with primary reference to religion and to be justified with respect to divine rather than popular will. It is not that normative factors are unimportant in other democratic systems. Liberal democracies, for example, are "willing to fight other types of states; and, in fact, their ideological beliefs can serve as a motivation for aggression (i.e., to bring others into the liberal fold)" (Morgan and Campbell 1991, p. 208). But states that seek to conform to the teachings of Islam judge other states not by whether the latter are democratic but by their attitudes and behavior with respect to Islam. Policies toward secular democratic states in the Middle East may be shaped by a desire to bring these countries into the Islamic fold, and aggressive behavior may be justified on that basis. Similarly, aggressive behavior may be directed at Western and other states deemed a threat to Islam, with no attention to whether or not these states are democratic.

This logic leads to several interrelated hypotheses that may be tested with data from the UAE opinion survey. First, in contrast to the proposition that is generally advanced in the literature on international relations, support for democratic values may not be positively related to favorable attitudes toward peace talks with Israel and cooperation with the West. Second, this relationship may actually be negative, either in general or to the extent that respondents also support political Islam. Table 6 presents data that may be used to examine these possibilities.

In presenting survey data to explore the interrelationships among democracy, Islam, and foreign policy, it must be acknowledged that data about individual attitudes do not provide a basis for accurately predicting the behavior of future democracies in the Arab world. There are obvious limits to the degree to which the study of individuals can shed light on the behavior of states. Nevertheless, given the importance of values and political culture in linking democracy and foreign policy behavior at the system-level of analysis, the examination of individual attitudes will help to explicate the relationship between democracy and peace and, in the Middle East, the importance of political Islam as an intervening variable.

Turning first to attitudes toward Israel, table 6 shows that the relationship between support for democracy and foreign policy attitudes is not the same among respondents with differing attitudes toward political Islam. Specifically, the tendency to view Israel as a threat to UAE national security, though strong overall, declines as a function of support for democracy among respondents who do not strongly support religious groups. Indeed, this anti-Israel view is least likely to be expressed by respondents who are at least somewhat supportive of democracy and opposed to political Islam. Conversely, the view that Israel is a threat to the UAE increases as a function of support for democracy among respondents who do strongly support religious groups. This pattern also means that support for political Islam and anti-Israel attitudes are negatively related among respondents with the most favorable attitudes toward democracy, whereas this relationship does not exist among respondents who are less supportive of democracy. The implication of these findings is that democracy may produce very different attitudes toward peace with Israel, depending upon whether or not those who push for and gain influence from democratization are supporters or opponents of Islamic political groups.

Table 6 also shows that anti-Israel sentiments are most likely to be expressed by respondents who oppose, or at least do not strongly support, political Islam, and who also oppose democracy. Over 70 percent of such respondents rank Israel as the most important national security threat to their country. The attitudes of these respondents appear to be heavily influenced by traditional Islam and the view that democracy is an alien, Western cultural phenomenon. It is among these traditional respondents, who may not be highly opposed to the existing regime, that there is the greatest tendency to oppose the existence of a Jewish state in the Middle East.

Table 6 also shows some interesting patterns in attitudes toward the U.S. Although differences are not as pronounced, nor as pertinent to the present study's concern with democracy and peace, it may be noted that anti-U.S. sentiments are not associated with attitudes toward democracy among those who strongly support political Islam, that these sentiments decline as a function of support for democracy among those who somewhat support political Islam, and that they increase as a function of support for democracy among those who oppose political Islam. Thus, anti-U.S. views are least likely to be expressed by respondents who oppose both democracy and political Islam, respondents who would appear to be traditional and conservative, and also by respondents

Table 6. Political Islam, Democracy, and Foreign Policy

Political Islam	Strongly Support Political Islam			Support Political Islam			Oppose Political Islam		
Democracy	Strongly support democracy	Less supportive of democracy	Oppose democracy	Strongly support democracy	Less supportive of democracy	Oppose democracy	Strongly support democracy	Less supportive of democracy	Oppose democracy
Foreign Policy: Perception of threat to the UAE from									
United States	20.0	21.4	25.5	6.9	19.7	17.5	16.4	13.0	9.1
Israel	60.0	56.5	49.1	55.2	63.4	73.9	47.3	47.8	72.8
Iran	4.0	5.6	1.8	13.8	2.8	4.3	12.7	6.5	4.5
Others	16.0	16.5	23.6	24.1	14.1	4.3	23.6	32.7	13.6
Total	100.0 (N = 25)	100.0 (N = 55)	100.0 (N = 55)	100.0 (N = 29)	100.0 (N = 71)	100.0 (N = 23)	100.0 (N = 55)	100.0 (N = 46)	100.0 (N = 22)

who favor democracy and are somewhat but not highly supportive of political Islam. Alternatively, anti-U.S. views are most likely to be expressed by respondents who oppose democracy and strongly support political Islam, respondents who oppose the status quo but seek an Islamic rather than a democratic alternative.

Conclusion

What are the prospects for the emergence of stable democracies in the Arab world today? What is the relationship between political Islam and democracy and can democracy flourish if it increases the influence of current religious groups? What are the main implications of democratization in the Arab world for foreign policy and the resolution of regional conflicts?

The Gulf states are less authoritarian than many other Arab states. This is the result of several factors, including the political style of their leaders, policies of accommodation and moderation in dealing with internal political opposition, and welfare policies that lead to a lack of widespread opposition to the status quo. Thus, the extreme measures associated with authoritarianism are absent in the Gulf states. On the other hand, the Gulf states are hardly democratic; they provide few opportunities for political organization and political dissent and they also lack internal factions beyond major merchant or tribal families. The Gulf states also lack some of the conditions necessary for greater democratization. Political legitimacy continues to be derived largely from tribal identities, there is no active associational life based on such groups as political parties and unions, and the middle class is weak and has little influence on the political process.

Nevertheless, data from the UAE opinion survey show strong support for increased political participation, suggesting that democratization will be an important political issue in the Gulf in the 1990s. This is particularly true since the survey was conducted among university students, men and women whose attitudes will be particularly influential in the years ahead. There is thus considerable likelihood that political elites in the UAE, as well as other Gulf states, will permit an opening up of political life in the future. At the very least, they may "view democracy as a means to other goals, such as prolonging their own rule, achieving international legitimacy, [and] minimizing domestic opposition" (Huntington 1984, p. 212).

There are various views about the impact of Islam on the process of democratization in the Arab world. A number of scholars suggest that Islam and democracy are compatible and that most Islamic groups support a transition to democracy. However, the liberal tradition of Islam that attempted to make Muslim teachings compatible with democracy does not at present enjoy widespread support and is not a viable alternative. Rather, traditional and conservative interpretations of Islam are dominant in the Arab world today. Current religious groups are not committed to democratic values; they merely want to acquire political power in order to establish an Islamic sociopolitical order, which they define as the "common good." Therefore, those who support the argument that religious groups will eventually become more democratic are misinterpreting the ideology of political Islam. As explained in a recent issue of *The Economist* (1992, p. 14), " . . . people who suggest that an Islamic reformation may speedily be followed by a liberating Islamic renaissance should be warned: many of the Islamic movement's leaders, with first-hand experience of Western society, are determined not to repeat any Western pattern."

Iran and Sudan are countries where religious groups have been in power for several years, and these states are anything but democratic. On the whole, the current regimes in these countries are as authoritarian as the regimes they replaced. Iran is an example of a religious democracy. Candidates in Iranian parliamentary elections are screened by a religious committee, and a number of candidates have been banned from elections because they did not meet the state's religious standards. The prospects for liberal democracy under the rule of Iran's religious leaders thus seem unlikely. The situation in Sudan is even worse. The current Sudanese regime has no democratic characteristics and has been particularly harsh in its suppression of political opposition.

This situation presents supporters of democracy in the Arab world with a serious predicament. The strength of Islamic groups is in large part a response to the oppressive nature of the state in the Arab world. Arab rulers have not allowed secular opposition and have consequently created from their own style of governance a radical, religious opposition. Islamic groups are the only route for effective dissent in the Arab world today; a lack of institutionalized channels for political participation and the exercise of political influence has enabled underground movements calling for Islamic solutions to gain widespread support among a disaffected public seeking greater government accountability. Yet the long-term prospects for democracy may be diminished rather than enhanced should such movements come to power as regimes respond to demands for political reform. Thus, for the present at least, Arab political life will be shaped by the conflict between authoritarian states and quasi-totalitarian op-position movements, with the prospects for sustained democratization uncertain at best.

As far as issues of foreign policy are concerned, the relationship between democracy and foreign policy in the Arab world would seem to depend on two highly interrelated considerations: the nature of Arab political culture and the role and importance of political Islam. The relationship between democracy and foreign policy is mediated by considerations of political culture, and in this connection the attitudes and beliefs that shape assessments of other states "may be traced not only to the growth of democratic values but also to their roots in a country's historical and cultural traditions" (Diamond, Linz, and Lipset 1990, p. 17). In addition, traditional Islamic values will be critically important to the extent that governmental decisions take popular sentiment into account, and the ideological predispositions of governments themselves will place less emphasis on liberalism and democracy when judging other states if democratization does indeed allow Islamic opposition movements to gain power.

For both of these reasons, political reform may lead to the establishment of religious rather than liberal democracies, and religious democracies may not be more inclined than authoritarian regimes to resolve peacefully the Arab-Israeli conflict and other regional and international disputes. These possibilities suggest that it is necessary to treat considerations of political Islam as an important intervening variable when seeking to examine the relationship between democracy and peace in the Arab and Islamic world. And turning to prediction rather than explanation, they also suggest that democratization in the Middle East may not at the present historical juncture take place in a way that increases the prospects for regional peace.

NOTES

1. Demands for democratization and political reform were expressed in a conference held in Sharja, United Arab Emirates, in September 1991. Similar conferences were held in Jordan, Lebanon, and Cyprus in 1991 and 1992. See, for instance, *Al-Mustaqbal Al-Arabi* (Arab future) 149 (July 1991): pp. 158 ff.

2. These pressures have been reported by a number of scholars in different societies. For more details on the role of external pressure in the process of democratization,

see Diamond, Linz, and Lipset (1990, pp. 31–34); Huntington (1984, pp. 205–207); Allison Jr. and Beschel Jr. (1992, pp. 81–98); and Diamond (1992, pp. 25–46).

3. The usually short-lived parliamentary experience in Kuwait can best be described as a minority democracy. If implemented and reformed, Kuwait's constitution would be a powerful document for stable democracy. Although the constitution emphasizes equality, freedom, and justice, political rights are limited to all males who have "first degree citizenship." In 1959, the government issued the nationality law, Article 1 of which states that "the Kuwaitis are basically those people who inhabited Kuwait before 1920 and have continued to reside there until the date of publication of this law." By 1992, this category did not exceed 20 percent of the population of the country. Thus, women and naturalized citizens have no political rights. In the National Assembly election law of 1962, Article 1 states: "Every Kuwaiti male over 21 years has the right to vote . . . excluded from this category [is] the nationalized citizen who has been in the country less than 20 years." Naturalized citizens, moreover, have not been given the right to vote even after twenty years of residence in Kuwait.

4. For a detailed discussion of the evolutionary nature of democracy, see Martins (1986, p. 72); Arat (1991, pp. 87–88); Diamond, Linz, and Lipset (1990, pp. 257–58); and Huntington (1984, p. 214).

5. Quasi-totalitarian opposition is used here to refer to antidemocratic opposition movements that aspire to regulate broad aspects of sociopolitical life.

6. Max Weber has had a major influence on the scholarly understanding of secularism in modern society. In fact, Weber's theory of secularism as a product of capitalism and Protestantism has become the basis of most theories of democracy and modernization. Weber's position on secularization is summarized as follows in Turner (1974, p. 156; see also Fenn 1969, p. 161):

> Capitalism as an economic embodiment of rationalization produces institutional and cultural differentiation and specialization of different social spheres—politics, economics, religion, morality. While social life as a whole becomes more calculable, each sphere of activity is autonomous and has no claim to universal relevance or communal authority. In a secular world, the only place for religion is in the area of interpersonal, rather than public relations.

7. A number of scholars emphasize the high correlation between Protestantism and democracy (e.g., Huntington 1984, pp. 207–209). As Robertson (1970, p. 44) suggests, "By christianization of society, Parsons means basically that the social values implicated in Christian culture have become institutionalized in secular society; that is, they have become part and parcel of the everyday operation of social life."

8. Hassan Hanafi (1982, p. 65) describes political life in the Arab world today:

> . . . every week, a government ministry in Cairo prepares a model sermon and then distributes it to the preachers throughout the country who either read it or put its contents and meaning into their own words. In them, government policies are es-

poused and backed up with quotations from the Quran and the Sunnah. The government solicits from the ulama formal legal opinions (*Fatwas*) on a wide range of subjects, including birth control, land reform, nationalization, scientific research, foreign policy, and social affairs.

See also Ajami (1981).

9. Diamond, Linz, and Lipset (1990, p. 23) explain that one of the major dilemmas of democratic theory is "how to restrain the power of the state so that its incumbents remain responsive and accountable to the people."

10. See the writings of early Muslim modernists such as Khayr al-Din al-Tunisi, Jamal al-Din al-Afghani, Muhammad Abdu, Abdu Rahman al-Kawakibi, and Qasim Amin. See also the writings of current Muslim activists such as Amin Huwaidi, Ahmad Kamal Abu al-Majd, and Muhammad Salim al-Awa. For a discussion, see Rahman (1970, 1982); al-Awa (1991); and Esposito and Piscatori (1991).

11. This position is in evidence in the writings, programs, speeches, and actions of the leaders of current religious groups; for instance, one leader argues: "Not everyone who claims to be a Muslim is one. Only those who accept and live by the tenets of the groups of Muslims are good Muslims. Others are infidels." For further details, see Muhammad Faraj, *Al-jihad: al-Farida al-Ghaiba*, p. 16 (quoted in Jansen 1986, p. 7).

12. This is a major problem in the history of Islamic political and theological thought. The Quran is understood as a fragmented text rather than as a unified whole. Fazlur Rahman (1982, p. 20) explains:

In building any genuine and viable Islamic set of laws and institutions, there has to be a two-fold movement. First, one must move from the concrete case treatment of the Quran, taking the necessary and relevant social conditions of that time into account, to the general principles upon which the entire teaching converges. Second, from this general level there must be a movement back to specific legislation, taking into account the necessary and relevant social conditions now obtaining.

13. The literature on democracy also discusses a number of other prerequisites, such as a market economy and economic growth and development. For further details on the "preconditions" for democratic development, see Huntington (1984, pp. 198–209) and Rustow (1970).

14. Associational life refers to the role of voluntary associations such as the press, bar associations, student movements, labor and trade unions, women's organizations, business associations, and societies of intellectuals and opinion leaders.

15. For useful discussions of political regimes, leaders, and opposition movements in the Arab world, see Bill and Springbord (1991); Anderson (1987a, 1987b); Adams (1986); Dekmejian (1985); and Reed (1981).

16. See evidence for this conclusion in Al-Suwaidi (1990).

17. For further details on Islam and democracy, see Al-Awa (1991, pp. 30–41); Esposito and Piscatori (1991, pp. 434–38); and Wright (1992, pp. 131–45).

18. Although Saddam Hussein is not a religious leader, he was able to exploit the feelings of the Arab masses toward Israel and gain broad support when Iraq invaded Kuwait on August 2, 1990.

REFERENCES

Adams, Charles J. 1986. "Islamic Resurgence: Religion and Politics in the Muslim World." In *Cities of God: Faith, Politics and Pluralism in Judaism, Christianity, and Islam*, ed. Nigel Biggar, Jamie S. Scott, and William Schweiker. New York: Greenwood Press.

Ajami, Fouad. 1981. *The Arab Predicament: Arab Political Thought and Practice since 1967*. Cambridge: Cambridge University Press.

Allison, Graham T., Jr., and Robert P. Beschel, Jr. 1992. "Can the United States Promote Democracy?" *Political Science Quarterly* 107 (Spring), pp. 81–98.

Anderson, Lisa. 1987a. "Lawless Government and Illegal Opposition: Reflections on the Middle East." *Journal of International Affairs* 40 (Winter/Spring), pp. 219–33.

———. 1987b. "The State in the Middle East and North Africa." *Comparative Politics* (October), pp. 1–18.

Arat, Zehra. 1991. *Democracy and Human Rights in Developing Countries*. Boulder, CO: Lynne Rienner.

Al-Awa, Muhammad S. 1991. "Al-Ta'adudia Al-Syassya Min Mandur Islami" (Political pluralism from an Islamic perspective). *Al-Arabi* 395 (October), pp. 30–41.

Bill, James A. 1984. "Resurgent Islam in the Persian Gulf." *Foreign Affairs* 63 (Spring), pp. 108–27.

Bill, James A., and Robert Springbord. 1991. *Politics in the Middle East*. Boston: Little, Brown & Co.

Crystal, Jill. 1992. "State and Society in the Gulf." Paper presented to the Council on Foreign Relations: Symposium on the implications for U.S. foreign policy of political developments in the Gulf Cooperation Council countries (January).

Dahl, Robert A. 1971. *Polyarchy: Participation and Opposition*. New Haven, CT: Yale University Press.

David, Eric. 1984. "Ideology, Social Class and Islamic Radicalism in Modern Egypt." In *From Nationalism to Revolutionary Islam*, ed. Said Amir Arjomand. Albany: State University of New York Press.

Dekmejian, R. Hrair. 1985. *Islam in Revolution: Fundamentalism in the Arab World*. New York: Syracuse University Press.

Diamond, Larry. 1992. "Promoting Democracy." *Foreign Policy* 87 (Summer), pp. 25–46.

Diamond, Larry, Juan J. Linz, and Seymour Martin Lipset, eds. 1990. *Politics in Developing Countries: Comparing Experiences with Democracy*. Boulder, CO: Lynne Rienner.

Dougherty, James E., and Robert L. Pfaltzgraff Jr. 1981. *Contending Theories of International Relations*. New York: Harper and Row.

Economist, The. 1992. "Living with Islam." April 5, pp. 13–14.

Esposito, John L., and James P. Piscatori. 1991. "Democratization and Islam." *The Middle East Journal* 45 (Summer), pp. 427–40.

Fenn, Richard K. 1969. "Max Weber on the Secular: A Typology." *Review of Religious Research* 10.

El-Guindi, Fadwa. 1986. "The Mood in Egypt: Summer Heat or Revolution in the Air." *Middle East Insight* 4.

Halliday, Fred. 1991. "The Gulf War and Its Aftermath: First Reflections." *International Affairs* 67 (April), pp. 223–334.

Hanafi, Hassan. 1982. "The Relevance of the Islamic Alternative in Egypt." *Arab Studies Quarterly* 4 (Spring), pp. 54–74.

Hudson, Michael C. 1980. "Islam and Political Development." In *Islam and Development: Religion and Socio-Political Change*, ed. John L. Esposito. New York: Syracuse University Press.

———. 1991. "After the Gulf War: Prospects for Democratization in the Arab World." *Middle East Journal* 45 (Summer), pp. 407–26.

Huntington, Samuel P. 1968. *Political Order in Changing Societies*. New Haven: Yale University Press.

———. 1984. "Will More Countries Become Democratic?" *Political Science Quarterly* 99 (Summer), pp. 193–218.

Imara, Muhammad, ed. 1972. *Muhammad Abdu: Al-Amal Al-Kamila*. Beirut: Al-Mu'assasah Al-Arabiyyah Li'l-dirasat Wal-nashr.

Jansen, Johannes J. G. 1986. *The Neglected Duty: The Creed of Sadat's Assassins and Islamic Resurgence in the Middle East*. New York: Macmillan.

Kedourie, Ellie. 1966. *Afghani and Abdu: An Essay on Religious Unbelief and Political Activism in Modern Islam*. London: Frank Cass.

Martins, Luciano. 1986. "The Liberalization of Authoritarian Rule in Brazil." In *Transitions from Authoritarian Rule: Comparative Perspectives*, ed. Guillermo O'Donnell, Philippe C. Schmitter, and Laurence C. Whitehead. Baltimore: Johns Hopkins University Press.

Morgan, T. Clifton, and Sally Howard Campbell. 1991. "Domestic Structure, Decisional

Constraints, and War: So Why Kant Democracies Fight?" *Journal of Conflict Resolution* 35, no. 2 (June), pp. 187–211.

Nagel, Jack H. 1987. *Participation*. New Jersey: Prentice Hall.

Al-Naqeeb, Khaldoun H. 1990. *Society and State in the Gulf and Arab Peninsula.* London: Routledge.

Pateman, Carol. 1970. *Participation in Democratic Theory.* New York: Cambridge University Press.

Rahman, Fazlur. 1970. "Islamic Modernism: Its Scope, Method, and Alternatives." *International Journal of Middle East Studies* 1, pp. 317–33.

———. 1982. *Islam and Modernity: Transformation of an Intellectual Tradition.* Chicago: University of Chicago Press.

Reed, Stanley. 1981. "Inside Assad's Syria: Little Brother and the Brotherhood." *The Nation,* May 16, pp. 592–96.

Robertson, Ronald. 1970. *The Sociological Interpretation of Religion.* New York: Schocken Books.

Rosenberg, Morris. 1968. *The Logic of Survey Analysis.* New York: Basic Books.

Rustow, Dankwart A. 1970. "Transitions to Democracy: Toward a Democratic Model." *Comparative Politics* 2, no. 3 (April), pp. 377–83.

Sanad, Jamal A. See below, Al-Suwaidi, Jamal.

Smith, Donald E. 1974. *Religion and Political Modernization.* New Haven, CT: Yale University Press.

Strayer, Joseph R. 1958/59. "The State and Religion: An Exploratory Comparison in Different Cultures." *Comparative Studies in Society and History* 1 pp. 38–43.

Al-Suwaidi, Jamal. 1990. [Sanad, Jamal A.] "Islam and Socio-Political Change: A Comparative Study of Egyptian, Kuwaiti, and Palestinian Attitudes." Ph.D. diss., University of Wisconsin-Milwaukee.

Tessler, Mark, and Emile F. Sahliyeh. 1991. "Some Propositions about Democracy in the Arab World and Its Relationship to the Israeli-Palestinian Conflict." Paper presented at the 25th annual meeting of the Middle East Studies Association of North America, Washington, DC, November 23–26.

Turner, Bryan S. 1974. *Weber and Islam: A Critical Study.* London: Routledge Kegan Paul.

Voll, John O. 1982. *Islam: Continuity and Change in the Modern World.* Boulder, CO: Westview.

Wright, Robin. 1992. "Islam, Democracy, and the West." *Foreign Affairs* 71 (Summer), pp. 131–45.

6

ISLAM AND DEMOCRACY

SHUKRI B. ABED

THIS CHAPTER EXAMINES the theological underpinnings of Islam's attitude toward democracy, giving particular attention to the views associated with Islamic fundamentalism. In recent years, fundamentalist leaders—in Iran, Sudan, Pakistan, Jordan, Algeria, and Tunisia—have carried their traditionalist message to Muslim multitudes in Asia, the Middle East, and North Africa. Further, their arguments, stressing the need for Muslims to return to tradition and to reject foreign or "imported" solutions to the pressing problems of the contemporary Islamic world, are gaining credence among the Muslim faithful. Against this background, the present chapter analyzes the arguments advanced by contemporary Islamic fundamentalists about democracy and related political concepts such as secularism and the nation-state.

Islam's attitude toward democracy and other political concepts of non-Muslim origin is not monolithic. Indeed, Islamic history is marked by intense debates about whether or not it is desirable to utilize these concepts along with others that are purely Islamic in order to organize the societies in which Muslims live. This chapter begins with a summary of these debates and presents the reasoning of intellectuals who have sought to incorporate foreign ideas into Muslim society. Explication of the diverse views that have historically characterized the Muslim community makes clear that Islam and fundamentalism are not synonymous.

Turning next to the views of Islamic fundamentalism, or traditionalism, the chapter examines the writings and speeches of major theoreticians and explores the reasoning they advance in support of absolute adherence to Islamic principles, which in practice often translates into the rejection of non-Muslim ideas and values. The goal of these theoreticians is to bring the Muslim community back to the Islamic fold, back to the "fundamentals" of Islam, and their point of departure in all cases is the strict interpretation and application of

Islamic law. In many cases, too, fundamentalists regard democracy as alien and irrelevant to Muslims and assign it a prominent place among the foreign ideas to be resisted in the name of Islam.

Finally, focusing on politicians rather than theoreticians, the chapter explores the attitudes and behavior of those fundamentalist leaders who see no contradiction between Islam and democracy and even, in some cases, speak positively of democracy and call for its incorporation into the Islamic solution they advocate. Many of these politicians have become quite influential, and although there is sometimes a significant gap between their rhetoric and their practice, they thus represent, at the level of ideological discourse, a stream of fundamentalism that regards democracy as a suitable organizing principle for political communities governed in accordance with Islamic law.

Diversity within the Muslim Community

Although there has always been a diversity of views within the Muslim community, belief in the perfection and completeness of the Islamic system has been a guiding principle in Muslim life since the inception of Islam in the seventh century A.D. Viewing itself as the right path, indeed the only path that believers should follow, Islam—when strictly interpreted—essentially shuts its door to new ideas that have no Islamic foundation. At the very least, it puts the burden of proof on those who would introduce such ideas. They must show that these ideas either have an Islamic basis or, at a minimum, are compatible with Islam.

Islam's antipathy toward things non-Islamic may well be inherent in the comprehensive nature of Islam itself. Seeking to govern more than just the spiritual life of its flock, Islam presents itself as the right and only path to a good life on earth and to the salvation of the soul in the next life. Islam explicitly claims that the Prophet Muhammad, the founder of Islam, is the "seal" of the prophets, which means that his message is the culmination of all that came before and cannot be exceeded in terms of perfection and comprehensiveness. By definition, then, Islam considers itself both a necessary and sufficient doctrine, to be followed rigorously by those who seek moral, social, and political perfection.

At the same time, however strongly Islam may have wished to resist contamination from without, there have been times in its history when contact with things foreign has been unavoidable, when Muslim peoples have had to react to and interact with new realities, new political systems, new social orders, and even new scientific ideas, the sources of which were not Islamic. There are two particularly important historical periods during which this was the case: the first, when Islam served as an occupying power over vast regions during the early stages of its development; and the second, reaching into our own century, when Muslim lands and peoples became the subject of domination and occupation by non-Muslim powers.

On each of these occasions, there was a split among Muslim religious, philosophical, and political thinkers on the issue of the correct Islamic attitude toward foreign things and ideas. There were, during both historical periods, those who believed it possible to accommodate the exigencies of the new reality to the path prescribed by the Muslim religion; but there were also those who staunchly defended the notion that Islam is the true and only path to a good society. At times this sharp contrast created a virtual chasm in Muslim societies between those who supported adoption of or even adaptation to new, non-Muslim ideas, and those who rejected any deviation from Muslim doctrine and principles.

From the earliest stages, then, there were heated debates between those who defended openness and accommodation to non-Muslim political, social, and even metaphysical world views, and those who looked upon these same views with suspicion and disapproval. Greek thought, for example—to which Western thought and culture owes such an incalculable debt—was perceived by many Muslims in medieval times as a veritable anathema to Islamic culture, and it was therefore the object of strict censure by the Islamic establishment and its supporters.[1] These critics were not about to allow such "foreign" sciences to flourish in Islamic lands, when in their view these sciences stood in basic contradiction to the word of God as revealed in the Holy Quran.

Put on the defensive, proponents of the Greek legacy in the medieval Islamic world—philosophers (*falasifah*) and, in a certain sense, rationalist theologians (*al-mutakalimun*)—set out to prove that there is no essential contradiction between reason and revelation, an argument that was to become a major theme in their writings, particularly those of the philosophers. The very fact that the Muslim supporters of Greek science chose this line of defense early on suggests that they were seeking legitimacy within the Islamic community and had no wish for a head-on conflict with Muslim orthodoxy. Rather, they felt it was necessary to defend their positive attitudes toward non-Muslim views by demonstrating the compatibility of these views with Islam.

More recently, beginning with the advent of Western colonialism in the nineteenth century and stretching forward to the present, Islamic civilization has found itself at a similar cultural crossroads. Confronted by the ideology of secularism, many Muslims today feel that Islam faces a major challenge to its most basic tenets. Never before have the Muslim lands and Islamic culture been so sweepingly and so insidiously penetrated by Western scientific, political, economic, and military achievements. Understandably, Muslim societies are more than ever driven to defend their culture from the perceived threat of these invading forces. Indeed, modern Islamic thinkers often ask whether it is possible to remain a true Muslim when new, non-Muslim values have become such an inescapable part of Muslim life. More specifically, they ask whether one can maintain his or her Muslim identity despite constant interference from the West and its world view.

These questions have divided contemporary intellectuals in the Islamic world, like their medieval counterparts, into two main camps. There are those who hold that the question should not be phrased " . . . *whether* it is possible," but rather " . . . *how* it is possible" to remain a Muslim while acquiring new, non-Muslim values. This group of thinkers assumes that to do so is clearly possible, the only question being that of how to achieve the desired harmony among differing systems of belief. For these Muslim thinkers, Islam and modernity (which, in this context, amounts to the acquisition of Western ideas and values) are compatible, once both are properly understood.

This was the main thesis of Muslim reformists of the nineteenth and early twentieth centuries, the most important of whom were Jamal al-Din al-Afghani, Muhammad Abdu, Rashid Rida, and above all Rifat al-Tahtawi. Al-Tahtawi, for example, considered a pioneer of cultural Westernization in Egypt, maintained that "what is called freedom in Europe is exactly what is defined in our religion as justice [*adl*], right [*haqq*], consultation [*shura*] and equality [*musawat*]. . . . This is because the rule of freedom and democracy consists of imparting justice and right to the people, and the nation's participation in determining its destiny."[2] Basically, then, al-Tahtawi and his intellectual disciples reformulated Western democratic principles using Islamic terms. Very much like the views of early Islamic philosophers and rational theologians, those of the reformists or accommodationists in the modern era are based on the principle of finding common ground, indeed of harmonizing the Muslim point of view with Western political, social, and economic concepts.

This trend has intensified during the past few decades, as the defenders of Westernization in the Muslim world continue to use Islamic terminology to justify the application of Western political and social concepts to Muslim realities.[3] Faced with overwhelming Western technological, military, and economic superiority, the reformists among Muslim thinkers have set themselves the task of interpreting various aspects—political, social, and economic—of Muslim life in a manner that accommodates the influx of new concepts from the West. And Western democracy is one of the new concepts to which this effort has been applied. The increasing application of democratic principles in other lands renders it difficult for Muslims to resist the temptation to incorporate it, at least in part, into their own political and legal systems.

Accommodation, reformulation, and harmonization have thus been the guiding principles by which many contemporary political leaders have attempted to define new secular identities for their nation-states. By affirming that Islamic and Western world views are broadly compatible, these reformist political leaders and thinkers in effect legitimize the application of Western values in Islamic countries. To be sure, they hold Islam to be the official religion of the state. At the same time, however, through the free and liberal interpretation of Islamic law and values, they seek to introduce Western concepts into the social and political life of Muslims. For reformists, then, there is no doubt that Western ideas may be applied to Muslim society. The only important questions concern the manner in which this should be done and the way in which such action should be understood and justified from an Islamic point of view.

Democracy in Islamic Fundamentalist Thought

The accommodationist perspective of Islamic reformers has been challenged by a second group of Muslim intellectuals who maintain that "the weakness of the modernists is inherent in the very nature of the hopeless task of attempting to make the incompatibles compatible."[4] Proponents of this second view demand, among other things, "that [the modernists] put an end once and for all to interpreting Islam through foreign criteria and summon the courage to stand up and defend unadulterated Islam."[5]

These Muslim intellectuals, who may be termed fundamentalists or traditionalists, reject the harmonization thesis of the modernists and instead advocate a "Muslim solution." In the eyes of such traditionalists, Western concepts such as democracy, secularization, and the nation-state represent a direct contradiction of Islamic religious and political thought since they rely for their authority on human rather than divine legislation and are formulated through secular rather than God-given laws. This group believes that "nobody can reconcile conflicting ideologies unless he is willing to accept intellectual dishonesty, spiritual blasphemy, moral cowardice and psychological confusion—a sure prescription for mediocrity.... "[6]

In sharp contrast to the reformists, Muslim traditionalists wish to Islamicize what they believe to be a corrupt and immoral world. In their view, reality as it exists is not the criterion according to which Islam must measure itself and evolve; rather, it is reality that must be revised to suit the Islamic point of view. This perspective can be seen in the writings of the Egyptian Sayyid Qutb, a major traditionalist figure executed by Egyptian authorities in 1966 for his active role in advancing the concept of an "Islamic Solution." As Sayyid Qutb writes:

> The first sign of defeat is considering "reality" [al-waqic] as the source [al-asl] upon which God's legislation [shariah] must model itself. Rather, Islam considers God's path and his legislation as the standard against which people must measure themselves and the model reality must be modified to suit. Islam, when it first appeared, faced an ignorant society that was worldwide; it corrected it according to its special path, then it urged it forward.[7]

Implicit in the traditionalist position is dissatisfaction with those Muslim thinkers who have accepted the "reality" imposed by the Western powers as a prism through which Islam must view itself and reevaluate its position on social and political issues. Sayyid Qutb, as seen, considers the acceptance of such an externally imposed reality as "the first step toward defeat" and calls upon Muslims to fight against a trend that considers the non-Muslim point of view to be the appropriate criterion and the standard for Muslims.

Many Muslim thinkers agree with Sayyid Qutb. Moreover, some of these thinkers not only reject the idealization of Western values, they find these values corrupting to the human soul and to society and regard them as a force against which Muslims must struggle. Witness, for example, the following tirade against "the three principles of Western civilization" offered by al-Mawdudi, an influential Pakistani thinker and a contemporary of Sayyid Qutb:

> We believe that the three principles [on which modern Western life is based] are wrong and corrupt [fasidah]. In fact, we believe very strongly . . . that these are the source of the evils, disasters and tragedies that have befallen humanity, and we have taken it upon ourselves to fight and destroy them, until we uproot them, with all the means and methods we possess.[8]

The "three principles of Western civilization" that al-Mawdudi vows to destroy are none other than secularism, the nation-state, and democracy.[9] Indeed, these principles have been a favorite target of fundamentalist, or traditionalist, Muslim thinkers.

According to al-Mawdudi, for example, it is the combination of these interrelated concepts that is the source of the world's current unfortunate situation.[10] Al-Mawdudi's critique of democracy is based on the notion that this concept, in its modern sense, has put man on "God's throne" by granting him the ability to legislate and produce laws. "Democracy," in his view, puts the entire governmental structure and its power at the service of man, so that man can obtain whatever he wants.[11] This is a prescription for disaster, al-Mawdudi believes, and the sovereignty of God and the caliphate of the believers should therefore replace the sovereignty of the people and the rule of the masses [*jamahir*].

Al-Mawdudi accepts the idea that there is no essential disagreement between Islam and Western democracy with respect to the goals that the two systems advocate: legal equality, equal opportunities, opposition to oppression, and discrimination on the basis of race, class and origin. He writes, for example, that if "democracy means that no one individual, family or class [of citizens] has the right to impose its will on millions of other people and use them to satisfy its greediness and egoism [*anainyyah*], then this concept, no doubt, is right and not against the truth."[12] If these matters are the essence of Western democracy, "then there is no dispute with our Islamic Democracy, which the Muslims have come to know throughout their history. In fact, Muslims gave democracy practical interpretations based on sound [*salihah*] patterns centuries before the birth of Western democracy."

The problem, al-Mawdudi continues, is that alongside this positive and bright side of the picture, democracy has come to mean providing unchecked freedom to each nation to fulfill its desires, which in fact reflects the wishes of the majority rather than an ideal and reasonable set of values. The laws of a democratic country, its principles and regulation of ethical, social and political issues, are considered to be valid and just not by any ideal or objective standard but only by virtue of the fact that they reflect the desires of the majority of its citizens.[13] The man-made laws and regulations of such a nation, therefore, may be changed arbitrarily according to the desires and wishes of the majority rather than "according to fixed and sound rules, which are not subject to change and alteration."[14] For these reasons, al-Mawdudi concludes, a nation that has absolute freedom in ruling itself, a nation that legislates its own laws according to the needs and desires of the majority of its citizens, is very similar to a wild (*sharis*), defiant (*jamih*) and shameless (*fajir*) individual.

Despite some kind words about the goals of Western democracy, al-Mawdudi is thus firmly convinced that Islam and Western democracy are inherently incompatible and indeed contradict each other. Specifically, while Western democracy adopts the principle of the absolute sovereignty of the people, which is restricted and controlled only by what the people decide for themselves, "we [Muslims] consider this principle to be invalid [*batilan*] as it leads to evil and destructive consequences [*awaqib wakhimah haddamah*]."[15] According to al-Mawdudi, God alone is sovereign since He created the human race, controls people's fate, and manages the world's affairs; and "any [other] claim to sovereignty within the domain of God's sovereignty and control is invalid, superficial [*sakhif*], and without substance, whether this claim comes from an individual, a class of people or the so-called masses [*jamahir*]."[16]

Summarizing this argument, al-Mawdudi turns to his fellow Muslims at the end of his book and addresses them as follows:

> I say to the Muslims openly that Secular National Democracy is in opposition to your religious belief, and if you succumb to it, this would be like leaving the Book of God behind you, and if you contribute to the process of building it or maintaining it, that would be like betraying your messenger whom God has sent to you. . . . The Islam that you believe in . . . differs substantially from this despicable order, resists its very spirit, and fights against its basic principles. . . . There is no harmony [*insijam*] between the two in any detail, however unimportant [*tafihan*] because they are contradictory. Wherever this order exists, we do not consider Islam to exist, and wherever Islam exists, there is no room for this order.[17]

Said Hawwa, a disciple of Sayyid Qutb who has become the major New Radicalist thinker in Syria,[18] gives concrete expression to these views in an influential book entitled *Jund Allah* (The soldiers of God), published in Beirut in 1977:

> The shura is by no means identical to democracy, and, in certain regards, it is even its exact opposite. . . . Democracy is a Greek term which signifies sovereignty of people, the people being the source of legitimacy; it is the people who legislate and rule. As for the shura, it denotes consultation [by the ruler] with a person or persons with regard to the interpretation of a certain point of Islamic law. In Islam, the people do not govern themselves by laws they make on their own, as in a democracy; rather the people are governed by a regime and a set of laws imposed by God, which they cannot change or modify in any case.[19]

An echo of these views is found in the works of the Egyptian Yusuf al-Qardawi (born 1926). In an influential book[20] published in 1977, al-Qardawi presents and analyzes what he considers to be the basic elements of Western thought that have been erroneously applied to the Arab countries:[21]

(1) secularism (*ilmaniyyah*), i.e., separation of church and State;

(2) nationalism (*al-nazah al-wataniyyah al-qawmiyyah*);

(3) the capitalist-bourgeois economy;

(4) personal freedom—in the Western sense, and particularly the freedom of women in terms of restraint and mixing *(al-tabarruj wa-l-ikhtilat)*;

(5) the application of the foreign secular laws; and

(6) the appearance of parliamentary process and the declaration that the nation is the source of authority.

Like al-Mawdudi, al-Qardawi asserts that these interrelated elements are Western products and that their influence on the Muslim lands has been pernicious. Both believe that the West adopted these principles as a reaction to the domination of church and clergy in medieval Europe and not as a reaction to religion per se,[22] and since Islam is free from church bureaucracy there is no justification for adopting similar principles in order to combat constant interference by the church in the lives of individuals.

Al-Mawdudi and al-Qardawi both believe that the application of these man-made principles has been the "source of the disastrous and tragic situation from which humanity suffers what it does today."[23] All men, they claim, have been the victim of this civilization, which is based solely on man's own vision and principles, which by definition are limited, imperfect and therefore doomed to failure. Al-Qardawi's chief concern, however, as reflected in the title of his book, is what he considers to be the negative impact of these man-made and Western principles on Muslim societies. Al-Qardawi states that the Western liberal-democratic scheme, and the application of secular laws in particular, has had decidedly negative consequences for Muslims. He argues, for example, that Western law has pushed aside Islamic law in such areas as the production and drinking of wine and sexual relationships outside marriage, both of which are forbidden by Islam.[24]

With respect to the parliamentary process, yet another aspect of liberal-democracy, al-Qardawi at first seems to view it in positive terms:

> The most positive side of the liberal-democracy—in my view—is the political aspect manifested in the parliamentary process. Through this system people can choose the representatives of whom the 'legislative branch' is composed. . . . Through this elected body, the people rule themselves, and 'the nation becomes the source of authority.' This picture as a whole is, theoretically speaking, good and acceptable from an Islamic point of view—provided it is implemented in such a way that the mischief and evils which accompany it can be avoided.[25]

But al-Qardawi also emphasizes the negative aspects of this system, which stem from the unlimited power of the parliamentary body to enact legislation. He believes that this elected body should not have the authority to legislate in areas covered by God-given law; God is the supreme legislator and human beings may legislate for themselves only where He permits them to do so, namely where there is no explicit law concerning their earthly affairs:

> . . . it should be said that the nation is the source of authority only within the limits of the Islamic law. Furthermore, there should be in the legislative body a group of fuqaha [Muslim jurists] . . . who examine the validity of the laws [adopted by this body]. The democratic regime [of Egypt], however, does not require this, despite the fact that its constitution states that the religion of the state is Islam.[26]

Al-Qardawi and the other traditionalists realize that the existence of a contradiction between Islam and Western democracy—while clearly supporting the inapplicability of this Western concept to Islamic countries, if they wish to remain Muslim—is not in and of itself sufficient to discredit democracy. Therefore, they move on to pinpoint what they perceive to be the deficiencies and weaknesses of the democratic system as applied in the West. They claim that this system has failed in that it has brought moral and social degeneracy to the West itself. Sayyid Qutb, for example, who lived in the United States, describes this situation in detail, stating that democracy is a type of government that has reached the point of virtual bankruptcy and that the West has no "values" to offer the world. His conclusion is that if democracy and related political concepts and values are showing signs of bankruptcy in the West, they should not be imported to the Middle East.[27]

Al-Qardawi, too, examines this system and makes the following observations: (1) Because of the way the system is run, those who have power and money can manipulate the system and gain more power. They can pay their way into public office. Elected officials, in other words, are not necessarily elected on the basis of their virtuous character or their ability to lead people. Corrupt people can be, and often are, elected to public offices. (2) The percentage of those voting is usually very low.[28]

In addition, al-Qardawi examines the example of Turkey, a Muslim country that adopted Western values and, allegedly, ignored its Islamic heritage. Ataturk, according to al-Qardawi, forced the Muslims of Turkey to live according to Western standards. But "did the secular state of Turkey succeed in creating a strong and coherent society? No. Turkey has lost the Islamic way of life, and yet she remained a burden on the West in terms of [their] supplying her with technology and arms. Neither did she maintain her spiritual heritage, nor [did she] achieve any significant material progress...."[29]

The case of Turkey, the only secularist state with a Muslim population, is also taken up by al-Mawdudi. In a speech delivered to the Jamiat ul-Tulaba (university student organization) in Karachi on December 10, 1963, al-Mawdudi said:

> Turkey, for example, has been an independent nation since 1924, but can it boast of any great progress in industry or trade? During the same period, Japan and China have made remarkable progress in practically all fields and now stand among the most advanced nations of the world. Obviously, the reason for Turkey's failure to progress lies in the internal conflict to which she has been subjected by her secularist rulers. Those in power have striven all along to impose Western civilization upon the country, whereas the people want an Islamic order. The same story has been repeated more or less in every Muslim country.[30]

Democracy in the Discourse of Fundamentalist Politicians

The traditionalists whose views are discussed above are primarily theoreticians or intellectual leaders. Some have attracted followers and established or given new direction to religious-political movements. This is particularly true of Sayyid Qutb, who made an important contribution to the Muslim Brothers movement, founded by Hasan al-Banna in 1928. Yet none of these individuals can be considered political leaders in the strict sense of the term. All are either intellectual or, in the case of Qutb and al-Mawdudi, spiritual leaders. Their role has been mainly to provide the theoretical justification for an Islamic revolution, a role similar to that often ascribed to the intellectuals behind the French Revolution.

A distinction between the intellectual and political leaders of traditionalist Islam is important because the latter, although they of course advocate an Islamic solution, have somewhat different attitudes than the former about democracy and related concepts. There are many Muslim political movements in the Islamic world and they are not all the same. Nor are the views of their leaders, meaning that any generalizations will of necessity be incomplete. Yet the views about democracy held by many fundamentalist political leaders appear to be less negative, or at least more ambiguous, than those of the spiritual and intellectual leaders discussed above. Indeed, most declare openly that they are committed to the democratic process and the principles it embodies.

For example, Rashid al-Ghannoushi, leader of the outlawed Tunisian Islamic movement En-Nahda (the renaissance), speaks in the most positive terms about democracy and political pluralism: "We accept [the fact that we must] work within the legal framework with the hope of improving it by making it more democratic and pluralistic."[31] In another interview, on December 15, 1991, al-Ghannoushi defined the movements he leads in the following terms:

> Ennahdha (*sic*) is a school of Islamic thought that aims to play a political role and has rejected and still rejects violence both physical and verbal and this has been its methodology. . . . We believe in giving everyone the chance to run for the government and we believe in giving the people the right to choose through voting in an environment of democracy and human rights. . . . [32]

In a series of articles collected in a three-volume book,[33] al-Ghannoushi seems consistent in his commitment to the democratic process, which most likely would have brought his movement to power had the process been allowed to continue unimpeded in Tunisia. There is nothing in these essays to indicate that al-Ghannoushi is advocating democracy merely as a vehicle for attaining power. Algerian Muslim leaders, too, often speak of the democratic process, defending it and promising to adhere to it, as do the leaders of the various Muslim groups in the West Bank and Gaza Strip.[34]

Hassan al-Turabi, leader of the Sudanese National Islamic Front and behind-the-scenes mastermind of the Sudanese Muslim regime, also uses the term "democracy" in his speeches and interviews in a positive way. In a speech he delivered in 1988, one year before the Muslim takeover in Sudan, he repeatedly spoke of democracy, true democracy, and asserted that he and his movement wanted "democracy as a criterion of absolute value [*aqidah mutlaqat al-qimah fi l-dhat wa-l-ghayr*], equally applied to everybody—the self and others—rather than as a self-serving device [*hilah*]."[35] And in a recent lecture tour in the United States, al-Turabi expressed a commitment to "Islamic emancipation of women and respect for individual dignity and property." Islam "does not believe in coercion," he stated.[36]

While the statements of al-Ghannoushi, al-Turabi and other fundamentalist politicians may legitimize democracy among the supporters of their movements, and thus, to an extent, undermine the antidemocratic arguments of Sayyid Qutb, al-Mawdudi, and other traditionalist theoreticians, it is also necessary to ask what happens once an Islamic movement takes over. Is the declared commitment to democracy respected in practice? Are elections allowed in a country governed by the strict application of Islamic law, and do Islamic-dominated governments allow other parties to compete in elections?

Government leaders in several Middle Eastern countries, most notably Algeria and Tunisia, have in recent years taken action based on a belief that Islamic political groups and their leaders cannot be trusted. Algerian military and civilian authorities, for example, halted their newly instituted election process once it became apparent, in 1990 and 1991, that Islamic parties were making striking gains at the polls. They cancelled the second round of balloting for the National Assembly and subsequently ceased altogether any movement toward democracy. The Tunisian government, too, did not trust the declarations offered by leaders of the Islamic movement. Acting on the assumption that democracy would come to an end once an Islamic government was in power, they refused to grant En-Nahda legal status as a political party and thereby prevented it from participating in the elections of 1989 and 1990.

Although some have questioned the motives of Algerian and Tunisian government officials, charging that their primary objective has been to remain in power, these officials insist that the problem resides in the antidemocratic character of the Islamic solution advocated by Muslim political groups. Notwithstanding the many liberal views embodied in Islamic law, and the liberal interpretations of that law offered by Islamic modernists, these officials assert that fundamentalist politicians, no matter what they may say, are committed to an exclusivist interpretation that would not allow any permanent place for foreign ideas and concepts, including democracy.

Developments in Sudan during recent years only serve to confirm the fears and suspicions of many observers concerning the future of democracy under a government committed to the imposition of Islamic law. Less than a decade ago, Sudan was perceived as the Arab country with potentially the most liberal and open political system. Suwar El-Dahab, leader of the group of officers that overthrew Numeiri, set up a transitional government that emphasized citizen participation. He allowed parties to organize, and in April 1986 elections were held for a new parliament. A coalition government headed by Sadiq al-Mahdi was formed, and the democratization process seemed well on its way.

In June of 1989, however, this process was reversed when Brigadier General Omar al-Bashir, supported by the National Islamic Front led by none other than Hassan al-Turabi, forced the elected government of Sadiq al-Mahdi from power. Since then, the country has been under military rule, and the military government and its supporters have not hesitated to use violent means to suppress their opponents.[37] Many point out, naturally enough, that al-Turabi's declarations in support of democracy and the protection of individual rights cannot be reconciled with the actions of the present Sudanese government, and they accordingly raise questions about the sincerity of his pronouncements.

The case of al-Turabi and Sudan suggests that expressions of support for democracy by fundamentalist political leaders may in at least some cases be motivated by tactical considerations. Advocacy of democracy and pluralism strengthens an Islamic movement's appeal and, paradoxically enough, legitimizes it in the eyes of those it seeks to defeat. Fundamentalists realize that they need legitimacy in a world that increasingly advocates and adheres to democratic values, and they accordingly use terms like "democracy," "human rights," and "pluralism" without hesitation, merely placing them in an Islamic context. Interestingly enough, secular and liberal politicians frequently employ a similar strategy; they use Islamic terminology in order to legitimize the adoption of Western concepts.

There is disagreement about the extent to which generally applicable lessons can be drawn from the experience of Sudan. At the very least, however, the Sudanese case emphasizes the importance of asking about practice and performance, as well as language and rhetoric. And in the years ahead, as Islamic political leaders continue to make their case for participation in the political process, there is certain to be much discussion about the seriousness and sincerity of their declarations of support for democracy.

Conclusion

This discussion of Muslim attitudes toward democracy and related Western political concepts has both noted the diversity that exists within the Muslim community and given particular attention to the views of intellectuals and politicians associated with fundamentalist Islam. While reformists believe in the universality of concepts like democracy and assert that the Islamic and Western worlds have the same needs and, therefore, that what is good for the West is good for Muslims, fundamentalists, or traditionalists, believe not only that Western political concepts are inapplicable to Muslim communities but that they have a negative, indeed a corrupting influence on the human soul.

Traditionalists, however, address the issue of democracy with two voices, that of the theoretician and that of the politician. The theoretician's attitude is characterized by an open, straightforward critique of Western political concepts, a critique that rejects their application in the Muslim world and even questions their effectiveness in Western societies. Fundamentalist politicians, on the other hand, while strictly adhering to the principles of an Islamic solution, employ the language of modern political discourse. They present themselves as defenders of democracy and human rights, although they seek the meaning of these terms in the shariah rather than in Kant and Rousseau.

The struggle between the reformist and traditionalist streams within Islam is almost as old as the religion, having manifested itself in various forms throughout Muslim history. There were debates between theologians and philosophers in early Islam, and later, in the modern period, between fundamentalists on the one hand and liberal intellectuals and nationalists on the other. Moreover, this struggle is bound to continue, and possibly even to intensify, in the future. The debate between competing ideologies purporting to offer solutions to the Muslim world's problems appears to be sharpest during difficult and dynamic times when Islam is exposed to real or perceived external challenges. It is also driven, at present, by the unfortunate state of affairs in the Muslim world, including problems that have not been alleviated by governments identified with non-Islamic political formulas. Indeed, given the current malaise in many Middle Eastern countries, it is likely that the fundamentalist stream of Islam will continue to gain ground, with Muslims in general, and Arabs in particular, seeing Islam as a last resort in their search for a better life. Should this indeed be the case, questions about the beliefs and practices associated with Islamic fundamentalism will be more important than ever.

NOTES

1. Concerning the general attitude toward logic and science in medieval Islam, see Ignaz Goldziher "Mawqif ahl al-sunnah al-qudama' bi-iza' ulum al-awa'il," in *Al-turath al-*

yunani fi-l-hadarah al-islamiyyah, ed. Abd al-Rahman Badawi (Cairo: Maktabat al-nahdah al-misriyyah, 1940), pp. 123–72.

2. Quoted in Hamid Enayat, *Modern Islamic Political Thought* (Austin: University of Texas Press, 1988), p. 131.

3. Thus, the celebrated Egyptian intellectual Abbas Mahmoud al-Aqqad wrote a book entitled *Al-dimuqratiyyah fi'l-islam* (Democracy in Islam) (Cairo: 1952), in which he attempted to defend the similarity between the liberal thought of Islam and that of Western thought as expressed through democratic values.

4. Maryam Jameelah, *Islam Face to Face with the Current Crisis* (Lahore: Sunnat Nagar, 1979), p. 29. Maryam Jameelah (formerly Margaret Marcus), an Englishwoman who converted to Islam in 1961, became one of the most outspoken critics of the reformist view.

5. Mohammad Yusuf Khan, *Correspondence between Maulan Maudoodi and Maryam Jameelah* (Lahore: Evergreen Press, 1969), p. 85.

6. Jameelah, *Islam Face to Face*, p. 29.

7. Sayyid Qutb, *Al-Islam wa-mushkilat al-hadarah* (Islam and the problems of civilizations) (Cairo: Dar ihya al-kutub al-arabiyyah, 1962), p. 189.

8. Abu al-ala al-Mawdudi, *Al-Islam wa-l-madaniyyah al-hadithah* (Islam and modern civilization) (Cairo: Dar al-Ansar, 1978), p. 18.

9. Ibid., p. 17.

10. Ibid., p. 28.

11. Ibid., p. 29.

12. Ibid., pp. 15–16.

13. Ibid., pp. 16–17.

14. Ibid., p. 17.

15. Ibid.

16. Ibid.

17. Ibid., pp. 41–42.

18. See Emmanuel Sivan, *Radical Islam: Medieval Theology and Modern Politics* (New Haven: Yale University Press, 1990), p. 43.

19. As quoted in ibid., pp. 73–74.

20. Yusuf al-Qardawi, *Al-hulul al-mustawradah wa-kayfa janat ala ummatina* (The imported solutions and how they brought disastrous consequences upon our nation] (Cairo: Maktabat Wahbah, 1977) (henceforth: al-Qardawi, *Hulul*). The importance of the views expressed in this book can be seen, for example, from the reaction to them in *Azmat al-dimuqratiyyah fi al-watan al-arabi* (The crisis of democracy in the Arab homeland) (Beirut: Markaz dirasat al-wahdah al-arabiyyah, 1984).

21. Al-Qardawi, *Hulul,* p. 46.

22. Ibid., p. 111; al-Mawdudi, *Al-Islam,* pp. 10–11.

23. Al-Mawdudi, ibid., p. 18; al-Qardawi, *Hulul,* p. 117.

24. Al-Qardawi, *Hulul,* p. 66.

25. Ibid., p. 70.

26. Ibid., pp. 70–71.

27. Sayyid Qutb, *Maalim fi'l-tariq* (Landmarks along the road) (Beirut: Dar al-Shuruq, n.d.), pp. 3ff.

28. Here al-Qardawi bases his observations on the Egyptian elections before the 1952 revolution. His point seems to be that as only a few participate in the elections, this process does not necessarily express the will of the majority.

29. Al-Qardawi, *Hulul,* p. 123.

30. Quoted in Maryam Jameelah, *Who is Maudoodi?* (Lahore: Mohammad Yusuf Khan, 1973), pp. 32–33.

31. Interview in *North African News* (September/October 1991): 6.

32. *Tunisian Observer* 1, no. 3 (January 1992).

33. Rashid al-Ghannoushi, *Harakat al-ittijah al-islami* (The Islamic movement), 3 vols. (Kuwait: Dar al-qalam, 1987).

34. For the position of these leaders, consult Ziad Abu-Amr, "Palestinian Islamists and the Question of Democracy," in Edy Kaufman, Shukri B. Abed, and Robert L. Rothstein, eds. *Democracy, Peace, and the Israeli-Palestinian Conflict* (Boulder, CO: Lynne Rienner, 1993).

35. Hassan al-Turabi, *Al-harakah al-Islamiyyah fi'l-Sudan* (The Islamic movement in the Sudan) (Kuwait: Dar al-qalam, 1988), p. 115.

36. Quoted in Judith Miller, *New York Times,* May 17, 1992, sec. E, p. 3.

37. To quote Benaiah Yongo-Bure's description:

Repression has prevailed in Sudan in every period, but whereas earlier it had targeted particular groups, the present regime spares no sector of society. Previous governments operated on the basis of the same dogma of Islamizing and Arabizing the country, but they felt constrained, for a variety of reasons, from vigorously enforcing their cultural and political hegemony. The regime of Omar al-Bashir has shed all constraints and hesitancy. (*Middle East Report* [September/October 1991]: 9)

PART THREE

DOMESTIC POLITICS AND INTERNATIONAL BEHAVIOR

7

DEMOCRACY IN THE ARAB WORLD
AND THE ARAB-ISRAELI CONFLICT

MARK TESSLER AND MARILYN GROBSCHMIDT

THIS ANALYSIS TAKES note of pressures for political liberalization and democratization in the Arab world and advances the thesis that additional movement in this direction would have a positive impact on efforts to resolve the Arab-Israeli conflict. After an introduction to the concern for political liberalization that presently characterizes much of the Arab Middle East, the chapter (1) reviews scholarly literature in the field of international relations which reports that disputes among democracies are almost never resolved by means of war; (2) speculates about some of the mechanisms by which democracy and peace may be linked in the Middle East in the manner posited by this literature; and (3) considers and offers a rejoinder to the arguments of those who contend that the conclusions of the international relations literature are not applicable to the Middle East, and that democracy in the Arab world would in fact increase the prospects for armed conflict between Israelis, Palestinians, and other Arabs.

The assertion of a positive relationship between democracy and peace in the Middle East is not intended to divert attention from the underlying causes of the Arab-Israeli conflict, including, above all, the statelessness of the Palestinian people and the unwillingness of both Israeli and Arab hard-liners to accept a solution based on territorial compromise and mutual recognition between Israelis and Palestinians. Supporters of Israel sometimes argue, usually in response to condemnations of the Jewish state's actions in the occupied territories, that a lack of democracy in the Arab world is among the most important obstacles to peace. *The Jerusalem Post* editorialized on June 5, 1991 (p. 7), for example, that "pointing a finger at Israel as the chief obstacle to peace is puzzling indeed.... [The real problem] is the unelected leaders of the Arab world who refuse to negotiate an end to the Arab-Israeli conflict." This is not the position of the present analysis. Attention to the relationship between de-

mocracy and peace is not intended to suggest that responsibility for the continuing conflict rests exclusively or even primarily with the Arabs, or that Israeli opposition to an exchange of land for peace and an accommodation with
Palestinian nationalism is of no more than secondary significance. But greater
political liberalization and democracy in the Arab world may nonetheless reduce the likelihood of armed conflict between Arabs and Israelis, and it may
also create a climate in which diplomatic efforts designed to address the underlying causes of the conflict will have a greater chance of success. These possibilities are the subject of the present inquiry.

Popular Complaints and Pressures for Democratization

The complaints of ordinary Arab men and women appear to be similar in
all but a handful of oil-rich states (Tessler 1991a). First, masses of people live
in impoverished conditions; and for much of the population, especially the
young, the prospects for social mobility and a higher standard of living are
declining rather than growing brighter. Second, there is a large and growing
gap between rich and poor, meaning that the burdens of underdevelopment
are not shared equitably and that, despite economic difficulties, there are is-
lands of affluence and elite privilege, often involving luxury and excess. Third,
there is a widespread belief that elite membership is determined in most instances not by ability, dedication or service to society but, rather, by personal
and political connections. The result, it is charged, is a system where patronage
and clientelism predominate in decisions about public policy and resource allocation. Fourth, there are few legitimate mechanisms by which the populace
can register complaints in a way that will have a meaningful impact on the
political process, and none whatsoever by which it can remove senior political
leaders whose performance is judged unsatisfactory. Finally, expressions of discontent are tolerated, if at all, only to the extent they do not threaten the established political and economic order.

Numerous scholarly and journalistic investigations confirm that these complaints are both widespread and intensely felt. Describing the situation in Jordan, for example, a country that experienced popular unrest in the late 1980s,
one analyst reports that "a system of cronyism is pervasive," with opportunities
for enrichment channeled by insiders to their friends and with top positions
always going "to the same old faces, families and clans." This situation contributed directly to the outbreak of rioting in April 1989, since many Jordanians

simply "were not willing to tighten their belts to pay for an economic crisis they felt was the result of widespread corruption" (Amawi 1992, p. 27).

Circumstances are similar in other Arab countries. Algeria, like Jordan, was shaken by rioting in the late 1980s, with both mass poverty and elite indulgence contributing to popular anger. An American scholar wrote in 1988 that people were no longer impressed by tales of their leaders' struggle for independence: "They want[ed] to know, as one student bitterly stated . . . why more than half of them are jobless 'while we earn billions per year from natural gas, and [the former head of the ruling party] lives like a king' " (Vandewalle 1988a, p. 2). A political scientist of Algerian origin makes the same point, reporting that "in the midst of an economic and managerial crisis, a few people succeeded in not only increasing their wealth but also displaying it in the form of late-model cars, new villa construction and new businesses," and that this in turn "exacerbated the frustration of the masses" and "made them potentially rebellious against a state of affairs they neither liked nor understood" (Layachi 1992, p. 3).

Accounts of the rioting that shook Tunisia and Morocco in 1984 also emphasize the gap between rich and poor and popular indignation over the perceived squandering of national resources (Paul 1984; Tessler 1986). In Tunis, thousands of students, workers and unemployed young men from the city's slums roamed the streets, shouting anti-government slogans and attacking symbols of authority and wealth. Thousands more shouted encouragement from open windows and rooftops. Moreover, as reflected in the attacks on shops selling luxury goods and incursions into elite neighborhoods, anger was directed not only at the government but also at the consumption-oriented middle and upper classes, population categories perceived to be prospering at a time when the circumstances of the masses were deteriorating and the regime was asking the poor to tighten their belts even more. Similar sentiments were observed in Morocco. For example, some protesters carried pink parasols to express their disdain for royal pomp and their indignation at the excesses of the king and the elite.

Popular grievances are political as well as socioeconomic in character. People complain about what they often describe as the problem of the Arab regimes, or the crisis of leadership and legitimacy in the Arab world. Summarizing the findings of several recent surveys in Morocco, for example, one scholar reported in 1987 that "while the state is feared, it is also often resented, if not hated . . . [and is] widely recognized as not representative of the people. This produces two main reactions, either complete apathy or at least passivity (sometimes viewed as acceptance), or alienation and activism in some anti-establishment form or medium" (Suleiman 1987, p. 113). Writing of Algeria in 1988, another scholar asserted that the overall cause of political alienation is a "system of power, patronage and privilege that entrenched interests in the party, government and economy are unwilling to sacrifice in the name of some larger good" (Entelis 1988, pp. 52–53).

More generally, according to a Jordanian journalist who wrote of the situation during the 1990–91 crisis in the Gulf, opposition to existing regimes and established patterns of governance constitutes an "essential message reverberating throughout the Arab world. . . . [There are everywhere] signs of a profound desire for change" (Khouri 1990, p. 4). The central problem, he wrote in another article, is the pervasiveness of "autocratic rulers and non-accountable power elites [who] pursue whimsical, wasteful and regressive policies" (Khouri 1991, p. 15). A similar conclusion is advanced in a recent article by two scholars with long experience in the Middle East: "Since the end of World War II, the power of the Arab state has reached appalling levels. . . . Its chief executive is almost a god, protected by layer upon layer of secret police. He is obeyed out of fear or the desire to secure individual advantage" (Muslih and Norton 1991, p. 5).

This situation has led many Arabs to call for political reform and democratization. According to the Jordanian journalist quoted above, the demand is "for democracy and human rights, for social equity, for regional economic integration, for the accountability of public officials, for morality in public life, for the fair application of international law and U.N. resolutions, and for a new regional order characterized by honesty, dignity, justice and stability" (Khouri 1990, p. 4). A recent scholarly analysis also makes this point, noting that "the demand for human rights, participation and democracy comes from across the political spectrum. . . . The call for democracy is the subject of meetings, conferences and academic studies" (Kramer 1992, p. 23). Thus, for example, at a conference held in Amman, Jordan, in June 1990 and attended by approximately sixty prominent Arab intellectuals, participants called for a "new Arab order" and declared in their final communique that "democracy should take priority in the pan-Arab national project. It should not be sacrificed for any other value or cause—including Arab unity itself" (Halasa 1991, p. 3).

During the mid- and late 1980s, leaders in a number of Arab states responded to public discontent and demands for political change with measures involving movement in the direction of democratization. In particular, Egypt, Morocco, Tunisia, Algeria, Jordan, and Yemen, which between them have over half of the Arab world's population, took steps to open up political life. Measures taken include the release of political prisoners, greater press freedom, the acceptance of opposition political parties, and the holding of competitive elections. These developments led one scholar to conclude in 1990 that "however inadequate may be their polyarchal tendencies . . . political life in Egypt, Algeria, Jordan, Yemen and several other Arab countries is more complex and participant, and less authoritarian, than it used to be" (Hudson 1990, p. 24).

Serious obstacles to democracy remain in virtually every instance, and the motivation of most Arab leaders has been to contain and diffuse popular discontent, not to establish mechanisms of political change whose outcomes they cannot control. Thus, while there was indeed a meaningful degree of political liberalization in a number of Arab countries during the mid- and late 1980s, the governments of these countries are not committed to political openings that will bring full and genuine democratization. Moreover, there has in some instances been a retreat from the democratic path during the early 1990s. This has been the case, most notably, in Algeria and Tunisia. In both countries, the government has carried out a harsh crackdown on opposition parties and movements associated with Islam, preferring to abandon previous political openings rather than run the risk that Islamic groups would acquire power in fair and competitive elections.

Nevertheless, despite these important limitations and setbacks, pressures for political accountability remain intense and aggregate trends in the Arab world appear to indicate movement away from authoritarianism. At the very least, even though additional reverses can also be expected, the degree to which there are further political openings and progress toward democratization will be a major preoccupation of Arab politics during the remainder of the 1990s.

As a result, there is at least the possibility, and perhaps even a strong likelihood, that the years ahead will bring a continuing transformation of the patterns of political economy and political culture that characterize the Arab world. A reasonable projection is offered by Hudson, who sees continuing problems in the short term but nonetheless concludes that "the process of developing an effective civil society . . . is driven inexorably by the socioeconomic changes, even the painful ones, that are ubiquitous throughout the Arab world," and that consequently "it is likely [the Arabs] will demand—and finally achieve—more representative government than they have had in the past" (Hudson 1991, p. 426). To the extent that this is indeed a plausible scenario, it is important to ask whether political liberalization and movement toward democracy would have consequences not only for the domestic politics of various Arab states but also for Middle Eastern international relations and for the evolution of regional disputes, the most important of which is the Arab-Israeli conflict.

Scholarly Research about Democracy, War, and Peace

If the Arab world does experience additional movement in the direction of democracy, one important consequence may be a significant increase in the prospects for a peaceful resolution of the Arab-Israeli conflict. Providing support for this proposition is a growing body of theoretical and empirical literature in the field of international relations which indicates that democratic states are highly unlikely to resort to war to resolve disputes with other democracies. To the extent that the conclusions of this literature are applicable to the Middle East, democracy in the Arab world will not only bring about a much-desired transformation in the character of domestic political life, it will also reduce the prospects for armed conflict between Israelis, Palestinians, and other Arabs and thereby create a climate in which efforts to resolve the lingering Middle East dispute will have a greater chance of success. This analytical projection assumes, of course, that Israel will remain an effective and functioning democracy.

Although a number of studies have demonstrated that democracies, in general, are no more peaceful than non-democratic states (Small and Singer 1976; Chan 1984; Weede 1984), there is compelling evidence that democracies do not go to war against one another. As expressed by Rummel, "libertarian systems mutually preclude violence," in other words, "violence will occur between states only if at least one is nonlibertarian." By libertarian, Rummel means those states that "[emphasize] individual freedom and civil liberties and the rights associated with the competitive and open election of leaders" (Rummel 1983, pp. 27–28).

One study providing evidence in support of this conclusion was conducted by Babst, who examined 116 major wars from 1789 to 1941 and found that "no wars [had] been fought between independent nations with elective governments" (Babst 1972, p. 55). In another investigation, Doyle examined "liberal" regimes dating back to the eighteenth century and found that "even though liberal states have become involved in numerous wars with nonliberal states, constitutionally secure liberal states have yet to engage in war with one another" (Doyle 1983, p. 213). Doyle defined liberal states as "polities that are externally sovereign . . . [where citizens] possess juridical rights . . . [and are ruled by a] representative government" (ibid.). A third study was conducted by Maoz and Abdolali (1989), who reported that while democracies are no more peaceful than other states, they almost always go to war with nondemocratic regimes, rather than other democracies.

There has been some debate about whether the relationship between democracy and peace is spurious. For example, arguing that societies with greater wealth have more to lose and are therefore reluctant to go to war, one analyst suggests that the correlation may be an artifact of the high level of economic development that characterizes most democratic countries (Mueller 1989, p. 264). Yet empirical studies report that the relationship between democracy and peace holds when statistical controls for wealth and other variables are introduced. Studies by Maoz and Russett (1992, pp. 245–46; 1991, p. 30) demonstrate that peace among democracies cannot be explained by level or rate of development, by political stability, or by the lack of common borders. Also, with respect to the impact of wealth and economic development, Ember, Ember, and Russett (1992, p. 575) correctly observe that this does not explain the peace that existed among democracies prior to industrialization. Nor does it explain the outbreak of World War II, which pitted " 'advanced capitalist . . . states against each other.' "

Although the pathways that link democracy to peace are not fully understood, scholars have identified two categories of constraints that appear to push toward peace in democratic polities. Maoz and Russett (1991) describe these two types of causal mechanisms as "structural" and "normative." The former focuses on the institutional checks and balances that exist within democratic societies and make it difficult for leaders to gain the consensus needed to go to war. The latter calls attention to the political norms and standards of behavior that permit democratic societies to resolve domestic disputes in a peaceful manner. Doyle, too, discusses the salience of both structural and normative constraints (1983, pp. 229–30), and in this connection he draws heavily upon Immanuel Kant's classic study from 1795 which predicted that "perpetual peace . . . [would result] from the world-wide establishment of republican governments."

There are actually two kinds of structural constraints, one involving the electorate and the other flowing from competition among elites. Doyle (1983, p. 229) argues that in democratic countries, the electorate serves as a strong check upon the executive due to the inordinate burden placed upon ordinary citizens in times of war. These citizens experience, first hand, the fighting and losses associated with armed conflict, and they will therefore be reluctant to support leaders who take military action before exhausting peaceful methods of conflict resolution. Leaders, for their part, are constrained by this situation. Knowing they are accountable to the electorate, they will be reluctant to launch initiatives that may be costly in terms of lives or resources and will do so only when able to convince the public that these initiatives are legitimate and unavoidable. Rummel (1983, p. 28) also makes this point, observing that leaders in a democracy are dependent on the support of an electorate that is "unwilling to bear the cost . . . of foreign adventures and interventions unless aroused by an emotionally unifying issue, [and] even then the public cannot be trusted to pay the price of foreign violence for long." The leaders of undemocratic governments, by contrast, are less constrained since the maintenance of their authority does not depend on popular support. According to some analysts, authoritarian regimes may in fact derive benefit from militarized interstate conflict. Lake, for example, argues that such conflict may simplify the task of domestic political control and enhance the state's rent-seeking ability (Lake 1992, p. 30).

Doyle, Rummel, and others also suggest that competition among leaders and political institutions may check the war ambitions of a democratically elected head of state. According to Morgan and Campbell, for example, a democratic structure imposes constraints that push toward peace to the extent that competing politicians scrutinize and critique one another's policies or that a decision to go to war must be approved by various leaders and institutions. Indeed, they argue, these may be the most important structural constraints, since "no modern democracy puts a decision for war to a vote of the entire electorate" (1991, p. 189). Morgan and Campbell also present empirical evidence in support of these propositions, although their findings are clear-cut only in the case of major powers. In yet another study that considers the structural characteristics that push democracies toward peace, Kilgour (1991, p. 282) argues that the likelihood of war involvement is diminished by the diffusion of decisional responsibility and the existence of an effective opposition.

So far as normative constraints are concerned, several analysts suggest that military conflict among democracies is discouraged by the legitimacy that citizens of one state accord to the behavior of the other, presumably because this behavior is based on the decisions of a government that represents and is accountable to its people. As explained by Doyle (1983, p. 230), who again borrows heavily from Kant, "domestically just republics, which rest on consent, presume foreign republics to be also consensual, just, and therefore deserving of accommodation." Russett makes a related point. He suggests that there is an expectation of reasonable behavior and of a willingness to compromise that allows democracies to approach problems amongst themselves in a conciliatory fashion. Specifically, "the norm for behavior within democratic systems [is that] peoples *ought* to be able to satisfy common interests and work out compromise solutions to their problems, without recourse to violence or the threat of it" (Russett 1989, p. 248; original emphasis).

These normative constraints are absent when the citizens of a democracy evaluate the behavior of nondemocratic states. The actor in this case is not a legitimate government that must be presumed to represent the people it rules and whose behavior in the domestic political arena has demonstrated a commitment to pluralism, compromise and respect for the rule of law. Consequently, it may be easier to justify resorting to violence against a nondemocratic state.

As noted, the functioning of these and other mechanisms that purport to explain the relationship between democracy and peace are not fully understood. Nevertheless, whatever the reasons, it is clear that militarized conflict among democracies is extremely rare, and this, in turn, makes plausible an expectation that the Arab-Israeli conflict would evolve in a very different manner were the Arab world to become more democratic. To the extent that the international relations literature discussed above holds lessons which apply to the Middle East, conflicts among opposing democratic governments in Israel and various Arab states would be addressed with far less likelihood that one side or the other would resort to war. Moreover, the prospects for a peaceful and permanent resolution of the Arab-Israeli dispute would increase significantly under these circumstances.

Democracy and Peace in the Middle East

There are at least two sets of reasons to believe that democratization in the Arab world would increase the prospects for a peaceful resolution of the Arab-Israeli dispute. First, the processes and calculations shaping political decision-making in Arab states would be vastly different than they are at present, which would lead to at least some diminution of these states' belligerent attitude toward Israel. Second, at the level of regional international relations, attendant changes would have an important impact on Israeli perceptions and, more specifically, would reduce the security concerns that play such a significant role in the formation of Israeli foreign and defense policy.

It is reasonable to assume, as a general principle, that Arab democracies would be no different than other democracies with respect to the functioning of structural and normative constraints that push toward peace. To the extent that decision-making about war and peace is diffused, for example, or subject to scrutiny by rival politicians and by a public that must ultimately bear the costs of military conflict, it is likely that Arab governments would resort to war only in the last resort and that at least some military confrontations would therefore be avoided.

Applying this logic to the Arab world retroactively, a recent analysis argues that both the Iran-Iraq War and the 1990–91 Gulf War might have been avoided had the governments of Iraq and other states in the region been less authoritarian. Writing of the war over Kuwait, for example, Muslih and Norton assert that while the immediate causes were the ambitions and obsessions of Saddam Hussein, the "root causes lie in Arab society and politics," and especially in the absence of democratic political processes. More specifically, they contend that "had there been a minimum level of parliamentary activity and political consultation in Iraq, Hussein could not have blundered into a senseless eight year war with Iran followed by a suicidal adventure in Kuwait," and that "by the same token, had these two ingredients existed in the Arab states allied against him, a political solution could have been found to avert war" (Muslih and Norton 1991, pp. 4–5).

Moreover, the leaders of undemocratic Arab states have not necessarily blundered into interstate disputes but have sometimes deliberately involved themselves in regional conflicts in an attempt to enhance their legitimacy and deflect attention from domestic grievances. Such behavior includes but is not limited to Arab involvement in the conflict with Israel, although the Arab-Israeli dispute is certainly the best known and perhaps the most important of the regional antagonisms that undemocratic Arab leaders have sought to exploit for their own purposes. Such behavior also includes expressions of belligerence and other actions that help to perpetuate regional conflict, even though they stop short of initiating military hostilities.

This sort of behavior is strongly encouraged by the crises of leadership and legitimacy discussed earlier, at the center of which is the absence of political mechanisms through which citizens can hold their governments accountable. Involvement in foreign conflicts, in other words, is an instrument by which political regimes with little or no domestic support can attempt to maintain their authority. On the one hand, the leaders of such regimes can use foreign adventures to divert public attention from domestic political and economic grievances. On the other, by insisting that national unity is necessary in the face of an external challenge, they can put forward a justification for the suppression of political dissent. It is in this connection, writes a specialist on the Arab world, that "state elites inevitably find foreign threats to the nation easier to manage than the domestic threats to the regime engendered by social and economic transformation," and that for this reason many Arab leaders are "more-than-willing players in this game of nations" (Anderson 1992, p. 166).

These kinds of motivations for involvement in foreign adventures, including a posture of hostility toward Israel, would greatly diminish were Arab governments to gain genuine legitimacy through their performance and accountability in the domestic political arena. There are admittedly limits to the changes that would occur. There are real issues associated with the Arab-Israeli conflict, issues such as Palestinian statelessness which transcend whatever cynical motivations Arab leaders may possess. If these issues go unaddressed, the conflict will fester no matter how democratic the Arab world might become. It would also be naive to expect that democratically elected Arab leaders would be able to satisfy all of the demands and aspirations of their citizens and that they would thus have no further interest in using foreign policy to shore up their popularity or to divert attention from domestic problems. Nevertheless, despite these limits, democratization would bring a fundamental and qualitative change in the way Arab leaders formulate policy and calculate their own interests and those of the citizens to whom they are accountable. The leaders of Arab democracies would be obliged to allocate more resources and give much greater priority to domestic social and economic problems, including poverty, corruption, the skewed distribution of opportunities for advancement, and arbitrary state interference in the lives of ordinary citizens. Leaders would have to address these problems sincerely and effectively in order to remain in power, and in so doing they would acquire greater legitimacy and eliminate, or at least significantly diminish, the need to point to foreign problems in an attempt to diffuse popular anger.

The likely connection between democracy and peace can be seen at popular as well as elite levels in the Arab world. On the one hand, as the preceding suggests, democracy would almost certainly bring a significant transformation in the outlook of ordinary citizens. Attitudes toward government would become much more positive if people were convinced that their problems were receiving serious attention and if citizens knew that they could replace those leaders who failed to make meaningful progress in dealing with these problems.

On the other hand, and perhaps even more important, the availability of legitimate channels for public debate and protest would most likely reduce the

---

frequency and intensity of popular demonstrations over real and alleged foreign grievances, including those relating to the conflict with Israel. This is not to say that ordinary Arabs would become less sympathetic to the Palestinian cause. This cause would continue to receive strong support, and quite properly so. But it is probably of secondary importance to most Arab men and women, receiving an emphasis disproportionate to its salience because it has traditionally been one of the few issues with respect to which public protest and expressions of opposition are tolerated. Under conditions of greater democracy, it would no longer be needed as a proxy for complaints that are in fact much higher on most people's agenda but which governments prevent from being the focus of serious political discourse.

All of these developments would have an important and positive impact on Israeli perceptions of the Arab world, and herein lies the second set of reasons to believe that Arab democratization would increase the prospects for a peaceful resolution of the Arab-Israeli dispute.

Israelis have long asserted that most Arab regimes oppose peace and prefer the status quo because the conflict with Israel provides a convenient distraction from their failures in the domestic arena. This is the message of the *Jerusalem Post* editorial quoted earlier, which asserted that the principal obstacle to peace lies in "the unelected leaders of the Arab world who refuse to negotiate an end to the Arab-Israeli conflict." Although Israelis sometimes advance such arguments for their own purposes, alleging that Arab leaders are untrustworthy in order to justify their own rejection of opportunities for progress toward peace, it is ironic that the traditional Israeli view of Arab leaders and regimes is to a significant degree shared by ordinary Arab citizens. In any event, Israeli arguments about the intransigence of Arab governments suggest that a change in the political culture and political economy of key Arab states could have a significant psychological impact within the Jewish state, making it more difficult for Israelis to argue, and in many cases believe, that peace with the Arab world is impossible and that any search for compromise and accommodation would be meaningless. In particular, Israeli hard-liners would find it more difficult to reject calls for an exchange of land for peace—as did Prime Minister Yitzhak Shamir in a 1989 speech, one of many that could be cited—by insisting that advocates of territorial compromise are misguided because "it is the Arab states that are the problem" and that without their intransigence "the Palestinian problem could easily have been disposed of" (*Jerusalem Post*, January 26, 1989).

A related and equally important consideration is that Arab regimes governed by democratic institutions would be far less fragile, and this in turn would make it less reasonable for Israelis to worry that it is dangerous to make peace with an Arab leader today because the volatile and violent nature of Arab politics may tomorrow turn out his regime and replace it with that of a new strongman, who might have a different agenda and political calculus. Authoritarian governments of this sort are sometimes cynically labelled "one-bullet regimes," meaning that the political orientation of an entire country is heavily dependent on the preferences and inclinations of a single individual and that this orientation could change radically were that individual, for whatever reason, to disappear from the scene. This possibility led some Israelis to question the wisdom of signing the 1978 Camp David accords with Anwar Sadat and of returning the Sinai Peninsula to Egypt. Thus, even though Israel did withdraw from Sinai and the treaty with Egypt survived Sadat's subsequent assassination, Israelis would have far more confidence in some future agreement that depended on the commitments of a government that was deemed legitimate by its own people and whose policies were the product of open competition among institutions representing different philosophies and interests, rather than the unchallenged dictates of a handful of unaccountable elites, or even a single individual.

Greater democratization might also lead to a significant reduction in military budgets and expenditures for arms purchases by Arab governments, and this, too, would contribute to a change in Israeli perceptions of the threat coming from the Arab world. Arab leaders accountable to their people would almost certainly be under pressure to allocate a larger share of the state's resources to domestic development, rather than to the armed forces. In addition, these leaders would no longer have reason to view a large military and an associated domestic security apparatus as necessary for the containment of popular discontent and the survival of their regimes. Under these conditions, if challenged to make peace by an Arab world that was less militarized, as well as less volatile, Israelis might be more inclined to conclude that the security of their state would not be compromised by withdrawal from the occupied territories. Indeed, this prospect has been discussed explicitly by some Arab advocates of democratization, who add to their arguments in favor of political liberalization the possibility that "Israel might be much less intransigent" if it faced a Middle East characterized by greater stability and democracy ("Jordan and the 1990 Gulf Crisis" 1990, p. 6).

The importance of Israeli perceptions of the Arab world lies in the Jewish state's understandable preoccupation with national security and in the way this preoccupation enters into the country's ongoing debate about whether its conflict with the Arabs can be resolved on the basis of a land-for-peace formula. Israel is in fact deeply divided on this issue, with a majority willing to see the country relinquish at least some of the occupied territories in return for credible security guarantees and a smaller but nonetheless substantial number opposing any territorial concessions. Questions about security and Arab intentions are central to both positions (Tessler 1991b, pp. 79–86). Advocates of territorial compromise state that their arguments will be convincing only to the extent that Israelis believe the country will remain secure, and that this in turn depends heavily on an assessment of what can be expected from the Arabs. This assessment also plays a central role in the thinking of many who oppose territorial compromise. Although some opposition is based on ideological or religious conviction, many and perhaps most Israelis who support hard-line politicians do so for security-related reasons. As expressed by a former central committee member of the Likud Union, the hard-line party of Yitzhak Shamir, nine out of ten who support Likud and Shamir "will compromise on territory if their questions about security are satisfied" (Ben-Yishai 1988, pp. 6–7; Tessler 1991b, p. 79).

Assessing Counter-Theses

Some analysts believe that conclusions drawn from the international relations literature on democracy, war, and peace are not applicable to the present-day Middle East. Some even suggest that increased democratization in the Arab world would make it more difficult, not less difficult, to establish peace between Arabs and Israelis. In addition to arguing that too little is known about the mechanisms that discourage democracies from fighting one another to permit confident projections, those who take this position offer two interrelated propositions about the Middle East and the Arab-Israeli conflict: (1) there is deep antipathy among the Arab masses to the existence of Israel, so that if governments were more accountable to their citizens they would actually have less flexibility to seek an accommodation with the Jewish state; and (2) democracy in the Arab world would permit the acquisition of power by Islamist movements that oppose peace with Israel on any conditions, meaning that there would be increased intransigence at the governmental as well as the popular level.

One scholar recently put forward these arguments in the following manner: "Can democracy in the Middle East establish the preconditions for peace? Probably not. First, a truly satisfactory explanation for why democracies fail to fight one another has yet to emerge. Second, democracy represents the means of rule, not its ends. In those Arab countries where democratic reforms have emerged, notably Egypt, Algeria and Jordan, Islamic fundamentalist candidates have fared well, and these tend to be candidates who adopt a rejectionist stance toward Israel. Therefore, democratic reforms might promote the very foreign policy behavior that [advocates of peace] would like to discourage. . . . [These] comments are not meant to belittle the virtues of democracy, but simply to temper the optimism of those who believe democracy in the Middle East would establish the conditions for peace" (Barnett 1991, p. 109).

Other analysts, too, worry that if democracy were to come to the Arab world the results might actually be detrimental to peace and stability (Kemp 1991), and this possibility appears to be of particular concern to some American officials and also to some elites in the Arab world. Several observers note that American officials and commentators frequently discuss Islam as they once discussed Communism, with an emphasis placed on the need to contain this dangerous ideology, and that "self-styled liberals in the Arab world" seek to exploit American fears by arguing that "the West must support the governments in power, for however much they fall short of democracy they are more congenial than the supposed fanatics with whom they will otherwise be replaced" (Anderson 1992, p. 177; see also Miller 1992, p. 42).

While these arguments deserve to be taken seriously, their accuracy is not self-evident. So far as the Arab masses are concerned, the question, as nicely posed by Rothstein, is "whether their expectations are or can be made realistic and pragmatic. . . . [Whether ordinary citizens] will only be satisfied with the defeat or destruction of Israel, the expulsion of foreign influences, the installation of Islamic fundamentalist governments . . . [or whether there is some other reason that] they are rejecting the status quo and demanding change" (Rothstein 1991, pp. 140–41).

As discussed in the introductory section of this chapter and elsewhere (Tessler 1991a; Tessler 1993), grievances related to Israel are not among the most important determinants of the anger and militancy that are growing among ordinary Arab men and women, anger which has given rise to riots in a number of Arab countries. Nor are this anger and militancy the product of any innate, primordial, religious or culturally induced extremism. Thus, despite the stereotypes about Arabs and Muslims that are sometimes put forward by Western analysts, it is difficult to disagree with the characterization offered by Muslih and Norton (1991, p. 19): "The Middle East is . . . populated by people with aspirations for peace, pragmatic justice, freedom from arbitrary rule, and a decent life for their children."

It therefore seems reasonable to view popular expressions of anti-Israel sentiment at least partly as a way of venting the pent-up anger that derives from domestic political and economic complaints about which protest is not permitted, and thereafter, perhaps, as a more general complaint about the foreign policy failings of Arab governments rather than as a considered rejection of any compromise with Israel. Opposition to Israel is not all proxy and symbolism, of course. There are real, substantive grievances that receive strong expression as well. But in most cases these involve either anger at perceived, or real, Israeli intransigence in the face of Arab calls for compromise or denunciations of specific policies and actions undertaken by the government in Jerusalem. So, again, expressions of anti-Israel sentiment may not mean, and probably do not mean, that ordinary Arab men and women demand and would be satisfied with nothing less than destruction of the Jewish state.

The public enthusiasm in Egypt that initially greeted Anwar Sadat's overtures toward Israel and his promise of a peace dividend also suggests the absence of deep-rooted feelings that would prevent an Arab government accountable to its citizens from accepting a compromise that included recognition of Israel's existence. Were this the case, Egyptians would have told Sadat that a peace dividend was of no interest, since a more important moral principle was involved. This did not happen, however; most of the opposition expressed at the time came from intellectuals and leftist politicians, rather than from the masses, and even many of the former declared that they were not opposed to peace per se but rather to this particular peace because it failed to make adequate provisions for Palestinian self-determination. Thus, with many ordinary Egyptians concluding that their country had made its contribution to the Palestinian cause and that it was now time to devote greater attention to domestic needs, the lesson would seem to be that peace will be accepted, indeed welcomed, if it involves a fair compromise and is seen as bringing real opportunities for dealing with critical problems at home.

Findings from original survey research recently carried out in Egypt lend additional and somewhat more systematic support to this assessment. A heterogeneous sample of 292 Cairo residents was interviewed in mid-1988, and several questions dealing with Israel were included on the interview schedule. Details about construction of the sample, administration of the survey instrument, and measurement validity and reliability are provided in the appendix. The questions dealing with Israel include: (1) Which statement best describes your attitude toward the Arab-Israeli conflict: (a) peace efforts are desirable, or (b) peace is impossible; and (2) Which is the best solution to the Arab-Israeli conflict: (a) a diplomatic solution, or (b) a military solution? Responses to these two questions are highly intercorrelated and the items were therefore combined to form a single scale measuring attitudes toward peace with Israel.

Findings from the survey show broad support in Egypt for a peaceful resolution of the Arab-Israeli conflict. Specifically, as shown in table 1, 70 percent of the respondents favored peace, whereas only 14 percent said peace is undesirable or impossible. The remaining 16 percent were unsure. It might also be noted that the survey was conducted at a time when the Palestinian uprising in the West Bank and Gaza, the intifada, was particularly intense, so that anti-Israel sentiment may actually have been somewhat inflated by concern about the harsh measures Israel was using in an attempt to suppress resistance in the occupied territories.

Demographic patterns based on a regression analysis also lend support to the proposition that there is little primordial, mass-based opposition to Israel's existence. Less well-educated individuals tend to hold more traditional cultural values but are no less supportive of peace with Israel than better educated persons. Further, although older individuals are also more traditional, they are actually more likely than younger persons to favor an accommodation with the Jewish state. Finally, attitudes toward Israel are unrelated to gender, indicating that support for peace is broadly based among both men and women.

The survey was also carried out in Kuwait, where both Kuwaiti citizens and Palestinian residents were interviewed, and support for peace with Israel was lower among both groups than among respondents in Egypt. These findings, which are also shown in table 1, suggest several conclusions that are relevant for the present analysis. First, only 44 percent of the Kuwaitis and only 56 percent of the Palestinians viewed peace with Israel as either impossible or undesirable. These figures are not as low as in Egypt, but they are still low enough to suggest that there is not overwhelming, mass-based opposition to a peaceful resolution of the Arab-Israeli conflict. In addition, as in Egypt, demographic correlations show that more traditional individuals, those who are either older, less well educated or both, are not more opposed to peace than others.

Finally, and perhaps most important, the difference in attitudes expressed in the quasi-democratic political environment of Egypt and in the undemocratic political environment that characterized Kuwait in 1988 is consistent with the proposition that there are constraints which push toward peace in relations among democracies. It is not possible to determine statistically whether political system differences, or some other attributes that differentiate between the two countries, account for the fact that support for peace is more common in Egypt. Greater Egyptian support for peace may to some extent be the result

Table 1. Attitudes toward Peace with Israel by Sample Group (1988)

Frequency Column Percent	Egyptians	Kuwaitis	Palestinians	Total
Opposes peace with Israel	38 13.7%	120 44.0%	142 56.3%	300 37.4%
Unsure	45 16.2%	89 29.7%	69 27.4%	203 25.3%
Favors peace with Israel	194 70.0%	72 26.4%	41 16.3%	307 38.3%
Total	277	281	252	802

of a decade of diplomatic relations with Israel. Another possibility is greater war-weariness in Egypt, which is consistent with the fact that older Egyptians are more likely to favor peace than younger Egyptians. In any event, since attitudes toward Israel are clearly more pacific in the more democratic country, the data at the very least lend additional credibility to the argument that generalizations about a positive relationship between democracy and peace may be extended to the Middle East. And further, so far as the views of the masses are concerned, the comparison between Egypt and Kuwait reinforces the contention that there is not a primordial, indigenous "Arab" orientation but, rather, that views about Israel and peace are shaped by variable present-day experiences and circumstances, at least some of which are political or economic in nature.

The Question of Islam

The arguments of those who believe that democracy will provide Islamist parties with an opportunity to influence national policy have some merit. Islamist movements and candidates have indeed done well in those Arab countries that have in recent years permitted competitive elections, most notably Algeria, Jordan, Tunisia and Egypt. But the reasons for growing popular support of Islamist challenges to the status quo deserve careful scrutiny, as does the contention that this support demonstrates an inverse relationship between democracy and peace in the Middle East.

It is probably the absence of democracy and the existence of unresolved domestic economic and social problems that have produced most of the current support for movements with Islamist tendencies, rather than anything that has to do with Arab culture or even, in a direct sense, the religious faith of ordinary citizens. With secular regimes tied to the U.S. (or until recently to the USSR) lacking legitimacy in the eyes of their own people, it is not surprising that many have responded positively to slogans which proclaim that "Islam is the solution." This is the conclusion of many analysts of the contemporary Arab world, and it may be understood in the context of observations offered earlier about the bases for popular discontent and demands for accountable government.

As expressed by Jamal Al-Suwaidi in his contribution to the present volume, "As long as Arab governments resist political participation and refuse to tolerate different political opinions, the strength of Islam as an alternative political ideology will continue to grow." A similar conclusion is offered by a prominent journalist with long experience in the Middle East, who writes that "Islam's victories, of course, have not happened in a vacuum. . . . Islam's appeal has grown because of economic hardship, political failure, social turmoil or a combination of all three" (Wright 1991, p. 140). Assessments of particular Islamist movements also make this point. Reporting on developments in Tunisia, for example, one scholar notes that "feelings of dislocation and alienation among Tunisia's Muslims gradually turned an essentially apolitical [Islamist] group into an activist organization" (Vandewalle 1989/90, p. 5), and "[The growth of this movement is] only a symptom of a deeper malaise within Tunisian society" (Vandewalle 1988b, p. 617).

Findings from the opinion surveys carried out in Egypt and Kuwait provide more systematic evidence that considerations unrelated to the faith and religious attachments of ordinary citizens are producing much of the support for contemporary Islamist groups. The data also indicate, by extension, that this support does not necessarily reflect a belief that existing political systems should be replaced by patterns of governance based on Muslim legal codes. Separate attitudinal scales were developed to measure two distinct Islamic orientations: (1) support for political Islam and contemporary Islamist groups, and (2) personal piety and attitudes toward the social salience of Islam. The items and procedures used to construct each scale are shown in the appendix.

Although there is a statistically significant relationship between these two scales, a surprisingly large proportion of the individuals with highly favorable attitudes toward Islamist political movements have relatively low ratings on the

Table 2. Support for Political Islam by Personal Religiosity among Egyptians, Kuwaitis, and Palestinians in Kuwait

	Frequency Row Percent Column Percent	Refers to Islamic teachings when making important personal decisions		
		Sometimes or Less	Always	Total
Support for contemporary Islamic political organizations	Strong	207 53.3% 40.5%	181 46.7% 51.0%	388 44.8%
	Moderate or Weak	304 63.6% 59.5%	174 36.4% 49.0%	478 55.2%
	Total	511 59.0%	355 41.0%	866 100.0%

scale measuring personal piety and attitudes toward the social salience of Islam (Tessler 1992). This pattern is illustrated in table 2, which cross-tabulates a leading indicator item from each scale. The table shows that approximately half of the most religious respondents are not highly supportive of Islamic political organizations, and that about half of those who *are* highly supportive of these groups are among the less religious of the individuals surveyed.

These findings are consistent with the conclusions of other analysts. Henry Munson, for example, who has written extensively on Islam and politics, insists on differentiating the ideology of Islamist political movements from the traditional religious attachments of Muslim men and women. He contends that the former "is not how most Muslims understand their religion" and that "a politicized conception of Islam differs radically from how Islam is normally understood by ordinary Muslims" (Munson 1992, p. 13). Jamal Al-Suwaidi's contribution to the present volume makes a similar point. He asserts that the "ideology and the sociopolitical programs of religious groups are too political to appeal to traditional mainstream Muslims."

The preceding establishes the strong possibility that many Arabs who support Islamist parties are not genuinely persuaded that Islam is the solution to the political and economic problems they face. It is true, of course, that political slogans based on Islam have particular resonance in societies where many are devout and where religion puts forth a normative model for societal organization as well as personal morality. Nevertheless, Islamist groups have to a considerable extent succeeded simply because they are the most effective vehicle available for registering opposition to an undesirable status quo.

Prominent among the reasons for the Islamists' success are organizational and ideological considerations having little to do with the religious attachments of ordinary citizens. For one thing, in the undemocratic environment that has prevailed in most Arab countries, mosques and other religious establishments offer opportunities to recruit and organize followers that are unavailable to more secular movements. Further, in some countries, Islamic groups have built support through community assistance projects carried out under the banner of religion. Such activities require a measure of organization that political authorities are usually required to tolerate, even though these activities may foster a belief that Islamic groups are more dedicated to helping ordinary men and women than are government officials. Yet another important consideration is the collapse of Communism and the diminished credibility of ideologies based on socialism, which have greatly reduced the appeal of opposition movements that seek to challenge the government from the left side of the political spectrum.

That support for an Islamist movement does not always imply an unqualified endorsement of its philosophy and platform is illustrated by an account of the 1990 local and regional elections in Algeria. One Algerian informant told an American journalist, for example: "I voted for the FIS [Islamic Salvation Front] out of revenge" (Ibrahim 1990). According to a second informant: "In this country, if you are a young man . . . you have only four choices: you can remain unemployed and celibate because there are no jobs and no apartments to live in; you can work in the black market and risk being arrested; you can try to emigrate to France to sweep the streets of Paris or Marseilles; or you can join the FIS and vote for Islam" (ibid.).

The tendency to vote for an Islamic party in order to protest the status quo was also evident in the March 1992 elections for the Chamber of Commerce in Ramallah, an important town in the Israeli-occupied West Bank. Candidates associated with the Islamist Hamas movement handily defeated those identified with secular nationalism and the PLO. According to press reports, many Palestinians complained of PLO officials who live lavishly and whose bank accounts contain funds that should be spent in the occupied territories, and it is for this reason, at least in part, that Hamas candidates were victorious in "a city with a large number of Christian Palestinians who normally would never vote for an Islamic fundamentalist" (Ibrahim 1992).

Having distinguished Islam in general, that is, the Muslim faith and the religious attachments of the masses, from the militant ideologies of Islamist political organizations, it must be asked whether the former will nonetheless influence democratic governments in ways that move them away from peace rather than toward it. In other words, will ordinary men and women, to the extent they refer to Islam when making important decisions, demand from governments obliged to respect their wishes a foreign policy orientation that is militant, rejectionist, confrontational and even militaristic in its approach to Israel, and perhaps to the West more generally as well? Is it indeed the case, as an American journalist wrote during the 1990–91 crisis in the Gulf, that "the passion of Muslims against the West is . . . inevitable, unstoppable, a terrifying phenomenon based on justified anger and the Koran" (Rosenthal 1991)?

Despite the fears of some U.S. officials and others, both empirical evidence and scholarly opinion suggest that this is unlikely to be the case. A regression analysis of the survey data from Egypt and Kuwait shows that attitudes toward peace with Israel, the dependent variable, does not bear a significant relationship to the attitude scale measuring personal piety and views about the social salience of Islam ($b = .026$; $p = .50$). This finding, presented in bivariate form in table 3, contrasts with the pattern observed for the scale measuring support for political Islam and contemporary Islamist groups, which bears a significant inverse relationship to support for peace with Israel ($b = -.283$; $p = 0000$).

This pattern is consistent across a series of regression analyses using different combinations of independent variables. It is also found both in Egypt and among Palestinians in Kuwait, when data from these populations are analyzed separately. The findings are somewhat different among Kuwaitis insofar as the scale measuring personal but not political aspects of Islam is inversely related to pacific attitudes toward Israel. The relationship is just barely statistically significant, however, and not strong enough to account for a meaningful amount of variance ($b = .147$; $p = 0427$). Thus, even in this case, and certainly more generally, it appears that Islam, as understood at popular levels and reflected in personal religious attachments, is not seen by believers as requiring opposition to an accommodation with the Jewish state.

There is also a body of scholarly opinion that seeks to explicate Muslim attitudes toward war and peace and, more specifically, to make clear that Islam does not incline its followers toward a political orientation characterized by

Table 3. Attitudes toward Peace with Israel by Strength of Personal Islamic Attachments among Egyptians, Kuwaitis and Palestinians in Kuwait

Frequency Row Percent Column Percent	Personal Piety and Social Salience			
	Very Religious	Religious	Less Religious	Total
Opposes peace with Israel	72 24.6% 40.0%	119 40.6% 39.7%	102 34.8% 33.8%	293 37.5%
Unsure	45 23.7% 25.0%	62 32.7% 20.6%	83 43.6% 27.5%	190 24.3%
Favors peace with Israel	63 21.1% 35.0%	119 39.8% 39.7%	117 39.1% 38.7%	299 38.2%
Total	180 23.0%	300 38.4%	302 38.6%	782 100.0%

extremism, intolerance, ideological rigidity, belligerence, and a preference for confrontation over compromise. Implications for the Arab-Israeli conflict are rarely a specific concern of these analyses. But they do serve to combat the notion, often expressed in Western stereotypes of the Arab and Muslim world, that governments will of necessity be bellicose and anti-Western if they are required to respect the wishes of citizens whose policy preferences may be influenced by their Islamic attachments.

John Esposito is prominent among the American scholars who have addressed this issue in recent years. In congressional testimony in 1991, for example, he denounced "the assumption that the mixing of religion and politics [in the Muslim world] necessarily and inevitably leads to fanaticism and extremism." So far as conflicts with the West are concerned, he asserted that disagreements "are more often motivated by objection to specific Western policies than by civilizational hostility" (Esposito 1991; also Esposito and Piscatori 1991, p. 440). According to another knowledgeable specialist, "by and large the focus of Islamic law is on the peaceful settlement of disputes." More specifically, he continues, "the preponderant focus in the Quran and the Traditions of Prophet Muhammad is on removing the causes of violence and war, the management and peaceful resolution of discord and conflicts . . . and the promotion of holistic development and peace. . . . [This] requires an intensive effort or struggle, or jihad, . . . against one's own propensity towards moral and rational lapses. . . . [The term] 'Jihad' is not 'holy war' as commonly misunderstood" (Husaini 1991, p. 50).

Islamist Groups in the Political Process

Even if many of the men and women who support Islamist groups do not seek governance based on a politicized conception of Islam, and do not themselves understand or practice their religion in this manner, it is very likely that political liberalization would, in the short run at least, increase the political influence of parties and movements that campaign under the slogan "Islam is the solution." These movements would probably be well represented in the national assembly, for example, which would not only give them a prominent platform for the expression of their views but would also enable them to make gains through participation in legislative bargaining. There is also a strong possibility that Muslim political groups would become members of the ruling coalition in some Arab countries. Thus, quite apart from the impact of popular religious attachments, it is necessary to ask about the implications for public policy, including foreign policy, of any increase in the power of Islamist political movements that would result from democratization.

Islamist opposition to Israel is easily documented. Even before the Islamic resurgence of the last two decades assumed major proportions, Muslim theologians were active in putting forth an Islamic case against the Jewish state, as when two dozen jurists, academicians and others gathered at Cairo's al-Azhar University in 1968 to offer their views on Israel and the Jews (Green 1976). A summary discussion of Islamist opposition to Zionism and Israel at the time of the recent Gulf crisis, and of Saddam's Hussein's attempt to exploit this opposition, is provided by Piscatori (1991, pp. 5–6). According to the 1987 statement of a leading religious scholar from Saudi Arabia, whom Piscatori quotes, "the Palestinian problem is an Islamic problem first and last. . . . [Muslims] must fight an Islamic jihad against the Jews until the land returns to its owners." Among the other examples that could be given is the May 1991 statement of a Muslim Brotherhood spokesman in Egypt, who criticized the announcement that Gulf Arab states might attend an international conference to discuss peace with Israel and then declared that his movement rejected "all political projects proposed to resolve the Palestinian issue" (Associated Press, May 28, 1991).

Nevertheless, while democracy in the Arab world would probably increase the political influence of Islamist movements, many of which are indeed opposed to peace with the Jewish state, other factors significantly reduce the challenge this presents to the proposition that Arab democratization would improve the prospects for a resolution of the conflict with Israel. At least three interrelated considerations are relevant in this connection: the heterogeneity of Muslim political groups and the opinions they hold, the variable nature of popular support for movements with Islamist tendencies, and the way that Muslim groups and movements may themselves be influenced by the opportunities associated with democracy.

First, there are major differences among Islamist groups, scholarly observers routinely making a distinction between "moderates" or "pragmatists" on the one hand and "radicals" on the other (Brumberg 1991, p. 190). According to one analyst, Muslim groups which are "legalist" or "political" differ from those that are "radical" or "militant" in that they renounce violence, emphasize incrementalism and "focus on propagating al-da'wa [the call] and on 'purifying' individual minds and social beliefs from traces of secularism" (Karawan 1992, p. 172). Moreover, this analysis continues, it is groups of the latter type, rather than those that are more extreme, which have been most effective in attracting followers and gaining influence. This is the case in Egypt, Syria, Jordan, Tunisia, Morocco and Algeria (ibid., p. 173).

An example of an influential but comparatively moderate Islamist movement is Tunisia's En-Nahda party, whose leader, Rashid al-Ghannoushi, writes that "what is not permitted to Muslims or non-Muslims is to resort to violence or aggression in resolving disputes" (1991, p. 179). A statement of moderation relating to Israel was recently offered by Hassan al-Turabi, a Sudanese scholar who is at present one of the most influential Islamist theologians in the Arab world. Al-Turabi told a group of Arab and American scholars during a dialogue-debate in 1992 that Islam can accept the existence of Israel so long as a political settlement is freely negotiated between Israelis and Palestinians, rather than imposed by force, and so long as this settlement respects the collective political rights of the latter people as well as the former (Lowrie 1993). Some observers question Turabi's sincerity, noting that the oppressive nature of the Islamist regime in Khartoum reveals a large gap between rhetoric and practice. From a theological perspective, however, it is highly significant that a prominent and influential Islamist scholar would publicly declare that there are conditions under which Islam would not oppose the existence of a Jewish state in the Middle East.

Other examples of the attitudes toward Israel held by Islamic movements are provided by Johannes J. G. Jansen, whose important study of political Islam in Egypt reveals militant opposition as well as moderation but, overall, makes clear that there is no single opinion which characterizes all Muslim groups. The Sufi movement, for example, shows little concern for Israel and Zionism (Jansen 1986, p. 67), and even the ideological leader of the radical faction that assassinated Anwar Sadat declared the liberation of Jerusalem and the Holy Land to be of secondary importance. It is more important to struggle against the enemy who is near than the enemy who is far away, he wrote; indeed, to fight Israel and other manifestations of imperialism is a useless waste of time: "We must concentrate on the real problem of Islam, the establishment of God's law, beginning in our own country" (ibid., p. 18). Thus, again, while the militant opposition to Israel expressed by some Muslim groups must be recognized and taken seriously, it is also important to avoid monolithic and unidimensional characterizations of political Islam. As expressed by Esposito and Piscatori (1991, p. 440), it is essential to recognize "the diversity of ideological interpretations and the even greater diversity of actual practice in Muslim societies."

Second, in addition to taking note of the diverse opinions expressed by Muslim movements, it is necessary to recognize that the relative strength of these movements is highly variable and that the popular support they enjoy at present may decline significantly in the future. One relevant consideration has already been emphasized: it is the existence of unresolved political, economic, and social problems, rather than cultural traditions or the religious faith of ordinary Arabs, that has produced most of the current support for movements with Islamist tendencies. As explained in one recent study, echoing judgments reported earlier, "we cannot adequately understand resurgent Islamic sociopolitical movements without taking into consideration the impact of a severe, multi-dimensional, and protracted crisis faced by many regimes in the Arab world" (Karawan 1992, p. 162). This is what one Arab sociologist has termed "azmatology," from *azmah*, the Arabic word for crisis (quoted in Dwyer 1991, p. 20). The implication of these assessments, as noted, is that Muslim political groups are strengthened by the absence of democracy and the lack of legitimate political opposition and, accordingly, they may lose much of their appeal should political systems become more open and governments more accountable.

A related point is that democracy and political liberalization may erode support for Muslim political groups by exposing the deep political and ideological cleavages that exist among those who proclaim Islam to be the solution to the

Arab world's problems. This is one of the conclusions of a recent study of Islamic "fundamentalisms" in four Arab states, the Israeli-occupied West Bank and Gaza Strip, Iran and Pakistan (Brumberg 1991, pp. 187, 195). Therefore, the strength of Islamic groups is variable and, despite some uncertainty, political openness may actually diminish the credibility and appeal of those who speak in terms of Islamic absolutism.

Perhaps most important of all in this connection is the different way that Islamist movements are likely to be viewed once they are permitted to enter the arena of legitimate politics and, if successful, to share responsibility for dealing with unresolved political and economic problems. Under these circumstances, Muslim groups will become less attractive as a vehicle for the expression of political discontent and rejection of the status quo. Even more important, their claim that Islam is the solution will lose much of its appeal if, as seems inevitable, the problems confronting ordinary men and women persist.

Support for these conclusions is provided by accounts of Jordan and Algeria, where there has been public dissatisfaction with the performance of Islamist politicians who acquired positions of national or local leadership after their parties scored successes in the elections of 1989 and 1990 respectively. In the latter case, for example, several recent studies report that leaders of the Islamic Salvation Front were criticized for serious shortcomings in the operation of local government and for failing to deliver on a number of the promises they made in the electoral campaign (Ibrahim 1990; Layachi and Haireche 1992, p. 79). In the former case, the Muslim Brotherhood became the dominant party in the Jordanian National Assembly following the elections of 1989 but lost support in the balloting of November 1993, retaining only 16 of the 32 seats it had held previously. Moreover, while diminished support for the Brotherhood was due to a variety of considerations including the Israeli-PLO agreement signed two months earlier, observers report that the party was also hurt by disenchantment with the performance of some of its cabinet ministers after 1989.

Yet another example is that of Sudan; Islamists have come to power and university students, once their passionate supporters, have largely turned against the ruling National Islamic Front (Miller 1992, p. 38). Thus, overall, as expressed by a senior Egyptian scholar, "the early results [of democratization] show that when Islamic activists gain power and in fact exercise it, they will not necessarily fare much better than the liberals before them, or the socialists before them or the nationalists before them. They will make their mistakes" (quoted in Wright 1991, p. 144).

Third, participation in the democratic process may alter to some degree the

views and leadership structure of Muslim political movements and, in particular, it may further moderate and "normalize" those Islamic groups that acquire
a share of legitimate political power. According to one knowledgeable American observer, Islamists in Egypt, Jordan and elsewhere have demonstrated that
they "can work within the system and adhere to the rules of the new political
game" (Wright 1991, p. 140).

This point is also made by other analysts, both Western and Arab. James P.
Piscatori asserts, for example, that many Islamists are not "unbending dogma-
tists" but, on the contrary, are "at ease with the complex political calculus of
means and ends, constraints and values which we in the West assume to be the
normal stuff of politics" (Piscatori 1991, p. 23). Thus, in the judgment of Ghas-
san Tueni, a seasoned Lebanese political observer, "Islamist movements are capable of being absorbed into the political mainstream" (quoted in Wright 1991,
p. 140). Indeed, according to Saad Eddin Ibrahim, the Egyptian scholar quoted
above, the Muslim Brotherhood in Egypt "is becoming a fairly respectable
movement, like Christian Democrats or Euro-Communists. They're learning
how to win and lose gracefully" (quoted in Miller 1992, p. 42). The same might
be said of Jordan, where parliamentarians affiliated with the Muslim Brotherhood opposed participation in peace talks with Israel but in June 1991 accepted
King Hussein's decision to name a new cabinet to lead the country into these
negotiations. Indeed, as noted, the party accepted its defeat in the elections of
November 1993, suggesting that Islamists who gain power through the ballot
box are not necessarily unwilling to surrender that power. This conclusion is
also suggested, admittedly at the local level, by the behavior of the Palestinian
Islamist movement, Hamas, during elections for a number of university councils and municipal committees in the West Bank and Gaza.

Another interesting illustration, although not linked specifically to democracy, is the action taken by Islamic leaders in Egypt following the conclusion
of that country's 1979 peace treaty with Israel. In May 1979, jurists and theologians at the Islamic al-Azhar University declared that the treaty was *not* contrary to Islamic law (Jansen 1986, p. 44; Hopwood 1982, p. 119), thereby contra-
dicting the view that had been expressed by scholars assembled at al-Azhar in
1968. At the theological level, this episode reinforces the point made earlier, that
Islam is subject to diverse interpretations and that widely differing views may
be expressed by sincere and knowledgeable Muslims, including different Muslim scholars and different Islamic groups. Even more important, however, the
episode also shows that those who speak in the name of Islam frequently behave as do secular politicians, making bargains, exchanging favors, and taking

positions that are at least partly shaped by instrumental considerations. The issue, then, is not whether the "true" Islamic position was expressed at al-Azhar in 1968 or in 1979, it is rather that the attitudes and behavior of Muslims and even Islamists are variable and cannot be separated from their social and political context.

These observations do not invalidate the arguments of those who see serious challenges and even dangers in the opening that democratization in the Arab world may give to Islamist political movements. They do suggest that such concerns may be exaggerated, however, or at least that they offer only a partial view of the possible results of a genuine political opening. Thus, challenges and dangers notwithstanding, the conclusion to be drawn from the present analysis is that the overall effect of political liberalization and democracy would be much more positive than negative with respect to the Arab-Israeli conflict. Democracy would make governments more accountable to ordinary citizens, whose greatest concern is with performance in the domestic policy arena and whose cultural and religious orientations do not appear inhospitable to a settlement with Israel based on compromise and mutual accommodation. In addition, governments themselves would be subject to structural and normative constraints that push away from the use of military force in international disputes. Equally important, they would have less reason to try to deflect public anger or enhance their legitimacy through involvement in foreign adventures. Finally, the appeal of radical Islamist groups would diminish as leaders become more accountable to their people. Increased attention to the concerns of ordinary men and women would reduce popular anger and diminish the tendency to express opposition to the status quo by supporting Muslim political movements. In addition, the Islamists' own participation in the political mainstream would force them to be more pragmatic while demonstrating that there is no magical "Islamic formula" for solving the country's problems.

None of this alone would solve the Arab-Israeli conflict. A resolution of the conflict depends in the final analysis on the willingness of Israel to relinquish land for peace and accept the exercise of Palestinian self-determination, and on a corresponding Palestinian willingness to recognize Israel's right to exist on a portion of the territory of Palestine. But the prospect for movement toward this sort of compromise itself depends, in significant measure, on the broader context of Middle East politics and international relations, on a reduction in the threat of war in particular and on the elimination of popular grievances that promote extremism more generally. For this reason, given the way that democratization in the Arab world would most probably affect the political, ideological and security environment of the Middle East, it appears that greater political liberalization and democracy in key Arab countries would not diminish, and would probably significantly increase, the prospects for a peaceful settlement of the conflict between Israelis, Palestinians and other Arabs.

Appendix: Public Opinion Data from Egypt and Kuwait

Public opinion surveys carried out in Egypt and Kuwait in mid-1988 deal with issues of religion and politics and also include questions pertaining to the Arab-Israeli conflict. Two samples were drawn in Kuwait, one of Kuwaiti citizens and one of Palestinians residing in the country.

Stratified samples of adults were selected in Cairo and Kuwait. All respondents are Sunni Muslims; Egyptian and Palestinian Christians and Kuwaiti Shiites were not included. Each sample includes both men and women, and each is also heterogeneous with respect to age, education, socioeconomic status and neighborhood. Although better-educated individuals are somewhat overrepresented, the samples are generally representative of the active, adult, urban population. The distribution of each sample with respect to gender, age and education is presented below.

The surveys were carried out under the direction of Professor Jamal Al-Su-

	Total (N = 885)	Egyptians (N = 292)	Kuwaitis (N = 300)	Palestinians (N = 293)
Gender:				
Male	51%	52%	48%	54%
Female	49	48	52	46
Age:				
Under 30	62	55	67	68
30–39	29	32	27	18
40 and over	9	13	6	14
Education:				
Intermediate or less	19	25	13	19
High school	28	27	28	26
Some post-secondary	22	17	28	23
University	31	31	31	32

waidi of the United Arab Emirates University. Interviews were conducted by teams of research assistants, or "intermediaries," who were selected on the basis of previous experience in survey research administration. Intermediaries were also given a four-day orientation and the survey instrument was pretested in both countries.

The survey items pertaining to Israel and the Arab-Israeli conflict, listed in the text and used in the construction of tables 1 and 3, are strongly correlated with one another. This gives evidence of their reliability and also increases confidence in their validity. In addition, factor analysis shows that they load highly on a larger battery of items pertaining to foreign policy issues, which includes questions about relations with the United States.

As discussed in the text, factor analysis was used to measure two distinct dimensions of attitudes toward Islam, one dealing with personal piety and social salience and the other with the relationship between religion and politics and attitudes toward Islamic political organizations. The items and the strength of their association with each factor are shown below.

Item	Factor 1	Factor 2
	(Personal Piety/ Social Salience)	(Religion and Politics/ Islamic Groups)
30	**.72945**	.00153
32	**.68098**	.13009
31	**.67403**	.21164
15	**.66808**	.22825
36	**.55939**	.11639
38	.01436	**.80070**
62	.12740	**.76350**
72	.16159	**.61355**
69	.32806	**.53887**

(1) *Personal Piety and the Social Salience of Islam*
  30. Would you support anyone in your family who wants to study in a religious institution?
  32. How often do you refer to religious teachings when making important decisions about your life?
  31. Do you support the application of Islamic law in social life?

15. Do you support the application of Islamic law to deal with civil and criminal matters?
36. How often do you read the Quran?

(2) *Religion and Politics and Islamic Political Groups*
38. Do you agree or disagree that religion and politics should be separate?
62. What do you think of the following statement: religious practice must be kept private and must be separated from sociopolitical life?
72. Do you support current organized Islamic movements?
69. What do you think of the religious awakening now taking place in society?

REFERENCES

Amawi, Abla. 1992. "Democracy Dilemmas in Jordan." *Middle East Report* 174 (January/February), pp. 26–29.

Anderson, Lisa. 1992. "Remaking the Middle East: The Prospects for Democracy and Stability." *Ethics and International Relations* 6, pp. 163–78.

Babst, Dean V. 1972. "A Force for Peace." *Industrial Research* 14 (April), pp. 55–58.

Barnett, Michael. 1991. "From Cold Wars to Resource Wars: The Coming Decline in U.S.-Israeli Relations?" *Jerusalem Journal of International Relations* 13 (September), pp. 99–119.

Ben-Yishai, Ron. 1988. "What Do the Generals Think about Territorial Compromise." *Yediot Aharonot* (supplement), June 10.

Brumberg, Daniel. 1991. "Islamic Fundamentalism, Democracy, and the Gulf War." *Islamic Fundamentalisms and the Gulf Crisis*, ed. James Piscatori. Boston: American Academy of Arts and Sciences.

Chan, Steve. 1984. "Mirror, Mirror on the Wall: Are the Freer Countries More Pacific." *Journal of Conflict Resolution* 28 (December), pp. 617–48.

Doyle, Michael W. 1983. "Kant, Liberal Legacies, and Foreign Affairs [Part 1]." *Philosophy and Public Affairs* 12, no. 3 (Summer), pp. 205–35.

Dwyer, Kevin. 1991. *Arab Voices*. Berkeley: University of California Press.

Ember, Carol A., Melvin Ember, and Bruce M. Russett. 1992. "Peace between Participatory Polities: A Cross-Cultural Test of the 'Democracies Rarely Fight Each Other' Hypothesis." *World Politics* 44 (July), pp. 573–99.

Entelis, John. 1988. "Algeria under Chadli: Liberalization without Democratization or, Perestroika, Yes; Glasnost, No." *Middle East Insight* (Fall), pp. 47–64.

Esposito, John L. 1991. "Democracy in the Middle East." Testimony at a U.S. Senate hearing, May 4.

Esposito, John L., and James P. Piscatori. 1991. "Democratization and Islam." *Middle East Journal* 45 (Summer), pp. 427–40.

Al-Ghannoushi, Rashid. 1991. "Hukuk al-Muwatana fil Islam." In *The Renaissance Party in Tunisia: The Quest for Freedom and Democracy.* Washington, DC: AMC.

Green, D. F. 1976. *Arab Theologians on Jews and Israel.* 3rd. ed. Geneva: Editions de l'Avenir.

Halasa, Serene. 1991. "Arab Scholars Call for New Order Based on Democracy, Urge End to Iraq Sanctions." *Jordan Times,* May 30–31.

Hopwood, Derek. 1982. *Egypt: Politics and Society, 1945–1981.* London: Allen & Unwin.

Hudson, Michael C. 1990. "The Democratization Process in the Arab World: An Assessment." Paper presented at the annual meeting of the American Political Science Association, San Francisco, August 30–September 2.

———. 1991. "After the Gulf War: Prospects for Democratization in the Arab World." *Middle East Journal* 45 (Summer), pp. 407–26.

Husaini, S. Waqar Ahmed. 1991. "An Islamic Assessment of Development and Belligerence in the Sub-Himalayan Countries: Policy Implications for India, Pakistan, Bangladesh, USA, and Global Development Planning." Working paper from the Hoover Institution, Stanford University.

Ibrahim, Youssef. 1990. "Militant Muslims Grow Stronger as Algeria's Economy Grows Weaker." *New York Times,* June 25.

———. 1992. "PLO Is Facing Growing Discontent." *New York Times,* April 5.

Jansen, Johannes J. G. 1986. *The Neglected Duty: The Creed of Sadat's Assassins and Islamic Resurgence in the Middle East.* London: Macmillan.

"Jordan and the 1990 Gulf Crisis." 1990. Amman, Jordan: World Affairs Council.

Karawan, Ibrahim A. 1992. " 'Reislamization Movements' According to Kepel: On Striking Back and Striking Out." *Contention* 4 (Fall), pp. 161–79.

Kemp, Geoffrey. 1991. "Conditions for a Stable and Lasting Peace in the Middle East." *Perspectives on War and Peace* 8 (Spring), pp. 1–6.

Khouri, Rami G. 1990. "The Arab Dream Won't Be Denied." *New York Times,* December 15.

———. 1991. "A Lesson in Middle East History and Humanity." *Jordan Times,* May 28.

Kilgour, D. Marc. 1991. "Domestic Political Structure and War: A Game-Theoretic Approach." *Journal of Conflict Resolution* 35 (June), pp. 266–84.

Krämer, Gudrun. 1992. "Liberalization and Democracy in the Arab World." *Middle East Report* 174 (January/February), pp. 22–25.

Lake, David A. 1992. "Powerful Pacifists: Democratic States and War." *American Political Science Review* 86 (March), pp. 24–37.

Layachi, Azzedine. 1992. "Government, Legitimacy and Democracy in Algeria." *Maghreb Report* (January/February).

Layachi, Azzedine, and Abdel-kader Haireche. 1992. "National Development and Political Protest in the Maghreb Countries." *Arab Studies Quarterly* 14 (Spring/Summer), pp. 69–92.

Lowrie, Arthur L. 1993. "Islam, Democracy, the State and the West: A Round Table with Dr. Hassan Turabi." Monograph of World and Islam Studies Enterprise. Tampa, FL.

Maoz, Zeev, and Nasrin Abdolali. 1989. "Regime Types and International Conflict, 1816–1976." *Journal of Conflict Resolution* 33 (March), pp. 3–35.

Maoz, Zeev, and Bruce M. Russett. 1991. "Normative and Structural Causes of Peace." Paper presented at the annual meeting of the Peace Studies Society, Ann Arbor, MI, November 15–17.

———. 1992. "Alliance, Contiguity, Wealth, and Political Stability: Is the Lack of Conflict among Democracies a Statistical Artifact?" *International Interactions* 17 (February), pp. 245–68.

Miller, Judith. 1992. "The Islamic Wave." *New York Times Magazine*, May 31.

Morgan, T. Clifton, and Sally Howard Campbell. 1991. "Domestic Structure, Decisional Constraints, and War: So Why Kant Democracies Fight?" *Journal of Conflict Resolution*, 35, no. 2 (June), pp. 187–211.

Mueller, John E. 1989. *Retreat from Doomsday: The Obsolescence of Major War*. New York: Basic Books.

Munson, Henry. 1992. "Islamist Political Movements in the Middle East." Paper prepared for a USAID project on "Politico-Religious Movements and Development in the Near East," June 1992.

Muslih, Muhammad, and Augustus Richard Norton. 1991. "The Need for Arab Democracy." *Foreign Policy* 83 (Summer), pp. 3–19.

Paul, James. 1984. "States of Emergency: The Riots in Tunisia and Morocco." *MERIP Reports* 127 (October).

Piscatori, James P. 1991. "Religion and Realpolitik: Islamic Responses to the Gulf War." In *Islamic Fundamentalisms and the Gulf Crisis*, ed. James Piscatori. Boston: American Academy of Arts and Sciences.

Rosenthal, A. M. 1991. "Neither God Nor Infidel." *New York Times*, February 15.

Rothstein, Robert L. 1991. "Change and Continuity in the Middle East." *Washington Quarterly* 14 (Summer), pp. 139–60.

Rummel, R. J. 1983. "Libertarianism and International Violence." *Journal of Conflict Resolution* 27 (March), pp. 27–71.

Russett, Bruce M. 1989. "Democracy and Peace." In Bruce M. Russett, Harvey Starr, and Richard Stoll, eds. *Choices in World Politics: Sovereignty and Interdependence.* New York: W. H. Freeman.

Small, Melvin, and J. David Singer. 1976. "The War-Proneness of Democratic Regimes." *Jerusalem Journal of International Relations* 1, pp. 50–69.

Suleiman, Michael W. 1987. "Attitudes, Values and the Political Process in Morocco." In I. William Zartman, ed. *The Political Economy of Morocco.* New York: Praeger.

Tessler, Mark. 1986. "Explaining the 'Surprises' of King Hassan II: The Linkage between Domestic and Foreign Policy in Morocco; Part I: Tensions in North Africa in the Mid-1980's." *Universities Field Staff International Reports* 38.

———. 1991a. "Anger and Governance in the Arab World: Lessons from the Maghrib and Implications for the West." *Jerusalem Journal of International Relations* 13 (September), pp. 7–33.

———. 1991b. "The Impact of the Intifada on Israeli Political Thinking." In Rex Brynen, ed., *Echoes of the Intifada: Regional Repercussions of the Palestinian-Israeli Conflict.* Boulder, CO: Westview.

———. 1992. "The Origins of Popular Support for Islamist Movements: A Political Economy Analysis." Paper prepared for a USAID project on "Politico-Religious Movements and Development in the Near East," June 1992.

———. 1993. "The Alienation of Urban Youth." In I. William Zartman and W. Mark Habeeb, eds. *Polity and Society in Contemporary North Africa.* Boulder, CO: Westview.

Vandewalle, Dirk. 1988a. *Autopsy of a Revolt: The October Riots in Algeria.* Hanover, NH: Institute of Current World Affairs.

———. 1988b. "From the New State to the New Era: Toward a Second Republic in Tunisia." *Middle East Journal* 42, pp. 602–20.

———. 1989/90. "Ben Ali's New Tunisia." *Universities Field Staff International Reports* 8.

Weede, Erich. 1984. "Democracy and War Involvement." *Journal of Conflict Resolution* 28 (December), pp. 649–64.

Wright, Robin. 1991. "Islam's New Political Face." *Current History* (January).

8

DOMESTIC POLITICAL VIOLENCE, STRUCTURAL CONSTRAINTS, AND ENDURING RIVALRIES IN THE MIDDLE EAST, 1948–1988

ZEEV MAOZ

Introduction

THE MIDDLE EAST has been—perhaps more than any other single regional sub-system—the site of some of the most manifest international rivalries in the post-World War II era.[1] Given the way the international system has evolved, and with the apparent resolution or disappearance of most significant super-power rivalries in the late eighties and early nineties, the international rivalries in the Middle East stand out as an island of international concern. Indeed, over the period from 1946 to 1992, nine out of a total of twenty-one interstate wars occurred among Middle East states. More importantly, four of the five international wars that broke out in the 1980s and 1990s took place in the Middle East.[2] These were also among the longest and bloodiest wars of the nuclear era.

The end of the U.S.-Soviet rivalry, and the concomitant disappearance of the U.S.-China and Soviet-Chinese conflicts, reduced substantially the risks of global conflagration. Yet the dissolution of the Soviet empire may well have some negative consequences in terms of the risks associated with the escalation of enduring regional rivalries. For one thing, the likelihood of nuclear prolif-eration has apparently increased as a result of the deterioration of centralized control over nuclear weapons in the political entities that once formed the So-viet Union (Mearsheimer 1991). Second, the restraining influence that the ma-jor powers had on their regional clients during the Cold War has diminished substantially (Miller 1992). The emerging global order may be perceived by some regional actors as directly harming some of their vital interests. This may prompt such actors to initiate conflicts that would impose faits accomplis on the major powers, and these could, in turn, serve as a basis for renewed super-power intervention on behalf of global stability.

One important feature of the dramatic international system changes during the eighties is the influence of domestic factors on system transformation at the global level. Economic and social pressures were instrumental in bringing about fundamental domestic and foreign policy reforms in the Soviet Union during the Gorbachev era. Renewed nationalistic aspirations led to the disintegration of states that had been held under authoritarian rule in the post-World War II era. The process of global democratization is perhaps the most distinguishing political characteristic of the 1980s. This systemic transformation may well represent an unprecedented historical process: a revolutionary change in the global system that took place without a major war.

This change may be due more to domestic political forces than to any other cause, a striking conclusion in light of the major theoretical works that influenced the scholarly literature in international relations during the period: most principally the neorealist writings of such people as Waltz (1979, 1986) and Gilpin (1981). This literature focused on system-level forces and structural constraints on foreign policy behavior. It also emphasized the key role of international war in inducing systemic change.

In light of the prevailing international developments, and the apparent doubt these processes cast on many of the key theoretical themes of the eighties, it may be instructive to reassess the impact of domestic processes and structures on the key enduring rivalries in the Middle East. Accordingly, this study addresses the following three issues:

(1) What are the key patterns of the major international rivalries in the Middle East in the nuclear era?

(2) Can some of the key features of these rivalries be accounted for in terms of domestic structures and processes of the actors participating in them?

(3) If the answer to question two above is positive, what are the implications of these findings for the future of these rivalries and the ability of the indigenous actors or major powers to manage and resolve them?

Domestic Politics and International Conflict:
A Theoretical Overview

In contrast to the top-down approach of systems theory (Maoz 1990, pp. 547–48) that was prominent in international relations literature after World War II, there is a body of literature that explores international processes as the outcome of intrastate structures and processes. Some of these works focus on the relationship between political, economic, and social change in states and those states' foreign policy behavior. Other works look at the potential effects of the structural characteristics of states on their foreign policy behavior. Finally, a third body of literature attempts to understand national behavior as the result of the microlevel decision-making processes of political leaders. The third body of research has produced a large number of empirical studies but only a few of the large-N type. Moreover, though there is a generally accepted view that international processes are the result of chains of national choices, there has been almost no empirical application of this logic (Maoz 1990, pp. 374–77; Maoz and Astorino 1992). Therefore, the concluding section of this study will consider the implications of the data presented here for that view.

The general idea of the two other bodies of literature is that national or dyadic factors affect systemic processes. These factors can be highly dynamic or fairly static in nature. Dynamic domestic factors include processes such as rapid government changes, coups, social protests, changes in rates of unemployment, and so forth. Domestic factors of a more static nature include such structures as the type of political system, the degree of constraint on the executive, the social and ethnic composition of society, and the market structures of the national economy.

Until recently, the literature on domestic politics and foreign policy could be grouped into two rather general categories. The first category focused on domestic processes and international behavior. The second category focused on domestic structure and international behavior. The literature on domestic processes and national behavior covers dynamic relationships between domestic and international behaviors. The work on domestic structure and international behavior focuses on fairly static aspects of this relationship.

Space constraints preclude elaborate discussion here of the key works associated with each of these bodies of literature. There are several excellent critical surveys that can be consulted by the interested reader: Stohl 1980; Russett 1983, 1990; Levy 1988, 1989; Ray 1992. I would like to outline some of the main trends and puzzles associated with these bodies of literature, as well as a seeming convergence of empirical findings in recent years around some key points.

Efforts to relate domestic processes to external foreign policy behavior have met with mixed success. The central efforts of this genre were designed to test different versions of the "scapegoat" hypothesis by finding a systematic relationship between domestic conflict and the foreign conflict behavior of states. Until very recently, no consistent findings confirming this hypothesis had been reported. Levy (1989) argued that there is a wide gap between the political science studies that have made use of quantitative aggregate data and the historical studies that have uncovered numerous examples of a systematic relationship between these two processes.[3] He suggested that the problem may lie in the realm of quantitative analysis, specifically in model specification, in the focus on cross-sectional rather than on longitudinal analysis, and so forth.

However, more recent research has revealed some increasingly persistent patterns. The first stems from a general observation, made originally by Wilkenfeld (1968), that different political systems exhibit different forms of relationships between domestic and external conflict. In democracies, a fairly persistent linkage has been found between decline in the leadership's public popularity and conflict initiation. (See a discussion of this literature in Russett 1990, pp. 20–51.) A similar link has frequently been posited for the relationship between economic stagnation or decline and conflict initiation in democratic political systems. Finally, it has been found that conflict participation patterns in democracies seem to be linked to electoral cycles (Barzilai and Russett 1990). In authoritarian states, conflict initiation patterns seem to follow periods of economic upswing.

A second interesting set of results stems from analysis of the relationship between state creation processes, domestic political change, and conflict behavior patterns. Revolutionary state formation and regime transformation processes lead to high levels of conflict involvement of states in the first few years following a change, but evolutionary state formation and evolutionary processes of political change in existing states are followed by lower-than-average patterns of conflict involvement in those states. Patterns of revolutionary state formation seem to evoke patterns of spreading contagious conflict in the system (Maoz 1989).

Finally, the relationship between domestic politics and international conflict involvement patterns is not unidirectional. Conflict involvement, particularly war participation, can profoundly affect economics and domestic politics. War participation has important state-building functions, for it strengthens the coercive capacity of state institutions (Gurr 1988). War participation also evokes strong economic growth patterns that supersede prewar levels (Organski and Kugler 1980; Rasler and Thompson 1989).

The conclusions concerning relationships between regime types and patterns of international conflict are clearly among the most significant scientific contributions of the last decade. After a fairly long period of debate on this issue, a general convergence seems to have taken place among scholars regarding two results linking democracy to conflict. The conclusions drawn are that (1) democracies are about as conflict and war-prone as are other political systems, but (2) democracies have rarely clashed with each other in militarized conflict and—according to some reasonable criteria—have not fought each other in a full-scale war during the last 177 years (Small and Singer 1976; Rummel 1983, 1985; Chan 1984; Doyle 1986; Maoz and Abdolali 1989; Bremer 1992a, 1992b). These results appear to be extremely robust and nonspurious, that is, they seem to hold up even when controls are introduced for potentially confounding factors (Maoz and Russett 1991, 1993).

Yet consensus on the validity of these findings does not translate into consensus on an explanation. Although arguments against a "democratic peace" result have been undermined, a positive explanation of the phenomenon requires addressing the causes of peace between democracies. This explanation, as Maoz and Russett (1993) have pointed out, must simultaneously account for both aspects of the democratic peace result. Initial efforts to explain the democratic peace result focused on two fundamental models: structural and normative (Morgan and Campbell 1991; Morgan and Schewbach 1992; Maoz and Russett 1993).

The structural model argues that the complexity of political mobilization in democracies imposes considerable constraints on executive decisions to resort to force. These constraints can be circumvented when democracies face authoritarian opponents because of the fear that the latter could exploit the hesitations of the former to carry out surprise attacks. However, when the opponent is another democracy, it is impossible to avoid a lengthy process of persuading the public, the legislature, and a wide variety of interest groups of the need to resort to force. Because the opposing democracy faces similar problems, time allows for a peaceful solution to the conflict.

The normative model claims that political systems externalize—to the extent possible—the norms of political conduct developed within their own state. Hence democracies attempt to base their international dealings on notions of free competition, resolution of political conflict through bargaining, negotiation, and compromise. Their attitudes toward opponents are based on notions that the rights of losers in political contests are guaranteed. On the other hand, authoritarian norms are based on zero-sum notions of political competition where opposition must be suppressed and eliminated and conflicts are decided by the elimination of the opponent. Hence, in an anarchic international system, confrontations between democratic and authoritarian norms are dominated by the latter because the resort to democratic norms in such situations can be exploited by the authoritarian state. Yet, in conflicts between two democracies, both states are willing and able to exert their "natural" norms. Hence, most disputes between democracies do not even reach a militarized level involving the threat, display, or use of military force. And almost none of the conflicts that reach the militarized level escalate to all-out war.

Initial tests of these two models suggested that both are supported by the data. However, the influence of factors associated with the normative model on levels of conflict and conflict escalation appears to be more robust than levels of structural constraints (Maoz and Russett 1993). Some implications of the normative model regarding the ways democracies resolve conflicts with each other also suggests that normative factors lead them to increased use of international mediation (Dixon 1993).

This review of the literature suggests that recent research on the relationships between domestic and international processes has apparently resulted in a consensus that domestic structures and processes have profound implications for international politics. These conclusions are related to the revolutionary changes in the international system, such as the end of the Cold War, the global process of democratization, the apparent institutionalization of international norms, and the growing significance of economic, national, and ethnic factors in world politics. The following section will discuss the implications of both the theoretical and empirical shifts for the Middle East.

Constraints, Norms, and Middle East Politics

At first glance, the empirical patterns discussed in the previous section would appear to have little relevance for the various conflicts that have plagued the Middle East subsystem in the post–World War II era. To begin with, the major conflicts in the region seem to be rooted in national struggles, territorial disputes, and—during the Cold War—strategic competition between the superpowers. Moreover, during that period, Israel appeared to be the only democracy in the region.[4] Hence the hypothesis suggesting the lack of war and the relative absence of conflict between democracies cannot be tested on the Middle East conflict.[5]

Nonetheless, it is possible to use certain aspects of the relationship between domestic and international conflict, as well as other aspects underlying the various explanations of the democratic peace phenomenon, to analyze some of the enduring rivalries in the Middle East. The following discussion is an attempt to understand the ups and downs of two of the major Arab-Israeli rivalries during the period from 1948 to 1986.

One key characteristic of the Middle East subsystem is the endemic instability that characterizes many of its member states. The Middle East is suffused as much by internal as by international conflict. It is therefore natural to link the two processes. Recent studies show a consistent relationship between revolutionary political change within states and international conflict (Maoz 1989) and emphasize that states which undergo such change are not necessarily the initiators of conflict. On the contrary, they may become victims of conflict initiated by other states. Neighbors as well as more distant powers: (a) may fear that the revolutionary changes that occurred in the focal state could spill over into their own societies, or (b) see an opportunity for cheap and successful conflict initiation due to a perception that the military power or political will of the focal state has been weakened by such changes.

This finding seems logically linked to conclusions about the causes of the democratic peace phenomenon. Maoz and Russett (1991) found that political stability, measured in terms of the number of years a political system has preserved its structure, is the only factor that can be used to predict a relative lack of conflict, both between democracies and between democracies and other political systems (or between nondemocracies and other nondemocracies). This stability can be interpreted strategically or normatively. The strategic interpretation holds that conflict initiation against a highly stable state—democracy or nondemocracy—is perceived as a far more costly venture than conflict initiation against a highly unstable state. Stable states seem to be better equipped to resist the challenge than nonstable states.

The normative (cultural) explanation is that the longer a political regime persists in a state, the more likely it is that its norms become rooted in that society. If these are democratic norms emphasizing free competition, preservation of losers' rights, and peaceful resolution of conflicts, then the constraints on the resort to force increase markedly.

To understand how these factors may have worked in the Arab-Israeli conflict, we can examine the two key interstate rivalries in that conflict: the Israeli-

Israeli–Egyptian Conflict Interactions
and Egyptian Regime, 1948–1988

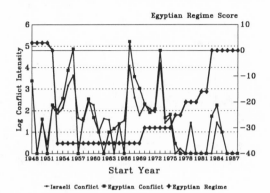

Fig. 1: Israeli-Egyptian Interactions
Sources: Conflict Intensity: compiled by the author; Regime Score: Gurr et al.
1989

Egyptian rivalry and the Israeli-Syrian rivalry. The conflict interaction patterns of these rivalries are depicted in figs. 1 and 2.[6]

Figures 1 and 2 show the log intensity of Israeli-Egyptian and Israeli-Syrian
conflict interactions,[7] measured on the left-hand Y-axis. The regime scores of
Egypt and Syria, respectively, are measured on the right-hand Y-axis.[8] Not surprisingly, conflict interactions in both the Israeli-Egyptian and Israeli-Syrian
rivalries appear to exhibit high levels of reciprocity. This clearly suggests a
great deal of strategic responsiveness, which implies that a significant portion
of the variance in the interactions depicted by these figures can be accounted
for by the opponent's behavior. Moreover, the major peaks in this interaction
correspond with the five Israeli-Egyptian and four Israeli-Syrian wars. However, if we look at the over-time peaks and valleys of these two rivalries, and
relate them to domestic changes in the participant states, some interesting observations can be made.

Let us consider the Egyptian-Israeli rivalry first. In general, both Egypt and
Syria responded to the violent emergence of the State of Israel in 1948. Both
opportunities and threats were involved in this intervention. A Jewish state represented a challenge to the image of commitment to the Palestinians, but there
was also the threat that Abdullah of Jordan might have his way if Egypt or
Syria failed to get involved. The apparently weak Jewish foothold in Palestine
presented an opportunity. Following the war, and as long as the constitutional

Israeli–Syrian Interactions and Syrian Regime, 1948–1988

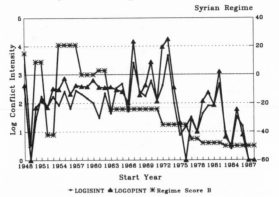

Fig. 2: Israeli-Syrian Interactions
Sources: Conflict Intensity: compiled by the author; Regime Score: Gurr et al.
1989

monarchy in Egypt held, the level of conflict between Egypt and Israel was fairly low. This level rose immediately following the 1952 coup and escalated sharply in 1954 when Nasser took over. This coincides with the sharp change in the regime score of Egypt shown in fig. 1. Levels of conflict interaction remain high up to the Sinai war of 1956.

While the 1956 war helped settle a number of outstanding strategic issues between Egypt and Israel, it also served to establish Nasser's internal status in Egypt (and to a large extent across the Arab Middle East). However, Middle East turmoil in the late fifties is also reflected in a number of hostile interactions, involving virtually no casualties, on the Israeli-Egyptian border. Most of these incidents consist of reports concerning aerial incursions for intelligence purposes. The intensity of conflict remained relatively low up to 1967. The termination of the Six Day War led to some reduction in intensity, yet conflict intensity remained relatively high through the death of Nasser in October 1970 and the internal struggle over his succession that ended in May of 1971 with the total victory of Sadat. The intensity of the conflict again exhibits a sharp rise in 1973, not surprisingly after renewed riots early that year in Egypt. Subsequently, levels of conflict drop steadily, with the last upswing following Sadat's assassination and peaking just prior to the Taba settlement.[9]

Let us now trace the Israeli-Syrian patterns. In the early fifties, when Syria exhibited some of the characteristics of a democracy, there are numerous clashes, mostly of a low-level and contained nature. As Syria began to experience frequent political upheaval, levels of conflict increased markedly. Though war did not break out during this period, levels of hostility remained high. The 1962 coup resulted in heightened levels of hostility in the conflict, correlating quite closely with the high levels of instability inside Syria (Bar-Siman-Tov 1983). Following the Six Day War, the leadership struggle inside the Ba'ath party was accompanied by frequent clashes between the two states, culminating in the futile Syrian intervention in the September 1970 Jordanian-Palestinian civil war.[10] As Assad's regime stabilized, the level of conflict dropped considerably in the late seventies and early eighties, with a new peak during the 1982 war in Lebanon, which became the major area of conflict between the two states after the mid-seventies.

Intuitively, therefore, there appears to be a solid factual basis for the argument that domestic and external conflict patterns are closely related. It remains to be seen just how these patterns are supported by a more rigorous empirical analysis. This analysis is guided by the following hypotheses:

(1) The intensity of interaction in the Arab-Israeli conflict is affected by prior levels of domestic instability.

(2) Levels of hostility in the Arab-Israeli conflict are affected by changes in domestic political systems. The move toward democracy by these states reduces the intensity of conflict interaction.

These hypotheses stem from review of the domestic-external literature and can be used to examine whether and to what extent the more general findings on domestic-external linkage and on democracy and conflict apply to the Arab-Israeli conflict. The tests of these hypotheses are discussed below.

Research Design

Enduring Rivalries

The study of enduring international rivalries (EIRs) has received considerable attention from students of conflict over the last few years (Diehl and Goertz 1993). A small set of dyads has accounted for a substantial portion of conflict activity in the international system over the last two centuries, and these dyads have also tended to generate considerable conflict in their environment as other states on the periphery of the conflict have become involved from time to time. An enduring international rivalry is a set of repeated militarized interstate disputes between the same set of states over time. EIR disputes must meet all of the following conditions:

(1) The Severity Condition: There must be at least five reciprocated Militarized Interstate Disputes (MIDs) between the same two states, each lasting at least thirty days.[11]

(2) The Durability Condition: There must be at least twenty-five years between the outbreak of the first dispute and the termination of the last dispute.

(3) The Continuity Condition: The gap between any two disputes (the termination date of the first dispute and the start date of the second dispute) must not exceed ten years. Alternatively, if the gap between two disputes is wider than ten years, two disputes between the same states will be considered as part of the same EIR only if the territorial domain and the issues at stake remain unresolved and there is at least one dispute within a period of twenty-five years (Huth, Jones, and Maoz 1990; Diehl and Goertz 1993; Geller and Jones 1991).

In the Middle East, the Egyptian-Israeli and Syrian-Israeli dyads clearly meet these conditions.[12] Hence we focus on patterns of interaction within those rivalries.

Spatial and Temporal Domain

The empirical domain is clearly suggested by the choice of EIRs for the present investigation. The entire period of the dyads' existence seems to provide a suitable time frame for analysis. This is evident from the fact that despite the peace treaty between Israel and Egypt, a certain level of conflict activity is present, though the number of fatalities due to this rivalry is almost nil. These have obviously been the bloodiest and most severe rivalries in the Middle East, and they therefore suggest themselves as candidates for analysis.

Data Sources

This study relies on a number of different sources for its data. The sources are specified in relation to the relevant variables cited here.

Conflict data.

The conflict dataset was generated by the author as part of an international effort to collect systematic data on enduring international rivalries. The conflict dataset is based on Egyptian, Syrian, and Israeli sources, principally daily newspapers, that list conflict events. The general format for collection of incident data is that used by the Correlates of War project to generate the Militarized Interstate Dispute dataset (Gochman and Maoz 1984). Specifically, each incident is listed in terms of the start date, initiator, target, type of actions undertaken by each,[13] outcome of incident, fatalities to each party, and whether or not there was a formal settlement of the incident. Subsequently, all incidents are aggregated into distinct disputes, following the coding rules specified by Gochman and Maoz (1984).

Political regime and political structure data.

The principal source for the data on political structure, changes therein, and regime types is Gurr et al. (1989). This general dataset contains yearly coding of key variables describing states' political systems, changes in these variables, and the nature of these changes.

Domestic conflict data.

The data on domestic political events were derived from the *World Handbook of Political and Social Indicators* (Taylor and Jodice 1983), which contains figures on deaths from domestic political violence, on political executions, armed attacks, protest demonstrations, and riots. Data on political deaths and political executions have been updated following the coding instructions in the original source, using data from Keesing's *Contemporary Archives* for the 1983–88 period.

Definition of Variables

Intensity of conflict interactions.

Each dispute in a relationship is composed of a set of incidents wherein one state initiates the threat, display, or use of force. These incidents are rated on a scale of hostility from low hostility (0) to war (100). There are eighteen types of military confrontation actions (MCAs), and each is given a level of hostility on that scale.[14] Rather than aggregate over the course of the entire dispute, all incidents occurring in the course of a given year are aggregated by level of hostility. This measure reflects how conflicted the interaction is during a given year. Two continuous measures have been developed to reflect the intensity of interactions. The first variable (Intensity of Conflict) is measured in the year following the incident. Each action initiated by a state during an incident is given a scale value from 1 (threat to blockade—low severity) to 100 (war—high severity), based on the scale developed by Maoz (1982, pp. 217-25). Using this severity value, the formula given below is applied to measure the raw intensity (CI) of an incident.[15]

The raw intensity of an incident is aggregated to an annual figure which is simply the sum of all CIs that have started in a given year.

The robustness of the results has been tested using the Militarized Interstate Dispute dataset (Gochman and Maoz 1984). For each year, the dichotomous variable is coded zero (no new dispute eruption that year), or one (at least one new dispute erupting that year).

Regime type.

This measure is discussed in great detail in Maoz and Russett (1991, 1993) and will therefore be mentioned only briefly here. In general, this measure is based on the Polity II dataset and incorporates three distinct variables that capture the nature of the regime and its clarity: the degree of democracy (scale ranging from 0 = none to 10 = maximal), the degree of autocracy (same scale values), and power concentration (same scale values). The principal idea is based on the notion discussed by Gurr (1974) that regime type need not be a linear scale: a state's political system can possess simultaneous features of democracy and autocracy. Moreover, the power concentration index defines the extent to which a system is autonomous and sovereign as reflected by the ability of its formal institutions to make and impose laws. Hence, the regime score is obtained by using the following formula:

$$REG = (DEMOC - AUTOC) * CONCEN$$

where DEMOC is the state's democracy value, AUTOC is the state's autocracy value, and CONCEN is the state's power concentration value. This measure ranges from −100 (highly authoritarian) to 100 (highly democratic). Low positive values and low negative values of this measure indicate what Gurr (1974) called anocracy, that is, a political system that either contains mixed democratic-autocratic features, or one in which the power concentration score is low, indicating that the regime lacks a clear monopoly on the making and imposition of laws.[16]

Following Maoz and Russett (1991), I collapsed the continuous regime measure into the traditional Democracy-Anocracy-Autocracy classification at the following points: Democracy (Regime Type 1) is a regime with a score exceeding +30, Anocracy (Regime Type 2) is a state with a regime score between −25 and +29, and Autocracy (Regime Type 3) is a state with a regime score lower than −25.[17] This categorical variable has been used in order to examine the trend effect of regime change on patterns of conflict interaction.

Domestic instability.

Two measures of domestic political instability have been used here. The first, based on the Taylor and Jodice (1983) data, measures the number of deaths from domestic political violence with a one-year lag. The other measure is the number of political executions by the regime with a one-year lag.

Data Analysis Methods

Two major procedures have been used to test the hypotheses. The first is a time-series regression analysis using Conflict Intensity as the dependent variable. This method is used in two different ways. First, the immediate effects of independent variables (regime score, domestic conflict, opponent's conflict intensity) are estimated by regressing these variables on the dependent variable (CI). Second, in order to examine whether regime changes had some enduring effect on the intensity of conflict, we have regressed the dependent variables on the year and controlled for regime type. If a regime change had an enduring effect on the patterns of conflict interaction, then a major shift of regime type (for example, from an anocratic political system to an autocratic one), would change the slope of the coefficient of conflict intensity over time, or even the direction of the slope.

The other procedure is probit analysis using the dispute (war) dichotomy as the dependent variable and regime and domestic conflict as independent variables. Because this definition of the dependent variable does not focus on who did what to whom but on whether a dispute or war broke out, opponents' actions are not used to predict conflict.

Empirical Results

Table 1 examines the relationships between the two conflicts. It is worth noting that less than 5 percent of the 570 incidents in both disputes suggest direct coordination between Egypt and Syria, or a direct linkage of an Israeli action on one front to its actions on the other front.[18] Yet the table clearly suggests that, by and large, the intensity of conflict on one front exhibits a moderately high correlation with the intensity of conflict on the other front.[19] There are two explanations for this, not including political coordination between the two

Table 1. Cross-Rivalry Relationships: Correlations between Interactions on One Front and Interactions on the Other Front, 1948–1988

Initiator-Target in Rivalry A with Initiator-Target in Rivalry B	Israel-Syria with Israel-Egypt	Syria-Israel with Egypt-Israel
Conflict Intensity	0.61**	0.53**
Number of Years	41	41

** $p < .001$

states. First, Israel may well have treated the two conflicts as parts of a whole strategic problem and managed the two conflicts as if they were one. Second, the very strong mutual effects between Israeli and Arab conflict interactions caused the Egyptians and Syrians to react not so much to each other's actions toward Israel, but rather to Israel's actions toward each of them separately. This will become more evident below. However, it is important to note that ups and downs in the Arab-Israeli conflict—at least in terms of two of its principal rivalries—exhibit a significant degree of interdependence. This interdependence is reflected not only in terms of the period of heightened conflict activity, but also in terms of the more pacific periods in the rivalries.

Table 2 lists the results of the time-series regression analysis relating regime factors and domestic stability factors to conflict interactions. A few words of explanation are required for this table. First, it is obvious that a state's actions and the opponent's actions have a strong mutual effect. Thus a full-blown model examining the effects of domestic and regime factors on conflict intensity would have to take that fact into account. This would yield a model with the following form:

[1] $CI_{ij} = \alpha + \beta_1 CI_{ji} + \beta_2 Regime_i + \beta_3 Domestic\ Conflict_i + \epsilon$

where i and j are two states, CI_{ij} is the conflict initiated by state i toward state j and CI_{ji} is the conflict initiated by state j toward state i.

However, it turns out that in the case of Egyptian and Syrian conflict, there is a significant colinearity in the model. Specifically, significant correlations exist between the key measures of domestic conflict and the intensity of conflict initiated by Israel.[20] For that reason, I have used two interaction terms: INT_1, defined as $INT[1] = CI[is-eg] * Political\ Executions[eg]$ where is = Israel, eg = Egypt, and INT_2, defined as $INT[2] = CI[is-eg] * Death\ from\ Political\ Vio$-

Table 2. Regression Analysis of Domestic Effects on Conflict Intensity in the Arab-Israeli Conflict, 1948–1988

Model	Independent Variable	Israel to Egypt	Egypt to Israel	Israel to Syria	Syria to Israel
Non-Inter-active	Regime Type*	−0.03^{+++*}	−0.04^{++}	0.13^{+}	0.02^{++}
(Opponent's behavior not included)	Deaths from domestic political violence	−0.01	0.06^{++}	0.00	0.01^{++}
	R^2 Durbin-Watson	0.06 1.86	0.31 1.98	0.09 1.84	0.27 1.94
Interactive	Regime Type	−0.01^{+}	−0.03^{++}	−0.00	0.02^{++}
(Opponent's behavior in-cluded)	INT$_1$ (Deaths from domestic political violence—IS)***	0.01	0.02	0.00	0.04^{++}
	INT$_2$	—	0.08^{++}	—	0.02^{++}
	Opponent's CI	0.66^{++}	—	0.73^{++}	−2.09
	R^2 Durbin-Watson	0.77 1.92	0.36 1.90	0.85 1.99	0.34 2.00
Trend Model	Year	−0.04^{+}	−0.03	−0.01	−0.01
	Regime Type*	0.91^{+}	0.96^{+}	−0.35	−0.38
	R^2 Durbin-Watson	0.26 1.91	0.09 1.96	0.07 1.86	0.05 1.95

Key:
* Regime Type refers to the regime type of Syria or Egypt. Israel's regime type does not exhibit any variation during the period and is fixed at +50.
** NA = Not available. No variation on this variable for the Israeli case (only one political execution, Karl Adolf Eichmann, since 1948).
*** In the case of Israeli conflict initiated toward Egypt and Syria, no significant colinearity exists in equation [1] above. Hence the full equation is used.
$^{++}$ $p < 0.01$
$^{+}$ $p < 0.05$

lence[eg] [is = Israel and eg = Egypt]. INT₁ refers to the effects of deaths from domestic political violence in Israel on Israel's behavior. INT₂ refers to the effects of deaths from domestic political violence on Egypt's (Syria's) behavior toward Israel. In each case it refers to an actor's domestic political conflict levels. The table also lists the separate effects of the domestic factors on each state's conflict intensity, without controlling for an opponent's actions. Finally, the trend model displayed in this table shows the effects of regime type change in Egypt and Syria on the patterns of temporal shifts in the conflict behavior of the protagonists. This is reflected in equation 2:

[2] $$CI_{ij} = \alpha + \beta_1 \, Year + \beta_2 \, Regime \, Type_i$$

As the table suggests, though the relationship is at times weak and somewhat inconsistent, there appears to be some support for the two hypotheses. In the Israeli-Egyptian case, the support is fairly clear. There is both an immediate effect as well as a trend effect of the regime type on the intensity of Egyptian conflict initiated toward Israel. Interestingly, even when we control for the intensity of the opponent's conflict, Israeli actions appear to be sensitive to changes in the Egyptian regime. This is evident both in terms of the immediate effects in the model and in the long-range trend effects.

But this relationship is not the same for both rivalries. As the level of democratization in Egypt increased, Egypt deescalated the conflict toward Israel and Israel deescalated its conflict toward Egypt. However, as the level of democratization in Syria decreased, Syria deescalated its conflict toward Israel. Yet Israel's conflict toward Syria seems less clearly sensitive to changes in Syria's regime. We will examine below just how robust these findings are. Table 3 examines domestic and regime effects on the outbreak of disputes. The previous results are basically replicated except for the lack of sensitivity of Israeli-Syrian disputes to changes in Syrian regime type.

These results, though tentative in nature, suggest that beyond the strategic aspects of the Arab-Israeli conflict, domestic factors seem to affect the interactions as well as the more general patterns of these enduring international rivalries. The implications of these results are discussed below.

Conclusion

The study of enduring rivalries in general, and of enduring rivalries in the Middle East in particular, is in its infancy. Though the number of works on

Table 3. Probit Analysis of Domestic and Regime Factors in
Dispute Outbreak in the Arab-Israeli Conflict, 1948–1988

Dependent Variable	Independent Variable	Egypt-Israel	Syria-Israel
Dispute	Regime Type*	-0.05^{++}	-0.01
	Deaths from domestic political violence	0.06^{++}	-0.01
	Political executions	0.01	0.11^{++}
	R^2	0.45	0.35
War	Regime Type$^+$	-0.05^+	-0.02
	Deaths from domestic political violence	0.10^+	0.02
	Political executions	0.18^+	0.04^+
	R^2	0.73	0.23

Key:
*Regime Type refers to the regime type of Syria or Egypt. Israel's
regime type does not exhibit any variation during the period.
$^+$ $p < 0.10$
$^{++}$ $p < 0.05$

specific rivalries—including the Arab-Israeli conflict—is staggering, the systematic exploration of the effects of domestic processes and the structural characteristics of political systems on the course of enduring rivalries has received only scant attention. This study provides initial evidence that this research is worth pursuing.

The findings of this study can be summarized as follows:

(1) Domestic processes seem significantly to affect the conflict interactions of states experiencing enduring international rivalries, even when we control for the principally strategic nature of such conflicts. In the case of Egyptian and Syrian actions, the intensity of conflict

initiated by these states toward Israel seems to be affected by the level of domestic violence within their own societies.

(2) Regime factors seem also to play an important role in the interactions of states in these rivalries. Given the fact that Israel preserved its regime structure throughout the conflict, the variability in the regime structure of Egypt and Syria seems to have affected both immediate conflict intensities as well as long-term patterns of interaction.

(3) As Egypt exhibited signs of liberalization in the mid-seventies and throughout much of the eighties, conflict levels decreased significantly. Israel also seems to have reacted in kind to this pattern. It exhibited more trigger-happy behavior during the reign of Nasser's authoritarian regime and more restraint during Sadat's liberalization process in the seventies and Mubarak's in the eighties.

(4) On the other hand, as Syria showed some signs of liberalization in the early and mid-fifties, conflict intensity was fairly high, though the levels of actual violence were quite low. When Assad's regime had stabilized, conflict levels seem to have dropped somewhat. The effects of regime type on conflict behavior—both in terms of Syrian conflict targeted at Israel and Israel's actions directed at Syria—seem far less stable than in the Israeli-Egyptian rivalry. The trend effect in the former case is also less evident than in the latter one.

What is the explanation for these patterns? A plausible hypothesis, not directly examined here, is that the interaction between regime structure and political stability is the key to understanding the relationship between domestic politics and conflict behavior. This result stems from recent studies that give renewed credence to the linkage politics theory. This implies that when political systems stabilize, either in the form of an increasingly liberal political structure or an increasingly authoritarian one, the pressure for externalization of internal conflict declines because the severity of political conflict itself decreases. The ability of a political system to cope with challenges to the governing groups through regulated mechanisms of order enables the leaders of that system to deal directly with the issues at stake in the international conflict.

The Egyptian system survived key challenges to the slow but persistent path of liberalization during the food riots of January 1977, during the Sadat assassination in October 1981, and—more recently—during the Gulf crisis. The regime's ability to cope effectively with the threats to the political system while maintaining some clear signs of democratization such as limited freedom of the press and multiparty elections, seems to go hand in hand with the implementation of the peace agreement with Israel. Israel's principal concern upon signing the peace treaty with Egypt was that peace might hinge on one individual's good will. Because this does not appear to be the case, Israel could respond in very mild terms to minor Egyptian provocations in the Gulf of Eilat during 1984 and 1985.

In Syria, domestic instability has been a pathological feature of politics up to the rise of power of Hafiz al-Assad in late 1970. Since then, the Syrian polity has become increasingly autocratic, with more and more of the power concentrating in the hands of the Alawite group and in Assad's hands, in particular. This system also faced several challenges to its existence, principally from radical Muslim groups. However, over time, Assad managed to stabilize his regime using various coercive mechanisms. As a result, and with the exception of Israel's attack on Syrian forces in Lebanon in June of 1982, the eighties exhibited an unprecedented level of stability in the Israeli-Syrian rivalry. This culminated, of course, in Syria's joining the Madrid Peace Talks framework in 1991.

Whether stability is accomplished through increased legitimacy or by crushing the opposition, stable leaders can reverse trends in their countries' international relations (Handel 1981). This suggests that a possible joining of the Middle East states to the growing club of democratic nations can lead to peace if democracy in the Arab states proves to be a viable, effective, and stable political system. If it does, leaders will feel that they can afford to change course regarding peace with Israel. And because democratic leaders are dependent on their constituency, and their constituency responds to success and failure in foreign policy, they would be willing to risk violating peace only if this would lead to meaningful benefits. If the risks of violating peace are high, democratic leaders would be more reluctant to choose this option. In unstable systems, policy shifts are more likely because of the feeling that short-term gains could be the key to retaining power.

This does not mean that peace is possible only between stable democracies. Rather, peace is more likely to be made and to hold if maintained by stable political systems. Democracy, as the general evidence on this topic shows, imposes considerable constraints on the use of force against other democracies. There is some initial evidence in the present study that this general trend may well apply to the Arab-Israeli conflict.

NOTES

1. This study is part of a larger project on Enduring International Rivalries, funded by a grant of the Ford Foundation through the Israeli Foundation Trustees. I would like to thank Allison Astorino, Gil Hanan, and Hanit Schwartz for helping me in data collection and data processing. Additional data sources for the empirical study include collection efforts by various people and institutions. These are acknowledged specifically in subsequent sections of the study. However, none of the individuals and projects that provided me with data is responsible for the analyses and interpretations contained herein.

2. The wars of the 1980s were the Soviet-Afghanistan, the Iran-Iraq, the Falklands, the Lebanon, and the Gulf Wars. Sources include Small and Singer (1982) and Maoz and Russett (1993).

3. This is also typical of studies focusing on the Middle East. See, for example, Burrowes and Spector (1973) versus Bar-Siman-Tov (1983).

4. Though Lebanon may be characterized as a democracy over the period from 1947 to 1974, most experts agree that it was not a real democracy due to the lack of clearly central institutions of law enforcement even during that era. Similar aspects can be attributed to Syria in the late forties and the early fifties, but there, too, the lack of stable institutions of governance seems to suggest that Syria never crossed the democratic threshold. Some of these features will be presented below.

5. If Turkey is included—as it typically is—as a Middle Eastern state, then the absence of any conflict between Turkey and Israel—the former an occasional democracy, the latter a permanent democracy—can be cited as probably the only relevant case in this context. However, too much cannot be made of this fact because Turkey and Israel are noncontiguous. Hence, despite the fact that they are in the same region, they cannot be described as "politically relevant" states, that is, states that, a priori, have a high likelihood of conflict interactions (Maoz and Russett 1993).

6. The precise coding of levels of hostility will be explained below.

7. The precise measures of conflict intensity will be discussed in the following section. Logs were used for convenience of presentation but not for statistical analyses.

8. Following Maoz and Russett (1991, 1993), a state is considered a democracy to the extent that its regime score is equal to or larger than +30. An autocracy is considered a state if the regime score is lower than −25. Between these two scores, states are considered to be anocracies, that is states with mixed characteristics or with a low level of power concentration. A more detailed discussion of this variable is given in Maoz and Russett (1991).

9. The Taba settlement was an international decision made by arbitration in 1985 on a territorial dispute between Israel and Egypt over a strip of land south of Eilat. This dispute had not been settled during the peace negotiations in 1978–79. Bilateral nego-

tiations on this issue failed to reach an agreement and—in accordance with the terms of the peace treaty—the parties turned to an international tribunal which ruled in favor of Egypt.

10. This intervention can also be viewed in direct connection with the struggle for the leadership of the Baath party between Jadid and Assad (Seale 1988).

11. By reciprocated disputes I mean that each of these states, during the dispute, initiated military confrontation actions that included the threat to use military force, the display of military force, and the actual use of military force.

12. The Israeli-Jordanian rivalry and (if we are willing to include nonstate actors) the Israeli-Palestinian rivalry also qualify. Presently, data are available only for the Israeli-Syrian and Israeli-Egyptian rivalries. Future investigations of these issues will focus on the other rivalries as well.

13. Based on the fourteen Military Confrontation Action (MCA) types employed by COW (Maoz 1982). Another type of MCA was added here to denote violation of border by air, sea, or land.

14. Scale values are displayed in Appendix 1 in Maoz (1982). The definition of Militarized Interstate Disputes (MIDs) is given in Gochman and Maoz (1984, p. 586).

15. This measure takes into account the severity of the incident in terms of the kind of verbal, demonstrative, or physical force used as well as its severity in terms of fatalities. Intensity is defined simply as severity per day of conflict. The log of the annual CI is the log intensity given in fig. 1 above.

16. Maoz and Russett (1993) show that the measure provides robust results when compared with more traditional measures of regime types based on ordinal or categorical scales.

17. Maoz and Russett (1991) discuss the rationale of and some tests for this classification.

18. Each incident coding contained a joint action variable which indicated whether a clear coordination existed between the initiator's behavior or the target's behavior, and that of another actor.

19. In terms of war events, the record is, in fact, mixed. Only three of the six Arab-Israeli wars show explicit Egyptian-Syrian coordination: the 1948 War of Independence, the 1967 Six Day War, and the 1973 Yom Kippur/Ramadan war. In the other three cases, no meaningful coordination existed. This includes the 1956 Sinai War, the 1969–70 War of Attrition—though in that case there was significant short-of-war activity on the Golan Heights—and the 1982 Lebanon War. One may also question the effectiveness of Egyptian-Syrian coordination in the former wars as well (see, e.g., Seale 1988).

20. The correlations between political executions, deaths from domestic political violence, and Israeli conflict intensity are, in the Egyptian case, 0.41 and 0.45, respectively ($p < .01$). In the Syrian case, 0.35 and 0.39 ($p < .05$).

REFERENCES

Azar, E. E. 1980. "The Conflict and Peace Data Bank (COPDAB) Project." *Journal of Conflict Resolution* 24, no. 3, pp. 379–403.

Bar-Siman-Tov, Yaacov. 1983. *Linkage Politics in the Middle East.* Boulder, CO: Westview.

Barzilai, Gad, and Bruce M. Russett. 1990. "The Political Economy of Israeli Military Action." In Asher Arian and Michal Shamir, eds., *The Elections in Israel, 1988.* Boulder, CO: Westview.

Bremer, Stuart A. 1992a. "Dangerous Dyads: Conditions Affecting the Likelihood of Interstate War, 1816–1965." *Journal of Conflict Resolution* 36, no. 2, pp. 309–41.

———. 1992b. "Democracy and Dyadic Dispute Participation, 1816–1976." Paper presented at the 33rd annual meeting of the International Studies Association, Atlanta, GA, March 31–April 4.

Burrowes, Robert, and Bertram Spector. 1973. "The Strength and Direction of Relationships between Domestic Conflict and Cooperation: Syria, 1961–1967." In Jonathan Wilkenfeld, ed., *Conflict Behavior and Linkage Politics.* New York: McKay. Pp. 294–321.

Chan, Steve. 1984. "Mirror, Mirror, on the Wall: Are the Freer Countries More Pacific?" *Journal of Conflict Resolution* 28, no. 4, pp. 617–64.

Diehl, Paul F., and Gary Goertz. 1993. "Enduring Rivalries: Theoretical Constructs and Empirical Patterns." *International Studies Quarterly* 37, no. 2, pp. 147–71 .

Dixon, William J. 1993. "Democracy and the Management of International Conflict." *Journal of Conflict Resolution* 37, no. 1, pp. 42–68.

Doyle, Michael W. 1986. "Liberalism and World Politics." *American Political Science Review* 80, no. 4, pp. 1151–69.

Geller, Daniel, and Daniel M. Jones. 1991. "The Effect of Dynamic and Static Balances on Conflict Escalation in Rival Dyads." Paper presented at the annual meeting of the American Political Science Association, Washington, DC, August 29–September 1.

Gilpin, Robert. 1981. *War and Change in World Politics.* Cambridge: Cambridge University Press.

Gochman, Charles S., and Zeev Maoz. 1984. "Militarized Interstate Disputes, 1816–1976: Procedures, Patterns, and Insights." *Journal of Conflict Resolution* 28, no. 4, pp. 585–615.

Gurr, Ted Robert. 1974. "Persistence and Change in Political Systems, 1800–1971." *American Political Science Review* 68, no. 4, pp. 1482–1504.

———. 1988. "War, Revolution, and the Growth of the Coercive State." *Comparative Political Studies* 21, no. 1, pp. 45–65.

Gurr, Ted Robert, Keith Jaggers, and Will H. Moore. 1989. "Polity II Handbook." Mimeographed. Boulder: University of Colorado.

Handel, Michael. 1981. *The Diplomacy of Surprise.* Cambridge: Harvard University Press.

Huth, Paul, Daniel M. Jones, and Zeev Maoz. 1991. "An Operational Definition of Enduring International Rivalries." Mimeographed. Ann Arbor: University of Michigan.

Levy, Jack S. 1988. "Domestic Politics and War." *Journal of Interdisciplinary History* 18, no. 1, pp. 653–73.

———. 1989. "The Diversionary Theory of War: Quantitative and Historical Evidence." In Manus I. Midlarsky, ed., *Handbook of War Studies.* Boston: Unwin Hyman.

Maoz, Zeev. 1982. *Paths to Conflict: International Dispute Initiation, 1816–1986.* Boulder, CO: Westview.

———. 1989. "Joining the Club of Nations: Political Development and International Conflict, 1816–1976." *International Studies Quarterly* 33, no. 2, pp. 199–231.

———. 1990. *National Choices and International Processes.* Cambridge: Cambridge University Press.

Maoz, Zeev, and Nasrin Abdolali. 1989. "Regime Type and International Conflict, 1816–1976." *Journal of Conflict Resolution* 33, no. 1, pp. 3–35.

Maoz, Zeev, and Allison Astorino. 1992. "Waging War, Waging Peace: Decision Making and Bargaining in the Arab-Israeli Conflict, 1970–1973." *International Studies Quarterly* 36, no. 4, pp. 373–99.

Maoz, Zeev, and Bruce M. Russett. 1991. "Alliance, Contiguity, Wealth, and Political Stability: Is the Lack of Conflict among Democracies a Statistical Artifact?" *International Interactions* 17 (February), pp. 245–68.

———. 1993. "Normative and Structural Causes of Democratic Peace, 1946–1986." *American Political Science Review* 87, no. 3, pp. 624–38.

Mearsheimer, John. 1991. "Back to the Future: Instability in Europe after the Cold War." *International Security* 15, no. 1, pp. 5–56.

Miller, Benjamin. 1992. "Explaining Great Power Cooperation in Conflict Management." *World Politics* 45, no. 1, pp. 1–46.

Morgan, T. Clifton, and Sally Howard Campbell. 1991. "Domestic Structure, Decisional Constraints, and War: So Why Kant Democracies Fight?" *Journal of Conflict Resolution* 35, no. 2, pp. 187–211.

Morgan, T. Clifton, and Valerie L. Schewbach. 1992. "Take Two Democracies and Call Me in the Morning: A Prescription for Peace?" *International Interactions* 17, no. 4, pp. 305–20.

Organski, A. F. K., and Jacek Kugler. 1980. *The War Ledger.* Chicago: University of Chicago Press.

Rasler, Karen, and William R. Thompson. 1989. *War and State Making.* Boston: Unwin Hyman.

Ray, James Lee. 1992. *Global Politics.* 5th ed. Boston: Houghton Mifflin.

Rummel, Rudolph J. 1983. "Libertarianism and International Violence." *Journal of Conflict Resolution* 27, no. 1, pp. 27–71.

———. 1985. "Libertarian Propositions on Violence within and between Nations." *Journal of Conflict Resolution* 29, no. 3, pp. 419–55.

Russett, Bruce M. 1983. "International Interactions and Processes: The Internal vs. External Debate Revisited." In Ada W. Finifter, ed., *Political Science: The State of the Discipline.* Washington, DC: American Political Science Association. Pp. 541–70.

———. 1990. *Controlling the Sword: The Democratic Governance of National Security.* Cambridge: Harvard University Press.

Seale, Patrick. 1988. *Asad.* Berkeley: University of California Press.

Small, Melvin, and J. David Singer. 1976. "The War-Proneness of Democratic Regimes." *Jerusalem Journal of International Relations* 1, no. 4, pp. 50–69.

———. 1982. *Resort to Arms: International and Civil Wars, 1815–1980.* Beverly Hills: Sage.

Stohl, Michael. 1980. "The Nexus of Civil and International Conflict." In Ted Robert Gurr, ed., *Handbook of International Conflict.* New York: Free Press. Pp. 297–330.

Taylor, Charles L., and David A. Jodice. 1983. *World Handbook of Political and Social Indicators.* 3rd ed. New Haven: Yale University Press.

Waltz, Kenneth N. 1979. *Theory of International Relations.* Menlo Park: Addison-Wesley.

———. 1986. "Reflections on 'Theory of International Politics': A Response to My Critics." In Robert O. Keohane, ed., *Neorealism and Its Critics.* New York: Columbia University Press. Pp. 322–46.

Wilkenfeld, Jonathan. 1968. "Domestic and Foreign Conflict Behavior of Nations." *Journal of Peace Research* 1, no. 1, pp. 56–69.

9

DEMOCRACY AND FOREIGN POLICY IN THE ARAB WORLD

MICHAEL C. HUDSON

AT FIRST GLANCE, one would expect any essay on democracy and foreign policy in the Arab world to be a very short one. Democracy is almost nonexistent today in the politics of the Arab states; and in any case, Arab foreign policy decision-making, according to a well-known study, is predominantly shaped by external factors (Korany and Dessouki et al. 1991, pp. 20, 30–31). In the index to that book one looks in vain for the heading "democracy" and must settle for scattered references to the "domestic environment" or "internal politics." "The primacy of the executive, particularly in the development of a presidential [and/or, we might add, monarchical] center . . . dominates the political process," they write; and this is "due to the absence of a free press or a strong opposition" (p. 20).

These empirical observations may be placed in the context of the theoretical debate in international relations which has pitted the "realist" school (and its recent variants) against the "sociological" school in what one might call a war of paradigms (Lijphart 1974). The realists have insisted on the causal priority of the international security environment in explaining the foreign policy of states, assuming that states are the primary unit of analysis and that they act according to rational calculation of interests. "Classical" realists (and neorealists) have emphasized the importance of the balance of power, security threats, and the causal importance of the international system (Waltz 1959; 1979); while more recent dependency analysts have stressed the imperatives of political economy (Korany and Dessouki et al. chap. 2). Both, however, have downplayed domestic politics; and some students of diplomacy have scarcely concealed their concern that democratic forces could impede the proper calculation and execution of policies relating to the national interest by the foreign-policy elite.

Stephen M. Walt's *The Origins of Alliances* (1987) uses the Middle East to illustrate the neorealist contention that actors are primarily driven by perceptions of a "balance of threat" to maneuver incessantly in a shifting pattern of coalitions that repeatedly contradicts the ideological agendas which regimes feel they require to manage their domestic environment.

The "sociological" school, on the other hand, derives its intellectual momentum from the behavioral movement in American political science and focuses on the domestic environment as the principal causal locus for the external behavior of states. Foreign policy behavior, including going to war, is best explained by studying individual attitudes, social structure and relations, economic conditions, institutional patterns, political culture, leaders, and decision-making processes. Middle East applications include Brecher's study of Israeli foreign policy (1972) and various case studies of Arab foreign policy-making (Korany and Dessouki et al. 1991, chaps. 4–12). It follows from this perspective that a major change in the domestic environment might be expected to produce changes in external behavior and international relations. To adherents of the "sociological" school, the realists' construction of the state as a rational, monolithic, self-help actor in an "anarchic" environment is a simplistic abstraction. Rather, the roots of conflict lie *within* the state and society.

Any discussion of democracy as a factor in shaping Arab foreign policy, therefore, can go forth fruitfully only by assuming, first, that the domestic societal environment in general plays a significant role in policy formation. If the formidable realist objections to this assumption can be refuted or at least set aside, there is still a second question: Would a "democratic" domestic environment bring about foreign policy behavior among Arab regimes significantly different from their past foreign policy behavior? And in what way might it be different? As liberal American scholars we perhaps are predisposed to imagine that democratically generated foreign policies in the Arab world might be pragmatic, accommodating, peace-loving, and generally benign—but we could be completely wrong. It does not take much thinking to imagine regimes being driven by emotional populist forces, generated by democratically elected majorities, into policies and behavior that would substantially raise tension levels and induce new conflicts in the region.

This paper does not pretend to settle any of these issues definitively. Instead, I propose to take a speculative look at the relationship between democracy and foreign policy in the Arab world by raising a historical question and posing a counterfactual proposition: The historical question is whether we can ascertain any such relationship during those relatively infrequent periods of "democracy" in recent Arab politics. The counterfactual proposition asks: What if Arab regimes had been "democratic?" Would they have pursued policies vis-à-vis Israel other than the ones they have actually pursued? Would some greater degree of Arab unity or cooperation have been achieved? Would they have positioned themselves differently vis-à-vis the United States? Finally, I would like to address briefly the prospects for democratization in the Arab world and ponder how governments more representative of societies torn by socioeconomic dislocations and ideological ferment, yet increasingly intruded upon by "the new world order," might behave in their external security, diplomatic, and economic relations.

The Recent Historical Record

Without insisting on a purist's definition of democracy, let us suggest for the sake of argument that the existence of several political parties, a parliamentary electoral system, and a relatively free press comprise the minimum requirements. Perhaps the term "limited liberal parliamentary system" is more accurate, if also more cumbersome. Even by these modest criteria, it is clear that the Arab world has not experienced much "democracy" since World War II. But it has experienced some. The principal examples are Egypt until the 1952 revolution; Syria from independence in 1943 until the military regimes (1949–54), 1954 until the 1958 merger with Egypt, and 1961 to 1963 (between the end of the union and the Baathist takeover); Iraq (in a much more restricted sense) until the 1958 revolution; Jordan (with a limited parliamentary system) from independence in 1946 until the 1957 nationalist challenge; and Lebanon until 1975. Most of these cases require various qualifications, and other cases that one might think of (Morocco, Sudan, or Kuwait at various times) require stretching the definition even more. The main difficulty is the extent to which "the people," or society as a whole were "represented," the extent to which executives were accountable—and the extent to which politically significant sectors perceived that the system was "democratic." Bourgeois parliamentary systems, some of them chaperoned by Britain or "guided" by strong monarchies, may have been formally democratic, but they were generally not popular. By the middle to late 1950s, nearly all of the main parliamentary systems had given way to authoritarian single-party, populist regimes dominated by nationalist military officers, or to successful assertions of royal authoritarianism.

If we confine ourselves to Egypt, Syria, Iraq, Jordan, and Lebanon from the mid-1940s to the mid-1950s, is it possible to draw any conclusions about the relationship between their relatively liberal, pluralistic practices (compared at least to what would come later) and their foreign policy behavior? Before making the attempt, four points need to be made. First, we should recall that the issues of imperialism, full independence, and nationalism dominated the foreign policy agenda. Second, the crisis over Palestine and Israel had traumatized Arab opinion. Third, the issues of social justice, corruption, and reform were weighing heavily on new and fragile governmental structures and practices. Fourth, political movements outside the formal political structure were articulating these demands in a manner that challenged the legitimacy of the established order and that led regimes to regard them as subversive. Thus challenged, these fledgling "democratic" regimes were compelled to pursue defensive and reactive foreign policies.

Egypt

In Egypt after World War I there were three centers of power: the monarchy, the British, and the Wafd party—the main representative of the nationalist movement. But there were also other parties represented in the elected Egyptian parliament. Between the two world wars, the Communist Party and the Muslim Brotherhood also developed grass-roots strength. During and after World War II, a succession of prime ministers alternately challenged and accommodated the British presence but failed to move forward on this paramount national issue fast enough to forestall the 1952 coup (Vatikiotis 1969, chap. 15). As domestic tensions increased, a Wafdist government under Mustafa Nahhas came to power in 1950. Notwithstanding its belated steps forward on pressing social issues, it found itself head-to-head with a British government that firmly resisted growing nationalist demands for withdrawal. The government abrogated the 1936 Anglo-Egyptian treaty in October 1951, antagonizing the British. The Egyptian nationalists remained undeterred from their growing guerrilla warfare against the British. When the British retaliated with force, the Nahhas government dithered. "In these conditions," writes Vatikiotis (1969, p. 371), "the opposition groups assumed correctly that the Wafd government was not prepared to risk armed combat with British troops." A bloody clash in Ismailia triggered the "burning of Cairo" on January 26, 1952. During the next five months, before the July 23rd revolution, there were three governments, none of which could arrest the slide toward populist authoritarianism.

Foreign policy under Egypt's parliamentary, multiparty constitutional monarchical system was hardly pacific. King Farouk and Prime Minister Nahhas both sought to enhance their popularity by backing the Palestine cause and Arab unity. There was strong public backing for military intervention to help save Palestine for the Arabs. But the unexpected and humiliating defeat of the Egyptian army in the 1948 war not only further delegitimized the parliamentary system and the monarchy itself, but also deepened the salience of this issue in Egyptian politics for years to come.

Elsewhere in the region, Egypt sought to project hegemony in the Sudan and influence in Arab Asia and North Africa. But highest on the agenda was the continuing British imperial presence. The delegitimizing effect of the British presence on the monarchy and on a seemingly ineffectual governmental system certainly contributed to the nationalist revolution of 1952. Defeat in Palestine was another nail in the coffin. Perceptions of domestic corruption and of socioeconomic policy failures further discredited the liberal order. Whatever the moral virtues of a liberal political system may be, I see no obvious indications of exceptional foreign policy restraint, tolerance, or competence that can be associated with Egypt's form of government at this time.

Syria

In Syria, the republican era began unsteadily with independence from France in 1943. The National Bloc, which had led resistance to the Mandate, transformed itself into the National Party, and its head, Shukri al-Quwwatli, became president. However, the National Party and other parties that soon appeared were narrowly based groupings dominated by wealthy businessmen and landowners; and the parliamentary system in the late 1940s had a reputation for corruption and incompetence (Seale 1965 [1986], chaps. 4, 5). One policy that was strongly endorsed by both the Syrian political elite and public opinion was support for the Palestinians against Zionist encroachment. Quwwatli, in particular, had been an ardent advocate of assistance to the embattled Palestinians during the unsuccessful Palestinian uprising of the late 1930s. So there was powerful domestic backing for Syria's military involvement in the 1948 war, even though the French had evacuated the country only in 1946, leaving just a small, inexperienced, and ill-equipped army.

Syria's military debacle in 1948 had even more devastating political repercussions than had Egypt's. Rocked by humiliation, scandal and intrigue, the military staged no fewer than three coups d'état in 1949, initiating an era of instability that ended only when another officer, Hafiz al-Assad seized control in 1970. Despite the early military interventions, Syria continued fitfully to manifest some parliamentary and party activity until an elected government sought the country's merger with Egypt in the short-lived United Arab Republic (1958–61). Competition between the traditional bourgeois parties of notables and broader-based movements such as the Parti Populaire Syrien, the Communists, the Muslim Brothers, and the Baath (all of which were struggling against each other, as well) continued during the brief restoration of parliamentary government between 1954 and 1958. But the country was unable to maintain an effective liberal-democratic system.

Syria's foreign policy during its short pluralist era was affected by frustrated nationalist and irredentist goals—Lebanon, enlarged by the French in 1920 at the expense of what most Syrians considered Syrian territory, Alexandretta Province, ceded by the French to Turkey in 1938, and (from an Arab nationalist perspective) Palestine (also known as "southern Syria") in 1948. Loss of the Golan Heights in 1967 has only exacerbated these frustrations. Notwithstanding its intervention in Palestine, Syrian foreign policy in this "liberal" period was essentially defensive. Damascus was cross-pressured by competing regional ideological currents and by powerful and intrusive neighbors: Iraq, Turkey, Jordan, Saudi Arabia, and on the international level France, Britain, the U.S. and (later) the USSR. Within an intense domestic ideological environment featuring powerful Arab nationalist, greater Syrian, Islamic radical, socialist, and communist movements, Syrian politicians fended off (and engaged in) intrigues and maneuvers to balance (and exploit) the ambitions of regional neighbors, notably the Hashemite rulers of Iraq and Jordan, the Saudis, and the Egyptians. Syria's foreign policy at this time may have been generated within some kind of liberal democratic framework, but it is difficult to discern that this framework shaped policy in any consistent and coherent way. Indeed, inconsistency and improvisation seem to be the main hallmarks of that policy.

Iraq

Created in 1921 by the British out of the Mesopotamian provinces of the defunct Ottoman Turkish Empire, the Kingdom of Iraq was a constitutional monarchy ostensibly in the image of its British sponsors. Its first parliamentary elections were held in 1924, and the state remained, in form at least, a parliamentary system until the military-led Arab nationalist revolution of 1958, which ushered in the era of single-party, bureaucratic-authoritarian politics that has continued through the rule of President Saddam Hussein. Iraqi politics under the monarchy, however, could be called "liberal" only in the most qualified way. Riven by ethnic and sectarian conflicts (Kurds, Assyrians), by Sunni-Shiite schisms, and by tribal rebellions, Iraqi political life was more conspiratorial than democratic. Rising nationalist, communist and anti-imperialist sentiments could only erode the legitimacy of a regime so closely connected to Britain (Batatu 1978). A small elite of merchants, former Ottoman officials, and landowners—predominantly Sunni Muslims—dominated parliamentary and governmental affairs. At the same time, Iraq began a remarkable process of economic and social development that would make it one of the most advanced countries in the Arab world. A talented and skilled labor force gradually appeared, replete with the educational, scientific, manufacturing, and bureaucratic talent that might have underpinned—ceteris paribus—a vibrant civil society and liberal political order. Instead, however, the ruling elite remained isolated and corrupt; and growing ideological opposition movements found expression in mass organizations that occasionally erupted with massive demonstrations, and in the military, which bears the distinction of having staged the first coups in contemporary Arab politics in 1936 and 1941. These nationalist, anti-British efforts were thwarted; and the British, who had installed the Hashemite family (from the distant Hijaz) on the throne after World War I, now found in Nuri al-Said, a former nationalist and Ottoman officer, a capable and willing ally to run the country.

Under the autocratic management of Nuri al-Said, parliament was held firmly in check (summarily dissolved when deemed necessary), and political parties were routinely harassed and suppressed. Nevertheless, there was more political freedom in activity in Iraq at this time than there would be under the much more authoritarian single-party nationalist regimes to come. Nuri and the regent, Abdul-Ilah, might have been dictatorial, but they could not totally ignore other political forces. For during the same period, the politicization of Iraqi society—and the growth of mass and cadre parties—led to periodic violent upheavals, as in 1946, 1948, 1952, and finally, the revolution of 1958 (cf. Batatu 1978, pp. 526 ff., and chaps. 22, 32).

How did this nominally liberal political system affect (if at all) Iraqi foreign policy? Despite—perhaps because of—its British "taint," the regime did its best to display nationalist credentials. This may explain Iraq's decision to intervene in the Palestine war of 1948, even though it was a noncontiguous actor. Iraq also sought to promote its own version of Arab unity—a "Fertile Crescent plan" which would have embraced Syria, Jordan, and perhaps Lebanon as well under Baghdad's hegemony. But when it came to larger strategic relationships, Nuri and the royal family decided to cast their lot with Britain and the West. In spite of apparent public opposition, Nuri (with British encouragement) took Iraq into treaty commitments with Turkey and Iran, leading to the formation of the Baghdad Pact. Nuri had no trouble generating overwhelming parliamentary support for these ventures (Gallman 1964, pp. 43–56), despite their unpopularity outside parliament. If Iraq's "democracy" could not prevent the regime from pursuing its own unpopular foreign policy interests, neither could it save that regime from the eventual consequences of such policies. The Iraqi "liberal" period is, I believe, too clouded with ambiguities to permit any clear conclusion about whether the form of government affects the "peaceful-ness" of its foreign policy behavior. If we classify this government as "demo-cratic," we must count its war with "democratic" Israel in 1948 as an exception to the "democracies do not fight democracies" proposition of the international relations scholars. Yet if Iraq had been more democratic, its involvement in Pal-estine might have been even more extensive. Similarly, if one regards Nuri's pro-British stance as evidence of "peaceableness," "pragmatism," or "states-manship" (a most problematic kind of judgment, in my opinion), then one has to observe that he pursued this course against what was probably Iraqi public opinion on this matter even though he commanded formal parliamentary majorities.

Jordan

When Transjordan declared its independence in 1923, neither its British in-ventors nor the mainly nomadic inhabitants of the arid territory had any in-tention of establishing a liberal, democratic form of government. In reward for services rendered by the Hashemites, the British installed Amir Abdallah as ruler and were more concerned about developing a competent army (the Arab Legion) than a liberal democratic political order. Politically, Transjordan was less a state than the possession of a prince, whose family (even though not in-digenous to the territory) enjoyed Islamic and tribal legitimacy. Nevertheless, the emirate held its first elections in 1929, and in the 1930s, several political parties came into existence.

The turbulence between Zionists and indigenous Palestinian Arabs in Man-date Palestine during the 1930s dominated Transjordan's political agenda. As the conflict reached its climax toward the end of World War II, Britain's deci-sion to withdraw galvanized the various claimants: the Zionists, the Palestinian Arabs, and the neighboring Arab states—foremost among them Amir Abdallah's Transjordan. In 1946 the emirate had achieved full independence from Britain and subsequently issued a constitution establishing a bicameral legislature with an elected lower house. The Chamber of Deputies was given legislative power but no authority over finance or government appointments (Patai 1958, p. 46). But the 1947 elections were effectively dominated by the progovernment party, with the opposition preferring to protest from outside the country. The legislature fully supported Abdallah's continuing cooperative relations with Britain, even though nationalists objected. And Abdallah was able to pursue secret talks with Zionist (and later Israeli) leaders through which he hoped to arrange a peaceful partition of Palestine between himself and the new Zionist state. Ultimately, of course, such a partition occurred, although not peacefully. What is noteworthy for our purposes, however, is that Abdallah's actions clearly contradicted the collective position of the newly created Arab League, which was to reject the Zionist project with force if necessary. Had Transjordan been democratic—with effective contestation and participation—one wonders whether Abdallah could have pursued his policy of what Shlaim (1987) calls collusion with the Zionists. In 1951, a Palestinian Arab nationalist bent on punishing King Abdallah's "treason" assassinated him at the Mosque of Omar in what had become Jordanian east Jerusalem.

Following the accession of Abdallah's grandson Hussein in 1952, the young new king (like his cousins ruling in Iraq) sought to pursue his family's traditional alignment with the British, but more discreetly. Discretion was necessary: As a result of the 1948 war, Jordan now had a very large population of dispossessed and angry Palestinians. Arab nationalism was galvanizing the masses throughout the Arab world. Most Arab regimes and all the nationalist-progressive parties reviled the Hashemites for "selling out" Palestine. At first, the young king tried to build his legitimacy by allowing parliament and parties to function fairly openly. For about five years he presided precariously over what in hindsight may be called Jordan's brief liberal experiment. It was the freest and most free-wheeling period in Jordanian politics until the king's new democratic opening in 1989. He tried riding with the Arab nationalist current by sacking Glubb Pasha, the legendary commander of the Arab Legion and symbol of Britain's continuing presence. But in 1957 he drew the line when the pro-Nasser officer Ali Abu Nuwar and the Arab nationalist government of Suleiman Nabulsi appeared to be going too far; after an attempted military-nationalist coup, liberalism gave way to some three decades of "emergency" rule during which political freedoms were drastically curtailed.

Jordan's brief liberal experiment in the 1950s was a good deal freer than the more cosmetic parliamentary life in Hashemite Iraq. But there were similarities in foreign policy. Both regimes pursued a British (and later an American) connection and looked upon the pan-Arabism emanating from Egypt as a serious threat, even though this ideology was very popular among their own people. King Hussein proved far more astute than his Iraqi cousins in handling what, for them, proved indeed to be a mortal danger. King Hussein sought to ride the tide of popular outrage over the loss of most of Palestine rather than to let himself be engulfed by it. This meant engaging in strong rhetorical Arabism while trying not to provoke Israel. It also meant supporting diplomatic compromise rather than forceful confrontation. Hussein's disastrous decision to attack Israeli Jerusalem in the early hours of the 1967 war is the exception (and an understandable one, on political grounds) to a stance that most Western policy-makers have called "statesmanlike." Many Palestinians and other Arabs have less flattering words for it. Evaluations of the "quality" of a foreign policy often depend on the situation of the evaluators.

Be that as it may, our question here is whether Jordan could have pursued such a course had its political system been more liberal and democratic than it was. Again, it is hard to say, but it is worth noting that during the 1950s "liberal" period, Jordanian policy briefly became more nationalist. The king also declared solidarity with the *fidayyin* (Palestinian guerrillas) in 1968 during another brief period when his royal authority was being challenged by Palestinian guerrillas. In general, however, it is hard to imagine that the king could have been as "statesmanlike" as he was if there had been a more participant and competitive political process in Jordan.

Lebanon

The case of Lebanon is especially interesting because it was the most democratic of all the Arab countries. With all its flaws, Lebanese politics was distinctly more liberal and pluralistic, and less authoritarian, than the other regimes we have just mentioned. Although the Lebanese president had much more power than the prime minister, the cabinet, or the Chamber of Deputies, he was far more limited than his neighboring counterparts as a result of Lebanon's consociational structure. The blueprint for that structure was the National Pact of 1943. It embodied two compromises designed to manage Christian-Muslim tensions, one of which involved Lebanon's future foreign policy. The newly independent state would foreswear any entangling alliances either with the West (France) or the Arab East (Syria). We have here a unique case of an Arab country's foreign policy orientation fixed in a quasi-constitutional pact. If Lebanon's democracy thus shaped its foreign policy, it is also true that an unbalanced foreign policy could destroy Lebanon's democracy—and, indeed, its very stability.

This is indeed what almost happened. In 1948 Lebanon participated (albeit rather passively) with its Arab League partners in the Palestine war. It dispatched four battalions to the border and supported Lebanese and Palestinian irregular forces in holding (for a time) some of central Galilee. Not to have done so would almost certainly have alienated the Muslim communities and created a disastrous rift in the new and delicate Lebanese polity; but some Maronite Christian leaders were opposed, or at least lukewarm, to Lebanon's involvement even in token form. Then, in the mid-1950s, the regime of President Camille Chamoun and Foreign Minister Charles Malik maneuvered to align Lebanon overtly with Western security projects at a time when Arab nationalist currents were running strong among Lebanon's non-Christian majority (and in the Greek Orthodox Christian community as well). It was not the Chamber of Deputies but rather fear of popular protest that kept Chamoun from bringing Lebanon into the Baghdad Pact in 1955. The parliament that was elected in 1957, in what opposition politicians claimed was a rigged election, supported Lebanon's adherence to the Eisenhower Doctrine. Following the brief civil war of 1958, the new president, General Fuad Shihab, steered the country's foreign policy back toward a centrist stance—friendly but not tied to Nasser's United Arab Republic, and friendly but not tied to Washington and Paris. Shihab understood that Lebanon's domestic environment of pluralistic power-sharing required such a position.

A decade and a half later, however, another Lebanese president, Suleiman Frangieh (less sophisticated than President Shihab), faced a foreign policy crisis far more difficult than the 1958 episode. His regime split apart as Sunni prime ministers (with a large popular following) supported the activities of the Palestinian resistance movement against Israel, while Maronite Christian politicians, officers, and militia organizations turned to violence in order to oppose what they saw as an unacceptable violation of the National Pact's stipulation of balance and (perhaps) noninvolvement in regional disputes. The formal structures of Lebanese democracy were inadequate to sustain a foreign policy of noninvolvement and the concurrent restrictions that would have been required on Palestinian activities, and the country split into opposing, warring camps. Equally explosive domestic issues deepened the split. Would a less democratic Lebanese political system possibly have been able to steer the country clear of the fifteen-year civil war that ensued? Or was the problem that Lebanon was not democratic enough? With all its imperfections, Lebanon's quasi-democratic system did reflect the deep popular polarization over foreign policy—for better or for worse.

Implications of the Case Studies

What, if anything, do these episodes of imperfect democratic practice tell us about Arab foreign policy-making? Clearly, caution should be exercised in drawing any conclusions: the regimes were far from being truly democratic, the cases need fuller study, and the historical conditions were different from those of today. Nonetheless, I am struck by the lack of an obvious or simple relationship between political structure and policy outcome. It is not intuitively obvious that a different kind of decision-making process (either more or less "democratic") would have led to different foreign policy decisions in the cases discussed.

Surveying these historical episodes, I am also struck by the disjunction in every case between the formal structure of "democracy" and the popular political arena. As we have seen, the disjunction is greater in some cases (e.g., Iraq) than in others (e.g., Egypt or Lebanon). We may be right in thinking that foreign policy by dictator (or a small "ruling circle") can lead to disasters, but it does not follow that the truer the representation, the wiser the foreign policy. The popular political arena in the Arab world in the decade following the creation of Israel in 1948 was turbulent and unruly—not very different, perhaps, from the situation today. Too faithful a replication at the parliamentary level of various militant, radical tendencies found at the popular level might have led not only to foreign policy excess but to domestic instability as well. Would political parties have been able to channel intensely held political agendas into an orderly policy process marked by compromise and tradeoff? We shall never know. But we do know that three of these imperfectly representative regimes (in Egypt, Syria, and Iraq) collapsed anyway. Democracy in the Middle East, of all places, cannot be risk-free, much as incumbent regimes would like it to be. Would the benefits have outweighed the costs? We cannot say. But to the extent that the legitimacy of regimes might have been strengthened by parliaments representative of the main political tendencies, these regimes might have been able to carry out their external relations with greater prudence, knowledge, and authority than would otherwise have been the case.

Arab Democracy and the Conflict with Israel

According to Russett (1990, p. 123), the proposition that "[w]ith only very marginal exceptions, democratic states have not fought one another in the modern era . . . is one of the strongest nontrivial or nontautological generalizations that can be made about international relations." The Middle East would seem to be a particularly arid testing ground for this proposition given the general absence of democracy, and its relevance to the Arab-Israeli conflict would seem to be nil. Yet as we have observed, there have been brief periods in which Arab states in conflict with Israel have been "democratic" to some extent. (It is beyond the scope of my paper to consider whether "democratic" Turkey's invasion of "democratic" Cyprus in July 1974 constitutes another Middle Eastern exception to Russett's proposition.) The most sustained such period happened to encompass the years 1947–49, the years of the first Arab-Israeli war during which Israel was established as an independent state.

At this time three of Israel's four contiguous adversaries actually had parliamentary systems and elected governments: Egypt, Syria, and Lebanon. As I have already noted, one can argue as to how "purely" liberal-democratic were the constitutional monarchy in Egypt, Syria's parliamentary republic, or Lebanon's peculiar consociational democracy; but in form—and arguably in reality—these governments, which went to war to try and prevent the establishment of Israel, would seem to meet the criteria specified by writers such as Dahl (1971) and Russett (1990). Were these Arab governments less democratic than the unelected Zionist regime (shortly to be established as the government of the new State of Israel)? Putting aside the possibility that Israel's government in 1948 was not democratic, it would appear that this war may constitute a nontrivial exception to the above-mentioned proposition. Russett's characterization of this war as the "nearest exception" to the rule on the basis simply of Lebanon's "peripheral involvement" (since he appears to dismiss the idea that Israel was undemocratic) understates the significance of the case. It is easy to understand why this example might not be widely cited. In the first place, Arab/Islamic political culture is widely (but, in my view, incorrectly) viewed as intrinsically incompatible with liberal democracy (see, e.g., Kedourie 1992); secondly, anyone familiar with the 1948 conflict would find little evidence for the logic of the proposition: Neither Arabs nor Israelis perceived of their adversaries as liberal, democratic, or legitimate. One can argue, however, that there was sufficient democracy, or at least populism, on both sides for genuine mutual antipathies to express themselves by resort to armed force.

There are two other episodes of Arab-Israeli warfare that also appear to deviate from the "democracies don't fight democracies" proposition. The first involves Israel's invasions of Lebanon in 1978 and 1982. (Doyle 1983a, p. 213, n. 7, refers somewhat vaguely to Israel-Lebanon fighting in the post-1967 period as a possible exception to the rule.) In effect, one democracy has twice invaded and occupied (indeed, still occupies) part of another democracy; and ongoing low-intensity conflict around the Israel-Lebanon frontier continues into the 1990s. One can counter this view in three ways. Perhaps what happened in 1978 and 1982 were not true wars but only limited interventions. This argument might conceivably be applied to 1978, but not, I think, to Israel's adventure in Lebanon between 1982 and 1985. It is also possible to argue that Israel, although a democracy, was driven by nondemocratic processes, at least in 1982 (i.e., the adventurism of a rogue minister of defense acting outside government procedures). Thirdly, perhaps the most persuasive counter-argument is that Lebanon at this time was not a democracy. Certainly, Israeli policy-makers and citizens alike felt that Lebanon as a state had disintegrated. The constitutionally elected parliament and legally formed government in Beirut was unable to control Palestinian and Lebanese armed groups that had been carrying out armed attacks against Israel and Israelis. This observation is indisputable. At the same time, the fact that Lebanon remained, in form and with continuity, a democratic government, with a legally elected president and parliament, is also a nontrivial observation. Lebanon throughout this period was a democracy, for better or worse, albeit almost fatally crippled.

The second episode is perhaps even more debatable, and yet I think it is worth raising: the recent "warfare" between Israel and the Palestinians. Whether the intifada (the Palestinian uprising that began in 1987) can be called a war is, of course, debatable. In its initial phases, at least, the weapon of choice for Palestinians was stones, not firearms. Moreover, Palestine was a state only on paper, and the leadership of the Palestinians is unelected. Nevertheless, the Palestinians indubitably displayed national consciousness and political capabilities, and they did possess certain important attributes of democratic politics, including a parliament (unelected but still representative of various sectors of the Palestinian people), parties, associations, and a greater degree of political freedom than was present in most Arab countries. I would not suggest that the Palestinian community had an indisputable claim to being democratic, but considering their difficult circumstances, one could argue that the Palestinians for many years had been engaged in significant political participation and contestation—Dahl's criteria for democratic behavior. I would venture to argue that the Palestinian community was hardly less democratic than was the Jewish community in British Mandate Palestine. If, for the sake of argument, one accepts these characterizations, then we must consider whether the conflict between "democratic" Palestine and "democratic" Israel constitutes another exception to the proposition that democracies do not fight each other.

Imagining Democratic Arab Regimes:
Foreign Policy Consequences

I turn now to three speculative counterfactual exercises. What if the main Arab state actors had been democratically organized over the past four decades or so? Would individual and collective Arab policies on the major issues of the time—Palestine, Arab unity, and relations with the West—have been much different? Thickets of alternatives present themselves, and it would take a very powerful computer to sort them all out. The methodological issues associated with counterfactuals are formidable; but as Fearon (1991) has pointed out, in small-N comparative research they are a virtual necessity and can yield important findings if used carefully. Not only must the counterfactual antecedent, when joined with appropriate theories and facts, imply the consequent, but the counterfactual antecedent must be " 'cotenable' with the facts or 'initial conditions' used to draw the inference, meaning that if the antecedent had actually occurred, the initial conditions could also have occurred" (Fearon 1991, p. 193). Whether the counterfactual assumption of "Arab democracies" meets the test of cotenability is obviously debatable; and I wish to reiterate that our speculations are intended not as a formal test but merely as an exploratory exercise.

First, we must imagine what "democratic" Arab regimes might look like. Let us take Turkey—the only long-functioning, indigenous Middle Eastern democracy (recognizing all its limitations)—as a heuristic model. Suppose that Egypt, Jordan, Syria, Iraq, and Saudi Arabia actually had a domestic political environment similar to that of Turkey. Imagine that each of them had two major parties, one dominated by conservative business interests respectful of religion and tradition (e.g., the Turkish Democrat/True Path party), the other dominated by left-of-center nationalists, technocrats, secularists, and statists (e.g., the Turkish Republican Peoples' Party/Social Democrat Populists). Imagine further (without getting into details) that transitions from one party to the other occurred occasionally and that there was some significant degree of freedom of political expression and association. We would expect, in addition, that there would be radical and transnational movements on the left and on the religious right which, although largely "outside" the formal system, would still exert influence derived from the "masses" and pose certain concerns for the organized mainstream parties. Policy outcomes—domestic and foreign—would reflect the outlooks and interests of the leading elements in Arab society: the "civil" elements like the business community, the landed elite, the professions, the intelligentsia, and labor; and also the military, which would play a "guardian" role.

I have proposed the Turkish model because it takes some account of the historical, social, and cultural milieu of the contemporary Arab political systems. Alternatively, I could have stipulated a "purer" philosophical model of liberal democracy, but to do so might have necessitated a greater suspension of analytical disbelief than would be acceptable to most social scientists or Middle East specialists. But there is a price for this greater empirical "fit" in relation to the proposition that "democracies" don't (often) fight each other. The logic of that proposition as explicated by Doyle (1983), Russett (1990) and others places considerable weight on the "liberal" character of democratic systems: mutual recognition of system legitimacy depends on genuine popular representation and individual rights and liberties. Does the Turkish model or any intuitively plausible Arab model exhibit enough liberalism to sustain the argument relating democratic structure to (nonwarlike) foreign policy behavior (toward other democracies)? For that matter, does the Israeli model do so?

Be that as it may, to speculate whether this hypothetical alternative to the actual "domestic environment" would have made any difference in foreign policy behavior forces us back to the core theoretical debate: would the imperatives of the international system, mediated through "rational" state actors, tend to produce the same positions and decisions on the part of these Arab governments, regardless of whether they were more-or-less "democratic" in structure, or more-or-less authoritarian? Let us look briefly at issues in three key areas, with particular attention to the Palestine conflict.

Palestine/Israel

If Arab regimes had been "democratic" in the manner stipulated above, would they have pursued policies vis-à-vis Israel other than the ones they have actually pursued? Generalizing very broadly, I am inclined to answer "probably not." If we first consider the Arab-Israeli saga from the Rhodes armistice agreements of 1949 up through 1967, a period when Israel was bent on demonstrating not just its survival capacity but its toughness, it is difficult to imagine political parties in a competitive environment calling for compromise. Indeed, the accommodations sought discreetly in the mid-1950s by the authoritarian Egyptian and Jordanian regimes would have been less likely under leadership more affected by public opinion.

Would more representative regimes have been able to avert the Sinai-Suez war of 1956, the Six Day War of 1967 or the War of Attrition along the Suez canal in 1969–70? It seems unlikely, because the perceptions of objective threat were so intense and pervasive among government decision-makers, but also— and crucially—because popular feelings on all sides were, to say the least, amenable to military action. It seems implausible to me that a democratic regime in Egypt would have been willing or able to curb domestic resistance to Britain's continuing presence in the Canal Zone, the cycle of low-level violence on the Egyptian-Israeli border, and Egypt's support for the Algerian rebellion against France—events that precipitated the tripartite (Israeli, French, and British) aggression against Egypt in 1956.

In the 1967 case, it is now generally agreed that Nasser did not intend to precipitate a war, notwithstanding his provocative action in blockading the Strait of Tiran and demanding the withdrawal of the UN force in Sinai; but the logic of threat (and opportunity) drove Israeli policy-makers to launch their devastating strike. Whether a democratic regime in Egypt at the time might have behaved more prudently is possible, of course, but such a government might well have been driven even more strongly by populist-nationalist pressures than was Nasser's. The same consideration leads me to suspect that a functioning parliamentary system in Jordan would have been more, not less, prone to involve that country in combat: We recall that kings Abdallah and Hussein in past conflicts (1948 and 1956) had sought to restrain rather than fan hawkish parties and public opinion. Syria in 1967 is a more complex case. Certainly the rhetoric and policies of the very radical "neo-Baath" regime contributed to the outbreak of war. It is certainly possible that a hypothetical multiparty parliamentary coalition might have been less provocative. Yet hostility toward Israel, based on real past and present grievances, was ubiquitous in Syrian politics. Whether such a coalition would have been sufficiently less provocative is, I think, doubtful. Israeli policy was not driven only by Syria's hostile rhetoric but by calculations of Syria's threat to Israeli security; and it is hard to imagine Syria's form of government figuring significantly in Israeli calculations. As events unfolded, of course, Israel attacked Syria and the government in Damascus, whatever its form, had no choice but to fight. After their resounding defeat in the Six Day War, the governments of Egypt, Syria, and Jordan—concerned about winning future elections—could hardly have opted for anything other than the three Nos of the Khartoum summit. Similarly, an external factor—the diplomatic impasse over securing Israeli withdrawal from Sinai—which drove Egypt to attempt the unsuccessful War of Attrition in 1969 would very likely have driven a democratic government to the same policy. Under conditions of national emergency, even established democratic governments (such as Israel's, to take a pertinent example) generally give a free hand to the national security establishment, so it is hard to imagine a less robust democratic system doing any less.

The more recent phase of the Arab-Israel dispute, since around 1970, presents greater complexity. It is easy to understand why hypothetical democratically elected governments in Egypt and Syria might have launched a war in 1973 for the purpose of jump-starting a demonstrably stagnant diplomatic process; one can imagine "national unity" governments enjoying massive parliamentary and public support across the political spectrum for a project that would liberate their occupied land in Sinai and the Golan Heights. And while Jordan did not participate (other than in a token way) in the 1973 war, it is plausible to imagine that it might have done so for the same reasons had it been governed by a more representative regime. But could democratic governments in Egypt and Syria have maintained the secrecy necessary for such an enterprise? That war might have been avoidable for the "technical" reason that democracies could not surreptitiously generate consent or maintain the deception.

Let us now consider the Camp David "peace process." We have been suggesting thus far that, contrary to the conventional wisdom, "democratic" Arab governments might have been as war-prone, or even more so, than the actual authoritarian Arab governments. Can we go even farther and suggest that "democratic" Arab governments might be less prone to make peace? It is hard to imagine a genuinely representative government in Egypt being able to muster consent for a dramatic unilateral peace gesture like Sadat's trip to Jerusalem and the subsequent Camp David agreement and peace treaty with Israel. Egyptians and others differ among themselves as to whether Sadat's initiative and Egypt's conclusion of a separate peace with Israel were wise or proper policies. But if one believes that this was "enlightened" foreign policy behavior, one might also be thankful that the leader did not have to answer to the people for it.

Turning finally to Arab government participation in the "peace process" organized by the Bush Administration, we should note first that the logic of Camp David, with its removal of Egypt as the keystone of Arab confrontation of Israel, has redefined the parameters of realism for other Arab governments. "Attentive publics," too, are imbued with a certain new pragmatism, even as other elements mobilize against further perceived sellouts. There was also modest democratization in Mubarak's Egypt and Hussein's Jordan, but greater

democratization did not, on the whole, make it easier for these Arab governments to participate in a process stringently defined by Washington in order
to meet irreducible Israeli requirements regarding Palestinian participation
and the ultimate shape of a solution. In Jordan, the most popular new force,
the Islamists, was (and is), of course, opposed to Jordanian participation. Had
almost all of the opposition in Egypt not boycotted what it felt was a biased
electoral process, might there not have been more resistance to Egypt's facilitating role? Syria's surprising and dramatic cooperation would have required
President Assad to expend some political capital had his dominance over parliament not been so total. If there had been a democratically elected parliament
in Saudi Arabia, with some power, it might have been quite difficult for the
government to meet face to face with the Israelis in Moscow, to receive a delegation of American Jews, and to endorse implicitly a peace process under
which Israel in all probability will maintain sovereignty over Jerusalem. In
short, more democratic systems might not only have had little positive effect
in preventing war but might also have made it more difficult to negotiate peace.

Arab Unity

If Arab regimes had been "democratic," would some greater degree of Arab
unity or cooperation have been achieved? The fact that nondemocratic regimes
have failed to achieve very much inter-Arab cooperation, let alone unity, does
not allow us to conclude that democratic regimes would have succeeded. Indeed, Arab integration projects initiated through more participatory domestic
processes might have been harder to achieve than those sponsored by individual leaders, inasmuch as the competing interests of various parties and groups
would have been brought into play. Once achieved in this manner, however, it
is likely that such projects would have endured longer than the ephemeral
schemes of populist-authoritarian presidents.

Arab politics in the post-World War II period were driven by the ideological
imperative of Arabism and by the realpolitik imperative of the ever-shifting
balance of power in what was, for the most part, a multipolar state system.
Would-be hegemons, notably Nasser, exploited the ideological resource of
unity to strengthen (at least in the near term) the raison d'état. But the pursuit
of hegemony inevitably brought into play balancing behavior and the formation of countercoalitions. Driven at the system level by "objective" security
considerations—and ambition—state actors regularly sacrificed unity for more
immediate concerns. I find it difficult to imagine that more democratic regimes

would have behaved much differently. But I can imagine one important miti-
gating factor. To the extent that wider participation might have induced more
intelligent policy-making—in particular, an appreciation of the many economic, cultural, and political advantages of integration—the pursuit of unity
might have elicited steadier, less emotional support. An incremental and functional approach to integration or unity would also have reduced the fears and
jealousies that the more grandiose and totalistic visions of unity aroused
among the less powerful states.

The glacial, detailed, tedious process of European integration, marked by
endless negotiations over agricultural and business issues, among many others,
seems the antithesis of the poorly planned ventures in Arab unity, such as the
United Arab Republic and assorted short-lived, empty "confederations." The
pluralistic, democratic character of the European state actors necessitated such
an approach, and it appears to have delivered many impressive results. Arab
countries, it should be noted, did not lack for the technical expertise to pursue
functional integration. The level of planning exhibited at the 1980 Arab "development" summit, for example, was impressive; but regimes proved incapable
of the systematic elaboration and implementation of the plans.

Relations with the U.S.

If Arab regimes had been "democratic," would they have positioned themselves differently vis-à-vis the United States? We begin with the observation
that the governments most closely and continually aligned with the U.S. since
the 1950s were not democratic—Saudi Arabia, Jordan, Tunisia, Morocco. Lebanon is a doubly qualified exception: a qualified democracy and a qualified
alignment. Of course, the Arab states aligned against the U.S. for much of this
period were not democratic either—Egypt under Nasser, Iraq, Syria, Libya under Qaddafi. Raison d'état, or more precisely raison de régime, was the rationale
behind pro-U.S. alignments: U.S. support was a bulwark against the security
threats of Arab nationalism and Soviet-backed communism; and the oil connection made for a very special relationship in the case of Saudi Arabia. These
considerations overrode distaste for American support of Israel.

Had "civil society" been more strongly represented in the councils of government in these countries, through political parties, interest groups, and a
freer press, I think the moral, national, and perhaps religious issue of Palestine
would have played a more prominent role than calculations of realpolitik. The
extent to which anti-U.S. regimes enjoyed broad popularity (though they were

undemocratic) resulted in significant part from their championing of the Arab position on Palestine and Israel. I think that it would have been more difficult for Washington to enlist Arab governments' support for containing Soviet expansionism and the spread of communism because parties and independents represented in Arab parliaments probably would have placed higher priority on national issues than on superpower rivalries in the region, and also because anti-U.S. groupings would have had substantial visibility and influence.

Let us not exaggerate or oversimplify anti-American feeling in Arab civil society. More democratic Arab political systems would presumably have represented (to one degree or another) a variety of group interests. Borrowing again from the Turkish model, it is conceivable that a conservative, business-oriented party might have come to dominate some Arab parliaments, or at least to be a significant minority party. Such a party might well have counseled a pragmatic approach to the U.S. and the West in general. The attractiveness of (or dependency on) U.S. economic, technological, and cultural resources, even at times of deep political animosity, would not have been inconsequential. In Saudi Arabia, for example, it is very likely that such a tendency would have played a leading role. But even in countries that became vociferously anti-American one can imagine a more temperate foreign policy climate than what actually transpired under populist-authoritarian rulers. Moreover, such a climate might have diminished the demonizing of the Arabs that occurred in the American policy arena, contributing possibly to a more evenhanded American stance in the Middle East.

There is some plausibility to a realist analysis that American interests were better served by undemocratic Arab regimes because authoritarian rulers could pursue regime interests without the distraction of unruly and unfriendly public opinion. This is fine as long as those dictators felt their interests lay with the U.S.—often, of course, they felt otherwise. On the other hand, democratically elected regimes might have engendered more popular respect for foreign policy positions, even controversial ones, than autocratic regimes perceived as colluding with hostile foreign powers. The logic of international politics (as realist theorists such as Waltz and historians such as Brown conceive it) suggests that an involved outside power like the U.S. is bound to be drawn into the balance of power "game" in the Middle East, making (and changing) both "friends" and "enemies," regardless of their democratic or undemocratic character. But to the extent that the domestic environment is represented in foreign policy decision-making, one might envisage a struggle between popular ideological positions (hostile to the U.S.) and particular interests (favorable to a U.S. connection).

Assessing the Counterfactuals

In his methodological analysis of counterfactuals, Fearon declares that it is not appropriate to criticize them simply by insisting that they could not have occurred; rather, the critic must show that "nothing else would also have been different in a way that would have materially affected the outcome" (Fearon 1991, p. 195). Taken very strictly, this "cotenability" requirement might doom most counterfactual analyses to inconsequence. This would appear to be especially true in the thicket of Middle East politics, where Brown, quoting an Arab diplomat, states that "everything is related to everything else" (1984, p. 16). Does the counterfactual implantation of Arab democracy into the situations discussed above "muddy the historical waters" so much that no valid inferences are possible? My inference—that, in general, "Arab democracy" would not have altered Arab foreign policy outcomes very much—is open to challenge on these grounds. But perhaps the challenge can be rebutted. Let me confine the discussion to the Palestine/Israel conflict. The "democracies don't fight democracies" hypothesis rests in part on mutual perceptions of what we might call liberal-democratic legitimacy. If Arab governments are imagined to have become democratic at time-1, we cannot make the ceteris paribus assumption that democratic Israel would not be influenced by that development and soften its aggressive policies at time-2, raising the possibility, therefore, that the democratic Arab regimes would (contrary to my inference) moderate their hostile policies at time-3, and so on. One might at this point conclude that cotenability is indeed impossible and that the whole historical environment would become so completely, and unpredictably, altered that the exercise is pointless.

Short of giving up entirely, however, one could ask the narrower question: How likely would it have been for Israeli decision-makers to alter their behavior if confronted with democratic Arab governments? My own reading of Israeli political dynamics does not convince me that key military and national security leaders would have "given the benefit of the doubt" to their Arab neighbors just because they were legitimately elected. The imperatives of Zionist ideology, the traumas of Jewish history, the givens of the balance of power, and the backing of the United States would all have driven Israel toward the tough stance that it in fact adopted. Even if hypothetical Arab democracies had been less "threatening" (an unlikely eventuality, as I have suggested), I find it difficult to imagine a reciprocal softening caused by the democratic nature of Israel. Israel is a democracy in many respects, but in studying its foreign policy behavior, one must wonder whether the liberal-democratic norms and expectations Doyle and others use to explain the "democracies don't fight each other" proposition have been operative in the domain of Israel's national security policy.

Prospects for Democratization and Foreign Policy

The following tentative conclusions can be drawn from our historical speculations: First, the Arab (and Arab/Israeli) cases do not clearly indicate a clear relationship between regime structure ("democracy") and foreign policy behavior. This is mainly because there is so little democracy in this region. Second, to the extent that there might be such a relationship, these cases suggest that "democratic" structures might be less "peace-prone" than authoritarian structures. In the few instances of Arab democracy, we do find examples of warfare and armed combat with "democratic" Israel. This conclusion is also supported by our counterfactual analyses. Third, the Middle East experience provides more compelling support for the corollary to the "democracies don't fight democracies" proposition, i.e., that democracies are quite belligerent in dealing with non-democracies, than for the main proposition itself. "Democratic" Israel fought wars with "undemocratic" Arab regimes in 1956, 1967, 1969–70, and 1973 (see Schweller 1992, pp. 264–67). It should be noted, however, that most writers on the Middle East do not identify regime type as a major cause of these conflicts but focus instead on "real" grievances, security issues, and ideological factors. Fourth, "regime type" is a clumsy variable—static, hard to define, and hard to apply. Perhaps it is more appropriate for long-term historical and global comparisons than for the dynamics of conflict in the contemporary Middle East. For the latter purpose, more promising political variables might include regime stability and regime capabilities. And for investigations of this level and scope, regime type may be less causally sensitive than regime identity. Who governs? The form may be parliamentary, but it matters whether the government is made up of conservative businessmen or radical professionals. It matters whether it is one-party dominant or a fragile coalition of disparate parties. And the degree of contestation and participation is also important. In short, refinements will be necessary for further fruitful investigation of the democratization and foreign policy question.

Finally, I would like to address briefly the prospects for democratization in the Arab world and ponder how governments more representative of societies torn by socioeconomic dislocations and ideological ferment, yet increasingly intruded upon by "the new world order," might behave in their external security, diplomatic, and economic relations. There are two contradictory trends at work in the post-Soviet, post-Gulf War Arab world. One is the growing disjunction between state and society, between regime and opposition that is creating a crisis of governance in which democratic "openings" are becoming possible. The other is the growing imperative for Arab states to accommodate themselves to the power and interests of the new world hegemon, the U.S.

The deepening of economic and social tensions exacerbated by the Gulf War has generated protest movements against incumbent regimes and systems, and the worldwide perception of democracy in the ascendancy has challenged regimes and civil society alike. The shift of economic development doctrines in a neoclassical direction—away from the state and toward the market—has strengthened the calls for a parallel devolution of political power. Simultaneously, Islamic political movements have in many places taken the lead in filling the participation vacuum. Although the sociological conditions for democratic opening may be favorable, it is by no means certain that democratization projects will succeed—as the Algerian example reminds us. But if they were to succeed, with Islamic parties in positions of influence, my guess is that foreign policy positions would take on a more anti-American, anti-Israeli, pro-unity character. But they would not be wholly doctrinaire or monolithic because the democratic process itself, and the accompanying process of economic liberalization, would generate competing interests and policy alternatives.

In addition, the second trend I have mentioned—the logic of the "New World Order"—is likely to generate "pragmatic," "realistic" conceptions of national interest which will further temper "extremist" impulses. The evolution of Iranian foreign policy under Ayatollah Khomeini's successor illustrates the dynamic. Democratization in the Arab world or anywhere else is not going to be "risk-free." But it is not going to lead inexorably to wars and regional crises either. Nor, on the other hand, is democratization a panacea that can eliminate regional conflict. In the long run, the dynamics of the international system take precedence over the domestic environment. Other things being equal, I would argue that democratic decision processes are marginally preferable to dictatorships because they reduce the chances of leaders making egregiously irrational mistakes.

REFERENCES

Bar-Siman-Tov, Yaacov. 1980. *The Israeli-Egyptian War of Attrition, 1969–1970.* New York: Columbia University Press.

Batatu, Hanna. 1978. *The Old Social Classes and the Revolutionary Movements of Iraq.* Princeton: Princeton University Press.

Bowie, Robert R. 1974. *Suez 1956.* New York: Oxford University Press.

Brecher, Michael. 1972. *The Foreign Policy System of Israel: Setting, Images, Process.* New Haven: Yale University Press.

Brown, L. Carl. 1984. *International Politics and the Middle East.* Princeton: Princeton University Press.

Dahl, Robert A. 1971. *Polyarchy: Participation and Opposition.* New Haven: Yale University Press.

Dann, Uriel. 1969. *Iraq under Qassem.* Jerusalem: Israel Universities Press.

Doyle, Michael W. 1983a. "Kant, Liberal Legacies, and Foreign Affairs [Part 1]." *Philosophy and Public Affairs* 12, no. 3 (Summer), pp. 205–35.

————. 1983b. "Kant, Liberal Legacies, and Foreign Affairs [Part 2]." 12, no. 4 (Fall), pp. 323–53.

Fearon, James D. 1991. "Counterfactuals and Hypothesis Testing in Political Science." *World Politics* 43, no. 2 (January), pp. 169–95.

Flapan, Simha. 1987. *The Birth of Israel: Myths and Realities.* New York: Pantheon.

Gallman, Waldemar J. 1964. *Iraq under General Nuri.* Baltimore: Johns Hopkins University Press.

Glubb, Sir John Bagot. 1957. *A Soldier with the Arabs.* London: Hodder and Stoughton.

Gubser, Peter. 1983. *Jordan: Crossroads of Middle Eastern Events.* Boulder, CO: Westview.

Insight Team of The London Sunday Times. 1974. *The Yom Kippur War.* New York: Doubleday.

Kedourie, Ellie. 1992. *Democracy and Arab Political Culture.* Washington, DC: Washington Institute for Near East Policy.

Khalidi, Walid, ed. 1971. *From Haven to Conquest: Readings in Zionism and the Palestine Problem until 1948.* Beirut: Institute for Palestine Studies.

Khoury, Philip S. 1987. *Syria and the French Mandate.* Princeton: Princeton University Press.

Korany, Bahgat, and Ali E. Hillal Dessouki et al. 1991. *The Foreign Policies of Arab States. The Challenge of Change.* 2nd ed. Boulder, CO: Westview.

Lijphart, Arend. 1974. "The Structure of the Theoretical Revolution in International Politics." *International Studies Quarterly* 18, no. 1 (March), pp. 41–74.

Neff, Donald. 1981. *Warriors at Suez*. New York: Linden Press/Simon and Schuster.

———. 1984. *Warriors for Jerusalem*. New York: Linden Press/Simon and Schuster.

Patai, Raphael. 1958. *The Kingdom of Jordan*. Princeton: Princeton University Press.

Russett, Bruce M. 1990. *Controlling the Sword: The Democratic Governance of National Security*. Cambridge: Harvard University Press.

Safran, Nadav. 1969. *From War to War: The Arab Israeli Confrontation, 1948–1967*. New York: Pegasus.

Schiff, Ze'ev and Ehud Ya'ari. 1984. *Israel's Lebanon War*. New York: Simon and Schuster.

Schweller, Randall L. 1992. "Domestic Structure and Preventive War: Are Democracies More Pacific?" *World Politics* 44, no. 2 (January), pp. 235–69.

Seale, Patrick. 1965 [1986]. *The Struggle for Syria*. London: Oxford University Press [repr. New Haven: Yale University Press].

Shlaim, Avi. 1988. *Collusion across the Jordan: King Abdullah, the Zionist Movement, and the Partition of Palestine*. New York: Columbia University Press.

Vatikiotis, P. J. 1969. *The Modern History of Egypt*. London: Weidenfeld & Nicolson.

Walt, Stephen M. 1987. *The Origins of Alliances*. Ithaca, NY: Cornell University Press.

Waltz, Kenneth N. 1959. *Man, the State, and War*. New York: Columbia University Press.

———. 1979. *Theory of International Politics*. Reading, MA: Addison-Wesley.

PART FOUR

CRITICAL CASES

10

DOMESTIC POLITICS AND
FOREIGN POLICY IN EGYPT

ANN M. LESCH

DEMOCRACY INVOLVES BOTH processes and values. Democratic processes include the rule of law, accountability of government, and competition among individuals and groups for positions of government power by means of regular elections. Democracy also involves upholding civic and political liberties, such as freedom of expression and organization. The values that underpin these freedoms are primarily learned through the actual experience of democracy. As groups struggle in the political arena, they discover the necessity of give and take: they must accommodate themselves to partial success or to the hope of winning through a competitive process.

In the Middle East, the popular call for democracy has mixed motivations. Some simply call for governments to be accountable to the people for the policies they formulate and execute as well as for the resources they receive and spend. Some add the demand for a share in decision-making power by the people. Others see democracy as a panacea that offers equality and freedom without commensurate obligations and responsibilities, or they seek to use the ballot box to impose their own political vision.

Analysts remain concerned that most Arab countries still lack the socioeconomic prerequisites for democracy, which include an autonomous civil society, competitive social and economic institutions and forces, and a significantly broad and active middle class. Only by freeing the economy from government domination, they argue, can power be partitioned and organizational pluralism become meaningful. Nonetheless, some analysts argue that democratization is feasible in the Middle East at present, despite numerous obstacles.[1] Others, however, are concerned that efforts to promote political liberalization will weaken the central authority of the state without promoting democracy. The lid on the pressure cooker will be lifted and deep-seated tensions will erupt. In particular, centrifugal ethnic and Islamist forces will be unleashed. Hilal Khashan, for example, urges that governments become more responsive to popular demands but argues that fully competitive political systems are "wishful thinking" today.[2]

Arab rulers face serious dilemmas. One dilemma involves the fact that governments have no choice but to liberalize, since they no longer have the economic and strategic resources with which they can buy acquiescence. Income from oil revenues and worker remittances has dropped in the past decade, and the public sector has decayed and been corrupted. Rulers cannot use their region's strategic importance in the Cold War as leverage to obtain armaments and economic aid. Governments seek to defuse public discontent and pressure for democracy by marginally widening the arena of public debate, allowing limited forms of collective action, and reducing restrictions on the private sector in agriculture, industry, and trade. Those measures, however, encourage processes that incubate political forces independent of the state. Measures that rulers adopt in order to contain protest may, in time, enable autonomous processes to develop that would support genuine democratization.

Another dilemma involves the dynamic interplay of Islamist movements and government policies. If governments forbid Islamists open expression of their views, they will be driven underground and become increasingly antisystemic. But if they are allowed to participate in the public arena, they can mobilize, gain popularity and try to change the system. It is not clear whether Islamist parties are generally antisystemic because they oppose democracy or because the current system is insufficiently pluralist. In any event, they can gain support from those who decry the limited liberalization of the regime as well as those who seek a transformed, Islamic polity. It remains unknown whether, should Islamist movements come to power through the ballot box, they would end democracy or adapt to its norms and processes.

A further dilemma involves the issue of whether governments can take the wind out of the sails of Islamist movements by meeting their demands to overhaul corrupt economic systems, provide employment, and foster moral societies. If the rulers can institute substantive reforms, then the social base of the Islamist movements might retract and they would remain a minority opinion, supported by the ideologically committed for whom material issues are not the sole motivation. Nonetheless, governments are likely to lack the funds and political will to meet even the minimal material demands of the public, and so the Islamists, as the principal opposition movement, can galvanize support on the basis of economic discontent.

The limited democratization in the Middle East and the challenge posed by Islamist movements have implications for the foreign policy of governments in the region. Given the lack of accountability of the regimes and the relative autonomy of government decision-making, foreign policy positions and actions need not reflect underlying public support. If a government diverges too radically from public viewpoints, it might be challenged by counterelites or mass protests. But government control over the media can ensure that its perspective dominates, and the regime can unleash the security forces to guarantee order in the streets. Moreover, governments can use foreign policy to distract public attention from domestic problems: criticism of Israel and the U.S. may be encouraged, whereas public protests over domestic issues can be crushed.

An argument can be made that enhanced democratization will alter the foreign policies of governments in the region. When governments become more accountable and citizens feel they have a voice in decision-making, Mark Tessler argues, public anger will be reduced and governments will be less apt to use foreign policy to deflect attention from domestic grievances.[3] Moreover, he maintains, institutional constraints will be enhanced since decision-making will be more diffuse and subject to greater scrutiny. Individual rulers will not be able to take arbitrary actions: a network of institutions will constrain them and public opinion will have autonomous modes of expression and action. The public will oppose activist foreign policies that would divert funds from domestic needs and risk the lives of citizens. A Saddam Hussein would have more difficulty launching a war with Iran or attacking Kuwait; a Mu'ammar Qaddafi would have to account for his adventures abroad.

On the other hand, the argument can also be made that democratization could lead to more bellicose foreign policies. Pent up anger, once released, could erupt over foreign as well as domestic issues. The anger at the United States that exploded in Iran in 1979, while channeled by the revolutionary government, reflected genuine grievances. Popular suspicion of Israel remains widespread and, in a crisis, could be difficult for a democratic government to contain. The public could press the government to respond strongly to provocations from abroad, reducing the government's room to maneuver. Moreover, even if the public is cautious about committing the country to an activist policy, the executive branch would retain considerable discretionary authority over foreign policy and would be able to manipulate public opinion to support its aims, as the American experience attests.

No Arab country has undergone a transition from autocracy to democracy since World War II, although Yemen made significant progress in this direction before the newly unified country came unglued in 1994. There is, therefore, no meaningful historical evidence of how democratization might affect regional foreign policies. Nonetheless, the Egyptian case is an interesting subject of examination and could illuminate some of the problems associated with democratization. The governing system has shifted from one-party authoritarian rule to limited democratization since the mid-1970s, permitting the relatively open expression of views on domestic and international issues. Political forces range across a wide spectrum, from left and liberal to Islamist. Nonetheless, power remains tightly held by the executive, which utilizes the dominant political party, the ramified bureaucracy, and pervasive security organs to implement and enforce its policies. Since the mid-1970s, rulers have significantly reoriented Egypt's foreign policy, with minimal consultation of public political forces and only pro forma approval by the parliament. Rulers have also tended to restrict political expression at critical moments when there was public dissent over policy moves. The cases of President Anwar Sadat's peace initiative toward Israel and President Hosni Mubarak's policy during the Gulf crisis of 1990–91 offer useful comparisons. The two presidents adopted differing approaches toward public opinion during those periods of high tension and policy change; yet each acted without consulting public political forces on the basis of his authority as chief executive.

Limited Democracy in Egypt

Egypt represents a particular blend of authoritarian and constitutional rule. Gamal Abdul Nasser's legitimacy was based on the revolution of July 1952. And yet that legitimacy was augmented by constitutional structures that provided for a strong executive and a one-party parliament. The constitutional system was bolstered by the orderly transition to the vice president, Sadat, when Nasser died in 1970 and to Mubarak when Sadat was assassinated in 1981. Nonetheless, under Nasser and Sadat, the rule of law was severely curtailed, the press censored, and organizational life restricted. Sadat did allow the formation of political parties in 1976, but he manipulated the parliamentary and local elections to ensure safe majorities for the ruling party.

Mubarak has emphasized the importance of the rule of law on the basis of the constitution.[4] He has upheld freedom of the press and multiparty political processes. Nevertheless, democratization has distinct limits. Military and security forces remain the key institutions underpinning the regime, and Mubarak has retained the restrictive state of emergency, in force since Sadat's assassination. Moreover, the governing National Democratic Party (NDP) maintains its dominance, relegating the other parties to minor roles. The governing elite's concern to control and manage social forces contrasts with the president's stated commitment to democratization. Mubarak himself has stopped short of full-fledged political liberalization. His preoccupation with stability—and his fear that civic order could crumble—outweigh his commitment to reform.

Indications of the limits to democratization include:

☐ The president is elected for a six-year term on the basis of a one-candidate plebiscite. In 1987 the speaker of parliament prevented other candidates from even nominating themselves. When the plebiscite was held that fall, the government claimed that 97 percent voted "yes" for Mubarak and that 88.5 percent of the electorate voted. (In parliamentary elections, voter turnout rarely exceeds 45 percent overall and 10 percent in the big cities, and so most observers viewed the presidential tally as substantially inflated.)

☐ In the elections for the People's Assembly, the governing party has never received less than three-quarters of the seats, guaranteeing itself the two-thirds needed to select the speaker, dominate committees, pass vital legislation, and nominate the president. The party's share was 82 percent in 1976, 88 percent in 1979, 87 percent in 1984, 78 percent in 1987, and 79 percent in 1990. The latter figure, however, masked a substantial decline: the NDP received only 58 percent, with the additional 21 percent reflecting MPs who joined the party after they won their seats as independent candidates.[5]

☐ During the parliamentary election campaigns, opposition parties have only a half hour to present their platforms on television and radio. In contrast, the president, his cabinet and the NDP make full use of the electronic media throughout the campaign.

☐ Elections are supervised by the Interior Ministry, which is controlled by the president and the NDP, rather than by impartial judicial officials as specified in Article 88 of the constitution. Government and public sector employees operate the election subcommittees. That exacerbated charges of election fraud and triggered a boycott of the 1990 parliamentary election by the major opposition parties.

☐ The movement of members of the assembly has been restricted, in violation of their parliamentary immunity. In one case, security officers searched a public bus traveling from Cairo to Suez and forcibly removed an Islamist MP. Utilizing emergency regulations, they prevented him from attending a religious rally in Suez and compelled him to return to Cairo.

❑ The electoral system for the upper house of parliament, called the Consultative Council (*Majlis al-Shura*), provides that the party that wins the most votes receives all the seats in that district. Since that system guarantees the NDP a monopoly in the Council, the opposition parties have boycotted elections since 1983, not wanting to legitimize a biased system.

❑ Since 1983, village-level councils are also elected under the winner-take-all party list system. The elections used to be contested vigorously, but the opposition parties subsequently boycotted them. When the opposition parties considered strengthening their hand by running coalition slates in 1988, the government rushed a bill through the People's Assembly prohibiting anyone from running under the label of another party. Without access to power and patronage at the grassroots level, opposition parties have no prospect of developing broad-based movements to challenge the NDP's control.

❑ In order to promote social peace, the constitution bans the formation of political parties based on religion, class, faction, or geography. The political parties law of 1977 also specifies that a new party cannot duplicate the program of an existing party. That prevents Islamist, Coptic, Communist, and Nasserite parties from being authorized. The Muslim Brotherhood circumvented the ban by running members either as independents, or under the rubric of the New Wafd party in 1984, or in alliance with the Labor and Liberal parties in 1987. In 1984, eight Islamists won seats, and in 1987 they gained 36, making them the dominant partner in the alliance but giving them only 8 percent of the seats in the assembly. Although the Coptic community comprises about 10 percent of the population, Copts spread their votes among several parties and their candidates are rarely elected. They rely on the president to select approximately four Copts among the ten MPs that he is authorized to appoint to the Assembly, a form of cooptation that some Copts resent since it means that those MPs do not represent the people's will but serve at the government's pleasure.[6] Nasserites and Communists formed an uneasy alliance in the Progressive Unionist (Tagammu) Party in 1976, since their own parties are banned; in 1990, several ran as independents. Nasserite parties have been refused registration on the grounds that the NDP is the sole heir to Nasser's legacy.

❑ The state of emergency gives the president the power to restrain the movement of citizens, forbid meetings, intern suspects, search persons or places, and ban publications. Under those regulations, security forces also cordon off villages, force their way into mosques, and retain in prison persons who have been acquitted by the courts.

The cumulative effect of these restrictions is to maximize the authority of the executive branch and its political party and to minimize the impact of the opposition groups. Even though they can field candidates and publish newspapers, they cannot gain the kind of grassroots following that would enable them to have a solid presence in the political arena. Some opposition MPs provide services to their constituents that guarantee them long-term support, but certain parties barely exist aside from their newspapers. Islamist groups have a distinct advantage: they have access to mosques, operate charitable societies, and promote Islamic banks and investment companies. They run medical clinics and literacy programs, provide low-cost clothes and books for students, and contribute food and even cash for the indigent. Given the deterioration in the quality of government services since the 1970s, the Islamic charities meet an important need. Thus, government restrictions on the formation of civic and political groups have disproportionately hampered liberal and left movements, while leaving loopholes for the religious groups.

The judiciary has played an important role in balancing the power of the executive. Under Mubarak, the Administrative Court of the State Council and the High Constitutional Court have decided landmark cases upholding constitutional freedoms. In 1983, for example, the Administrative Court allowed the New Wafd Party to resume functioning after it suspended operations in 1978. In early 1984, the court lifted the thirty-year-old ban on participation in political life by the leader of the Wafd. The High Constitutional Court ruled unconstitutional the electoral system that required citizens to run for parliament as part of a political party rather than as independents: the court compelled Mubarak to redraft the electoral law in 1986 and again in 1989, and this resulted in the return to the individual constituency system in the election of 1990. Moreover, in 1985 the High Constitutional Court placed restrictions on the president's right to issue decrees when the Assembly is not in session. The court ruled that decrees are only permissible for urgent business, not for issues that could be raised in the regular session of the parliament.

The opposition parties have come to rely on the courts to achieve reforms they cannot gain through the parliamentary process. In the wake of the 1990 elections, for example, the parties that boycotted the polls hoped that the High Constitutional Court would rule that the elections were invalid on the grounds that they violated the constitutional provision for judicial supervision. Cases that challenge the elections are still pending in the courts.

The judicial rulings have provided an important restraint on the executive. Significantly, Mubarak has not challenged the validity of the court rulings. In the case involving the president's power to issue decrees, he revoked the decree that the court annulled and submitted new legislation to the Assembly. In the electoral cases, he redrafted the electoral law, called referenda to endorse the reforms, dissolved the parliament, and held new elections according to the reformed system. The right of the Wafd and its leader to participate in politics was also not challenged.

Nonetheless, Mubarak has resisted additional reforms. He has not agreed to let the judiciary supervise elections; not opened up the electronic media to opposition parties; not lifted the state of emergency; and not altered the election system for the Consultative Council and local councils. Opposition parties' irritation at these restrictions culminated in the boycott of the Assembly election in fall 1990 by the Wafd, Labor, and Liberal parties, and by the Muslim Brotherhood.[7] Opposition leaders also criticize Mubarak for not meeting with them, much less consulting them about pending actions. Ibrahim Shukri (head of the Labor party) complained: Mubarak accuses the opposition of "deviating" from the national consensus, but he does not conduct a dialogue with the opposition through which a consensus could emerge.[8] The editor of *al-Wafd* noted in fall 1990 that the new election law should not be prepared in secret and sprung upon the Assembly and the public; rather, the parties, politicians, judges, and constitutional law experts should review its provisions. Such a discussion could serve as an important tool for making democracy a reality and transferring authority to the people.[9]

Mubarak has argued that limited liberalization is essential for Egypt. He talks of doling out "democracy in doses"[10] to a public that is only 60 percent literate, experiencing substantial unemployment, inexperienced in civic life, and potentially susceptible to interreligious strife. Suddenly and totally opening up the political system could destabilize social and political life, he argues. Mubarak justifies continuing the state of emergency by citing the violence carried out by extreme Islamist groups, including attacks on Copts in Cairo and rural areas as well as the assassination of the speaker of the Assembly in October 1990 and of a secular professor in June 1992. Mubarak expresses fears that

Islamist groups want to manipulate democracy's freedom of organization and expression of views in order to destroy the pluralist system and impose their own ideology.[11]

Skeptics note that such fears may have a real basis but that the government policies which flow from them may exacerbate the situation and prevent genuine democratization. Restricting the establishment of civil associations in itself prevents a pluralist political culture from evolving. Government measures to inhibit multipartyism often appear to be based on a desire to retain control, not on the opposition's potential antidemocratic nature. Until the 1990 elections, for example, the Muslim Brotherhood had resolved to participate in all parliamentary contests, even if the rules were stacked against them. (The decision to boycott apparently caused division within the Brotherhood, as some leaders argued that boycotting violated that resolution and denied the Brotherhood an opportunity to voice its views inside parliament.[12]) The platform of the Islamic Alliance in 1987 differed from the government's program since it called not only for a genuine multiparty system and complete freedom to form parties but also for the application of Islamic law and norms throughout the society. Nonetheless, the demand to introduce Islamic punishments (*hudud*), to Islamize the media and education, to close nightclubs, end gambling, and close factories that produce alcoholic beverages were subsequently presented in the Assembly through legislative procedure, indicating an acceptance of the norms and processes of the existing system. Moreover, several Islamist economic policy demands were congruent with the government's own approach, including the call to decrease the size of the public sector and to reinforce the private sector as the backbone of the economy.[13]

Following the 1990 elections, the political system faces a potentially serious crisis. The main opposition parties are not represented in the Assembly: the tiny opposition inside the Assembly consists of Tagammu, with 7 seats, 14 former Wafdists, and 3 Nasserites. The real opposition takes place in the streets, as the head of the Wafd remarked.[14] The Islamists, in particular, lack the safety valve provided by representation in parliament.[15] This creates the risk of reinforcing the extremists' argument that the democratic game is a waste and a fraud. Thus, the brakes put on democratization could exacerbate public alienation. That, in turn, could help spawn extralegal movements that resort to violence. Not all such movements need be Islamist, since secular and liberal groups are also estranged from the system. The vicious circle of repression and protest is thereby reinforced. The inherent contradiction in Mubarak's concept of "democracy in doses" is noted by Muhammad Abd al-Quddus, an Islamist columnist: Mubarak acts like an absolute ruler who controls the political process rather than like an elected leader who is controlled by the people.[16]

Sadat's Foreign Policy

Sadat sought political opening toward the West and toward the oil-rich Arab states in the Gulf which he thought would lead to financial aid for the faltering Egyptian economy and to diplomatic support and military aid. The *infitah* (open door) policy launched in 1974, following the October war, was designed to promote foreign investment and postwar reconstruction. Moderating the conflict with Israel was an essential component of that strategy: without peace, no U.S. support could be expected and no serious foreign investment contemplated. The disengagement accords of 1974 and 1975 enabled Sadat to reopen the Suez Canal, closed since June 1967, and to regain control over the oil fields in Sinai. Funds from the Gulf rulers helped to reconstruct the cities along the Canal and to underwrite the government budget. Egyptian workers and bureaucrats found jobs in the Gulf, where enhanced oil revenues led to ambitious development projects. The symbiotic relationship was disrupted, however, by the Camp David accords of September 1978 and the Egypt-Israel peace treaty of March 1979. The Gulf states severed diplomatic relations with Cairo and suspended aid and joint industrial projects, although they did not penalize Egyptian migrant workers. Sadat became dependent on the U.S. for financial assistance and became isolated strategically in the Arab world. But little Western investment was obtained, as Sadat remained reluctant to privatize the basic industries or to reduce controls on agriculture. Trade agreements were signed with Israel, but the Egyptian bureaucracy used delaying tactics to resist implementing them.

Sadat's sudden visit to Israel in November 1977 and his subsequent accords were carried out without prior warning to the public or consultation with parliament. Even close advisors dissented: three foreign ministers resigned and other diplomats expressed concern that Sadat's concessions to Israel were too one-sided. The tilt toward the U.S. also disturbed many bureaucrats and members of the NDP, who opposed privatization and feared neocolonialist pressures from the West.

Even though Sadat wielded a commanding majority in the People's Assembly and therefore was certain it would ratify the treaty with Israel, he became increasingly hostile to expressions of dissent. The left-leaning, Arab nationalist

Tagammu party strongly criticized Sadat's peace initiative on the grounds that it violated Arab unity, undercut nonalignment, and would lead to a unilateral agreement with Israel, leaving out the Palestinians and Syria. Sadat became irritated at the statements by Tagammu MPs in the Assembly and called elections in 1979, only halfway through the Assembly's term. He made sure that Tagammu was shut out of the parliament and that the NDP controlled nearly ninety percent of the seats. Sadat even inserted a restriction in the political parties law which banned the formation of parties that opposed the peace treaty with Israel.[17]

In the meantime, Sadat encouraged the formation in 1978 of the moderately socialist Labor party on the assumption that it would support his peace initiative. Labor accepted Camp David "with reservations" in 1979 and was allowed to win seats in the Assembly elections that spring. But the party soon began to express criticism: when Israeli President Yitzhak Navon visited Cairo in November 1980, Sadat had to cancel Navon's planned address to the People's Assembly because of Labor's objections. By early 1981, Labor turned sharply against Sadat's foreign policy and issued strong statements in support of the Palestinians.[18] Relations with the Coptic leadership also became tense when Pope Shenuda II instructed Copts to stay away from Jerusalem so long as its diplomatic status was not resolved and the Christian holy places were under foreign occupation.

Sadat's tacit alignment with the Muslim Brotherhood frayed, too.[19] The Brotherhood had supported Sadat's break with Moscow, his ties with conservative Arab monarchies, his economic liberalization, and his curtailment of the left and Nasserites. In return, the Brotherhood opposed violence by Islamist groups in 1974 and 1977 and tried to contain sectarian tension. But the Brotherhood criticized Sadat for opening Egypt to Western economic and cultural influences, establishing close ties with the U.S., and signing the peace accord with Israel. Israel was termed an illegitimate state, created on land that had been usurped from Muslims; the Brotherhood called for a *jihad* (holy war) to restore Palestine to the Muslim world. The Brotherhood intensified its criticism when Saudi Arabia and other conservative Arab states broke off relations with Egypt, since those states had close ties to the Islamist movement. But the Brotherhood did not seek a showdown with Sadat.

Sadat's reaction to criticism of his foreign policy illustrated the superficiality of his commitment to opening the Egyptian political system. He clamped down on the opposition parties and muzzled the parliament as soon as dissident voices began to express their views. The more isolated he became and the more difficulties his policies faced, the more autocratic his measures. Negotiations with Israel on Palestinian autonomy foundered, and the Israeli government embarrassed him not only by annexing East Jerusalem and the Golan Heights but also by bombing the Iraqi nuclear reactor the day after Sadat hosted a summit meeting with Prime Minister Menachem Begin in Sinai. As opposition mounted—including calls to sever relations and recall the Egyptian ambassador from Tel Aviv—Sadat arrested over 1500 politicians in September 1981. Leaders of the Brotherhood, Wafd, Labor, and Tagammu parties, heads of the journalists' and lawyers' associations, and dignitaries of the Coptic church were jailed alongside members of violent Islamist groups. Members of the Islamist group al-Jihad then assassinated Sadat.

One could ask what would have happened if a democratic system had already been in place in Egypt. Would Sadat have taken the bold and unilateral initiative of seeking peace with Israel? If he had been compelled to win support from parliament and debate his policies in public, would his actions have been curtailed by the Assembly? Might the MPs have refused to ratify the peace treaty? Raising those questions suggests that an authoritarian Sadat was necessary in order for the peace initiative to succeed. On the other hand, one could argue that Sadat's autocratic style made the criticism worse and more bitter. If he had adopted a consensual, open approach, might he have convinced the public that his moves were in Egypt's national interest? Might he have considered the options more fully and avoided the extreme isolation in which Egypt became trapped? Might he have bargained harder with Begin, knowing that they both had electorates to which they were responsible?

Such questions are unanswerable but tantalizing. In practice, Sadat was not willing to subject his foreign policy to public scrutiny and was quick to set aside political liberalization when it risked curtailing his autonomy of action. He paid the ultimate price for disdaining the opinions of his citizens.

Mubarak's Policies toward Israel

Before addressing Mubarak's actions during the Gulf crisis, contrasts could be noted between the ways in which Sadat and Mubarak handled the issue of Israel and relations with the Arab world. A comparison is difficult, since the circumstances differed. Mubarak, for example, could take advantage of Arab vulnerability during the Iran-Iraq war to reestablish Egypt's role in the Arab world without annulling the treaty with Israel. He could also win popular support for assisting Yasir Arafat in the wake of Israel's invasion of Lebanon in 1982 and the Syrian-supported attacks by dissident Palestinians on Arafat's forces in Tripoli. But he went further than that. On the heels of the massacre of Palestinian refugees at Sabra and Shatila in September 1982, he responded to the public outcry by recalling the Egyptian ambassador from Tel Aviv.[20] Mubarak allowed journalists and opposition parties to criticize Israel in the press (to the annoyance of the Israeli embassy), banned Israeli participation in several trade and book fairs in Cairo, did not pressure Egyptians to meet Israelis, and even permitted some anti-Israeli demonstrations on university campuses. Mubarak froze normalization and kept the ambassador away from Israel until the territorial dispute over Taba was submitted to judicial arbitration in September 1986 and Israeli troops had withdrawn from central Lebanon. He did, however, quietly continue the sale of oil, maintain bilateral agricultural accords, and allow the Israeli Academic Center to function in Cairo. His relations with Washington remained close and multifaceted and included basic food support, industrial and agricultural investment projects, and the sale of armaments.

The implications of Mubarak's relatively popular foreign policy for the democratization process are difficult to determine. The opposition parties had less grounds to criticize Mubarak than Sadat. They tended to accept the idea that he, too, was wary of the peace accord but had to maintain its terms in order to retain Sinai. They were pleased at Mubarak's tough style of negotiating with Israel and strongly supported his opening to the Arab world. In the 1984 and 1987 elections, the Wafd candidates (and, in 1984, the Liberals) supported Mubarak's foreign policy toward Israel, the Arabs, and the United States, even though they criticized his domestic policies. In contrast, in 1987 left-leaning Tagammu and the Islamic Alliance criticized Mubarak's unfreezing of relations with Israel and his close economic and military ties with the West. Tagammu argued that Egypt should return to the nonaligned, neutralist policies of Nasser. The Islamic Alliance called for special relations with Muslim countries in order to promote the self-reliance of the *umma* (Islamic community). The Alliance opposed superpower hegemony, encompassing both American penetration of the region and the Soviet military presence in Afghanistan. Islamists also called for support for the Palestinian jihad. Such verbal criticism was tolerated during the election campaign, but practical measures to assist the Palestinians were subject to surveillance. Material aid to the Palestinians in Lebanon and the occupied territories, for example, was carefully circumscribed and public gatherings were restricted to campuses and the premises of political parties. The government-controlled television presented few photos of the Israeli invasion of Lebanon and the Palestinian intifada or uprising.

Some Egyptian politicians argue that Mubarak could have utilized the broad support for his foreign policy in order to enhance democratization. He could have turned to the Wafd as well as his own party for votes in the People's Assembly and, on certain issues, might also have gained support from the Islamic Alliance. He did not, they argue, need to rule exclusively through the NDP. He could have attracted votes from a variety of parties and independent politicians, established his independent political base, and gained greater flexibility in his internal alliances. They even argue that Mubarak could have afforded to allow a second candidate to compete for the presidency in the fall of 1987. Mubarak's popular foreign policy and reputation for personal integrity guaranteed that he would win. A genuinely competitive election would have established his legitimacy on more solid grounds than the one-person plebiscite that he endorsed.

Instead, Mubarak maintained his halfway stance. He allowed critics certain opportunities to express their views, but carefully limited their impact. He adopted his policies with minimal consultation with the Assembly, except for the Taba dispute, and no prior dialogue with the opposition parties. Thus, the opposition remained discontented. They argued that the opportunity was lost to build a national consensus on foreign policy and feared that the autocratic style of policy-making had not diminished.

The Gulf Crisis

Mubarak rapidly adopted a firm position toward Iraq's invasion of Kuwait.[21] He argued that Egypt must participate in the effort to end the occupation of Kuwait or else Saddam Hussein would impose his will on the other Gulf states and become the hegemonic power in the Arab world. Mubarak preferred a negotiated solution under the auspices of the Arab League, but recognized that the League could not protect the Gulf states and that their governments therefore had the right to request American military support. Mubarak was cautious, however, about potential criticism that he was acting on behalf of Washington. He stressed that Egyptian forces were operating under Saudi, not American, command and denied that a deal had been made to forgive Egypt its military debt. (Nonetheless, the U.S. and France did write off $10 billion in debts for armaments, and the Gulf states forgave another $7 billion in loans.)

Mubarak also stressed the economic sacrifices that Egypt was making: trade, bank deposits, and remittances from Kuwait and Iraq were lost, and revenue from the Suez Canal and tourism dropped.

The government was able to galvanize public support for the strong stand against Iraq, in part because of the traditional rivalry between the two countries. Moreover, Iraqi treatment of Egyptian workers in the recent past was deeply resented and meant that there was little popular sympathy for Saddam Hussein. Hussein could also be criticized for bleeding Iraq during the eight-year war with Iran and then agreeing to return to the prewar borders in mid-August 1990 without any quid pro quo. A broad consensus emerged that supported the government.

Opposition politicians joined with Mubarak in denouncing the Iraqi invasion. The Wafd termed it a "barbaric crime," Tagammu called it an unprecedented violation of Arab solidarity, and the Muslim Brotherhood called the invasion "terrifying."[22] Both Tagammu and the Brotherhood feared that Israel and the West would exploit the situation for their benefit and therefore urged Iraq to withdraw immediately. Saddam Hussein, in their view, had violated the canons of Islam as well as Arab norms by seizing Kuwait.

However, divisions surfaced once the large-scale American military presence became evident. Politicians were sensitive to the U.S. presence in Egypt and feared that Washington would impose a hegemonic order on the region. They unanimously called for the swift replacement of foreign forces by Arab troops. Even the Wafd, whose newspaper often sounded more anti-Iraq than the government press, emphasized that Washington had pledged to withdraw U.S. troops as soon as the crisis ended.

Islamists became sharply divided. The editor of *al-Sha'ab* argued in mid-August that "the issue has changed from an Iraqi-Kuwaiti confrontation into an Arab-American one. . . . Now the question of who started it and whether he was right is meaningless. Arab and Islamic peoples are concerned now that armies of all the arrogant [powers] are flocking to hit an Arab-Islamic country."[23] Similarly, *al-Nur* editorialized: "America is a perfidious friend who loves neither the Arabs nor the Muslims," and wants to "swindle" Muslims of their money.[24] In contrast, the same newspaper included an article by a professor from al-Azhar University that maintained that Islam permits Muslims to enlist the help of non-Muslims as long as the purpose is defensive.[25] Similarly, a Liberal party newspaper justified the temporary presence of non-Muslim troops in Saudi Arabia, so long as they were stationed far from Mecca and Medina; its editor argued that Iraq, not the foreigners, threatened the holy places.[26]

The Egyptian government gained freedom to act because of the confusion within the ranks of the opposition. Within each party, some sympathized with Saddam and others denounced him; some supported his effort to link the occupation of Kuwait to the Israeli occupation of Palestinian territory, and others viewed that as cynical manipulation; some endorsed the use of foreign troops, and others rejected any foreign presence. In fact, one can argue that Mubarak decided to hold parliamentary elections on November 29 precisely because the government's popularity was high and the opposition was in disarray. Under normal circumstances, elections by individual constituencies—which the High Constitutional Court insisted be adopted—would have been risky for the NDP, since that system undermines party discipline and allows popular independent candidates to gain support.

Mubarak did not take advantage of the enthusiasm of the Wafd party for his foreign policy in order to reduce his dependence on the NDP and coopt that moderate opposition movement. Instead of rewarding the Wafd by including it in consultations over foreign and domestic policy, Mubarak held it at arm's length.[27] If Wafd leaders had been consulted over the changes in the election law, for example, they might have supported the elections. *Al-wafd* editorialized its fear that the government would use the Gulf crisis as a pretext to reduce democracy, just as the Palestine war had been used as an excuse in the past. Noting that "the Gulf catastrophe is the outcome of dictatorship in Iraq," the editor argued that "the national unanimity that appeared in Egypt in the midst of the Gulf crisis should encourage President Mubarak to repose confidence in the people, abandoning the illusionary party [NDP]. . . . Egypt will never be strong abroad unless it is strong inside."[28] However, Mubarak—and certainly the apparatchiks in the NDP—may have been pleased that most opposition parties boycotted the elections since that enabled the NDP to retain its control of the People's Assembly.

The opposition seriously misplayed its hand when it boycotted the elections. The parties faced a dilemma. They knew that they would have difficulty winning, given the broad support for Mubarak's Gulf policy and given their own divisions. However, they also thought that they could force the government to cancel the elections or yield to their demand for judicial supervision of the polls. They believed that the government would be sensitive to its international image as a democracy in the midst of the Gulf crisis. The respected columnist Mustafa Amin, for example, argued that Egypt was out of step with the rest of the world, which was shifting to genuine multipartyism while Egypt consolidated one-party rule.[29] They thought Mubarak would lose support from Washington if the elections went ahead without meaningful competition. But that perspective misperceived the bases for American support for Mubarak and the degree of American interest in democratization in Egypt. Instead of viewing the boycott as a sign of the regime's failure, the U.S. ignored the elections and Mubarak used them to consolidate his control. The opposition could not exert meaningful leverage through the boycott and, instead, lost even its minimal presence in parliament.

The government recognized that the public mood could be volatile as the crisis unfolded and banned all demonstrations, even those supporting its policy. Mubarak cracked down on Islamist groups and beefed up surveillance of Palestinian residents, particularly after the assassination of the speaker of parliament on October 12.[30] The government became particularly suspicious of the Islamic Alliance and the editors of the newspaper *al-Sha'ab*. The heads of the Labor party and Muslim Brotherhood and three journalists were briefly banned from traveling abroad to join an Islamic delegation that sought to mediate the crisis. Their loyalty was questioned: government-linked journalists hinted that the politicians were being paid by foreign governments to criticize Egypt. During the air war in January and February 1991, the security services apparently wanted *al-Sha'ab* closed for inciting opinion against the government, but Mubarak rejected such moves. Nonetheless, the government did take legal action against the editors when they violated the security act by publishing claims that American bombers were being serviced at an Egyptian air base.[31] The editor, in turn, complained that the government never provided information to the press: he could not verify whether U.S. B-52 bombers took off from Egyptian airports to hit Iraq or learn the exact mission of the Egyptian forces in Saudi Arabia.[32]

During the air war and the brief ground war, student protests escalated on university campuses. Even so, students tended to condemn both Iraq and the U.S.: they called for Iraq to leave Kuwait, demanded that the U.S. stop bombing Iraq, and urged an Arab, rather than imperialist, solution to the conflict.[33] The intensity of the demands grew after the U.S. bombed the air raid shelter in Baghdad and after the extent of damage to civilian areas became known. Demonstrators expressed fears that Washington aimed to destroy Iraq, not just liberate Kuwait, and that the U.S. was acting as Israel's agent in the attack.[34] *Al-Sha'ab* even called for Egypt to withdraw its forces from the front. On the eve of the ground war, all the opposition parties except the Wafd issued a joint appeal to Mubarak to support a negotiated settlement along the lines of the Soviet initiative. In contrast, the Wafd insisted that Egyptian troops remain in

Saudi Arabia and rejected a premature cease-fire.[35] In turn, government officials were careful to stress that Egypt aimed to liberate Kuwait, not occupy Iraq,
and that the Palestine issue must be confronted as soon as the fighting ended.[36]

The government was able to ride out the protests, given the divisions within
the opposition and given the brevity of the ground war. In the aftermath,
Egypt's only serious Arab rival was destroyed and Egypt claimed diplomatic
success when the U.S. initiated comprehensive negotiations among Israel, Syria,
Jordan, Lebanon, and the Palestinians. Egypt's centrality was symbolized by
the appointment of the former foreign minister as secretary-general of the
Arab League and the selection of an Egyptian diplomat as secretary-general of
the United Nations. Egypt's debt was slashed and relatively favorable terms
were negotiated with the International Monetary Fund. Thus, Mubarak
emerged from the Gulf crisis with unchallenged supremacy on the home
front.[37] The opposition parties were virtually shut out of the parliament and
uncertain what approach to adopt to recoup their losses.

The outcome was even less government accountability than before. The government had never involved the public in dealing with the debt problems or in
the decisions during the Gulf crisis. Whereas the American president had to
account to congress for his policies, leading to the dramatic January vote in
support of the use of force, Mubarak and his advisors could deliberate and act
without public accountability. An Egyptian human rights activist cautioned
that the Gulf crisis "arrested the slow progress of democratization" since "Mubarak formulated all policy and took all the decisions" with only insignificant
dissent in small opposition newspapers.[38]

Conclusion

Fundamentally the process of selective and partial democratization contains inherent contradictions. So long as democratization takes place from the
top down—as a grant to the people from the ruler—the process remains problematic. The ruler, under those circumstances, asks whether the public is ready
for democracy. He is apt to prefer stability and control over the perceived risk
of chaos.

The real question is whether the ruler is ready for the people's participation
since it would mean accepting limits to his own power and being held accountable to the public. Egypt shifted toward the rule of law under Mubarak, but
executive control remains tight. The contradictions inherent in the concept of
"democracy in doses" may undermine efforts to extend political reform.

Those contradictions also affect foreign policy. Opposition groups can ventilate their views through limited-circulation newspapers and carefully circumscribed public protests, along the lines of the student demonstrations on campuses. But they cannot influence the formulation of foreign policy, and the public remains ignorant of the rationale for particular measures. A sense of frustration builds up, especially when vital security and economic issues are at stake. In the 1970s, the public had no means to affect Sadat's diplomacy, and today the citizens cannot influence Mubarak through any structured system. Given the incompleteness of democratization in Egypt, the questions posed in the beginning of this essay cannot be answered. The imbalance in power between the government and the opposition can lead to tension in the domestic arena, make the opposition disillusioned with the parliamentary process, and prevent a pluralist system from evolving. Similarly, the imbalance can lead to stridency and mistrust in the diplomatic arena. An irresponsible opposition and an unaccountable executive are the worst possible combination for a stable, well-considered foreign policy.

NOTES

1. See Michael C. Hudson, "After the Gulf War: Prospects for Democratization in the Arab World," *Middle East Journal* 45, no. 3 (Summer 1991), and Muhammad Muslih and Augustus Richard Norton, "The Need for Arab Democracy," *Foreign Policy* 83 (Summer 1991).

2. Hilal Khashan, "The Quagmire of Arab Democracy," *Arab Studies Quarterly* 14, no. 1 (Winter 1992): 30.

3. Mark Tessler and Marilyn Grobschmidt, "Democracy in the Arab World and the Arab-Israeli Conflict," chapter 7, this volume.

4. The discussion of democratization in Egypt is based on the author's "Democracy in Doses: Mubarak Launches His Second Term as President," *Arab Studies Quarterly* 11, no. 4 (Fall 1989): 87–107.

5. *Al-Wafd*, December 9, 1990; as translated in Arab Press Review, Cairo (hereafter APR), no. 476 (December 10, 1990).

6. *Al-Watani* (Coptic weekly newspaper), November 4, 1990, APR no. 466 (November 5, 1990).

7. See, for example, the comments of Ma'mun Hasan al-Hudaybi, head of the Muslim Brothers in the parliament, in *al-Nur*, September 25, 1990, APR no. 456 (October 1, 1990).

8. Lesch, "Democracy in Doses," p. 95.

9. *Al-Wafd,* September 20, 1990, APR no. 454 (September 24, 1990).

10. In a statement on February 12, 1987, Mubarak said: "We are providing doses of democracy in proportion to our ability to absorb them" (quoted by Lesch, "Democracy in Doses," p. 107 n. 44).

11. Ibid., p. 94.

12. *Rose al-Yousef,* December 2, 1990, APR no. 474 (December 3, 1990).

13. Ann M. Lesch, "The Muslim Brotherhood in Egypt: Reform or Revolution?" in *The Religious Challenge to the State,* ed. Matthew C. Moen and Lowell S. Gustafson (Philadelphia: Temple University Press, 1992), p. 201.

14. Fuad Serageddin in *al-Wafd,* November 15, 1990, APR no. 470 (November 19, 1990).

15. *Middle East International* 390 (December 21, 1990), p. 12.

16. Lesch, "Democracy in Doses," p. 96.

17. That provision was struck down by the High Constitutional Court in 1988 on the grounds that it undermined the citizens' freedom to express their views.

18. Mona Makram-Ebeid, "Political Opposition in Egypt: Democratic Myth or Reality?" *Middle East Journal* 43, no. 3 (Summer 1989): 427.

19. See Lesch, "The Muslim Brotherhood," pp. 192–93.

20. For an overview of Egyptian policies toward Israel, see Ann M. Lesch, "The Guarded Relationship between Israel and Egypt," in *Israel after Begin,* ed. Gregory S. Mahler (Albany: State University of New York Press, 1990).

21. For a discussion of Egypt's policy, see Ann M. Lesch, "Contrasting Reactions to the Persian Gulf Crisis: Egypt, Syria, Jordan and the Palestinians," *Middle East Journal* 45, no. 1 (Winter 1991): 34–41, 49.

22. *Al-Wafd,* August 5, 1990, and *al-Hakika,* August 4, 1990, APR no. 440 (August 6, 1990).

23. *Al-Sha'ab,* August 14, 1990, APR no. 443 (August 16, 1990).

24. *Al-Nur,* August 8, 1990, APR no. 442 (August 13, 1990).

25. *Al-Nur,* August 29, 1990, APR no. 448 (September 3, 1990).

26. *Al-Hakika,* August 18, 1990, APR no. 444 (August 20, 1990).

27. Commentary by Adel Hussein, *al-Sha'ab,* October 23, 1990, APR no. 463 (October 25, 1990).

28. *Al-Wafd,* September 13, 1990, APR no. 451 (September 17, 1990).

29. *Al-Akhbar,* October 31, 1990, APR no. 465 (November 1, 1990). See also *Middle East International* 388 (December 23, 1990), p. 12, and 398 (April 19, 1991), p. 17.

30. The speaker was killed in broad daylight in the center of Cairo and the assassins escaped by motorcycle. The target was probably the minister of the interior, who was also expected to pass by that site. See *Middle East International* 386 (October 26, 1990), p. 12, and 387 (November 9, 1990), p. 12.

31. APR no. 496 (February 21, 1991) and *Middle East International* 393 (February 8, 1991), p. 19.

32. *Sawt al-Sha'ab*, February 23, 1991, APR no. 497 (February 25, 1991).

33. See reports on campus protests in *al-Wafd*, February 18, 1991, APR no. 496 (February 21, 1991), and Tagammu's *al-Ahali* 497 (February 25, 1991).

34. For example, *Misr al-Fatah*, February 25, 1991, APR no. 498 (February 28, 1991).

35. Adel Hussein in *al-Sha'ab*, February 19, 1991, APR no. 496 (February 21, 1991), and Fuad Serageddin in *al-Wafd*, February 21, 1991, APR no. 497 (February 25, 1991).

36. *Middle East International* 393 (February 8, 1991), p. 15.

37. *Middle East International* 398 (April 19, 1991), p. 17.

38. Ahmed Abdalla, "Human Rights and Elusive Democracy," *Middle East Report* 174 (January 1992): 8.

11

DEMOCRACY AMONG THE PALESTINIANS

EMILE F. SAHLIYEH

A GROWING BODY OF literature argues that democracies are less war prone and as such do not fight other democracies. This assertion is based on the assumption that democratic regimes are inherently peaceful.[1]

Writers on democracy and war offer three interrelated sets of explanations to account for this phenomenon. In his six-volume work on conflict and war, Rudolph J. Rummel sheds much light on the causes behind the nonviolent nature of democratic governments. He asserts that the peaceful nature of democracies is attributable to the fact that freedom inhibits violence and that the degree of democratization in a country is therefore positively associated with the reluctance of that state to initiate wars. Further, since the propensity of a state to engage in war declines as a function of the freedom of its citizens, violent interstate conflict is precluded between democratic political systems and war will almost always occur only when at least one undemocratic government is involved.[2]

Rummel emphasizes in the latter connection that totalitarian and authoritarian states are the sources of wars. The concentration of power in the hands of a few elites, control over the media and the capacity to incite public opinion, and the ability to suppress interest groups and political opposition are among the factors that enable such regimes to engage in violent conflict. Democratic governments' involvement in such conflict, according to Rummel, is a reaction to real or perceived aggression from autocratic regimes or movements.[3]

Other authors have gone beyond definitions of democracy and the composition of democratic political systems and have examined the "specific mechanism by which the decisions of leaders are constrained."[4] One argument advanced by these authors is that democracies are less likely to initiate wars because they are accountable to a public that is unwilling to incur the human and material cost of violent interstate conflict. A related argument is that the presence of a legislature and opposition parties, as well as the independence of the mass media and an inability to control public opinion, discourage war initiation and restrain the belligerent behavior of leaders and governments that desire to stay in office. As a result of these domestic structural constraints, the decision to go to war is complex and costly.

The research of Bruce M. Russett adds another dimension to the question of why democracies are more pacific than nondemocracies. After examining the industrial democracies in the West, Russett attributes the reluctance of these states to make war against each other to the presence of norms against the use of military force.[5] The political elites of these countries, as well as their populations more generally, believe in majority rule, minority rights, and the principles of equality, respect for human dignity, consent of the governed, and aversion to the use or threat of violence. According to Russett's analysis, the presence of these liberal democratic values contributes to the emergence of international normative standards that delegitimize war, and this in turn leads democratic states to seek to resolve disputes through nonviolent means.

In the present chapter, an attempt will be made to assess the relevance to the Palestinians of these various assertions about democracy and war. The discussion will first inquire about the degree to which democratic political processes operate inside the PLO and will then ask about the relationship between these processes and the PLO's attitude toward Israel and the Middle East peace process. The chapter will also seek to assess the likelihood that an independent Palestinian state would be democratic, the assumption being that war between Israelis and Palestinians would be unlikely if the latter as well as the former were citizens of a democratic state. In addressing these concerns, attention will accordingly be directed to the following interrelated questions: How democratic is the Palestinian nationalist movement? To what extent does political decision-making within the PLO adhere to democratic principles? What are the social and political forces that have contributed to democratic trends within the Palestinian political community? Has an increase in participatory politics among Palestinians led to significant changes in the PLO's position toward the conflict with Israel? And finally, what are the prospects for a stable, democratic and peace-oriented Palestinian state?

Prior to taking up the Palestinian case and addressing these questions, it may be useful to acknowledge and briefly discuss some of the imprecision that surrounds the definition of democracy. As with most complex and abstract concepts, the meaning of democracy is not self-evident and is therefore the subject of disagreement, or at least differing emphases. This is discussed more fully in Robert L. Rothstein's chapter in this volume. For the purposes of this chapter, which seeks merely to identify aspects of democracy to be considered when making judgments about Palestinian politics, it may be noted that political theorists who write about democracy fall into a number of distinct groups.

One group of theorists emphasizes procedural aspects of democracy, calling attention, specifically, to four procedural elements of democratic governance.[6] First, democracy requires universal suffrage, with all or at least most adult citizens being able to vote. Second, it presupposes political freedom, with citizens voting and engaging in other forms of political discourse unconstrained by coercion or intimidation. Third, democracy is based on political competition and majority rule; candidates of different political parties compete for political office through periodic elections in which results are determined by the electorate. Fourth, there must be governmental responsiveness and accountability, meaning that political legitimacy derives from respect for the will and wishes of the people as expressed through open and competitive elections.[7] These four procedural elements highlight the centrality of majority rule in the definition of democracy. They place emphasis on citizen participation in the electoral process and on governmental accountability to the people who either reelect or defeat public officials based on their performance.

In contrast to these procedural and majoritarian aspects of democracy, a second group of scholars focuses on political pluralism, in which organized interest groups are more visible than the mass public. Rather than being attentive to public opinion at large, the government is seen as responding, first and foremost, to important interest groups. Pluralist democracy thus presupposes a decentralized form of government, with the most critical political processes being those that involve competition among powerful, well-financed and well-organized pressure groups.

To a third group of scholars, democracy entails the presence of particular political institutions, including legislatures, an independent judiciary, executive public accountability, multiple political parties, and autonomous political groups and associations. A fourth group deems cognitive attributes to be an important part of the definition of democracy. Scholars in this category assume the presence of shared values and norms among the citizens of democratic polities, including the willingness of competing elites to compromise and accommodate one another and tolerance of political opposition by those in power.[8] Yet another group of writers focuses on the socioeconomic conditions believed to be conducive to democracy, among them a high level of economic development, the presence of a large middle class, and low levels of ethnic cleavage. Finally, still other theorists speak of substantive democracy; a democratic regime guarantees to its citizens a wide range of political and civil liberties, including both personal political freedoms and protection from discrimination based on race, religion, gender, or national origin.

Democracy and the Palestinian Nationalist Movement

From its inception, the modern Palestinian nationalist movement has not been characterized by many of the facets of democracy outlined in the preceding section. Particularly notable has been the absence of direct popular elections for the selection of leaders and the expression of policy preferences. This state of affairs is the result of the Palestinians' physical dispersal throughout the Middle East, Western Europe, and North America; of Israel's military occupation of the West Bank and Gaza Strip; and of the absence of a centralized Palestinian government. In addition, the antidemocratic and authoritarian nature of the Arab state regimes has not allowed Palestinians living under their authority to elect representatives to the Palestine National Council (PNC). All of this casts doubt on the relevance for Palestinian interests and aspirations of such democratic principles as universal participation, political equality, majority rule, and governmental accountability and responsiveness.

Yet the absence of direct elections at the national level does not mean either that decision-making within the PLO is arbitrary and authoritarian or that Palestinians fail to respect democratic practices when given an opportunity to do so within their local communities.[9] On the contrary, political diversity within the Palestinian community, as well as its physical dispersal and the absence of a centralized state, have tended to prevent the exercise of arbitrary rule within the PLO's political councils and have fostered the emergence of some forms of democratic pluralism. For example, policy-making within the PLO has been heavily influenced by competition among powerful and well-organized interest groups. In particular, the PLO's military and political factions, including Fatah, the Popular Front for the Liberation of Palestine (PFLP), the Democratic Front for the Liberation of Palestine (DFLP), and a number of smaller groups, have, over the years, shaped the PLO's foreign policy behavior and orientation through an elaborate process of negotiation and political bargaining. Moreover, this bargaining takes place before, as well as during, PNC meetings, with lengthy debates among the various PLO factions determining the Council's agenda.

The pluralistic and diverse composition of the PLO has thus compelled Palestinian leaders to use persuasion and consensus-building in the formulation of national policy, rather than to rely on direct elections to determine the will of the Palestinian people. But while the diaspora nature of Palestinian politics and the need to preserve national unity are behind the PLO's efforts to promote consensus-building and power-sharing, the resulting political processes are not inherently undemocratic. Indeed, the policy of consensus-building and inclusion is based on the view that debate is essential, that all points of view should be heard, and that dissent should not be suppressed. It is for this reason that smaller factions have seats on PLO political councils.

The emphasis on pluralism, proportional representation, and political bargaining is reflected in the composition and functioning of the PLO's three main political institutions—the Palestinian National Council, the Central Council, and the Executive Committee.[10] With respect to the PNC, Article 5 of the PLO's Basic Law stipulates that members should be directly elected, but this has thus far been impossible for the reasons set forth above. As a result, the distribution of seats within the PNC has come to be based on proportional representation, with allocations determined by geographic, political, and functional considerations.[11] More specifically, PNC membership consists of four categories: (1) 20 percent of the seats are allocated to PLO military and political organizations; (2) 26 percent of the seats are assigned to the mass organizations; (3) 44 percent are given to the representatives of the Palestinian communities, including refugee camps, Bedouin tribes, and well-known independent Palestinian personalities; and (4) the Palestine Liberation Army (PLA) is assigned 10 percent of the seats. While there are no seats reserved for the Palestinians living inside Israel proper, 180 seats are allocated to the occupied territories, although these are not counted in the quorum of the PNC.

The first two categories (military factions and mass organizations) designate their own representatives to the PNC. Every organization, interest group, or faction is assigned a number of seats and then given responsibility for the selection of its delegates. With regard to the selection of independent candidates, for a limited period those from Lebanon and Kuwait were directly elected. More generally, however, independent delegates are selected through informal consultation within their respective communities, primarily on the basis of their professional, social, economic, or cultural contributions to the Palestinian cause. The occupied territories' seats, held by prominent Palestinian personalities who have been deported by Israel, are filled in a similar way. With regard to the PLA's membership in the PNC, the chairman of the PLO, in consultation with members of the Executive Committee, designates the PLA's representatives to the Palestine National Council.

The Palestine Central Council (PCC) is another major political institution. Formed in 1973, the PCC was intended to serve as an intermediate body between the PNC and the Executive Committee, with responsibility for the implementation of PNC resolutions. The PCC's membership is drawn from the ranks of the PNC on the basis of proportional representation.

The Executive Committee, a third important political institution, serves as the PLO's cabinet and is in theory accountable to the PNC. Its fifteen members are selected by the PNC, again in accordance with the principle of proportional representation and, more specifically, in accordance with the distribution of power within that political organ.[12] The Executive Committee meets more regularly than does the Central Council and has first-line responsibility for implementing the PNC's policies and programs.

Although the existence of the PNC, the PCC, and the Executive Committee provides the PLO with some of the institutional facets of democratic governance, there are also major limits to the degree of adherence to democratic principles. Primarily because of the Palestinians' physical dispersal, the PNC and the PCC do not function on a full-time basis. In addition, most PNC members are not full-time politicians; the result is that their inability to interrupt business or other professional obligations also makes it difficult for the PNC to function as a full-time legislative body. This not only creates a host of logistic, financial, and administrative difficulties, it also limits the degree to which the principle of Executive Committee accountability to the PNC is respected in reality. To a very large extent, the Executive Committee operates as a delegate decision-making structure, with members serving as representatives of the outside interest groups to which they belong rather than as spokesmen of a consensus fashioned by the PNC. This situation accounts for much of the ambiguity and deadlock that have characterized PLO policy over the years.

The Democratic Process among West Bank Palestinians: Political Pluralism and Partisan Activism

While corporate and bureaucratic interests have dominated the PLO's national political institutions, thus reducing opportunities for the exercise of direct procedural democracy at this level, the situation has been different among Palestinians in the occupied territories.[13] Although politics in the West Bank was once the primary domain of the elite, with individuals from historically

prominent families controlling local politics, the West Bank's political landscape was significantly altered by Israel's military occupation in 1967. Far-
reaching socioeconomic, structural, and demographic changes were set in mo-
tion, and these changes in turn have both expanded significantly the circle of
participatory politics and fostered the emergence of political processes marked
by diversity and pluralism, partisan activism, and mass political involvement.

This competitive milieu developed in tandem with a generational change in
the political leadership of the West Bank and Gaza. The older elite was dominated by pro-Jordanian politicians from prominent families, many of whom
played a role in resisting Israel's military occupation soon after 1967. In the
1970s, however, a younger, better educated, and more occupationally diverse
group of politicians assumed control of West Bank politics.[14] The new elite was
less likely to emphasize ties to Jordan and it held a variety of alternative ideological positions, including support for Fatah, the Popular Front for the Liberation of Palestine, the Democratic Front for the Liberation of Palestine, and the
Arab Baath party. Still others followed the Communist line.

The new politicians used different symbols and created new political structures to consolidate their legitimacy and articulate their interests and demands.[15] In particular, the West Bank's new elite sequentially created two institutional frameworks for the articulation of local needs. The first, the
Palestine National Front (PNF), was formed in the summer of 1973 in order to
mobilize political support for the PLO among West Bank Palestinians and, at
the same time, to press the PLO to endorse the goal of forming a West Bank-
Gaza Palestinian state. The second institution, the National Guidance Committee (NGC), was established in the fall of 1978 in order to organize local opposition to the Camp David Accords. The NGC also articulated the broader
interests and demands of the Palestinian community.

In addition to this ideological and structural diversity at the level of the political elite, the democratic process among West Bank Palestinians was enhanced when the Israeli military government permitted the conduct of municipal elections in 1972 and 1976 in order to choose municipal council
members for twenty-four West Bank towns and cities.[16] This democratic trend
was further augmented when the Israeli military government amended Jordan's 1955 election law, which had limited the right to vote to landowning men
who had reached the age of 21. The new law extended universal suffrage to all
male and female adults who had reached the age of 21. Thus, by the late 1970s,
non-elites had been given important opportunities to participate in the political process.

Expansion of the circle of participatory politics in the occupied territories was also reflected by the late 1970s in a growing number of mass-based organizations, including, among others, labor unions, student organizations, and the women's movement.[17] These organizations have become particularly important vehicles for the sustained political involvement of non-elite sectors of society. Political participation and activism have also been enhanced by the formation of professional associations, such as the associations of lawyers, engineers, doctors, and journalists. The vast majority of these institutions follow democratic procedures in the selection of leaders, holding annual elections to choose the members of their steering committees.

Political competition within mass-based organizations is often intense, reflecting the ideological divisions noted above and adding further to the complexity and diversity of political processes operating among West Bank and Gaza Palestinians. Five distinct factions are particularly active: the followers of Fatah, the Popular Front, the Democratic Front, the Communists, and the Islamic movement. These groups regularly contest elections and compete for control of student councils, workers' unions, and other mass organizations and professional associations.[18] Moreover, these divisions represent not only a competition among ideological tendencies but also among institutional and political interests. To a considerable degree, factions represent their patrons within the PLO and seek to advance the interests and political programs of their mentors.

Popular participation among Palestinians in the West Bank and Gaza increased further during the intifada, when the entire social fabric of the occupied territories became heavily involved in demonstrations, protests and other political activities.[19] The uprising significantly expanded the scope of some existing forms of political participation and gave a clearer definition of the objectives of the national movement. Further, in addition to the pro-PLO mass organizations in existence since the late 1970s, the Popular Committees that were created in the early days of the intifada to perpetuate the uprising were the vehicles for a significant increase in the level of grass-roots activism. And even more important in the context of the present discussion, the work of the Popular Committees was not limited to political protest but rather gave primary attention to self-help and communal problem-solving activities. The primary purpose of these collective efforts has been to encourage the political and economic development of the occupied territories.

Pragmatism and realism have been two additional features of Palestinian thinking during the uprising. The intifada's goals included an end to Israel's military occupation, recognition of the Palestinian people's right of self-determination, agreement that the PLO should represent Palestinian interests in any political settlement, and the eventual establishment of a Palestinian state in the West Bank and Gaza. In a number of their directives, the leadership of the intifada sought to make clear that the aim of the uprising was not the destruction of the Jewish state; rather, Palestinians wanted to establish a state adjacent to Israel.

Although the West Bank and Gaza have experienced the emergence of political processes marked by institutional and ideological pluralism, partisan competition and popular political participation, all of which may legitimately be described as democratic or at least quasi-democratic in character, there are also dimensions of political life that show little respect for the tenets of cognitive democracy. In particular, support for political tolerance, accommodation and compromise has sometimes been absent, with the supporters of various PLO factions and the Islamic movement occasionally resorting to violence to settle their differences. During the intifada, especially after the first two years, this violence increased significantly as scores of Palestinians accused of collaborating with Israel were murdered. The existence and growth of such practices must be included in any assessment of the degree to which political life in the occupied territories has been marked by trends that incorporate important aspects of democracy.

In conclusion, despite the important limitations noted above, political competitiveness and the availability of numerous institutions and professional societies have fostered democratic processes and widened the circle of participatory politics among West Bank and Gaza Palestinians. Moreover, in addition to undermining traditional norms and values and transforming the social, economic, and psychological foundations of political behavior among Palestinians in the occupied territories, these democratic trends have influenced the policy-making process and the foreign policy behavior of the PLO.

The PLO'S Foreign Policy:
From Militancy to Political Accommodation

How do democratic processes among the Palestinians, limited as they are, influence PLO policy-making? More precisely, how does one explain the change in the PLO's foreign policy from a militant anti-Israel posture to an accommodationist orientation and diplomatic flexibility? What are the current political trends among the Palestinians, and how do these trends influence the peace process?

Since its inception in the 1960s, three distinct phases can be discerned in the foreign policy behavior of the PLO.[20] The first phase, from 1964 to 1968, encompassed the Palestinian goal of reconstructing Arab Palestine and returning refugees to their homeland. The task of liberation was regarded as a collective Arab responsibility. During the second phase, between 1968 and 1974, the PLO advocated armed struggle and Palestinian self-reliance. In contrast to the first phase, the PLO now considered liberation to be primarily a Palestinian task.[21] The organization also proposed establishing a secular democratic state in all of Palestine, in which Christians, Jews, and Muslims would live together harmoniously and with equal political rights.

The third phase, from 1974 to the present, involves the evolution of the idea of a two-state solution. In 1974, the PNC called for the establishment of an independent national authority on any part of Palestine that was liberated from Israeli control. The 1977 PNC meeting expanded upon the concept of a national authority, specifying that this meant an independent state. In 1983, the PNC called for a confederation between the future Palestinian state and Jordan, and a year later the PLO endorsed majority rule and abandoned consensus-building in the making of public policy. During this period, the Palestinian organization also reduced its emphasis on armed struggle and assigned a greater role to diplomacy. This phase matured in November 1988 with the PNC's declaration of an independent West Bank-Gaza state, the PLO's acceptance of U. N. resolutions 242 and 338, and the subsequent commencement of direct peace talks with Israel. It culminated in September 1993 when the PLO signed an accord with Israel.

Three categories of explanatory factors can be considered in an attempt to illuminate the nature and evolution of the PLO's foreign policy.[22] The first contends that changes in the PLO's foreign policy orientation are the result of bureaucratic rivalries and pressures. The second attributes foreign policy change to threats and opportunities emanating from the external environment. The third ascribes the alteration of PLO foreign policy attitudes and behavior to domestic restructuring and internal political changes, including the emerging democratic trend among Palestinians.

Based on this conceptual framework, the PLO's reliance on Arab countries during the first phase was primarily dictated by the presence of opportunities and pressures from the external environment. On the one hand, the Arabs accepted collective responsibility for the liberation of Palestine and, on the other,

Palestinian nationalism was captured by Arab nationalism. The ideological primacy of Pan-Arabism explains why Palestinians accepted a secondary role in the liberation of their land. During the second phase, in the late 1960s and early 1970s, bureaucratic advocacy and pluralist interests accounted for the primacy of military struggle. The dominance of Palestinian resistance groups made armed struggle, self-reliance, and national unity the core objectives of the PLO during this period. The centrality of these goals, and the political strength of the resistance groups, was the result of a need to avoid internal Palestinian divisions and to offer an alternative resistance strategy in the wake of the Arab armies' defeat in the war of June 1967.

After the 1973 October War, the PLO's foreign policy behavior was influenced by both new external developments and new domestic pressures. Among the key external developments, which led to Palestinian acceptance of a two-state solution by the early 1980s, are the Lebanese Civil War of 1975–76, Sadat's visit to Jerusalem in 1977, the signing of the Camp David Accords in 1978, the conclusion of the Egypt-Israel Peace Treaty in 1979, and Israel's war against the PLO in Lebanon in 1982. The crisis in the Gulf in the early 1990s brought additional challenges from the external environment, including Iraq's military defeat and the subsequent expulsion from Kuwait of hundreds of thousands of Palestinians, the suspension of financial assistance to the PLO from Saudi Arabia and other Gulf states, and a general reduction in Arab support for the Palestinian cause, particularly on the part of states in the coalition that had fought against Saddam Hussein. Finally, Palestinians were affected by the demise of the Soviet Union and the Communist regimes of Eastern Europe, which was coupled with a dramatic increase in Jewish immigration to Israel from the former Soviet Union, by the accelerated construction of Jewish settlements in the occupied territories, by the growing inconclusiveness of the Intifada, and by deteriorating economic conditions in the West Bank and Gaza. All of this compelled the PLO leadership to allow West Bank and Gaza Palestinians to enter into direct peace talks with Israel and to resign itself to a nonparticipatory role in these negotiations.

While the impact of external factors should not be underestimated, the change in the PLO's foreign policy behavior is also the result of two other critical factors: a decline in the influence of the military factions on PLO decision-making and the political ascendancy of the occupied territories. Around the mid-1970s, the PLO experienced profound internal stress when the hard-line groups, led by the Popular Front for the Liberation of Palestine, suspended their membership in the PNC and the Executive Committee. This took place between 1974 and 1978. In addition, in 1983, a split occurred within the ranks of Fatah;[23] and a year later the various Damascus-based Palestinian groups boycotted the seventeenth session of the PNC that convened in Amman, Jordan. Finally, the military factions' control over the PLO decision-making apparatus came under additional stress in the wake of the Gulf War and the assassination of some of their key historic figures.

Although this decline in the influence of military factions partly explains the previously discussed changes in the foreign policy of the PLO, factors associated with domestic restructuring and the emergence of new social forces among Palestinians in the occupied territories have played an even greater role in the redirection of the PLO's foreign policy behavior.

After the 1973 October War, the new generation of West Bank politicians broke away from the old order based on ties to the government in Jordan and demanded the formation of a Palestinian state in the West Bank and Gaza. Whether through local municipal councils or through the Palestine National Front and the National Guidance Committee, these nationalist politicians conveyed to the PLO the interests and wishes of West Bank and Gaza Palestinians. In this connection, the PNF, which enjoyed widespread popular backing and encompassed various social forces, reminded the PLO that the objective of liberating all of Palestine was unrealistic. Israel's massive military superiority and the opposition of world public opinion to the elimination of the Jewish state made the attainment of the PLO's long-term objectives illusionary.[24]

Like the PNF, the NGC also urged the PLO to adopt a new political program centered around creative diplomatic action in the pursuit of a West Bank-Gaza state. Representing a wide variety of Palestinian organizations and individuals, including mayors, journalists, professionals, welfare societies, and women's organizations, the NGC pressed the PLO to emphasize diplomacy rather than armed struggle and to work toward the establishment of a Palestinian state. It was in response to these political demands, articulated by popular and representative political forces in the occupied territories, that the PLO accepted the idea of an independent Palestinian state alongside Israel and began the search for a diplomatic solution to the Palestinian question.

A continuing expansion of the circle of participatory politics in the 1980s, and especially during the intifada, has increased the ideological and institutional pluralism that characterizes Palestinian political life. This political diversity is manifested both in continuing support for an accommodation with Israel and, among others, in an increasingly belligerent attitude toward the Jewish state. This pluralism has also been evident in the aftermath of the Israeli-

PLO accord signed in September 1993. Many Palestinians support the accord, which they hope will lead to a two-state solution. Others see the accord as flawed, however; although favoring a settlement based on compromise, they complain that the agreement does not require Israel to relinquish the occupied territories at the end of the transitional period. Finally, still other Palestinians, most notably those who support Islamic political movements, continue to reject any accommodation with the Jewish state and condemn Yasir Arafat for concluding the agreement with Israel.

The present-day Palestinian political landscape also embraces diverse opinions about how Palestinian society should be governed, with differing political formulas advanced by nationalists, secular leftists, Islamists, and conservative politicians, some with continuing ties to Jordan. Since the beginning of the intifada and the end of the Gulf War, these political groups have been engaged in intense debate about the future of the Palestinian national movement. Moreover, with the ideological competition between democratic and Islamic principles of governance a central preoccupation, this debate is not unlike that in many other Arab societies. Thus, at present, peace with Israel and the salience of democracy are the two main points of contention that divide pragmatists and radicals and animate Palestinian politics.

Moderates and Hard-Liners

There is both a moderate and a hard-line camp in Palestinian politics, and the issues of peace with Israel and democracy are central to the distinction between them. Moreover, the two issues are connected, with one camp both favoring the Arab-Israeli peace process and calling for greater democracy in Palestinian political life and the other, although heterogeneous, taking a more uncompromising stand toward Israel and the peace process and also expressing more qualified and conditional support for democratization. The moderate camp is much larger and predominates among the Palestinian elite, but the hard-line camp is important as well and retains considerable influence despite the agreement between Israel and the PLO.

The moderate camp, composed of secular nationalists, includes pragmatists within Fatah and Western-educated intellectuals and politicians inside the occupied territories. These Palestinians have been impressed with Israel's parliamentary democracy and free press. In addition, many have developed close ties with liberal Israeli Jews and groups who support the Palestinian people's right to self-determination. These moderate politicians thus have a compromise-oriented and pacifist perspective and are willing to end the conflict with Israel on the basis of land for peace. For example, most favor the "Gaza-Jericho First" agreement and the subsequent establishment of an interim self-governing authority throughout the West Bank during a period of transition. At the end of the transition period, an independent Palestinian state would be created, most probably in the context of a federation with Jordan.[25]

These Palestinian proponents of the peace process tell hard-line rivals that rigid stands are out of touch with reality. They argue that regional and international developments have left the Palestinians with only the diplomatic option and, noting that Israel is today stronger than ever, they dismiss the use of military force as a means to resolve the conflict. They also contend that time is working against the Palestinians. In addition, and more positively, moderates point out that the peace process has increased Israeli willingness to trade land for peace and recognize Palestinian rights,[26] and that it has also brought greater support for the Palestinian cause among the American public.

Apart from their views about peace with Israel, these pragmatic Palestinian politicians and intellectuals also call for the democratization of the PLO's institutions. They advocate such measures as the direct election of members of the PNC and the expansion of its size to include West Bank-Gaza Palestinians. Elections in the occupied territories would be conducted under the supervision of the U. N.[27]

Standing in opposition to Palestinian moderates are both secular leftists and Islamists. The leftists are centered around the PFLP, the DFLP, the hard-line group within Fatah, and the Damascus-based Salvation Front. These leftists offer a competing perspective, based on a belief that the United States and Israel have not accepted Palestinian national rights and that the peace process forces Palestinians to accept autonomy rather than independence. Leftists thus reject a two-stage peace process and instead urge an immediate termination of Israel's military occupation and the establishment of a Palestinian state in the occupied territories. These hard-liners agree that the regional and global balance of power favors Israel and the United States. They see this as an obstacle to a settlement, however, and argue that an end to Israel's military occupation can take place only if the prevailing power imbalance is reversed. According to leftists, Israel will compromise only if forced to do so by active Palestinian resistance and strong Arab support.

Concerning democratization and election to the PNC, hard-line groups are afraid that the elections may lead to further divisions within the PLO, split the occupied territories from outside Palestinians, and undermine the status of the

PLO as the sole legitimate representative of the Palestinian people. Further-more, hard-line groups do not believe that countries such as Israel, Jordan, and Syria would allow the conduct of free elections.[28] Nevertheless, despite their profound differences with moderates, Palestinian hard-liners have not with-drawn from the PLO since the beginning of the peace process and for the most part remain willing to function as a loyal opposition.

In addition to secular leftists, moderates are also challenged by the Islamic movement among the Palestinians, at the core of which are Hamas and Islamic Jihad in the occupied territories. Islamists oppose political reconciliation with Israel and reject a settlement based on the establishment of a West Bank-Gaza state. They insist instead on the formation of an Islamic state in all of Palestine and believe that this will take place only if Palestinians respect Islamic norms and abandon their secular attitudes and practices.[29]

With respect to the question of democracy and elections, Islamists believe that democracy is a Western concept and therefore alien to Islam. They are not necessarily opposed to the conduct of elections in the West Bank and Gaza, since they believe this would reveal their considerable strength relative to that of groups linked to the PLO. Indeed, many among them claim that this would enable the Islamic movement to obtain a majority and gain control of many West Bank and Gaza institutions, organizations, and unions. At the same time, support for elections does not mean that Islamists accept the notion of democ-racy. On the contrary, the pronouncements of at least some Islamic leaders in-dicate their intolerance of secular and nationalist political groups.[30] The Is-lamists demand that Islam be the guiding principle for any coalition with the secularists and state that they would comply with the decisions of a political majority only if such decisions have an Islamic orientation. It is for these rea-sons that the Palestinian Islamic movement did not join the PLO, although they were offered seats in its various councils. The Islamic movement made its par-ticipation conditional on a change in the PLO's secular orientation and policies.

Democracy, Peace, and the Future Palestinian State

Despite institutional pluralism, intense partisan competition and an ex-panding circle of citizen participation, Palestinian political life is still not char-acterized by the presence of institutions and leaders that are democratically chosen and hence publicly accountable in a formal and institutionalized man-ner. Democratic mechanisms and processes of this sort can come into existence only if there is a Palestinian state. For this reason, the remainder of this chapter will explore and propose answers to two critical questions about the emergence of a Palestinian state. First, if a Palestinian state is established, what is the likelihood that it will favor peace and stability in the region, rather than a military confrontation with Israel and perhaps other neighbors? Second, will the new Palestinian state be democratic in character and, if so, is there a danger that its policies will be heavily influenced by groups opposed to peace with Israel and that it will therefore be under pressure to adopt a belligerent foreign policy?

It is safe to argue that the existence of a Palestinian state, whether fully independent or associated with Jordan, would not compromise Israel's national security interests. As in other countries, the policies of a state of Palestine would be determined by its most important national needs and by a series of domestic and external constraints. And in the Palestinian case, the capacity of the political elite to engage in violence, even were this its inclination, would be severely limited by the primacy of needs related to domestic political and economic development, by the scarcity of financial resources, by a number of externally imposed limitations, and by the nature of its political system. In other words, both the self-interest of the new state's political leaders and the limits governing their freedom of action would greatly reduce the chance of aggressive conduct toward Israel.

An important constraint on the war-making potential of the new state would be its needs and priorities related to nation-building. Fostering a sense of belonging and communal solidarity among West Bank and Gaza Palestinians would be a crucial task, as would be the full integration of any new immigrants from the Palestinian diaspora. The accomplishment of these tasks would be facilitated by the cultural homogeneity of the Palestinian people and by the fact that the new state's government would, or could, provide for the inclusion of political elites from diaspora communities. But the prospects for success do not diminish the energy and resources that will be required or, in the present context, the likelihood that nation-building, rather than military struggle, would be the primary preoccupation of the new state.

Economic and natural resource considerations would further constrain the foreign policy behavior of the Palestinian state. Like nation-building, economic development will be a primary objective of the new government, which accordingly will be under pressure to spend its limited resources on the fight against poverty rather than on the procurement of advanced weapons. Moreover, since the Palestinian state will need international assistance to achieve development-related objectives, and since Saudi Arabia and the other conservative Gulf Arab countries, together with Western Europe and the United

States, will be its main financiers, the economic dependency of the new state will also constrain its behavior and ensure that it does not engage in belligerent behavior toward Israel. The need to attract private capital from wealthy Palestinians and individual Arab entrepreneurs will similarly discourage foreign adventures, since investment will obviously depend on the stability of the state of Palestine.

The constraints associated with domestic priorities and dependence on external assistance would be in addition, of course, to the limitations that a peace settlement with Israel would undoubtedly impose on the military capabilities of the Palestinian state. Given the probable terms of a final agreement, which can be expected to include demilitarization and restrictions on the arms given to local police, there is little likelihood that an independent Palestinian state in the West Bank and Gaza would be a threat to Israel or any other neighbor. In addition, under these conditions, the military would not be an influential force in domestic political life and, in contrast to the situation in some other Arab countries, would not be in a position to press for policies and resource allocations that emphasize the role of the military.

Nor is it likely, quite apart from these domestic and external constraints, that the new state's leaders would themselves be inclined toward violence against Israel. Ideological moderates from the West Bank and Gaza will strongly influence the government of the Palestinian state. These politicians will insist on playing a pivotal role in the politics of the new entity, in which, as elsewhere, political discourse will be shaped by internal political dynamics and conditions. The foundation for the preeminence of moderate mainstream nationalists from the occupied territories has been in place since the late 1980s, if not longer. As a result of the intifada, these inside Palestinians came to play a prominent role in the political life of the larger Palestinian community. That role was further enhanced during the period prior to September 1993 when the PLO engaged in indirect peace talks with Israel.

Mainstream PLO politicians will also play an important role in the politics of the new government. The pragmatism and moderation of these leaders has been reflected most recently, in the late 1980s and early 1990s, in their acceptance of U. N. Resolution 242, their renunciation of terrorism, their recognition of Israel, and their acceptance of the Madrid peace process, as well as the Israeli-PLO Agreement.[31]

The political moderation of the new state will also be sustained by the influence of the outside Palestinian community. Despite the views of extreme leftists and Islamic radicals, a broad consensus exists within the Palestinian community on the creation of an independent Palestinian state in the occupied territories. Both instrumental and sentimental considerations will tie most outside Palestinians to the new entity, which will provide them with a sense of belonging, a point of reference, a potential refuge, and a government to speak on their behalf. In addition, well-to-do Palestinians are likely to invest their capital in the economy of the new state, while still others will make it a place of retirement. All of these considerations will give Palestinians everywhere a stake in the security, survival, and development of the state, which in turn will give them a strong interest in regional stability and peaceful relations with Israel.

The orientation of the probable leaders and mainstream constituency of the Palestinian state indicates a preference not only for moderation in foreign policy but also for democracy in domestic political life. Democratic principles and values are strongly advocated by most of the West Bank and Gaza personalities who would form the backbone of the Palestinian government, and by many other professionals and intellectuals who would also be influential contributors to the political life of the new state.

This democratic impulse is also reflected, as discussed, in the quasi-democratic processes that mark both the functioning of Palestinian national institutions and the conduct of local and regional-level politics in the occupied territories. It is highly probable that these processes would be retained, refined and incorporated into the system of governance adopted by the Palestinian state. In addition, pluralism, diversity and political competition would be promoted by the continuing physical dispersion of the Palestinian people, which will encourage the diffusion of power and political organization based on considerations of society and culture as well as politics and ideology.

These considerations give credibility to the calls for democracy contained in the Declaration of Independence that the PNC adopted in 1988. The declaration spells out the normative principles that will guide the state of Palestine and emphasizes the importance of institutional, cognitive, and substantive aspects of democracy. More precisely, the Declaration of Independence endorses the principles of equality, social justice, freedom of religion, freedom of speech, freedom of the press, the right to organize and form political parties, and protection of minorities against all forms of discrimination. While the implementation of these principles may not be without problems, the declaration offers a clear expression of Palestinian intentions regarding the issue of domestic governance, and, as noted, it should be taken seriously since it is consistent with both the thinking of leading Palestinian politicians and with the practice of present-day Palestinian political institutions.

Although the political and ideological moderation of the Palestinian mainstream has properly been emphasized in the present discussion, there are also Palestinian extremists with a different world view and other priorities. Moreover, some of these extremists would undoubtedly try to disturb the peace between Israel and the Palestinian state and, further, they would be able to pursue their objectives by legal means if the state were democratic. Once a democratic Palestinian state was established, in other words, leftists and Islamic radicals would be able to compete for political influence and even to seek control of the new Palestinian government.

While leftists do not enjoy widespread popular support, the Islamic movement has been popular among West Bank and Gaza Palestinians since the early 1980s and would probably do well in national elections. Further, support for Islamic factions appears to have increased in late 1993 and early 1994 in the wake of continuing delays in implementing the "Gaza-Jericho First" plan agreed to by Israel and the PLO.[32] And since Islamic groups oppose any peace or territorial accommodation with the Jewish state, insisting instead on the creation of an Islamic state in all of Palestine, Islamist political gains might bring pressure for a change in the foreign policy of the Palestinian state.

Nevertheless, the prospect that the Islamic movement will exercise substantial political influence or power over the long term is not promising. With the resolution of the Palestinian problem and Israel's withdrawal from the occupied territories, a major reason for the Islamists' appeal will immediately vanish. Islamic political groups tell the Palestinian rank and file that moderation and compromise are flawed policies, that they do not lead to national independence but rather to continuing occupation. Although these arguments have been persuasive, they will be meaningless once the Palestinians have a state.

In addition, Islamic formulas for solving the economic and social problems of the new state are unlikely to be more successful than those proposed by secular nationalists, meaning that Islamists will probably lose much of their attraction should they come to share in the exercise of power. Nor is there reason to believe that Islamist politicians, as a group, will be any more intelligent, efficient or honest than other politicians, and thus, again, the Islamists' appeal can be expected to diminish should they leave the opposition and be forced to deliver solutions rather than merely to criticize. For both these reasons, as well as the end of Israeli occupation, it seems unlikely that democracy would result for any sustained length of time in the acquisition by Islamic groups of enough political power to compel the adoption of a foreign policy based on conflict and confrontation with Israel.

On the contrary, and perhaps most important of all in the long run, the propensity of the state of Palestine to engage in violence against its neighbors is likely to be constrained by the democratic and participatory nature of its political system. Unlike many Third World countries, discontent leading to political instability will not arise from a gap between participation and political institutionalization. The possibility of such a gap can be ruled out because of the existing democratic practices among West Bank-Gaza Palestinians, which includes the presence of political pluralism and institutional diversity and is reinforced by the high level of education and political competitiveness of the population. There is thus a firm foundation for active and effective citizen involvement in the political arena,[33] and there will also be popular pressure to ensure that citizens retain the right to form political parties and to organize and express their political views in other ways. Equally important, as discussed, citizens can be expected to use their political influence to press for maximum attention to domestic needs associated with nation-building and economic development.

To promote stability as well as democracy in this political environment, popular participation will be absorbed and directed by a strong central government. The Palestine National Council, which is well established and enjoys wide legitimacy, can be expected to evolve into a national parliament. In addition, the Palestinians have executive-related departments and a well-developed civil service system, and the new state's government will also accumulate power and resources by virtue of its central role in the promotion of political and economic development. The consolidation and construction of the Palestinian state will thus enable the government to extend its control and supremacy throughout the West Bank and Gaza and to work effectively for the preservation of domestic stability.

As argued previously, this situation is unlikely to be associated with a growth in the military power or militaristic inclinations of the state of Palestine. The priorities of the state will lie elsewhere, reinforced both by popular demands for attention to national integration and economic development and by the moderate ideological orientation of mainstream political elites. Nor will there be either a high level of citizen unrest fueled by political authoritarianism or a tendency toward domestic instability produced by government weakness. With the role and political influence of the military further reduced by the probable terms of a final peace settlement, there is thus little likelihood that an independent and democratic Palestinian state in the West Bank and Gaza would be a threat to Israel or any other neighbor.

Summary

The transformation from a nonstate actor to a nation-state will create a new constellation of expectations, constraints, and pressures for the Palestinians. Political self-interest, functional considerations, and domestic and external constraints will compel the leaders of the state of Palestine both to be democratic and to pursue a conciliatory policy toward Israel. The conditions for democratic governance are already in place. They are reflected in the pluralism, diversity, and competition that exists within Palestinian national institutions, in the ideological moderation and democratic orientation of mainstream Palestinian elites, and in the expansion of mass participation associated with political life in the occupied territories. For these reasons, as noted, it is reasonable to attach credibility to the affirmation of democracy contained in the Palestinian Declaration of Independence.

As far as belligerence toward Israel is concerned, the new Palestinian government will have neither the inclination nor the resources to pursue an aggressive foreign policy.[34] Its pacific orientation will be encouraged by the political moderation of those who can be expected to provide leadership and by democratic procedures that will ensure these leaders' accountability to a population concerned with domestic development and reluctant to endure the human and material cost of war. The attributes and circumstances of the Palestinian state more generally will also reduce the likelihood of aggressive behavior toward Israel. These attributes and circumstances include the state's small size and population, its limited natural resource base and associated dependence on foreign assistance, its encirclement by Israel and the latter's massive military superiority, and the additional limitations on its military capabilities that will be tied a peace settlement.

NOTES

1. Many of these arguments are attributed to the writings of Kant. See, for instance, Patrick Riley, *Kant's Political Philosophy* (Totowa, NJ: Rowman and Littlefeld, 1983); Hans Reiss, *Kant's Political Writing* (Cambridge: Cambridge University Press,

1970); and A. C. Armstrong, "Kant's Philosophy of Peace and War," *Journal of Philosophy* 28 (April 1931): 197–204. For a general discussion of this subject, see Steve Chan, "Mirror, Mirror on the Wall: Are the Freer Countries More Pacific?" *Journal of Conflict Resolution* 28 (December 1984): 617–48; Michael W. Doyle, "Liberalism and World Politics," *American Political Science Review* 80 (December 1986); Erich Weede, "Democracy and War Involvement," *Journal of Conflict Resolution* 28 (December 1984): 649–64; and D. Marc Kilgour, "Domestic Political Structure and War Behavior: A Game-Theoretic Approach," *Journal of Conflict Resolution* 35 (June 1991): 266–84.

2. Rudolph J. Rummel, "Libertarianism and International Violence," *Journal of Conflict Resolution* 27 (March 1983): 27–71.

3. Rudolph J. Rummel, *Understanding Conflict and War: War, Power, Peace* (Beverly Hills, CA: Sage, 1979), pp. 277–79 and 292–93.

4. T. Clifton Morgan and Sally Howard Campbell, "Domestic Structure, Decisional Constraints, and War," *Journal of Conflict Resolution* 35 (June 1991): 187–211. John E. Mueller, *Retreat from Doomsday: The Obsolescence of Major War* (New York: Basic Books, 1989) argues that it is a change in attitudes or patterns of thought that has prevented war in the liberal community (p. 24). He also discusses the aversion to war as citizens become richer and have more to lose (p. 252).

5. Bruce M. Russett, *Controlling the Sword: The Democratic Governance of National Security* (Cambridge: Harvard University Press, 1990), pp. 119, 121, 124.

6. Kenneth Janda, Jeffrey M. Berry, and Jerry Goldman, *The Challenge of Democracy: Government in America*, 3rd ed. (Dallas: Houghton Mifflin, 1992), pp. 53–54. See also Arend Lijphart, *Democracies* (New Haven, CT: Yale University Press, 1984), p. 8.

7. Robert A. Dahl, *Democracy and Its Critics* (New Haven, CT: Yale University Press, 1987), pp. 35–41.

8. Robert L. Rothstein, "Weak Democracy and the Prospects for Peace and Prosperity in the Third World," paper presented at the U.S. Institute of Peace conference on Conflict Resolution in the Post–Cold War Third World, October 3–5, 1990.

9. Rex Brynen, *Sanctuary and Survival: The PLO in Lebanon* (Boulder, CO: Westview, 1990); and Helena Cobban, *The Palestinian Liberation Organization: People, Power, and Politics* (London: Cambridge University Press, 1984).

10. Hamid Rashid, "What Is the PLO?" *Journal of Palestine Studies* 4 (1975): 90–109; Cheryl Rubenberg, *The Palestine Liberation Organization: Its Institutional Infrastructure* (Belmont, MA: Institute of Arab Studies, 1983); and William B. Quandt, Fuad Jaber, and Ann M. Lesch, *The Politics of Palestinian Nationalism* (Berkeley: University of California Press, 1973).

11. Sami Massalam, *The Palestine Liberation Organization* (Brattleboro, VT: Amana Books, 1988), p. 13.

12. Ibid., pp. 2–6.

13. Moshe Maoz, "Democratization among the West Bank Palestinians and Its

Relevance to Palestinian-Israeli Relations," paper presented at the opening session of a conference on Democracy, Peace, and the Israeli-Palestinian Conflict, University of Maryland, January 30, 1992.

14. A complete discussion of the factors that led to the demise of the pro-Jordanian politicians can be found in Emile F. Sahliyeh, *In Search of Leadership: West Bank Politics since 1967* (Washington, DC: Brookings Institution, 1988). See also, Ann M. Lesch, *Political Perceptions of the Palestinians in the West Bank and Gaza Strip* (Washington, DC: Middle East Institute, 1982), chapter 3.

15. Ibid., chapter 4.

16. Moshe Maoz, *Palestinian Leadership on the West Bank: The Changing Role of the Arab Mayors under Jordan and Israel* (London: Frank Cass, 1984).

17. Ibid.

18. For more information on the role of the Communists and the Islamic groups, see Sahliyeh, *In Search of Leadership*, chapters 5 and 7.

19. Jamal R. Nassar, "The Nature of the Palestine Intifada," *Journal of Arab Affairs* 8 (1989); Jamal R. Nassar and Roger Heacock, eds., *Intifada: Palestine at the Crossroads* (New York: Praeger, 1990); and Don Peretz, *Intifada: The Palestinian Uprising* (Boulder, CO: Westview, 1990).

20. Muhammad Muslih, "Towards Coexistence: An Analysis of the Resolutions of the Palestine National Council," *Journal of Palestine Studies* 19 (1990): 3–29; and Mohammed E. Selim, "The Survival of a Nonstate Actor: The Foreign Policy of the Palestine Liberation Organization," in *The Foreign Policies of Arab States: The Challenge of Change*, Bahgat Korany and Ali E. Dessouki, eds. (Boulder, CO: Westview, 1991).

21. For further elaboration, see Quandt, Jabber, and Lesch, *Politics of Palestinian Nationalism*, part 2.

22. The conceptual framework for the ensuing analysis is adapted from Charles C. Hermann, "Changing Course: When Governments Choose to Redirect Foreign Policy," *International Studies Quarterly* 34 (1990): 3–22.

23. Emile F. Sahliyeh, *The PLO After the Lebanon War* (Boulder, CO: Westview, 1986).

24. Ibid., pp. 52, 56–57.

25. One of the leading advocates of this new approach is Yaser Abd Rabu, who split from the DFLP and adopted Arafat's diplomatic flexibility. Abd Rabu urged the Palestinians to pursue a pragmatic political program predicated on the formation of a West Bank-Gaza state, the acceptance of U. N. Resolutions 242 and 338, and Palestinian readiness to recognize Israel and peacefully coexist with it.

26. Following the Israeli-PLO agreement, an opinion survey conducted in Israel by the Hanoh Smith research institute found that 47 percent of the Israeli public supported a Palestinian state, with 40 percent opposed.

27. Such ideas were endorsed by such prominent PLO figures as Khalid al-Hassan.

28. Paul Lalor, "The Debate within the PLO: Foreign Policy," *Middle East International*, December 20, 1990, pp. 15–16; and idem, "The Debate within the PLO: Calls for Reform within the Movement," *Middle East International*, January 10, 1991, pp. 16–18.

29. Ziad Abu-Amr, "Palestinian Islamists and the Question of Democracy," paper presented at the opening session of a conference on Democracy, Peace, and the Israeli-Palestinian Conflict, University of Maryland, January 30, 1992.

30. See the statements by Dr. al-Zahhar and Shaikh Basem Jarrar quoted in ibid., pp. 7, 8.

31. For more information, see Sahliyeh, *PLO after the Lebanon War*, chapters 4–7.

32. In the February 1994 elections for the Gaza Engineers Association, the Islamic Bloc's candidates won half of the votes; this is a clear indication that even the educated and conservative bourgeois classes are inclining toward the Islamic movement.

33. For a discussion of activism among the Palestinians, see Sahliyeh, *In Search of Leadership*, chapters 3–7.

34. Edy Kaufman and Shukri Abed, "The Relevance of Democracy to Israeli-Palestinian Peace," paper presented at the opening session of a conference on Democracy, Peace, and the Israeli-Palestinian Conflict, University of Maryland, January 30, 1992.

12

ISRAEL AND THE
LIBERALIZATION OF ARAB REGIMES

GABRIEL SHEFFER

Democracies, Liberalizing Authoritarian Regimes, and the Israeli Case

THE BEHAVIOR OF democracies has been compared to that of nondemocratic states and an expanding body of literature reveals a consistent pattern: democratic states are ready to engage in wars and other violent confrontations with nondemocratic states, but they do not wage wars on each other (Rummel 1983; Doyle 1986; Maoz and Abdolali 1989; Bremer 1992a, 1992b; Maoz 1992). At the same time, the literature tends to focus on quantitative and aggregate measures at the expense of theoretical and analytical issues, with the result that we do not know enough about the mechanisms linking regime type to foreign policy behavior related to war and peace (Maoz and Russett 1992; Maoz herein).

One issue receiving scant attention is the way democracies view liberalizing and democratizing authoritarian regimes, particularly those with which they are locked in protracted conflicts. Several questions emerge concerning the internal structures and processes in democratic states that are confronted with liberalizing regimes: What are the grass-roots and elite perceptions of the changes that occur in nondemocratic adversaries? What is the impact of these changes on the readiness of democratic governments to alter their behavior toward such adversarial regimes? What are the short and long-term implications of such behavioral changes so far as violent encounters between the states are concerned? What are the ramifications for the possibility of solving underlying conflicts between pairs or groups of states in this situation?

Longitudinal and aggregate quantitative studies do not provide an adequate foundation for addressing these kinds of questions. Qualitative analyses, by contrast, can provide valuable theoretical and practical insights into the attitudes and behavior of democratic states toward authoritarian but liberalizing regimes with which they are locked in conflict. Toward this end, the present chapter will discuss Israeli public and elite perceptions and Israeli governmental policies toward the state's Arab adversaries. The goal is to shed light not only on concrete, sensitive questions about the possibility of war initiation and avoidance in the Arab-Israeli conflict system, but also to make a more general theoretical and analytical contribution to the study of war and peace between democracies and liberalizing authoritarian regimes.

This essay rejects the widely accepted view that Israel is a unique case which offers little basis for generalization. The present analysis assumes, rather, that the Israeli case is not sui generis and that findings about it can shed light on comparable cases (Migdal 1989). There are accordingly several reasons why the qualitative study of Israeli reactions to incremental liberalization in neighboring Arab states is important for the theoretical purposes of this volume. Israel is a veteran member in the small club of democracies. Since its founding in 1948, it has functioned like many other established parliamentary democracies. Like other Western democracies, Israel has also been acquiring the distinct features of a democratic-corporatist regime during the last two decades (Schmitter and Lehmbruch 1979; Katzenstein 1984; Katzenstein 1985). Finally, as in other democracies of this type, the views of the political elite and various governments have not always followed public opinion. Indeed, they have on many occasions shaped public opinion.

During this period, Israel has both initiated and avoided wars with its Arab adversaries, confronting many different kinds of Arab regimes in the process. It has signed a peace treaty with President Anwar Sadat's authoritarian government in Egypt and has maintained what is often described as a "cold peace" with Egypt under the somewhat more liberal government of President Hosni Mubarak. Recently, Israel has witnessed half-hearted attempts at liberalization in Jordan, democratization in Lebanon, and a modest degree of internal and external moderation in Syria. Israel has also dealt with the PLO's demand to establish "a secular and democratic independent state." In addition, very recently, it has had to cope with growing Islamic fundamentalism in the occupied territories and in Arab countries, which, perhaps not paradoxically, has to a considerable extent resulted from liberalization in these states. The rightist Israeli Likud government reluctantly joined in both bilateral and multilateral peace negotiations with nondemocratic Arab states and the Palestinians, and Israel is today confronted with the gradual adoption by at least some of its Arab adversaries of pro-Western attitudes and more democratic political forms.

In addressing the theoretical and practical questions that arise from these features of the Israeli case, this essay devotes attention to three different topics. The first involves the principal structures and processes that characterize the Israeli democratic regime, including the problematic relationship between public attitudes on the one hand and elite views and governmental policies on the other.

A discussion of the Israeli democratic system provides needed background for an examination of the second main theme of this essay: how the Israeli public and political elites perceive the various attempts at liberalization taking place in some Arab countries, the bases of these perceptions, the degree of their firmness, and the possibility of their alteration. This is followed by a more focused examination of political elite and governmental reactions to the liberalization of some Arab regimes and to the implications of these reactions for peace-making in the region.

The third main topic concerns the long-term effects on Israeli democracy of the absence of peace and of Israel's on-going involvement in the Middle East conflict. The essay ends with an articulation and summary of the major theoretical conclusions to be derived from the Israeli case.

Political Structures, Processes, and Policy Networks in Israel

As in Holland and Germany, where changing patterns of stratification have undermined class consciousness, the Israeli state has been weakened and emphasis is now placed more on individual than on collective political rights. Since the 1970s, the Israeli democratic regime has discarded some of its previous consociational features (Lijphart 1969; Eisenstadt 1967; Gutmann 1977; Horowitz and Lissak 1978) and has acquired discernable democratic-corporatist characteristics (Yishai 1987). But this change has affected neither the main features of established decision-making networks nor the traditional behavior of senior policymakers, particularly in the area of national security policy. Patterns formed during an earlier period still exert considerable influence on the issues to be discussed in this chapter.

In the early 1990s, Israeli society still exhibits a deep ethno-religious cleavage between its Jewish and Arab citizens, but the famous cleavage between Sephardi and Ashkenazi Jews (those of Middle Eastern/North African and European/Anglo-Saxon origin, respectively) has almost disappeared (Horowitz and Lissak 1989; Shuval 1989). This results from intermarriage between Israeli Jews of various ethnic backgrounds; improved access to the political process, especially on the local level; better education; and changes in occupational structure that increase upward mobility. As a result, the old social-political blocs which were so important during Israel's early years, and which endowed the country's political system with many of its consociational features, are to-day considerably weakened.

While the distance between Sephardi and Ashkenazi Jews has diminished, other divisions within Israel's Jewish population have intensified. These include cleavages associated with religiosity, and ideological orientations related to the Israeli-Arab conflict. The main axes of Jewish fragmentation now run along these two lines and, more particularly, the interplay between them has produced and contributes to the persistence of three electoral blocs: the left/center-left, the right/center-right, and the religious bloc.

Yet these ideological blocs, too, have lost much of their clout, having been undercut by a multiplicity of interest groups (Yishai 1987). Interest groups have aggregated to form four loose democratic factions: the government, private business, the trade unions, and the professional associations, all of which now play a major role in the formation of social and economic policies (Horowitz and Lissak 1989). Thus, notwithstanding the stubborn persistence of the main features of Israel's parliamentary system, which is based on proportional representation, there has been a marked reduction in the power of ideological parties and of blocs and factions that articulate particular political opinions. The Knesset has similarly lost power and is becoming no more than a platform for the expression of views by political leaders and a rubber stamp for legislation initiated by the government. As stated, these developments are the result of structural changes in patterns of social stratification and an associated increase in the importance of interest groups.

Although particular interest groups and democratic factions now play a much more important role in the formulation and implementation of economic and social policy, national security policy continues to be dominated by the prime minister, by a small group of senior cabinet members, including the defense minister and to a lesser extent the foreign affairs and finance ministers, by members of the cabinet's Foreign Affairs and Defense subcommittee, and by senior Israel Defense Forces (IDF) officers and civilian defense officials. Thus, as in other Western democracies, the prevailing pattern in the intertwined spheres of defense and foreign affairs is not one of "bottom-up," but rather of "top-down" policy-making.

These latter observations mean that when inquiring about the most critical Israeli attitudes toward political liberalization in the Arab world, and about the ramifications of this liberalization for policy-making in Israel, the focus should be on political elites rather than on public opinion at large. Despite the weakening of traditional social institutions and changes in the policy-making process in a number of key areas, policy networks in the sphere of defense and foreign affairs remain state dominated and highly centralized. These networks are firmly controlled by the governing coalition, in which the prime minister and a few senior ministers play a decisive role. The concentration of power is further reinforced by the prevailing proportional representation system and related processes of coalition formation, according to which each government ministry is treated as the fief of whomever holds the portfolio and each "fiefdom" is jealously guarded against the intrusion and influence of public opinion (and other ministries) in order to protect the interests of the party or faction to which it has been allocated.

Public Opinion about Changes in Arab Regimes

As in other Western societies, the Israeli public is interested primarily in domestic affairs and only secondarily in international politics. Only major and very dramatic upheavals in foreign affairs, such as the collapse of the Soviet Union and the unification of Germany, have attracted considerable public attention. Indeed, the disintegration of Yugoslavia, the conflict between Armenians and Azeris, and ethnic rivalries in Czechoslovakia, although they have generated considerable attention in Europe and in the U.S., have aroused only marginal interest in Israel. By the same token, subtle changes in regimes, or even some of the more dramatic governmental reforms, such as those in Latin America or Asia, have generated only limited interest among Israelis. Thus, not surprisingly, the comparatively feeble attempts during the last few years to liberalize the regimes of Egypt, Lebanon, Jordan, Kuwait, and Algeria have generated little interest in Israel. This disinterest has also affected the pollsters, who have failed even to inquire about public attitudes toward these developments.

A second preliminary comment concerns the horizon and focus of Israeli public attention with respect to Middle Eastern affairs. Understandably, a majority of Israelis are interested primarily in the countries immediately bordering Israel, those Arab countries known as the confrontation states. With the exception of unusual and dramatic events, like those in Iraq during the Gulf crisis, less dramatic, gradual developments in Arab countries outside the immediate circle of the Israeli-Arab conflict are therefore of much less interest to most Israelis. In other words, while revolutionary transformations would attract some attention in Israel, incremental changes are much less likely to generate any significant degree of interest.

We may now briefly examine some basic historical trends in Israeli public opinion, beginning with the differences between the period from the establishment of the state through the 1960s and the period that followed, especially after the 1973 war. During the earlier period, there was a remarkable degree of consensus about Israel's foreign relations and about its defense posture. A vast majority of the Israeli public supported a pro-Western orientation, preventive strikes and military retaliation against Arab states that allowed Palestinian guerrillas to launch raids against Israel from their territory, refusal to accept the return of most Palestinian refugees, and use of the occupied territories (after 1967) as a bargaining chip in peace negotiations with Arab states (Arian 1973; Arian, Talmud, and Herman 1988; Barzilai 1991). During this period, disagreements about public policy were primarily in the economic, social, and educational spheres (Patinkin 1959; Halevi and Klinov 1979).

These tendencies were reversed during the latter period, however. There emerged a substantial consensus about economic and social directions, with most Israelis favoring greater economic liberalization and a measure of privatization, but this was accompanied by growing disagreement about issues of war and peace and the Arab-Israeli conflict, and particularly about the fate of the occupied territories (Arian 1980; Arian and Shamir 1990; Goldberg, Barzilai, and Inbar 1991). During the last decade, especially, public opinion polls have consistently shown polarized public attitudes toward the major issues associated with the Arab-Israeli conflict. The public is divided over the territorial question, for example, namely on whether and to what extent there should be withdrawal from lands that Israel captured in 1967, and also about the political and civic rights that should be granted to the Palestinians who live in these occupied territories. In addition, the public is divided about the desirability of participating in the peace process (Peres and Yuchtman-Yaar 1992; Goldberg, Barzilai, and Inbar 1991; Arian, Talmud, and Herman 1988).

Although these divisions constitute the main demarcation between "right" and "left" in Israeli politics (Diskin 1988; Horowitz and Lissak 1989; Inbar 1991), the general public does not show great interest in the intricacies and subtleties of underlying factors that may either perpetuate or contribute to solving the Arab-Israeli conflict. Instead, the public has tended to follow the country's political leaders and to focus its attention on those issues that leaders proclaim to be critical for Israel's security.

One such issue is the stability of Arab regimes, which surfaces whenever there are rumors about the weakening of a neighboring Arab government or about the threat of a revolution or coup d'état in a neighboring country. At the heart of this concern is the traditional underlying assumption of many Israelis that domestically beleaguered Arab regimes and rulers will try to divert the attention of their citizens from internal misfortunes to military adventures directed against Israel. This was a popular Israeli argument, for example, with respect to Nasser's military moves on the eve of the 1967 war, the actions of Presidents Assad and Sadat on the eve of the 1973 war, and Saddam Hussein's missile attacks on Israel during the 1990–91 Gulf crisis (Herzog 1967; Kimche and Bawley 1968; Safran 1969; Schiff 1974; Herzog 1975).

The Israeli public also tends to direct its attention to the personal security of Arab leaders, particularly in the context of their ability to respect promises and adhere to treaties. One frequently hears arguments concerning the possible demise of an Arab leader who makes an implicit or explicit agreement with Israel. For example, many Israelis pondered the implications of Nasser's death for the status quo established after the 1967 war, of Sadat's assassination for the Camp David accords, of threats on King Hussein's life for the various tacit understandings that he has forged with Israel over the years, and of the misfortunes of King Hassan of Morocco for his moderating influence on other Arab states.

In addition, the Israeli public is also sensitive to the cruelty with which Middle Eastern authoritarian rulers and nondemocratic governments sometimes treat domestic opponents. An important example is the brutality with which the Syrian regime suppressed a rebellion by Islamic opponents in Hama in 1981. Many Israelis believe that Arab regimes are insensitive to human rights and consider their heavy-handed actions against domestic opponents as proof that they are also capable of harming external enemies, particularly Israel. Such demonology was responsible for the great fear, bordering on panic, that the Israeli public demonstrated during the Gulf War, especially during and following the Iraqi missile attacks on civilian targets in Israel. It would be very difficult to persuade Israelis that not all Arab regimes are inclined toward the use of such tactics (Goldberg, Barzilai, and Inbar 1991).

Israelis are especially uneasy about the rise of Islamic fundamentalism in a number of Arab countries. Israelis responded with trepidation to the extreme positions toward the Jewish state adopted by the Iranian fundamentalist regime, to the immediate threats posed by the Shi'ites in southern Lebanon, and to the direct threats to the personal and collective security of Israelis posed by the Sunni Hamas movement in the West Bank and the Gaza Strip (Goldberg, Barzilai, and Inbar 1991). These Israeli apprehensions are intensified, moreover, by recent clashes between fundamentalist opposition movements and the Arab governments of Egypt, Tunisia, and Algeria. The popular appeal and electoral success of some of these fundamentalist groups contributes to the popular Israeli view that in most Arab countries liberalization will only give more influence to Muslim fundamentalism, which is one of the most dangerous threats to Israel's existence. In this respect there is no significant gap between public and elite attitudes.

More generally, many Israelis view the domestic situation in most of the Arab states as essentially static. They doubt the possibility of successful liberalization in these countries, including Egypt. This skepticism implicitly assumes that because of these countries' traditional social structure, the presumed antidemocratic nature of Islam, and the inherent cruelty and steadfastness of the regimes, which leads to the immediate suppression of every attempt at meaningful reform, the likelihood of genuine change is very slim.

This tendency is illustrated by the Egyptian case. Although the government has in recent years relaxed its hold over political life and given limited license to the formation of opposition parties (Yadlin 1989), this is not reflected in Israeli attitudes toward Egypt. Israeli public opinion makes no direct connection between the so-called "Israeli-Egyptian cold peace" on the one hand and, on the other, the character of the Egyptian regime, be it more authoritarian or more liberal. Most Israelis believe that restrictions on trade with and tourism to Israel, criticism of Israel's behavior during the war in Lebanon, the unyielding Egyptian demand for Israeli withdrawal from the Taba area, and Egypt's commitment to the Palestinian cause are all explained by Egypt's Arab and Islamic identity or by commercial and financial considerations. Regime change in Egypt, to the extent the possibility is considered at all by Israelis, would not be seen as having much effect in any of these areas involving relations with Israel.

The salience as well as the substantive content of Israeli public opinion must be considered, and here it is important to reiterate that both Labor and Likud governments have formulated their policies toward the Arab states without giving much heed to domestic public opinion. When adopting major defense policies that affect Israel and the region as a whole, the government generally succeeds in pursuing its own intentions without prior consultation with the opposition or even with its coalition partners in the Knesset. Recent examples have been the bombing of the Iraqi nuclear reactor and the launching of the

1982 war in Lebanon on the one hand (Naor 1986; Schiff and Yaari 1984; Shiffer 1984), and participation in the peace process on the other. In none of these dramatic cases was the Israeli public directly or indirectly consulted before a decision was taken. The government proceeded to execute its decisions in total isolation and without orderly consultation with the senior opposition leaders in the Knesset. This disregard of general and organized public opinion went beyond any reasonable concern for the secrecy that might be needed to ensure successful military operations (Lissak 1984; Galnoor 1982). Indeed, the government's action bordered on contempt for public opinion.

Yet there is little evidence that the Israeli public is unhappy with this situation. Despite Israeli military debacles early in the 1973 war, during the 1982 war, and in dealing with the intifada, and despite growing criticism of Israeli politics in general and of the policy-making process in particular, most Israelis still express great trust in the IDF. A recent poll found that 94 percent of Israelis have a high degree of trust in the IDF and the intelligence community, and even for the government in general the figure is 48 percent (Peres and Yuchtman-Yaar 1992). Many Israelis thus agree that it is legitimate for state institutions to determine defense policies in relative isolation (Galnoor and Peres 1992). The public believes, in other words, that "the authorities know and understand better than us simple people" questions of defense and security.

Although the Israeli public lacks the ability to directly and decisively influence elites and policy-makers, either to launch wars or to participate in peace talks, its inclinations and priorities do indirectly affect the formation of Israeli foreign policy. Through participation in periodic general elections, the public broadly determines the parameters of ruling coalitions, which in turn influence the main contours of the policies that governments adopt. Moreover, the electoral process is especially important in this respect since about 85 percent of all eligible voters take part in Knesset elections. Particularly strong tendencies in public opinion can thus sometimes pressure the government to adopt certain policies. The most clear-cut example of this was when the public dictated, albeit indirectly and after a long delay, both the formation of a national unity government in 1984 and the subsequent withdrawal of Israeli military forces from Lebanon (Horowitz and Lissak 1989).

But these were also exceptional cases. While public attitudes may have indirect influence on governmental policy, especially in cases where there is a clear public consensus, the more important point, as noted, is that public opinion follows rather than leads government decision-making. This is particularly true in the critical areas of foreign affairs and defense, where the government not only formulates and implements national policy but also leads and shapes public opinion to mobilize support for its decisions.

Elite Attitudes toward Liberalization in the Arab States

Most Israeli leaders who have dealt with defense and foreign affairs, including Yitzhak Shamir, Yitzhak Rabin, Shimon Peres, Ezer Weizmann, Mordechai Gur, Ariel Sharon, and Raphael Eitan, have long experience in these matters. They are generally well versed in the most relevant issues and in the strategic as well as tactical dimensions of the Arab-Israeli conflict system. In particular, they are well acquainted with the intricacies of Israel's positions vis-à-vis the various Arab states. Therefore, if these leaders hold any distorted images, unfounded beliefs, or rigid views about Israel's regional adversaries, these are due neither to the influence of public opinion nor to a lack of sufficient information about the actual situation in the Arab world.

Moreover, the information available to senior policy makers from the Israeli intelligence community, academia, and the media is comprehensive. It includes a myriad of details about the internal situation in each country, including both actual and potential regime transformations. Hence, any biases or blind spots that may exist among political elites should be attributed to either personal psychological traits or cognitive ideological positions.

There are important differences between the attitudes of "rightist" and "leftist" Israeli leaders regarding the issue of regime change in the Arab states. Leftist and left-of-center political leaders show greater sensitivity to the possibility of democratization, both in general and in the Arab Middle East. Some Labor leaders, especially Shimon Peres (Inbar 1991), as well as leaders of the three other left-of-center parties (which formed the Meretz list in the 1992 Knesset elections), have argued that Israel should pay close attention to such reforms and to their potential moderating effects on the Arab-Israeli conflict. Thus, in the aftermath of the collapse of the Soviet Union and in view of accelerating democratization in various other parts of the globe, these leaders have argued that any attempt at liberalization in the Arab countries should be welcomed and encouraged. In the view of these Israeli leaders, developments of this sort may enhance contacts with the West, moderate foreign and defense policies, and increase potential readiness to conclude reasonable peace treaties with Israel.

More hawkish leaders in the Labor party, such as Rabin and Gur, who are ideologically close to the Likud leaders, refrain from addressing the issue of

liberalization in Arab countries and its potential implications for the avoidance
of violent confrontations with the Arabs. Rabin, as well as former chiefs of
staff and ministers Gur and Haim Bar-Lev, epitomize the structural-realist approach to international politics. These three Labor leaders judge the intentions
of Arab states by a single yardstick, their policies and actions. A clear illustration of this attitude is the great suspicion of Egyptian intentions expressed by
Gur, then chief of staff, on the eve of Sadat's 1977 visit to Jerusalem (Inbar
1991).

On the other hand, most leaders of the right-of-center Likud party, and of
more extreme rightist and some religious parties, ridicule the possibility of
genuine liberalization in the Arab countries. They firmly believe that owing to
their complete domination by nondemocratic Islam, their traditional social
structure, and consequently their "primitive" level of political development,
Arab rulers and governments are incapable of any significant transformation
to Western-style liberal democracy. The "natural" order in these states is authoritarianism, they believe, and any attempts at liberalization will therefore
fail. Indeed, the results of democratic experiments will be either increased extremism and fundamentalism or greater authoritarianism. These leaders (and
most Israelis) cite Jordan and Algeria as examples of countries where processes
of liberalization have produced fundamentalism and then, in response, greater
authoritarianism. And since these Israeli leaders deny the possibility of any
meaningful breakthrough toward democracy in the Arab countries, they consequently believe Israel should make only minimal concessions, particularly regarding territory.

This skeptical view about liberalization in the Arab countries is dominant
among rightist Israeli leaders, and these nationalistic leaders have in turn
guided the public and influenced its attitudes about the Arab world. Specifically, they have encouraged among the Israeli rank and file negative perceptions
about the possibility of structural changes in the Arab states that could lead to
a reduction of regional tensions. These views, although presumably sincerely
held, are consistent with and support the rightists' general approach to war and
peace. Rightist preconditions for peace are based not only on the assumption
of enduring Arab enmity toward Israel but also on a belief in the Jews' overriding right to control all parts of Eretz-Israel. Thus, rightist leaders reject
"land for peace" formulas. They demand "peace for peace" and insist that negotiations with the Arabs are possible only on this basis, a position that gives
them strong normative reason to hold and disseminate their views about the
implausibility of democratization in the Arab countries.

Concerning the Assumption that Arab Regimes
Become More Democratic

It is not obvious that any Arab state is heading rapidly toward major liberal or democratic reforms. There has been some progress in a few recent instances, most notably Jordan, and Morocco, and Yemen before the civil war of 1994. On the other hand, there is little or no movement in many other Arab countries, and there have also been unpleasant reversals in a number of states, such as Algeria and Tunisia. Nevertheless, even if progress toward democratization remains uneven and limited for the foreseeable future, there is both theoretical and practical room for speculation about how liberalization in the Arab countries might affect Israeli perceptions, policies, and behavior toward any Arab states moving meaningfully in the direction of democratization.

Consider the previous wars that Israel initiated, the 1956 and 1982 wars, and also the Israeli peace initiative of the early 1950s led by then foreign minister and later prime minister Moshe Sharett. It is evident that decisions to launch both the wars and the peace initiative were undertaken with little regard for the internal political situation in the relevant Arab countries. Rather, these decisions were predicated primarily on Israel's perceived needs with respect to security and foreign relations (Sheffer 1987; Bar-On 1992; Naor 1986).

In the case of the 1956 war, for example, Nasser's dictatorial rule and aggressive personal traits (both Anthony Eden and David Ben-Gurion called him "the new Hitler") were mentioned by Israeli leaders as one essential cause of the war. Yet a year or two earlier, Israeli leaders had been willing to hold private talks aimed at making peace with this same leader and regime. Similarly, although President Assad of Syria is occasionally described as equally authoritarian and ruthless, present-day Israeli leaders of both the rightist and leftist political camps have been willing to negotiate with his representatives in the framework of the Madrid peace talks. This pattern suggests that the nature of the regime plays only a secondary role in Israeli decisions to participate, either formally or informally, in a peace process. And if the absence of democracy is not necessarily a barrier to peace talks, neither does it appear that greater liberalization, by itself, provides a strong incentive for peace-making. For example, Menachem Begin's public statements did not suggest that Egypt's relative liberalization under Sadat was one of the main reasons that his advisers were able to persuade him to sign the Camp David accords and the subsequent peace treaty with Egypt (Quandt 1986).

Most Israeli leaders subscribe to a structural-realist view of international politics. Even if they are aware of the connections between democratic regimes and war avoidance, they are unlikely to perceive initial Arab steps toward liberalization as a sufficient indication that Arab rulers and governments are more likely to have peaceful intentions toward Israel. They would give much greater weight to concrete and direct evidence of peaceful intentions, such as unilateral reduction in military expenditures and, especially, a demonstrated readiness to accept Israel's main preconditions for peace.

Any offensive military move or deployment by the Arab states, or any dramatic increase in their military outlays or clear signs of major progress toward acquiring nonconventional capabilities, would prompt a strong military reaction by Israel, possibly including preemptive war. Israel showed considerable restraint during the Persian Gulf crisis, but its inclination to adopt a very wide margin of safety has increased since the 1973 war and remains very strong. It is almost inconceivable that Israel would refrain from using its military power, if this appeared to be necessary for security reasons, even if the offending action was undertaken by an Arab state in the midst of a serious program of political liberalization. Thus, although it can perhaps be argued that the likelihood of such action would diminish in a democratic, or democratizing, Arab state, liberalization alone would probably not change to any great extent the security calculations of Israeli leaders.

The Impact of Continued Conflict on Israeli Democracy

Israeli leaders are unlikely to accept initial steps toward liberalization in Arab countries as sufficient indicators of the coming to the Middle East of "the end of history." But some leaders have considered the adverse implications of the continuing conflict for Israeli democracy.

Generally speaking, the introduction of formal democratic institutions and practices into the new Jewish state, immediately after its independence in the midst of the 1948 war, was "natural" in the sense that Israel was incorporating democratic traditions and arrangements that had prevailed in the Zionist movement and the Jewish Yishuv in Palestine. And throughout its subsequent existence, Israel has succeeded in preserving its formal democratic character. These patterns were primarily applied to the Jewish sector, however. Moreover, partly because of the Arab-Israeli conflict, even arrangements in the Jewish sector have been far from perfect. The extensive use of emergency regulations, for example, has detracted from the quality of the "living democracy" in this privileged sector of Israeli society (Hofnung 1991; Horowitz and Lissak 1989).

These are not the sole weaknesses of Israel's democracy. Although difficult to document and measure, political sociologists argue that the results of the 1967 war—particularly the protracted occupation of the territories—have created severe problems of social and political adjustment, changes in basic norms, and consequently deep gaps between utopian aspirations and actual achievements (Horowitz and Lissak 1989). Furthermore, continued occupation has blurred the state's social and political vision, weakened its social cohesion, and caused political polarization and severe problems of central control (e.g., over the settlers in the occupied territories, special military units serving in the territories, and specialized interest and protest groups). This situation has also created dilemmas concerning basic values, such as the choices between respect for universal civil rights and the rule of law on the one hand, and perceived needs to protect the polity against subversive elements on the other.

The 1967 war was a turning point in the development of the Israeli polity, but its real impact was felt only after the 1973 war. The military debacle at the beginning of that war stimulated the emergence of numerous interest groups and expedited the transition to democratic-liberalism. Since then, the Israeli system has undergone significant changes, including electoral reform for the direct election of the prime minister and completion of the basic laws that together would form the Israeli constitution.

These reforms affect mainly the Jewish sector. They were introduced because of mounting dissatisfaction with the old proportional representations system and demands for greater political participation from Sephardi groups, women, and younger Israelis, all of whom had experienced unofficial discrimination and hence a sense of relative deprivation.

The application of democratic principles among Israeli Arabs was more directly influenced by developments in the Arab-Israeli conflict and by the situation in the occupied territories. The perceived danger from this national minority did not prevent the formal granting of equal political rights to Israel's Arab citizens immediately after the 1948 war. But it did cause the imposition of a highly restrictive military government in areas where most of this population lived. Only with the reduction in regional tensions after the 1956 war and the coming to power of more moderate Israeli politicians was there a relaxation of some restrictions and, in the mid-1960s, after nearly two decades of statehood, the abolition of the military government (Lustick 1980).

The majority of Israeli Arabs enjoys personal and political freedoms that are almost equal to those of Israeli Jews. On the other hand, they certainly have not obtained a full and proportionate share of the benefits offered by the Israeli system. This is partly because many of these benefits are connected to military service, which neither Muslim nor Christian Arabs want to perform because of their ethnic connections to the Palestinians and, equally, or even more important, because of deep Israeli suspicion about their loyalty. The growing links between Israeli Arabs and the Palestinians in the occupied territories, together with associated Israeli fears about the emergence of an irredentist movement and the spread of Muslim fundamentalism among Israeli Arabs, further complicate this difficult situation. They especially hinder full political and economic integration and the elimination of unofficial but often quite serious discrimination and deprivation (Smooha 1978; Benziman and Mansour 1992).

Rule over the West Bank and Gaza also undermines Israeli democracy. The Palestinians in the territories have suffered most from the recurrent wars in the Middle East and from the intensification of intercommunal conflict. They are at the core of the Arab-Israeli conflict and tirelessly insist upon the fulfillment of their national demands for the establishment of an independent state. But this causes most Israelis to regard them as the greatest threat to their personal and collective security, which in turn leads occupation authorities to suppress Palestinian political activity and govern with a heavy hand.

It remains to be seen whether this situation can be changed. The September 1993 accord with the PLO commits Israel to giving Palestinians wide responsibility for the administration of the West Bank and Gaza. The agreement also provides for the establishment of a Palestinian police force, with responsibility for domestic security during a transitional period. Yet Israeli fears and security concerns have caused the government to proceed slowly in implementing the agreement. And in the face of continuing Israeli doubts about Palestinian intentions, as well as the determined opposition of Jewish settlers in the West Bank and Gaza, it is not yet clear whether any Israeli government will be able to grant the Palestinians meaningful political rights leading to self-determination and statehood, and thus alter the historic pattern of intercommunal conflict and mutual distrust.

A Few Conclusions

Mass public opinion in Israel has mattered less than in other democratic states with similar features that include a political system with an intermediate level of centralization, an increasingly heterogeneous society, weakening state institutions, and distinct liberal-corporatist features along with state-dominated policy networks (Risse-Kappen 1991). Except for the withdrawal from Lebanon in 1985, Israeli public opinion has had relatively little influence on crucial decisions concerning war and peace.

Moreover, liberalization of the regimes in certain Arab countries has not been a salient issue in Israeli public opinion. The general image of many Israelis has been that, because of the traditional social and political structures in neighboring Arab countries, there is very little chance for genuine reform. And, in addition, the experience of Algeria and Jordan is believed to show that efforts at liberalization only breed fundamentalism. Thus, overall, the Israeli public has paid little attention to issues of democratization in the Arab world and, to the extent that such issues are thought about at all, it appears that they have created negative reactions.

Furthermore, the Israeli government makes major decisions concerning defense and foreign affairs in relative isolation and secrecy. The analysis of Israeli foreign policy has for this reason focused primarily on elite perceptions about regime transformations in the Arab countries. Most Israeli leaders are skeptical about the possibility of significant progress toward democracy in the Arab world. Moreover, these leaders are convinced that liberalization processes, to the extent they continue and succeed, will have only adverse consequences as far as Israel is concerned. They will promote Muslim fundamentalism, which is perceived as the force most dangerous to the Jewish state.

Historically, escalation and relaxation of the conflict have depended on considerations of realpolitik. That is, Israeli governments have decided to launch wars or sign armistice agreements, as well as a peace treaty, mainly on the basis of traditional strategic considerations that put great emphasis on an adversary's military capabilities rather than on its political intentions or the character of its regime.

Despite the Labor party victory in the 1992 elections, Israeli politicians continue to make decisions that are informed little if at all by the nature of Arab regimes. Overriding importance continues to be attached to the Arabs' military capabilities and, most important, to their readiness to accept Israeli preconditions for progress in the peace process. Furthermore, regardless of the nature of the regimes in the Arab states, the possibility of Israeli preemptive strikes against specific targets, such as nuclear reactors or apparently aggressive Arab states, remains very real.

Finally, Israeli calculations have not changed appreciably as a result of the September 1993 accord with the PLO. Despite the revolutionary breakthrough, this analysis remains pessimistic because of deeply ingrained Israeli attitudes, as well as the lack of significant and sustained progress toward democracy in the Arab world. This situation may change in the future, particularly to the extent that military challenges and political opposition from major Arab states diminish as a result of Palestinian recognition of the Jewish state. Indeed, there has been some progress in this direction since September 1993, with potential to influence the assessments of Israeli leaders whose views are shaped by structural-realism. Again, however, it is these considerations associated with military capabilities and political behavior, far more than those associated with the character of Arab regimes, that will predominate in Israel's own political calculations.

REFERENCES

Arian, Alan. 1973. *The Choosing People.* Ramat Gan: Massada (Hebrew).

Arian, Alan, ed. 1980. *The Elections in Israel: 1977.* Jerusalem: Jerusalem Academic Press.

Arian, Alan, Ilan Talmud, and Tamar Hermann. 1988. *National Security and Public Opinion in Israel.* Jaffe Center for Strategic Studies, Tel Aviv University, no. 9.

Arian, Alan, and Michal Shamir, eds. 1990. *The Elections in Israel: 1988.* Boulder, CO: Westview, 1990.

Bar-On, Mordechai. 1992. *The Gates of Gaza.* Tel Aviv: Am Oved (Hebrew).

Barzilai, Gad. 1991. *Democracy at War.* Tel Aviv: Siriat Poalim (Hebrew).

Barzilai, Gad, and Efraim Inbar. 1992. "Do Wars Have an Impact? Israeli Public Opinion after the Gulf War." *Jerusalem Journal of International Relations* 14, no. 1.

Benziman, Uzi, and A. Mansour. 1992. *Subtenants: The Position of Israeli Arabs and the Policy toward Them.* Jerusalem: Keter (Hebrew).

Bremer, Stuart A. 1992a. "Dangerous Dyads: Conditions Affecting the Likelihood of Interstate War, 1816–1965." *Journal of Conflict Resolution* 36, no. 2.

———. 1992b. "Democracy and Dyadic Dispute Participation, 1816–1976." Paper presented at the 33rd annual meeting of the International Studies Association, Atlanta, GA, March 31–April 4.

Diskin, Abraham. 1988. *Elections and Voters in Israel.* Tel Aviv: Am Oved (Hebrew).

Doyle, Michael W. 1986. "Liberalism in World Politics." *American Political Science Review* 80, no. 4 (December), pp. 1151–69.

Eisenstadt, Shmuel Noah. 1967. *Israeli Society.* New York: Basic Books.

———. 1985. *The Transformation of Israeli Society.* London: Weidenfeld and Nicolson.

Galnoor, Itzak. 1982. *Steering the Polity: Communication and Politics in Israel.* Beverly Hills, CA: Sage.

Galnoor, Itzak, and Yohanan Peres. 1992. "Those Who Vote May Influence." In "Democracy. A Special Supplement." *Ma'ariv* (Summer).

Goldberg, G., Gad Barzilai, and Efraim Inbar. 1991. *The Impact of Intercommunal Conflict: The Intifada and Israeli Public Opinion.* Jerusalem: Leonard Davis Institute.

Gutmann, Emanuel. 1977. "Parties and Camps: Stability and Change." In Moshe Lissak and Emanuel Gutmann, eds. *The Israeli Political System.* Tel Aviv: Am Oved (Hebrew).

Halevi, Nadav, and Rinah Klinov. 1979. *The Economic Development of Israel.* New York: Praeger.

Herzog, Chaim. 1967. *Great Days.* Tel Aviv: Sifrit Ma'ariv (Hebrew).

———. 1975. *The War of Atonement.* London: Weidenfeld and Nicolson.

Hofnung, M. 1991. *Israel: Security Needs vs. The Rule of Law.* Jerusalem: Nevo (Hebrew).

Horowitz, Dan, and Moshe Lissak. 1978. *The Origins of the Israeli Polity: Palestine under the Mandate.* Chicago: University of Chicago Press.

———. 1989. *Trouble in Utopia: The Overburdened Polity of Israel.* Albany: State University of New York Press.

Inbar, Efraim. 1991. *War and Peace in Israeli Politics.* Boulder, CO: Lynne Rienner.

Katzenstein, Peter J. 1984. *Corporatism and Change.* Ithaca, NY: Cornell University Press.

———, ed. 1985. *Between Power and Plenty: Foreign Economic Policies of Advanced Industrial States.* Madison: University of Wisconsin Press.

Kimche, David, and Dan Bawley. 1968. *The Sandstorm: The Arab-Israeli War of June, 1967: Prelude and Aftermath.* New York: Stein & Day.

Lijphart, A. 1969. "Consociational Democracy." *World Politics* 21, no. 2.

Lissak, Moshe, ed. 1984. *Israeli Society and Its Defense Establishment.* London: Frank Cass.

Lustick, Ian. 1980. *Arabs in a Jewish State: Israel's Control of a National Minority.* Austin: University of Texas Press.

Maoz, Zeev, and Nasrin Abdolali. 1989. "Regime Types and International Conflict, 1816–1976." *Journal of Conflict Resolution* 33, no. 1.

Maoz, Zeev, and Bruce M. Russett. 1992. "Alliance, Contiguity, Wealth, and Political Stability: Is the Lack of Conflict among Democracies a Statistical Artifact?" *International Interactions* 17, no. 4.

Migdal, Joel S. 1989. "The Crystallization of the State and the Struggles Over Rulemaking: Israel in Comparative Perspective." In Baruch Kimmerling, ed., *The Israeli State and Society: Boundaries and Frontiers.* Albany: State University of New York Press.

Naor, Arye. 1986. *Cabinet at War*. Tel Aviv: Yediot Aharonot.

Patinkin, D. 1959. "Israel's Economy in the First Decade." In *The Falk Institute for Economic Research, 4th Report*. Jerusalem: The Falk Institute.

Peres, Yohanan, and Ephraim Yuchtman-Yaar. 1992. *Trends in Israeli Democracy: The Public's View*. Boulder, CO: Lynne Rienner.

Quandt, William B. 1986. *Camp David*. Washington, DC: Brookings Institution.

Risse-Kappen, Thomas. 1991. "Public Opinion, Domestic Structure, and Foreign Policy in Liberal Democracies." *World Politics* 43, no. 4.

Rummel, Rudolph J. 1983. "Libertarianism and International Violence." *Journal of Conflict Resolution* 27, no. 1.

Safran, Nadav. 1969. *From War to War: The Arab Israeli Confrontation, 1948–1967*. New York: Pegasus.

Schiff, Zeev. 1974. *October Earthquake: Yom Kippur 1973*. Tel Aviv: University Publication Projects.

Schiff, Zeev, and Ehud Yaari. 1984. *Israel's Lebanon War*. New York: Simon and Schuster.

Schmitter, Philippe C., and Gerhard, Lehmbruch, eds. 1979. *Trends toward Corporatist Intermediation*. Beverly Hills, CA: Sage.

Sheffer, Gabriel. 1987. "Sharett, Ben-Gurion and the 1956 War of Choice." *State, Government and International Relations* (Hebrew).

Shiffer, S. 1984. *Snowball: The Story behind the War in Lebanon*. Tel Aviv: Yediot Aharonot.

Shuval, Judith T. 1989. "The Structure and Dilemmas of Israeli Pluralism." In B. Kimmerling, ed., *The Israeli State and Society*. Albany: State University of New York Press.

Smooha, Sammy. 1978. *Israel: Pluralism and Conflict*. London: Routledge and Kegan Paul.

Yadlin, Rivka. 1989. *Egyptian Opposition: The Boundaries of National Consensus*. Jerusalem: Leonard Davis Institute.

Yishai, Y. 1987. *Interest Groups in Israel*. Tel Aviv: Am Oved (Hebrew).

CONTRIBUTORS

Shukri B. Abed is a Senior Research Fellow at the Center for International Development and Conflict Management (CIDCM) at the University of Maryland, College Park. He most recently coedited a book entitled *Democracy, Peace, and the Israeli-Palestinian Conflict.*

David Garnham is Professor of Political Science at the University of Wisconsin-Milwaukee and author of *The Politics of European Defense Cooperation: Germany, France, Britain, and America.*

Marilyn Grobschmidt is a doctoral student in International Relations and Comparative Politics at Indiana University. Her primary research interest is the relative influence of public and elite opinion on the formulation of foreign and domestic policies in the industrialized states.

Jo-Anne Hart is on leave from the Department of Political Science at Brown University and is currently Associate Professor in the Strategy Department at the Naval War College. She specializes in Middle East security issues and is completing a book on deterrence and compellance theory using the 1991 Gulf War as a case study.

Michael C. Hudson is Professor of International Relations and Seif Ghobash Professor of Arab Studies at Georgetown University. He is a past president of the Middle East Studies Association (MESA) whose publications include *Arab Politics: The Search for Legitimacy,The Precarious Republic: Political Modernization in Lebanon,* and as editor *The Palestinians: New Directions.*

Ann M. Lesch is Professor of Political Science and Associate Director of the Center for Arab and Islamic Studies at Villanova University. She worked in Egypt for seven years, first as Program Officer for the Ford Foundation and then as an associate of Universities Field Staff International. She is principal author of *Transition to Palestinian Self-Government: Practical Steps toward Israeli-Palestinian Peace* and coauthor (with Mark Tessler) of *Israel, Egypt, and the Palestinians: From Camp David to Intifada.*

Zeev Maoz is Professor of Political Science and Head of the Jaffe Center of Strategic Studies at Tel Aviv University and has also served as Professor and Chairman of the Department of Political Science and Director of the Center of Policy and Security Studies at the University of Haifa. His recent books include *Domestic Sources of Global Change, National Choices and International Processes,* and *Paradoxes of War: On the Art of National Self-Entrapment.*

James Lee Ray is Professor of Political Science at Florida State University, where he has served as Director of the International Affairs Program since 1985 and Director of the Peace Studies Program since 1987. His research focuses on the causes of war, various aspects of international political economy, regime transitions, and American foreign policy in Latin America and the Middle East. He is author of *The Future of American-Israeli Relations, Global Politics,* and *Democracy and International Conflict.*

Robert L. Rothstein is Harvey Picker Professor of International Relations at Colgate University and author of *The Third World and U.S. Foreign Policy: Cooperation and Conflict in the 1980s, Alliances and Small Powers,* and *Global Bargaining: UNCTAD and the Quest for a New International Economic Order.* He is currently writing a book on the interaction between democratization in the Third World and trends in the international political and economic systems.

Emile F. Sahliyeh is Associate Professor of International Relations and Middle East Studies at the University of North Texas. He is author of *In Search of Leadership: West Bank Politics Since 1967,* and *The PLO After the Lebanon War,* and coeditor (with Mary Morris) of *Unity Versus Separatism in the Middle East.* He is currently completing a book entitled *Jordan: Domestic Politics and Foreign Policy.*

Gabriel Sheffer is Professor of Political Science at the Hebrew University of Jerusalem and has served as Director of the Leonard Davis Institute for International Relations of the Hebrew University. He has published numerous books and articles on Israeli politics, foreign policy, relations with the Jewish diaspora, and the modern ethnonational diaspora. He recently completed a major political biography of Israel's second prime minister, Moshe Sharett.

Jamal Sanad Al-Suwaidi is Assistant Professor of Political Science at the UAE University in Al-Ain and Director of the Emirates Center for Strategic Studies and Research in Abu Dhabi. He is author of numerous articles on such subjects as the economic orientation of Kuwaiti women, women and religion, UAE public opinion on the Gulf crisis, and Arab and western conceptions of democracy.

Mark Tessler, Professor of Political Science and Director of the Center for International Studies at the University of Wisconsin-Milwaukee, has spent more than six years in the Middle East, doing research in Tunisia, Israel, the West Bank, Egypt, and Morocco. He is author of *A History of the Israeli-Palestinian Conflict* and co-author of *Political Elites in Arab North Africa* and (with Ann M. Lesch) of *Israel, Egypt, and the Palestinians: From Camp David to Intifada.*

I. William Zartman is Jacob Blaustein Professor of International Organization and Conflict Resolution and Director of African Studies at the Paul H. Nitze School of Advanced International Studies, Johns Hopkins University. His publications include *Destiny of a Dynasty, Problems of New Power,* and *The Political Economy of Morocco.*

INDEX